THE INVESTMENT MANAGER'S HANDBOOK

THE
INVESTMENT
MANAGER'S
HANDBOOK

James Essinger

CHAPMAN & HALL
University and Professional Division

London · Glasgow · New York · Tokyo · Melbourne · Madras

Published by Chapman & Hall, 2–6 Boundary Row, London SE1 8HN

Chapman & Hall, 2–6 Boundary Row, London SE1 8HN, UK

Blackie Academic & Professional, Wester Cleddens Road, Bishopbriggs, Glasgow G64 2NZ, UK

Chapman & Hall, 29 West 35th Street, New York NY10001, USA

Chapman & Hall Japan, Thomson Publishing Japan, Hirakawacho Nemoto Building, 6F, 1–7–11 Hirakawa-cho, Chiyoda-ku, Tokyo 102, Japan

Chapman & Hall Australia, Thomas Nelson Australia, 102 Dodds Street, South Melbourne, Victoria 3205, Australia

Chapman & Hall India, R. Seshadri, 32 Second Main Road, CIT East, Madras 600 035, India

First edition 1993

© 1993 James Essinger

Typeset in 10/12^{1}/$_{2}$ pt Times by Graphicraft Typesetters Limited, Hong Kong

Printed and bound in Hong Kong

ISBN 0 412 47290 2

A catalogue record for this book is available from the British Library

Library of Congress Cataloging-in-Publication data available

CONTENTS

vi Contents

FOREWORD

The Investment Manager's Handbook aims to provide comprehensive information which will be of practical use to investment managers around the world. It has been compiled with the needs of investment managers involved in cross-border investment particularly in mind, although investment managers who are involved solely in domestic investment should also find this Handbook of considerable utility.

The information in the Handbook is both of a conceptual and purely factual nature. I have chosen this approach because it seems to me that an investment manager of the 1990s needs not only factual information which helps him or her to work in the most efficient manner, but also detailed information about major *trends* within the investment management industry worldwide. Currently we are seeing great changes within the industry, especially trends which reflect the increasing importance of technology in relation to the investment management function. Between now and the new century, these changes look set to accelerate. *The Investment Manager's Handbook* provides a readable and readily comprehensible key to these changes.

The material in the book is organized into three parts:

Part One, 'Technology and its impact on the investment management industry', looks in detail at the role of technology within the industry, particularly in view of new types of analytical strategies which technology has made possible.

Part Two, 'An industry forum', is a collection of exclusive and especially commissioned thoughtpieces, prepared by external organizations, which focus on issues of topical interest within the investment management industry.

Part Three, 'Investment management around the world', provides detailed information on financial market regulation and custody facilities in the following countries: Australia, Austria, Belgium, Canada, Denmark, Eire, Finland, France, Germany, Hong Kong, Italy, Japan, Korea, Luxembourg, Malaysia, Mexico, the Netherlands, New Zealand, Norway, Portugal, Singapore, South Africa, Spain, Sweden, Switzerland, the UK and the USA.

I am grateful to the Zurich-based International Society of Securities Administrators (ISSA) and *Global Custodian* magazine for permission to reproduce copyright material, as well as to the Securities and Investments Board (SIB) for supplying the contact details of regulatory authorities. I also extend my gratitude to those organizations which supplied the thoughtpieces in Part Two, and to those investment managers who have been so helpful not only in sharing with me their thoughts on investment management, but also in inspiring me to put this book together. David Lowe of investment managers Singer & Friedlander was good enough to read through the manuscript and suggest improvements. Finally, my thanks are due to Alan Nelson, my editor at Chapman & Hall, for his enthusiastic reception of the initial idea for this Handbook and his subsequent support and encouragement.

I have taken all possible steps to ensure that this book does not contain any errors of fact; if, however, any have inadvertently crept in, I would very much appreciate being informed about them in order that future editions can be corrected accordingly. I would also be interested in hearing from organizations which may wish to contribute thoughtpiece articles for future editions.

James Essinger

PART ONE

Technology and its impact on the investment management industry

INTRODUCTION

George Ross-Goobey, a former chairman of the National Association of Pension Funds in the UK and one of the most senior and widely respected figures in the British investment management industry, tells a revealing story about his early days as an investment manager. Recalling those times, Ross-Goobey says:

> On joining Imperial Pension Funds in 1947, I noted that – in common with most other pension funds – they had bought a large tranche of Dalton 2.5 percent [a former British government gilt]. As was inevitable in an age when inflation was only a modest four percent, the price of the stock had dropped to 83. My first recommendation to the trustees was to sell it and take a 17-point loss. I was almost shown the door.

Ross-Goobey goes on to explain how, as an advocate of selling all gilts and buying nothing but equities, he found himself something of a lone voice, 'preaching a gospel without disciples'. Today, Ross-Goobey's idea that, other things being equal, pension fund managers and managers of other types of investment funds are most likely to safeguard and increase their clients' assets by investing in equities, rather than fixed-interest stock, is widely accepted and remains true in the long term, despite even substantial short-term fluctuations in equity prices.

Many investment managers view the opportunities which technology offers them much as Ross-Goobey's colleagues viewed, in 1947, his suggestions in favour of equity investment. By the very nature of their work which, after all, involves making extremely important strategic decisions that will have a profound, long-term effect on the fortunes of thousands of pensioners and other contributors, investment managers tend to be a cautious and conservative breed. It is, of course, in everyone's interest that they should be so. However, the danger of placing emphasis on caution and conservatism is that really good opportunities to do things better might be overlooked or ignored.

Ross-Goobey's contemporaries may well have said (and doubtless did) that investing in gilts was completely safe, whereas equity investment was not necessarily so. They might have argued (and doubtless did) that their primary obligation was to their pensioners, who had a right to expect that hard-earned pension contributions would be safeguarded. The obvious flaw in this thinking is that if the balance between risk and return which an investment manager selects for a client takes on too low a level of risk at the expense of reasonable expectations of higher return, then the investment manager is not safeguarding the interests of contributors at all – any more than, say, a gardener would be safeguarding his employer's interests by keeping a valuable-looking statue in a toolshed instead of submitting it for a professional valuation.

The investment manager of today can through the use of technology expect to come closer to fulfilling all the objectives of the investment management process, whether these are higher returns for clients, more effective management of financial information, more efficient overall operation of the investment management process, higher profits for the investment management organization or other objectives. There can, furthermore, be little doubt that the great expansion in the use of technology within the investment management industry since the early to mid-1980s has been among the most significant developments throughout the industry's history. None the less, there remain a surprising level of technological illiteracy among investment managers – a problem which may well extend most of all to senior investment managers, who learnt their trade in the late 1940s and 1950s, before the application of even the most rudimentary computers to the investment management industry. And since we all tend to disparage and fear what we do not understand, there are even now far too many otherwise gifted and highly capable investment managers whose technological illiteracy is inhibiting themselves or their organizations from maximizing fund performance and general efficiency, in the same way that George Ross-Goobey's colleagues were hampered by their perception that gilts should be favoured as investment instruments above equities.

Technology is not the only area of the investment management function that has seen dramatic change over the past few years and is likely to see further extensive developments between now and the year 2000. Investment management industry regulation and sweeping changes in national clearance and settlement procedures (particularly in line with the Group of Thirty's recommendations) are also important areas of ongoing change in relation to the investment management industry. However, there is relatively little that an individual investment manager can do about industry regulation or the clearance and settlement procedures of the countries in which he or she invests client funds, whereas opportunities to deploy technology effectively are in essence limitless. It therefore seems logical, in this Handbook, to place a particular emphasis on the opportunities which technology offers to investment managers.

The purpose of Part One of this Handbook is consequently both to inform and inspire: *inform* because the first requirement of any study of investment management technology must be to provide the kind of information about the nature of this technology which the practising investment manager needs; and *inspire* because the next step must be to suggest applications which offer interesting and potentially profitable opportunities to deploy the technology.

The four chapters that constitute the remainder of Part One set out to achieve these twin objectives of informing and inspiring. The first chapter, 'Investment management technology', looks in detail at the nature of the latest technology for investment managers and examines how this might most effectively be implemented. The three following chapters, 'Quantitative analysis', 'Indexation' and 'Custody', suggest three important specific areas of investment management activity where technology has greatly facilitated the area of activity.

Several of the thoughtpiece articles in Part Two of the Handbook take the technological discussion into more complex and provocative areas.

1 INVESTMENT MANAGEMENT TECHNOLOGY

DEFINITION

Investment management technology is: *a term that can be conveniently applied to any use of computer technology within an investment management organization.*

THE ELEMENTS OF A COMPUTER SYSTEM

Computer technology consists of computer systems which are used to carry out specific applications. A computer system is any self-contained computer tool. Systems for investment managers tend to consist of three specific elements, as follows.

1. *The principal computer that powers the system*: this is often a mainframe computer – the largest, most powerful and most expensive type of computer – but increasingly it is likely to be a minicomputer. Modern minicomputers usually have an equivalent amount of processing power as all but the very largest mainframes, and have the great advantage of being much smaller and far less expensive. The reason why minicomputers are now often effectively as powerful as mainframe computers is that advances in microprocessors – the tiny components at the heart of the computer that handle the information processing function – have made these components increasingly small and increasingly powerful. It is already difficult to define the boundary between the mainframe computer and minicomputers in terms of processing power. A more practical approach to defining the mainframe and the minicomputer is to categorize them in terms of size: a mainframe computer will fill a medium-sized room, while a minicomputer will fill a storage cupboard. The evolution of computer technology is so rapid that some powerful minicomputers (such as the Apollo and Sun machines) are already compact enough to sit on a desk. It is likely that by the mid-1990s the distinctions between mainframes and minicomputers will have become redundant.

    Whatever the nature of the computer, the function here is to act as the controller and central store of information for the system. In some cases, it is also possible to use a powerful desktop computer to power the system. Note that the principal computer is often referred to as the 'host' computer.

2. *The communications method*: this will typically be a dedicated telephone line which is able to relay data around the system. Where the computer system is entirely contained within the office of the organization using the system, the communications network is known as a *local area network* (LAN). Where the communications network includes computers located within the organization's office and also computers located externally, the communications network is known as a *wide area network* (WAN). When external communications are involved, these will usually take place via telephone lines leased from a telecommunications company, although in cases where the external communications extends to computers operated by the same organization, proprietary telephone lines are often used.

3. *The desktop computer*: the final element in the system is the desktop computer, more often known as a **personal computer** (PC). Computer technology has been able to produce computers small enough to fit a desktop since the early 1980s; and the power of PCs has developed to the stage where a powerful PC can be used to power a small LAN, although the heavy information processing requirements of investment management organizations make it more usual to employ a mainframe computer or minicomputer for this purpose. Until the mid-1980s, it was usual for desktop terminals within a LAN or WAN to be 'dumb', that is they acted only as screens to relay information but were themselves unable to carry out any complex processing (or any processing at all). The use of PCs within LANs or WANs is now widespread and gives the desktop computer user access not only to the information that is being sent via the communications network, but also to all the information processing capabilities of the PC itself.

The only limit on the number of PCs within a LAN or WAN is the processing and control power of the principal computer. In practical terms, the principal computer will always be powerful enough to handle the number of PCs which will be required by the investment management organization. A small investment management organization would require up to about 10 PCs, a medium-sized organization approx. 30 and a large organization approx. 100.

ADDITIONAL COMPUTING CONCEPTS

Usually it is not necessary for a practising investment manager to possess a detailed knowledge of computer operation. However, computer-literacy is increasingly important within the investment management industry, since the industry is itself increasingly dependent on computers for its growth and future direction. It is useful for an investment manager to be familiar with the following computing concepts.

Basic principles of computer operation

Computers are essentially huge collections of on/off switches. These on/off switches, which are themselves electronic components allowing electrons only to pass one way, are used within computers to manage the binary processing which is the basis of all computer functioning. This initial level of computer operation is the **electronics level**.

The second level of operation, the **operating system**, is a protocol for allowing the electronics of the computer to operate an application. The operating system 'instructs' the electronics to add one stored register to another. When this process takes place many millions of times a second, the computer can perform useful work by following the systematic 'instructions' of a program.

The past few years have seen a trend for operating systems to become standardized. Here the rationale is that if an organization buys a computer with a standard operating system, the organization not only is able to run a much wider variety of programs than would otherwise be possible, but will also be able to run programs that will be developed in the future. These advantages of standard operating systems are so great that the UNIX and DOS operating systems are rapidly becoming standard throughout the investment management community.

The third level of operation, the **programming language** (the language in which the program is written), 'sits' on top of the operating system and is a way for the human operator (the programmer) to instruct the computer to do a useful task. The programmer's job is to interpret the requirements of the job in hand in such a way that the computer can carry it out. The programming language is therefore literally a way for human beings to communicate with the computer.

There are at least a dozen programming languages which are particularly popular among investment management organizations. Examples of programming languages are FORTRAN, the classic scientific language; Common Business Oriented Language (COBOL), which was principally designed for business activities involving numerous different accounts; and the language known simply as C, a very powerful language which has the ability to process complex information extremely quickly.

The fourth level, the **applications language**, does not feature in every investment management application, but it is used where the application requires an additional level of programming complexity dedicated to a particular programming function or group of functions.

Fault tolerance

This is an attribute of a computer system and indicates that if a particular processing component in the computer suffers a fault, the computer will:

- continue operating in exactly the same manner as before;
- suffer no degradation in its functioning (i.e. suffer no loss of data, etc.).

Open architectures

Open architectures are computer system protocols which allow the user to exploit fully the advantages of standardized operating systems. A particular advantage to the investment management organization of utilizing an open architecture is that it should in the future permit the organization to introduce new and unforeseen types of software. Today's computer packages for investment managers are almost always built around open architectures.

Packaged computer systems

Packaged computer systems (or 'packages', as they are more commonly known) are computer systems which have been designed and tested for the application in question before being sold. A package offers investment management organizations the considerable advantages of being reliable and far less expensive than a fully customized system built from scratch. On the other hand, since many copies of the same package will in all probability be sold, the package will only offer the organization that uses it any competitive advantage once it has been to some extent customized.

Real-time processing and on-line transaction processing

These related terms refer to the way in which information is communicated across a communications line. When information is sent in **real-time** (or **'on-line'**), the information is being sent the instant that it becomes available.

Furthermore, the information reaches the recipient with a speed limited only by the speed of electromagnetic waves (where radio communications are used) or by the speed of electrons through a wire. Since these travel at the speed of light and one-sixth of the speed of light respectively, real-time and on-line communications are considered to be instantaneous, although where the sender or recipient is many thousands of miles away, slight delays in switching and in transmission may result in a delay of a few seconds.

On-line transaction processing, where transactions are processed in real-time, is often abbreviated to OLTP.

AREAS OF TECHNOLOGICAL IMPLEMENTATION FOR INVESTMENT MANAGERS

Broadly speaking, there are two areas of technological implementation for investment managers; these are as follows:

1. *Back-office* applications: implementations of technology which are directed at managing the administrative requirements of the organization.
2. *Front-office* applications: these cover any implementation of technology directed at managing the 'money making' side of the business.

For investment managers, the principal applications of technology in each area are as follows:

Back office

- *General accounting.* This includes the general accounting requirements of the investment management organization.
- *Client accounting.* This covers the specific accounting requirements of client funds, which will be kept separate from the organization's own funds.

- *Preparation of client reports.* Reporting to clients is an important area where computers can relieve investment managers of much tedious work, as well as maximizing the accuracy of the report.
- *Handling transactions.* Details of completed transactions will be relayed by the investment manager to the back office, where transactions must be logged, relevant accounts updated and the transaction settled with the counterparty. Computers can speed this process and greatly reduce the likelihood of an error.
- *Communicating with custodians.* Custodians handle a variety of administrative requirements relating to the custody and general financial management of securities held by the investment management organization. Technology allows communications with custodians to take place in real-time or through batch-processing.
- *Holding details of portfolios.* It is essential for investment managers to keep precise track of the contents of their portfolios on a transaction-by-transaction basis. Computers are not only able to manage this process, but provide investment managers with the option of having screen-based access to this information in the front office. This information can, if required, also include details of the funds available for investment for a particular client, and a client's credit rating.
- *Communicating with the front office.* A great advantage to technology is that it allows electronic communications from the back office to the front office. This greatly increases the speed, accuracy and convenience of these communications.

Front office

- *Receiving datafeeds from vendors of financial information.* Financial information vendors sell a wide range of information relating to the current or historical prices of securities and other investment instruments on financial markets around the world. This information is usually supplied on a real-time basis, although it can also be accessed on a batch basis. Technology allows investment managers to obtain this information on a constantly updated basis direct from exchanges, with the vendor reconfiguring the information instantaneously and so causing no delay in the provision of the information.
- *Processing this information into a variety of customized configurations.* Technology allows 'raw' datafeeds to be processed by the investment manager's computer into the most useful configuration for a particular investment manager's requirements.
- *Making use of a range of methods to obtain support with buying and selling decisions.* The final step in the sophistication of front-office systems is a system which provides specific guidance with decisions. Technology is constantly providing new tools to maximize the efficiency of the decision-making process.
- *Communicating with the back office.* Technology allows investment managers to benefit from instantaneous access to a wide range of useful information that would otherwise only be retrievable from the back office by a laborious manual process.

WHY DO INVESTMENT MANAGERS DEPLOY TECHNOLOGY?

It is useful to identify six principal reasons why investment management organizations deploy technology. In order of importance, the reasons are as follows.

1. *To relieve manual drudgery*: many tasks facing an investment management organization, particularly in its back office, are inherently tedious and repetitive. Computers are particularly good at handling tedious and repetitive tasks, thereby freeing administrative staff for tasks involving direct contact with clients or suppliers, and for strategic planning activities.

2. *To increase the accuracy of completed tasks*: a major problem with using people to carry out repetitive tasks is that human fallibility produces a large number of inaccuracies. In the formal world of investment management the professionalism of investment managers is – reasonably enough – at least partly assessed in terms of the accuracy of their client reports, client accounting and settlement. The use of computers in these and other areas can greatly reduce errors, or eliminate them altogether.

3. *To increase the speed with which tasks are completed*: computers process information at the speed at which electrons travel through wires, which for all practical purposes involving a LAN or WAN means that they process the information instantaneously. No manual processing can even approach the speed of computer processing.

4. *To save money*: where human labour can be replaced by a computer, it is almost always less expensive in the medium to long term to deploy the computer than employ a person. Here the qualification 'the medium to long term' is necessary because, in most cases, the initial capital expenditure of designing the software and installing the computer will make the computer system more expensive in the short term. However, this capital expenditure should soon justify itself. An obvious (but none the less huge) advantage which computers have over human labour is that computers do not require holidays or leisure time, but can if required be run continually.

5. *To deal with increasing volumes of data*: all investment managers complain that they have too much data, such as financial information, to process. Not only can computers process information more speedily and more accurately than humans, but computers are able to plough through large volumes of data.

6. *To obtain a competitive advantage*: the previous reasons all relate to the advantages which computers offer in terms of processing information more efficiently; however, even in an environment where the vast majority of investment management organizations have similar information processing capabilities, there is still a great deal of scope for investment managers to use computers as a means of establishing a competitive advantage over rival investment management organizations. In an increasingly competitive investment management industry, the competitive edge which computers can offer is of extreme importance. The following section looks at this in detail.

USING COMPUTERS TO GAIN A COMPETITIVE ADVANTAGE

Investment management organizations can derive a competitive advantage from technology in two distinct, but related, ways:

1. by using technology to improve the quality of service which they provide to clients;
2. by using technology to improve the performance of funds under management.

Generally speaking, technology makes its greatest contribution towards improving quality of service by being deployed to competitive advantage in the back office, and its greatest contribution towards improving fund performance by being deployed to competitive advantage in the front office. However, it is necessary to bear in mind that integration of front- and back-office function is an inevitable result of an increased deployment of technology.

Technology can link the administrative and money-making parts of the business to the extent that the barriers between these different departments' functions start to blur. For example, where an investment manager has screen-based access not only to real-time price information in customized configurations, but also to comprehensive information which the manager can use to compile a detailed client report, then the manager is obviously benefiting from the competitive edge which technology can provide, both in terms of helping to improve fund performance and quality of service. Analysing technology's contribution towards competitive advantage in terms of back-office and front-office applications is none the less a useful approach to a complex field.

The main areas in which investment managers can deploy technology to maximum competitive effect are as follows.

Back office: helping to improve the quality of service

1. Advantage to be gained from deploying technology: *handling clients' accounts more efficiently and cost-effectively.*
The client handling requirements of investment management organizations tend to be high value but low volume, with the number of accounts handled being relatively small compared with, say, accounts handled by financial institutions that deal directly with the public. However, each individual account will require much more attention than the average retail account.

The efficient handling of client accounts is an important way for one investment management organization to establish an advantage over another. Since technology plays a key role in efficient client handling, it follows that it can offer a major competitive edge here.

Technology's role would cover the following areas:

- information storage and retrieval;
- calculations and reconciliation;
- configuring information in a format customized to the client's requirements.

2. Advantage to be gained from deploying technology: *developing more effective data communications.*

Where the communications network is taking place within an LAN, efficient data communications will make the investment management organization itself more efficient and so indirectly improve service quality. Where the communications network is a WAN that includes one or more terminals within the client's office (i.e. the client is linked to the investment management organization in real-time or via a batch-processing system), efficient communications will make a direct contribution to the quality of service.

Efficient communications means:

*   Accurate and instantaneous transmission and reception of messages.
*   Secure communications, which are of great importance either within a LAN or a WAN (although they are at a premium within a WAN where external networking is involved). The security process must guard against messages being read by unauthorized persons, or corrupted (which can happen even if a message cannot be read by the person doing the corrupting). The defence against illicit reading of a message is known as **encryption**, involving encoding the message according to an 'encryption key'. An encrypted message is impossible to read without access to an encryption key, and the use of 'end-to-end' encryption – the safest form – involves the message remaining encrypted within the system, so that it never appears 'in the clear' (i.e. readable) except at either end of the communication process. The defence against illicit corruption of a message is known as **message authentication** and involves 'tagging' the message with a code which reveals any modification of the message. Messages can be both encrypted and made subject to message authentication.

3. Advantage to be gained from deploying technology: *making more effective use of custodians.*

Efficient liaison with custodians is an important means for an investment management organization to establish a competitive advantage over its rivals through providing a better service to clients. The specific benefits to clients of the investment management organization as a result of the organization's efficient liaison with the custodian are as follows:

*   clients will receive a better accounting service relating to their funds;
*   clients will receive more timely notification of corporate actions by the corporations in which they invest (e.g. rights issues, voting opportunities);
*   clients will receive more timely payment of dividends;
*   clients will be better informed regarding the general administration of their funds and the investments in which the funds are held.

4. Advantage to be gained from deploying technology: *helping the investment manager to prepare better client reports.*

For many investment managers, preparing client reports is simply a tedious and time-consuming task. The danger here is that the tedium of the task may lead investment managers to neglect to give it their full attention. In fact clients pay a great deal of attention to the quality of the reports that they receive and will often (at least partly) assess an investment manager's performance according to the quality of these reports and the promptness with which they are forwarded. Not only does technology allow comprehensive and accurate client reports to be prepared with great speed, but it also facilitates the creation of reports that are customized to the specific requirements of a client rather than simply following the investment management organization's 'house style', which will usually have been developed in line with the convenience of the investment management organization rather than that of the client. An increasing number of clients are seeking to obtain customized reports and, other things being equal, are likely to opt for the investment manager who can supply them.

Front office: helping to improve performance of funds under management

1. Advantage to be gained from deploying technology: *maximizing the efficiency of incoming datafeeds*.
If an investment manager is going to obtain maximized competitive advantage from using datafeeds, these must meet two requirements:

1. They must provide all the information necessary.
2. They must be as inexpensive as possible.

The first requirement ensures that the incoming datafeeds cover all the financial markets in which the investment manager is interested. The second requirement ensures that the investment manager's utility of datafeeds makes the maximum contribution to his organization's cost-effectiveness.

   The precise nature of the datafeeds which an investment manager uses will naturally depend on the nature of the manager's investment interests. In order of market penetration, the following are the best-known commercial vendors of financial information, with their principal areas of coverage in parentheses:

   Reuters (worldwide)
   Quotron (US specialization, but now increasingly worldwide
   Telerate (worldwide)
   Telekurs (continental Europe, increasingly worldwide)
   Quick (Japanese specialization, seeking to move worldwide)

It will be seen that the trend among information vendors is to provide worldwide coverage.

   In addition to these commercial vendors, there are also official vendors: stock exchanges and other types of financial markets which provide information feeds (and often screens as well) to traders and fund managers. In the UK the best-known example of an official vendor is the London Stock Exchange, which rents its TOPIC screens to users. TOPIC screens carry the Stock Exchange's Stock Exchange Automated Quotations (SEAQ) services.

   The key to using technology to maximize the breadth of information available from datafeeds and the cost-effectiveness of using the service is to use one vendor rather than a number of vendors. With the shift in the information vending market away from specialized vendors and towards vendors who provide international coverage, there should be no problem in selecting a suitable 'single-source' vendor. Hand in hand with this requirement is the need to deploy a screen-based system which features *integration* of the different datafeeds from all the markets under scrutiny, thereby allowing the investment manager fingertip control over which market developments are scrutinized at any one moment. Such an integrated system would provide access to any of the available information feeds on one screen, or else on a 'window' (i.e. a compartment of a screen) within the screen. Increasingly, the industry standard for windows is the Microsoft Windows protocol.

Information vendors have realized that the market for datafeeds is moving away from several different feeds, towards a market where the demand for single-screen, integrated access to information feeds predominates. As a result, most vendors now provide integrated packages based on architectures. These can be used not only to integrate all incoming datafeeds, but also to provide a wide variety of 'value-added' analytical information. The range of this type of information is examined below.

2.   Advantage to be gained from deploying technology: *maximizing the benefits of decision support systems.*

The term **decision support system** can usefully be applied to any screen-based system which provides any information other than simply a variety of different datafeeds. By giving investment managers the opportunity to make investment decisions based upon more in-depth or comprehensive information than their rivals, decision support systems offer investment managers the opportunity to gain a competitive edge in fund performance.

One important technical point must be made. Decision support systems can only process datafeeds and add value to this information if the original datafeed is being supplied in **digital form**. This means that the message has been digitized and so converted into a computer-readable format, which can then be manipulated by the computer according to the requirements of the system. Some information feeds are still supplied in **video format** (i.e. supplied onto a video screen). These cannot be manipulated and processed within a decision support system. Although the emphasis among most investment management organizations is now on obtaining digital feeds, video still retains an appeal for smaller managers who have chosen not to use extensive decision support systems, or in countries (e.g. Japan) where the principal information vendor (Quick) is still principally supplying information on video.

The range of decision support systems varies widely through the following hierarchy of systems.

1.   *Integrated datafeeds* available on one screen (often via windows).

2.   *Value-added analytics* applied to the datafeeds and showing changes in prices over predetermined past periods. The term 'historical' is applied to these past periods, even though they may be no longer than 30, 60 or 90 days into the past. Value-added analytics can also include spreadsheets, and systems which enable an investment manager to key a particular portfolio into the system and find out – on a regularly updated basis – information about such factors as what the portfolio is

worth, which are the best-performing assets in the portfolio and which are the worst.

There are a wide variety of value-added decision support packages available from numerous specialized vendors.

3. The *most advanced type of decision support systems*, which not only take in incoming datafeeds and add value to them in a variety of ways, but also use various techniques to make specific buying and selling recommendations, or to advise on strategic investment decisions.

There are two major methods of building an advanced decision support system:

- *systems based around a mathematical model*: these embody in their software a particular mathematical theory of a market. This category includes **quantitative systems** which arrive at buying and selling decisions by applying one or other theory of balancing risk and return within the market, and **technical systems** which represent in mathematical form any of a variety of more general theories of market behaviour.
- *systems which seek to emulate human decision-making processes*: the second category of advanced decision support systems consists of systems which seek, however crudely, to imitate human reasoning. Such an ambitious objective has led to these systems becoming very well known in the media under the generic name of **artificial intelligence** (AI) systems. The term is something of a misnomer: however useful some AI systems may be, they cannot be regarded as intelligent. Although definitions vary, one important aspect of intelligence, that of thinking for oneself and drawing completely new conclusions from a different set of data, is quite beyond the abilities of AI systems. These really do nothing more than slavishly follow instructions. None the less, a great deal of ingenuity has gone into designing today's AI systems; there are two types of AI system:

(i) *the rule-based system* – these derive from the idea that one way to try to replicate human intelligence in a computer system is to program the computer with rules (or, as they are often called, heuristics) which supposedly govern the thought processes of a human in a particular field of expertise. However, applying the theory is only partly successful. Much of human expertise is intuitive and **tacit**, to use the technical term, and as such is not available for articulation and embodiment in a rule-based system.

Despite these objections, rule-based systems have proven their worth as competent, if uninspired, replicators of human intelligence. Many rule-based systems have extremely useful commercial applications within investment management scenarios, although the high level of judgemental skill required within investment management means that this is an environment where the judgement-forming ability of rule-based systems will always be severely tested.

(ii) *neural nets* – these are also called neural networks or neurone nets and have, on occasion, caused considerable excitement and interest among information technology staff who believe that these nets offer the best possibility to date for replicating human thought. At an anatomical level, the human brain is known to consist of specialized nerve cells (neurones), connected by specialized connective links (synapses). The neural net is a configuration, simulated within the computer program by traditional software, that works on similar lines. The concept of **simulation** is fundamental; neural nets are not new forms of computer hardware designed to operate like the brain, but simulated configurations which are best imagined as rather like a spider's web, where if you touch any point in the web, all the tensions of the spokes will be rearranged until the web is again in balance. This is exactly how a neural net works. An input to the configuration causes activity to spread along the simulated synapses and among the simulated neurones according to an arbitrary rule devised by the programmer. By gradual modification of the strengths of connection between the synapses and neurones, a net can be 'trained' to produce a known output for a particular input. Once the net has been trained in this manner, it can produce new, useful outputs (which might be buying and selling recommendations) for a given input.

In practice, the simulated neural net works well but, to date, only at a relatively rudimentary level. A major problem with applying neural nets in the financial world is that although it is known how to digitize price information, it is not known how to digitize those subjective thoughts and impressions which play a key role in the thinking of an expert investment manager. For this reason, neural nets should be regarded as still being at the research and development stage as far as their application in investment management is concerned.

THE FUTURE OF INVESTMENT MANAGEMENT TECHNOLOGY

The following are likely to be the major trends in investment management technology until the mid-1990s:

- a greater reliance on open systems;
- a continued shift in the market-place towards integrated systems;
- a premium will be placed on investment management systems that provide the widest breadth of functions. Systems featuring powerful administrative capabilities, as well as advanced decision support facilities, will begin to dominate the market-place.

Investment management technology guru Professor Thomas Ho of New York systems house Global Advanced Technology has said:

A principal trend within the industry is for advanced decision support systems to be run on open standards that will maximize the integration of these advanced systems with the other front-office information, value-added and communications systems.

While Joseph Rosen, Chief Information Officer of the New York-based Dubin & Swieca Capital Management firm has stated:

> The advanced decision support and AI industry may eventually be a victim of its own success, with the advanced portion of decision support programs being seen as so useful – for all their limitations – that they start to lose their own identity and become seen as part of the trading or fund management organization's overall front-office weaponry. This increased anonymity of AI systems is perhaps inevitable in computing environments where a primary buzzword is integration.

APPENDIX: COMPUTER SECURITY FOR INVESTMENT MANAGERS

An investment management system will only operate to its maximum effectiveness if the system is safe from malicious outside interference and holds information securely and confidentially. Within the financial sector as a whole, information is an increasingly valuable asset, and its value increases in direct proportion to the extent that market regulators, and the accelerating deployment of information technology within the financial sector, combine to create a scenario where financial markets are increasingly international and 'perfect', that is where all market participants will tend to have access to the same information. In this scenario, information ceases merely to be a useful asset and acquires a value that can be very great indeed. The information held within investment management systems therefore might be said to be valuable for the following reasons:

- It may give the investment manager who holds it a competitive advantage over other institutional investors.
- It is essential for the smooth running of the investment manager's own business.
- The integrity of the information is essential for the discharging of all the investment management functions.

All investment managers should seek to maximize the security and integrity of their computer systems. Many do not, perhaps because they believe that the process of investment management is somehow too rarefied and complex for computer fraudsters and other illicit users of computer systems to pay the investment management industry any attention. This view shows a misplaced confidence in the ability of an unprotected investment management system to withstand the onslaught of a really determined computer criminal ('criminal' since most countries are rapidly putting in place legislation which makes such illicit interference with a computer system a criminal offence). Unfortunately, the devastating breach in an investment management's computer system which demonstrates how misplaced this confidence is can often seriously damage the victim's business and, in some cases, inflict such damage that the victim will not recover.

In summary, breaches of computer security can be:

- *costly*. In addition to loss of money through computer fraud, the victim will need to conduct an expensive survey of its computer system to assess the extent of damage; many victims whose computer systems have been breached will take elaborate and expensive precautions to ensure that this particular breach does not recur, but will not plug other vulnerable points in the computer network; another problem is that for the victim to have any chance of recovering lost funds, it would have to report the incident to the police, but many victims will be reluctant to do so because of the resulting bad publicity;
- *time-consuming*. Staff time will be devoted to limiting the damage of the breach to prevent a recurrence of the breach and, perhaps, to dealing with the police and the media;
- *morale-sapping*. The knowledge that an investment management organization has been the victim of a computer fraud or other computer security breach can strike a severe blow at staff morale;
- *acutely embarrassing*. If news of the breach reaches the media, the resulting publicity can be very harmful for the victim; even if the news does not reach the general public, it may reach the ears of the victim's competitors, which is both humiliating and embarrassing.

It is therefore much better for an investment management organization to *prevent* breaches in its computer system.

All the available evidence suggests that the vast majority of computer security breaches occur because users do not take sufficient precautions to prevent a breach. One important reason why some financial organizations do not give a greater priority to computer security appears to be that senior managers do not find computer security technology interesting, and even do not see it as remotely important to the organization's mainstream activities, which generate revenue rather than implement, as computer security does, what are inevitably defensive measures. In a nutshell, many financial organizations' senior management and financial directors are neglecting computer security because they do not see it as being intimately bound up with the visible, day-to-day operations of their organization.

It is possible to take measures which go a long way towards ensuring that a computer system used by an investment manager is highly secure against unauthorized interference. However, no solutions are offered here to the fundamental psychological problem that many users too often see no particular reason to prioritize the actual deployment of computer security.

Suppliers of computer security technology have developed a range of arguments to try to convince users to place a high priority on making provisions for computer security. Broadly speaking, these arguments aim to indicate that financial organizations cannot afford *not* to make technical provision for computer security. While deploying computer security technology certainly costs money, the outlay is small when compared with the potential loss if an unprofessional computer system is broken into.

Financial organizations would then generally recognize that a small outlay on computer security provides them with less security than would a larger outlay. Where budgets are tight, however, there will be considerable pressure on the organization to reduce its expenditure on computer security to a minimum. Computer security is not yet a statutory obligation for financial organizations around the world, although it may well become so in time. In the USA a number of states have already enacted legislation which makes it impossible for a financial organization to bring a prosecution against someone accused of computer-related crimes unless a recognized computer security framework was in operation at the time of the alleged breach. In many other countries such prosecutions do not require the existence of a computer security system, but future legislation may place a statutory burden on financial organizations to implement a workable computer security system.

There are three principal types of control which, if properly implemented, will maximize the security of financial institutions' computer systems. These controls reach out to all areas of the institution's operations, from management policy to procedural controls and purely technology precautions, as follows:

1. Personnel controls.
2. Procedural controls.
3. Technological controls.

(1) Personnel controls

Experience has shown that the vast majority of serious computer crimes are 'inside' jobs, with the perpetrator being a trusted member of the organization's staff, sometimes working in league with more experienced criminals who will, incidentally, have no compunction about leaving the insider to take the blame and face retribution if the heist starts to go wrong. Sometimes 'sleepers' are used, who will work inside the organization for a fairly long period of time and establish a record of trust before striking.

As a result of the importance of the insider, a financial organization's overall computer security policy must take into account the dangers posed by staff – particularly those working in the computer systems department – who are dishonest, disgruntled or merely incompetent.

Eight key recommendations for aspects of personnel control are:

1. In every computer system installation there are a number of key staff whose activities are of critical importance. They should be identified, given special attention by management and, as soon as practicable, back-up staff trained in order to reduce the organization's vulnerability.
2. Recruitment procedures should be designed to ensure, as far as possible, that staff are competent and honest. References should be obtained and always checked.
3. A probation period should be used in appropriate cases to verify competence.
4. Salary and incentives should be appropriate to the responsibilities of the staff concerned. This ensures that the interests and objectives of employers and employees coincide.
5. A comprehensive, practical training programme will encourage employees to consider career development within the organization, and avoid demoralization caused by lack of achievement.

6. Dismissal and resignation procedures must take into account the damage which can be caused by a dishonest or disgruntled employee while serving a period of notice. If an employee with access to the computer network is allowed to serve out his or her notice (which may not always be advisable), it is important to change logging on procedures so as to prevent them from using the network during this time.
7. Staff, particularly those with 'hands-on' responsibilities, should be obliged to take their annual holidays (failure to take leave usually displays a need to be continually near the system). It is often when a perpetrator is away that a fraud is detected.
8. The financial organization should ensure that facilities exist within the personnel department for staff with personal difficulties, such as financial problems, family difficulties or psychological problems, to obtain some form of counselling or referral to an outside counsellor. Many instances where insiders have played a major role in perpetrating a computer crime subsequently show that the fundamental source of the deviation from normal honest behaviour was the onset of a personal problem to which the employee could see no possible resolution.

(2) Procedural controls

Procedural controls, that is regulations governing how a financial organization operates, with a particular reference to its internal operations, play a key role in minimizing breaches in computer security. The most important procedural controls for financial organizations used by banks in relation to computer security are:

1. Segregation of duties – this is the policy adopted by the UK's clearing banks and many other financial organizations of taking all steps to prevent an individual member of staff from having access to, or being in charge of, every element in a particular computing function. For example, one major UK clearing bank does not allow computer programmers to undertake program analysis work. Similarly, the bank has a policy of spreading encryption keys and other security components among a number of people, to ensure that at any one time no single person has access to all the keys.
2. 'Four Eyes' principle – this policy, related to segregation of duties, means that a bank takes all steps to ensure that where a computing function offers the potential for fraud and theft, then wherever possible two people will be required to access that function (e.g. the need for two separate passwords to be keyed into a system or two separate cards to be swiped through a cardswipe before the function can be accessed). Similarly, computer programs themselves should be independently checked and approved before being entered into the computer.
3. Other procedural controls – these cover a wide range of additional banking procedures that are directed at maximizing the security of a computer installation. Such procedural controls would include, for example, the provision of audit trails (computerized records of who has used the system, and when), vetting of personnel and/or electronic token security.

(3) **Technological controls**

Computers are high-technology tools and it is not surprising that the range of technological controls to which a financial organization must attend when seeking to maximize its computer security is extensive and complex. Examining these controls, and the potential hazards which they are most adept at defending against, is an essential part of the control process.

The technological development of the greatest significance to the computer security industry during recent years is undoubtedly that of the microchip. It has permitted the construction of computer security technology that is compact, powerful, reasonably priced and therefore more widely available.

It could be argued that computer security technology in the 1990s is able to meet all the security challenges that face it, and that consequently computer security is in essence not a technical problem, but a management one. The technology is readily available, hence what matters is whether the organization has a budget for deploying computer security technology and, if so, how the organization intends to spend it.

Current research and development in the field of computer security technology lies in refining existing technologies rather than in developing new ones. The emphasis in this area is on consolidating existing technological innovations and convincing an increasing number of users that they need the technology rather than on hastening to break new technological ground.

Since most tactical computer security requirements (i.e. those relating to a specific hazard) can already be met, users are free to develop strategic approaches to computer security, which is less straightforward than simply meeting tactical needs. For example, one area of computer security where developing a strategic approach is of importance is disaster recovery, an area that is examined in greater detail below.

In what follows the main computer security hazards that face organizations and the types of technological controls which organizations can make in order to defend against them are examined. Readers should bear in mind, however, that technological controls are effective only when implemented in conjunction with the above sections on personnel controls and procedural controls. Unless these two 'common-sense' types of control are in place, no sophisticated technological control is likely to be fully effective.

As we have already mentioned in this chapter, most investment management systems will contain the following elements:

- a desktop workstation (which increasingly is often a personal computer);
- an in-house link to a switching system, or to a mini- or mainframe computer;
- a telecommunications link to external computer systems.

Within this framework the actual nature of the system operated by the investment management organization will take numerous forms; however, from a security angle the differences are less important than the technical resemblances. The security hazards examined in this section apply more or less equally to any financial organization which deploys currently available technology.

Security hazards and technological controls

These hazards, and the technological controls associated with them, are as follows.

1.   The *physical access* hazard – this is the hazard of any unauthorized person gaining physical access to the proximity of any computer terminal, or any other part of the computer system.
Control: Impose a strict security policy at the entrance to buildings, backed up with a personalized access control system, such as one requiring the use of an electronic token plus a codeword or number, that restricts access to specific rooms or areas within the building.
2.   The *electronic access* hazard – this is the hazard of an unauthorized person gaining access to a computer terminal or workstation.
Control: As with the physical access hazard, the best control here is to implement an 'electronic token plus codeword' system of personalized access control, restricting access to specific terminals to authorized staff.
3.   The *communications* hazard – this is the hazard of an unauthorized person being able to interfere with any computer data communications system that is sending data from one point to another, whether inside or outside the building.
Control: For any financial organization involved in global custody, the security of the data communications link between global custodian, sub-custodian (if applicable) and institutional investor is perhaps the most vulnerable element of the investment management system. (The techniques by which the security of the communications element of the system is safeguarded is therefore examined here in detail.)

Both an external telecommunications network and a local area network (LAN) must be secured against unwanted interference. Attention must be paid to both issues if the institution is to feel confident about its security arrangements.
As far as communications security is concerned, the practical problems are likely to be:

- The need for the rapid relay of information will militate against any security system which protects the messages transmitted but which slows them down by even a small amount.
- Investment management organizations may ultimately be unwilling to spend money on ensuring security in this area, as it is not easy to see where the money has been spent, since all the security precautions will be contained in software or hardware, rather than visible in the form of terminal access controls or electronic locks.
- There is considerable ignorance within the investment management industry regarding communications security measures.
- Since breaches of communications security are more difficult, and rarer, than attempts by unauthorized persons to breach physical and electronic access control, some organizations may come to think that the expense of ensuring security in this area is not worthwhile.

Maintaining the security of communications systems is a problem for all organizations, in particularly, those which rely on on-line transaction processing (OLTP), as with an on-line ATM network. Similarly, automated trading systems that involve an on-line communications link must also be made secure. Efficient security systems to guard against either an outside party seeing one's transmitted data, or – which could be much worse – this data being deliberately interfered with, do exist and are being marketed worldwide.

Investment managers wishing to protect their communications system from an external threat would do well to make their system unattractive to access. A high-ranking source at a US government computer crime investigation department said that hackers would generally not spend more than five minutes trying to get into a system if it does not interest them. The trick, he said, is to make it uninteresting. If, for example, the name of the computer system is given as a military or financial institution, hackers would get together and spend whatever time it takes to break into the system. A simple solution, if at all practicable, is to change the name of the system into something uninteresting such as 'Janitorial Supplies'. He pointed out that, in addition, organizations should ask for a great deal of information whenever someone wishes to gain entry to their systems, so the system might request the employee's name, social security number, date of birth, department name, supervisor's name, and so on. In actuality, the authorized user is instructed to disregard the requested information and merely enter his or her name, insert three spaces and enter the password. The request for all the other information should be designed to make the intruder believe it will be impossible to get into the system and discourage him or her from even trying.

Encryption and message authentication

Techniques for maximizing the security of communications between computer systems are of two kinds. The first type of technique, **encryption**, aims to encode the communicated message and thus prevent an unauthorized person from finding out what the message says. The second type of technique, **message authentication**, seeks to prevent an unauthorized person tampering with the communicated message, which would otherwise be possible, even if the message were in encrypted form. For maximum security of the communicated message, both encryption and message authentication are required, although few organizations currently go to these lengths; most normally rely on encryption only.

Encryption is an encoding procedure which takes place at the point of entry of the message to be communicated; it uses software that can be incorporated into the home network via the entry terminal. The message is sent to the external destination, where it is decoded by the same encryption process. The software governing the point of data entry process and the delivery of data process must use the same encryption key – i.e. a number which is used as the basis for generating the encrypted form of the message.

Encryption relies for its effectiveness on the fact that the encrypted form of the message is generated by a highly complex algorithm which would take so long to break through random trial and error, even if a powerful computer were used for this purpose, that the code is for all practical purposes unbreakable, or at least with the reservations below. Since an encryption algorithm is used only in conjunction with a specific key, it is possible for a proprietary algorithm to be supplied, with the algorithm then being 'customized' by the use of a key.

Probably the most commonly used algorithm worldwide is the **US Data Encryption Standard** (DES), which gives a total number of permutations of 2 raised to the power 56, minus 1. The algorithm is a product cipher employing 64-bit data blocks and a 64-bit key. Organizations using this and other algorithms would typically change the key on a regular basis. As long as both 'ends' of the encrypted system use the same key, they will recognize the encrypted message, so the actual message does not at any time need to appear 'in the clear' within the system. Apart from the people directly involved with sending the message, not even staff of the institution which sends the message would have access to it since the encryption process takes place within the system and the key serves only as a way for the encryption process to begin.

Another important encryption algorithm is the **Rivest-Shamir-Adlemann** (RSA); it is based upon the computational difficulty of factoring the product of large prime numbers (for this purpose, integers with several hundred decimal digits). Advocates of RSA believe that it offers a higher level of security than DES in view of advances in computer processing speed which, they claim, mean that it may be feasible for a computer to run fast enough to crack the DES within a reasonable time-frame.

For all practical purposes, the use of encryption means that a message communicated between two banks' computers should be safe from anyone reading it. This does not necessarily mean that it will be safe from being tampered with; for example, a malevolent hacker might, on seeing that his efforts to read the message must end in frustration, decide to swap elements of the message around, still in its encrypted form, thereby giving the recipient a different message from that originally intended. In order to prevent this from happening, message authentication must be used.

Message authentication helps to protect a user against his data being tampered with by enabling him to check when such tampering has occurred. The message authentication technique involves a special code being put into the data at point of entry and only allows the data to reach the recipient if the code has been transmitted along with the message, unimpaired. If anyone tries to tamper with the message, the message authentication system will alert the bona fide recipient that this has occurred.

A standard for message authentication encoding has been set down by the American National Standard Institute, in ANSI Standard X9.9.

The ideal situation for an institution, as far as its communications security requirements are concerned, is to deploy both encryption and message authentication. In due course, such precautions may be seen as essential.

Where wholesale organizations are communicating with each other via a data communications system, the techniques of **non-repudiation** and **sender authentication** are important. Non-repudiation is required where it is in the interests of either counterparty to be able to prove that a particular message was sent. Non-repudiation is a communications security technique which involves making use of a 'digital signature': in essence, a piece of code which an institution may choose to attach to all messages which it receives from or sends to counterparties. Since it is conveyed in encrypted form, the digital signature cannot be accessed or deleted by any party and enables either counterparty to prove that a particular message (such as to buy or sell stock) was sent. The evidence would be strong enough to use in court, if necessary.

Digital signatures are also important for 'sender authentication', which is used when the recipient wishes for proof that the sender is in fact who he says he is. This technique usually involves both counterparties agreeing in advance to a particular password, the use of which by the sender will constitute the proof of his identity. Sender authentication is a potent technique to prevent an institution being defrauded by acting on a bogus instruction such as a fraudulent order to transfer funds.

Some of the breaches in computer communications security which organizations most fear are summarized in two terms: 'hacking', and the computer 'virus'.

Hacking

In the 1970s a computer 'hacker' was simply someone who was enthusiastic about computers and liked using them; it is only since the late 1980s that the term has started to denote a more sinister figure, one who practises **hacking**, the process whereby an unauthorized user tries to gain entry to a computer network by defeating the system's access controls. A hacker might work in his victim's office, but is more likely to operate via an external communications system.

The computer virus

The computer **virus** is a rogue software element which typically gains access to a computer system via what is often legitimate software and then – in much the manner of a pathological virus – sets to work to damage its host by a variety of means that usually include continual self-replication.

Controlling hackers and viruses

The remedies available to the problem of hackers and viruses are relatively straightforward. A good way to deal with hackers is to install a specialized type of access control system for outside parties wishing to enter the communications network. This system is known as a **'dial-back' modem**, and requires any user to be called back by the system before the would-be user can access it. Since the system will be programmed such that it can only call certain prearranged bona fide numbers, a hacker who is not calling from these numbers is unable to access the system. In theory, it is hard for any hacker to fake his own telephone number, and the vast majority of hackers, confronted with such a system, would probably move on to some less secure system operated by another organization. However, some computer security experts argue that new technology now exists which reduces the difficulty to a hacker of faking his own telephone number.

Viruses can be combated in two ways. First, if an institution constantly makes back-ups of its data (at least on a daily basis), the risk of a virus damaging an entire databank is minimized. The best method of preventing the virus from entering the bank's computer system is to make regular (i.e. daily) use of a **'checksum' program**, which is able to detect whether a piece of software has been altered in any way. By making regular back-up copies of data and software, and deploying checksum programs, it should be possible for an institution to prevent virus access to its system.

Having discussed the most effective techniques for dealing with communications security, the two other major types of computer security hazard of interest to those within the global custody industry can be examined:

1. The *systems shutdown* hazard: this occurs when the entire computer system ceases to be operative. The causes are numerous such as power failure, fire, major physical accident, or major software or hardware failure.

Control: Deploy an effective disaster recovery strategy, ideally with a second site which is permanently ready for use. A cost-effective way of managing this is to join a syndicate, where a number of members all have access to the same facility.

2. The *electromagnetic induction* hazard: this is the hazard of an unauthorized person gaining access to, or interfering with, a computer system without any direct on-line interference, but by deploying a variety of techniques which exploit the fact that all elements of a computer system emit electromagnetic radiation which can be 'read' by an inductive process even some distance away from the physical siting of the hardware.

Control: Install all terminals as far away as possible from exterior walls. Where the hazard is very serious, place a copper screen between the source of the electromagnetic radiation and the possible siting of an illicit detection device.

2 QUANTITATIVE ANALYSIS

DEFINITION

Quantitative analysis is: *a form of analysis of investment instruments which is based primarily on the expected return and risk accruing from the different investment instruments within a diversified portfolio. Technology has both enabled quantitative analysis to become increasingly widespread and also nurtured its development.*

THE NATURE OF FINANCIAL MARKET PARTICIPATION

In general, there are two ways of making money by investing in investment instruments (i.e. securities): first, from dividends or interest received; and secondly, from capital appreciation (i.e. an increase in the price of the instrument).

The financial markets themselves are not markets in actual goods, such as soya beans or tin, but in investment instruments which – except in the case of a corporate liquidation – have no intrinsic value. The investment instrument may generate dividends or interest, or it may go up in price and generate a profit for the investment manager but, in the case of equities, the instruments have no value as claims on the assets of the company which issued them. It is true that where an investment management organization owns a significant proportion of the company's shares, then that company will take immense pains to promote a favourable view of the company's fortunes among the investment management organization, but the shares still give the investment management organization no claim on certain of the company's assets. The only value which the shares have at any one time is the price for which they could be sold in the financial markets.

The fundamental fact that investment instruments which are traded on financial markets have no intrinsic value leads naturally to the principle that the only determinants of the prices of these instruments will be the views, expectations and hopes of the people or institutions which participate within the markets.

This would not be the case if, say, the market were in soya beans. Soya beans have a definite intrinsic food value, and the price of soya beans will be a straightforward function of the supply of soya beans and the demand for them. On the other hand, if somebody had reason to believe that in the months to come soya beans might become very scarce, that person may choose to buy a large volume of soya beans and hoard them, hoping to sell the beans at a profit. In this case, the person may well be indifferent to the food value of soya beans for himself, indeed he might not even like them. In this instance, the soya bean market has become like a financial market, in that the reason for buying the soya beans is not to eat them (or sell them as food to others), but rather to invest in the soya beans and hope that they become more valuable in the future.

Note, incidentally, that in this instance the would-be hoarder does not even need to take delivery of the soya beans now. He could buy the **obligation** to take delivery of soya beans at some future date at the current price, and if soya beans did indeed become scarce between now and the time when the soya beans were due for delivery, he could sell the right at a profit. This of course is precisely the origin of futures markets. In this case, a soya bean **future** (i.e. the obligation to take delivery of the soya beans) derives from the actual market in soya beans. This is why futures (and options, where what is sold is not the obligation to take delivery, but the option of taking delivery) are known as **derivatives**.

Prices of investment instruments on financial markets depend on a very wide range of factors which influence the expectations of the people who participate in trading or investing on the market. There is not unfortunately much agreement on which factors are the most important. Even more significant, there is not even agreement on *how* the market – or individual investment instruments – should be analysed in order to generate maximum returns.

FUNDAMENTAL ANALYSIS AND TECHNICAL ANALYSIS

There is, however, an accepted polarity around three principal types of analysis which are acknowledged to be of the greatest benefit in terms of analysing how investment performance on a market can be maximized. Quantitative analysis is one important form of analysis; the other two are fundamental analysis and technical analysis. These require brief discussion here since it is necessary to understand how quantitative analysis differs from them.

Fundamental analysis is based upon the notion that one way of assessing how the price of an investment instrument is likely to change in the future is thoroughly to investigate the current and likely future performance and business activity of the company which issues the instrument, as well as the industry sector to which the company belongs. Fundamental analysis, which is mainly used when assessing the prices of equities, is the most 'obvious' type of analysis and until the 1970s was almost the only type of analysis used. Fundamental analysis might mean reading the company's accounts and performing sophisticated analysis on them. It might mean studying industry trends, or speaking to the company directly. As a result of such investigation, fundamental analysts decide whether a share is 'underpriced' or 'overpriced'. If it is the former, the fundamental analyst will advise his clients to buy the share (or will buy it himself). If it is the latter, the recommendation will be to sell: *the implication is that soon the market will realize that the share is under- or overpriced, and then the market will catch up.*

It is extremely important to realize that implicit in the rationale of fundamental analysis is the idea that the market for the company's shares is an **imperfect**

market: *a perfect market is one where all participants have access to the same information, while an imperfect market is one where not all participants have access to the same information.*

Note that this does not mean that in an imperfect market insider trading is permitted, or that no efforts will be taken by the particular stock exchange which runs the market that all price-sensitive information is disseminated to all participants the instant that it becomes available. The assumption is that insider information is not permitted, and that the information that is available is readily available. People who believe in the existence of imperfect markets believe that even when a market is fairly run by the exchange that operates it, there will still be what might be termed 'pockets of imperfection' which will give one dealer or investor the opportunity to make money at the expense of less well-informed participants. For example, a company's annual report – which is available to everybody – may say nothing about a detail such as the likely passage of overseas legislation which will give the company the opportunity to trade in a lucrative foreign market. This is the kind of detail which a fundamental analyst hopes to locate in order to obtain better information than his competitors.

Technical analysis is quite different from fundamental analysis; it is sometimes called **chartism**, although the term 'technical analysis' is usually preferred by its practitioners. Technical analysis pays little or no attention to the intrinsic nature of the company or industry sector, but instead concentrates on the *previous pattern of price movements.*

At first sight, this seems rather startling. Does it mean that technical analysts believe that the future performance of a share or other type of investment instrument – or the overall direction of the market – is principally dependent upon past performance? In fact this is exactly what technical analysts believe. They create charts of price changes and claim that they can perceive a pattern in these changes. From these patterns, which are analysed by a variety of methods (usually proprietary), they believe that future price movements are indeed predictable.

Like fundamental analysts, technical analysts believe that they can obtain an edge over the rest of the market's participants. Again, there is the unspoken assumption by technical analysts that information in the market is not understood equally well by everyone – that the market is not *informationally efficient.*

Note that technical analysts believe both that there are patterns in market prices and that some are able to understand and predict from those patterns better than others.

Like fundamental analysts, technical analysts do not claim to get their predictions right every time. They do acknowledge that there are surprises, and that their own preferred forms of analysis are sometimes wrong. *But they believe that unexpected changes are only evidence of the basic unreliability of the market – an unreliability by which they claim they can profit through their forecasting methods.*

It might reasonably be asked whether there can possibly be any truth in the notion that previous price performance (that is, fluctuation) can be any guide to future fluctuation. After all, even a layman might suppose that fluctuations on a financial market are no different from events such as tossing a coin or spinning a roulette wheel – examples of events which are known to produce random variables (i.e. the mathematical probability of any event occurring is distributed evenly among all the possible events). Events which produce random variables are of their nature unpredictable. So-called 'systems' for winning at bingo, roulette, lotteries or the football pools do not work. Probably the only reason why some people still believe that these systems do work is that the events themselves are sufficiently complex for the ineffectiveness of the system not to be obvious. But nobody has ever tried to sell a system for predicting whether a single tossed coin will fall heads or tails – simply because the chance of either happening is so obviously equal and a system would seem ludicrous.

However, technical analysts confronted with the above reasoning would not deny that events such as tossing a coin or spinning a roulette wheel produced random variables. Technical analysts indeed would argue that the above reasoning is irrelevant because price fluctuations on financial markets are not random: *they would say, in effect, that price fluctuations are the results of human actions, and that human actions are anything but random.*

Certainly it is true that major price fluctuations occur when important news items break. A drop in the rate of inflation, for example, will bring confidence to the market, just as news of a worsening balance of payments will reduce confidence. These events will tend to increase and decrease market prices respectively. But it does not necessarily follow from this that the *trend* in a market price, or price of an individual instrument, can be predicted. Nor is it only the layman who might believe that market price movements were probably random. There is an important school of thought among academic economists that market price fluctuations are themselves random variables.

THE NATURE OF QUANTITATIVE ANALYSIS

Quantitative analysis draws elements from both fundamental analysis and technical analysis. In that quantitative analysis looks very carefully at the expected returns from owning an investment instrument, and the risk of those returns actually occurring, it makes use of fundamental factors; and in that it involves the very important assumption that previous returns (and the risk of obtaining those returns) can be extrapolated into future expectations of returns and risks, then it might also be said to borrow some of the thinking of technical analysts. What is certainly true is that quantitative analysis claims to be a particularly useful tool for obtaining consistently good performance from a relatively large, diversified portfolio. Since obtaining such performance from a relatively large portfolio is precisely what the professional investment manager will probably want to do, quantitative analysis is playing an increasingly important role within the investment management industry. Its name derives from the fact that it focuses on *quantities* of return and risk for the investment instruments under investigation.

The efficient markets hypothesis

Integral to the reasoning behind quantitative analysis is the **efficient markets hypothesis** (EMH). This hypothesis, which has gained much ground in the USA and is becoming increasingly widely accepted in other countries, holds that while it is impractical to suggest that markets are perfect since some participants will at any one time have information which may give them the opportunity to gain a short-lived edge over other participants, *the prices in the market will none the less reflect all relevant available information.*

The notion of the EMH has extremely important implications for investment managers. If the EMH is valid, then the entire notion that abnormal profits can be *consistently* made on a stock exchange is revealed as nothing more than superstition; someone might be lucky enough to make abnormal profits, on occasion, but this only indicates good fortune. There are no real opportunities for consistent profits within stock exchanges because all opportunities evaporate through the pricing mechanism, which 'absorbs' and rapidly evens out the portions of imperfection which have given one participant the opportunity to make abnormal profits.

Furthermore, if the EMH holds, it follows that the claims of fundamental analysts and technical analysts to try to beat the market are invalid. Indeed fundamental analysts and technical analysts might be said to help to make the markets more efficient through their constant vigilance.

No definitive answer is available to the question of whether or not the EMH is valid. Despite the considerable efforts of dealers, investors and their advisers to try to beat the stock markets – efforts which millions of people make every day around the world – far less is understood about how markets really work than might be expected. A great deal is understood about the more simple elements of a market, such as how the price of a particular equity is likely to change if the company involved announces higher profits than expected, but overall the dynamics of the precise fluctuations of a market and the prices of instruments on those markets appear to be too complex for any one theory to provide a complete explanation of them. An analogy can be drawn with the human body, where doctors and surgeons have considerable knowledge of how individual elements of the body function, but a far less adequate understanding of how all the elements of the body function together in a living person, which explains why ailments affecting the whole person, such as stress, are far less likely to yield to medical treatment than ailments affecting one particular part of the body.

None the less, the EMH is gaining increasing currency among academics and many market participants as *probably* the best available explanation of how financial markets behave. The supporters of the EMH would agree that fundamental analysis and technical analysis can be useful tools, to an extent, but that they are likely to produce as many losses as gains. The protagonists of EMH argue that the only way to obtain consistent returns from a market that is efficient is to diversify assets according to certain principles which indicate – principally by mathematical means – how return and risk might be maximized for a given asset allocation. Conducting an analysis of these return and risk factors, and allocating assets according to the analysis, is what constitutes quantitative analysis.

THE OBJECTIVE OF QUANTITATIVE ANALYSIS

The objective of quantitative analysis is to provide consistently good returns over a period of time, probably a longer period than a short one. What are regarded as 'consistently good returns' will of course vary from investor to investor, but most quantitative analysis would be content if their portfolios produced a consistent performance in the 'upper quartile'; that is, in the top 25% of performance achieved by all participants. Some quantitative analysts aim to achieve a consistent performance that is more ambitious than this, such as a performance in the 'upper decile' (the top 10% of performance achieved by all participants), but in most cases this may be an unrealistic expectation. The point is that if, as the EMH suggests, there are no consistent opportunities to gain abnormal profits within a market, the best that a quantitative analyst can hope for is to deploy a quantitative strategy which takes the most ingenious approach to maximizing return and minimizing risk. Such a strategy would reasonably be expected to produce *consistently good results rather than consistently exceptional results.*

THE CONCEPTS OF RETURN AND RISK

The concepts of return and risk are essential to the theory of quantitative analysis. The return on an investment in a particular investment instrument consists of two elements:

1. The first is a cash stream flowing from the instrument; that is, the dividend or interest which the ownership of the instrument provides.
2. The second is the difference between the price originally paid for the instrument and its current market price (i.e. the price at which it could be liquidated).

Note that the first element may amount to zero (e.g. if a company issuing an equity declares no dividend or the government or organization issuing a bond defaults on interest payment). Similarly, the second element may be negative, if the current market price is less than that which the investor paid for the instrument. A return can therefore be negative as well as positive.

Of course an investor will always know what returns he has achieved *in the past.* If, for example, he invested £100 000 in equity A one year ago, and during the past year has received £6000 in dividends and the value of his holding has increased to £104 000, then his overall return is 10% although he will of course only receive the cash value of this if he liquidates the holding (he would then have to factor broker's commission into his final return). The important point here, however, is that while the investor knows what his return has been over the previous year (or whatever period in the past is under survey), *he cannot know what his return is going to be in the future.*

In quantitative analysis, the term 'risk' is used to denote the element of uncertainty that surrounds a future expectation of return.

The return on an investment in the future cannot be known, but an estimate of it can be made, based upon an expectation of future dividends or interests, added to the expectation of future growth in the market value of the investment: *for any estimated return, there will be a corresponding probability that this return will occur.*

Consider the following example, where an investor, Mr Money, is confronted

Table 2.1 Mr Money's investments

Expected return (%)	Estimated probability
Advertising Agency	
10	0.05
15	0.20
20	0.50
25	0.20
30	0.05
Industrial Concern	
2	0.05
12	0.25
20	0.40
28	0.25
38	0.05

with two possible investments: the first is in an advertising agency's equities, and the second is in an industrial concern's equities. Mr Money is concerned with the expected return on both of these investments during the year to come. He draws up a table which shows different expected returns over the next year, and the probabilities which he attaches to each of these returns (Table 2.1).

In the case of the advertising agency, Mr Money expects that the most likely return on his investment will be 20%, to which he attaches a 50/50 likelihood. Note that since these different expected returns contain what Mr Money regards as the only possible outcomes, the sum of the probabilities in the right-hand column is 1.00. Of course a return of less than 10% or more than 30% could be achieved, but Mr Money considers these insufficiently likely for them not to affect his planning.

With the industrial concern, as with the advertising agency investment, the most likely return envisaged by Mr Money is 20%, but he is slightly less optimistic that this result will be forthcoming. The probabilities in the right-hand column sum to 1.00, for reasons that correspond to those in the example of the advertising agency. We can usefully represent these results graphically, as shown in Fig. 2.1.

The two curves derived in the figure will be familiar to readers versed in statistical theory as indicating a **normal distribution**, that is a distribution around a mean (the average return: in this case 20% for both curves) where there is a greater tendency towards symmetry on either side of the mean, the greater the number of variables that are sampled. In fact, although the figures given in the examples were chosen deliberately in order to keep the distribution straightforward, the distribution of expected returns tends to follow a normal distribution in all cases.

In this example, the risk of investing in either the advertising agency or the industrial concerned has been expressed fairly simplistically in terms of different probabilities that are attached to different expectations of future return. On occasion, this form of analysis will be useful to an investment manager who is considering whether or not to invest in a particular instrument, and who has good reasons for believing that certain probabilities can be attached to different expectations of return. However, there are two serious problems with this simplistic analysis:

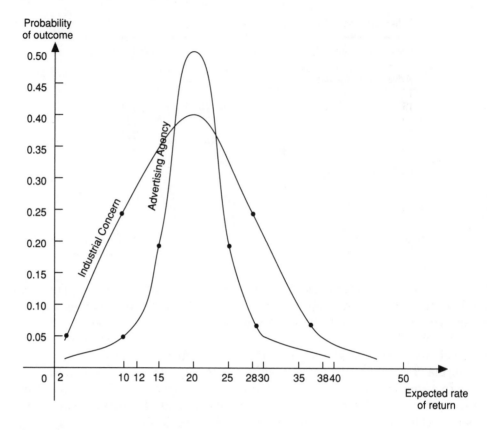

Fig. 2.1   Graph showing distribution of probabilities for expected return of two investments.

1. In practice it is very difficult to attach prior probabilities to expected outcomes on financial markets.
2. Investment managers will inevitably be interested in maximizing the performance of a portfolio composed of numerous instruments. The simplistic analysis does not appear to lend itself to such a requirement.

A much more popular method of evaluating risk than that of trying to attach probabilities to expected returns is the use of historic (i.e. past) returns as an indicator (in the absence of any better information) of the future risk. This method makes sense, in that the past is known with great precision, whereas the future is unknown. *On the other hand, it is important to note that basing an estimate of future risk on previous returns is not the same thing as knowing future risk.*

Clearly there is here a similarity between a quantitative analyst's technique of estimating future risk on past information and a technical analyst's belief that future price fluctuations can be, to some extent, predicted from historical fluctuations. However, quantitative analysts do not favour analogies to be drawn between aspects of what they do with the practice of technical analysts as it rather detracts from the intellectual and methodical aura with which quantitative analysts invest their work.

Table 2.2 Survey of Mr Money's £100 000 investment in Equity A over the past six years

Start of year	Value of investment (including all dividends received and market appreciation) (£)
1	100 000
2	122 000
3	112 240
4	85 300
5	93 830
6	112 600

The point that quantitative analysis is dealing with *estimates* of future risk based on previous returns is most important since the marketing literature of many quantitative analysts – one might even say, most of them – seems to suggest that they possess some special knowledge of the future risk of investing in a particular instrument. They don't.

Returning to Mr Money and the £100 000 that he wishes to invest, let us assume that he wishes to investigate the likely returns on investing in Equity A. He does this by looking at the returns on a hypothetical investment of £100 000 over, say, the past six years. This information is of course readily available. Table 2.2 shows examples of the returns that Mr Money would have obtained for his £100 000 at the end of each of the six year periods.

The return is calculated by subtracting the value of the investment at the start of the year from the value of the investment at the end of the year, and then dividing this by the value of the investment at the start of the year and expressing the result as a percentage; e.g. the return for the first year is:

$$\frac{£122\,000 - £100\,000}{£100\,000} = 22\%$$

and the return for the second year is:

$$\frac{£112\,240 - £122\,000}{£122\,000} = -8\%$$

So we can draw up another table which incorporates these percentage returns (Table 2.3).

Quantitative analysts are principally interested in the **mean** and **standard deviation** of the historic returns. The mean is the average return over the historic period surveyed. This is simply calculated by adding all the different returns together and dividing by the total number of returns. The formula for calculating the mean (m) is therefore:

$$m = \frac{R_1 + R_2 + R_3 \ldots R_n}{n}$$

Table 2.3   Hypothetical returns on Mr Money's £100 000 investment in Equity A over the past six years

Year	Value of investment (£)	Return (%)
1	100 000	
2	122 000	22
3	112 240	−8
4	85 300	−24
5	93 380	10
6	112 600	20

where n = the number of samples (i.e. 5).

In this case, the mean is:

$$\frac{22 + (-8) + (-24) + 10 + 20}{5}$$

$$= 20/5 = 4$$

So the mean return is 4%.

As statistically minded readers will be aware, standard deviation is a way of calculating divergence around a mean. In financial contexts, the word 'divergence' here can be usefully replaced by 'volatility'; i.e. standard deviation (usually represented as σ) shows to what extent the returns are likely to differ from the mean. *For this reason, the standard deviation of historic returns is the most usual way of estimating future risk from the given returns.*

The formula for calculating standard deviation is as follows:

$$\sigma = \sqrt{\frac{[(x_1 - m)^2 + (x_2 - m)^2 + (x_3 - m)^2 \ldots (x_n - m)^2]}{n}}$$

where m = the mean of the sample, and x_1, x_2, x_3, etc. are the items in the sample.

In this case, the standard deviation is as follows:

$$\sigma = \sqrt{\frac{[(22 - 4)^2 + (-8 - 4)^2 + (-24 - 4)^2 + (10 - 4)^2 + (20 - 4)^2}{5}}$$

$$\sigma = \sqrt{\left(\frac{1544}{5}\right)}$$

$$\sigma = \sqrt{(308.8)} = 17.57$$

So the standard deviation for the historic returns of Equity A is 17.57. Note, incidentally, that since the calculation of the standard deviation involves squaring, and the square of a positive number or a negative number is always positive, then the standard deviation is always positive, even though the mean can of course be negative.

Let us now suppose that Mr Money has a second investment possibility open to him, that is shares in Equity B. Using the same principle of investigating how a

Table 2.4 Hypothetical returns on Mr Money's £100 000 investment in Equity B over the past six years

Year	Value of investment (£)	Return (%)
1	100 000	
2	90 000	−10
3	87 300	−3
4	87 300	0
5	99 520	14
6	118 430	19

hypothetical investment over the past six years would have actually performed, we arrive at Table 2.4 for Equity B. Here, the mean return (4%) is the same as for Equity A, but the standard deviation of the price changes is only 10.83.

Quantitative analysis states that if Mr Money chose to invest in Equity A and Equity B in equal proportions, the return which he would expect to receive, *basing his expectation on previous experience only*, would be the mean of the two means of the investments involved; i.e.

$$\frac{m(\text{Equity A}) + m(\text{Equity B})}{n}$$

and since here $n = 2$ (because there are two investments under scrutiny), then the mean of the two investments is: $(4 + 4)/2 = 4$.

And what of the standard deviations, that is the risks involved in each investment? The standard deviation of Equity A is 17.57 and that for Equity B is 10.83. How do we arrive at the standard deviation of the combined investments, and hence the risk of the two investments?

The standard deviation for two two different investments cannot simply be arrived at by finding the mean of the two standard deviations, as each standard deviation said something about how the items diverge around their respective means, and the mean of the two standard deviations is not a useful figure. It should also be clear that the standard deviation of a combined investment will depend on the proportions of the two different investments within the overall portfolio.

There are two ways of finding the standard deviation of combined investments. The first method is not really practicable as it involves some very tedious calculations, but it is shown here in order to make clear what is going on. This method involves combining the two sets of returns, and creating a combined return. In this example, since Equity A and Equity B are being invested in equally by Mr Money, the combined return for each consists of the mean of the two returns for each respective time-period, which is worked out by adding the two returns together and dividing the sum by two. Drawing up a new table for the combined investments gives the results given in Table 2.5.

Calculating the standard deviation of the combined returns around the mean of 4 gives 11.44, which is less that the mean of the two standard deviations of the returns on Equity A and Equity B.

Table 2.5 The combined estimated returns for Equity A and Equity B (percentages)

Equity A – Return	Equity B – Return	Combined Return (= A + B/2)
22	10	6
–8	–3	–5.5
–24	0	–12
10	14	12
20	19	19.5

The second method of arriving at this figure for the standard deviation of the combined returns involves use of a formula; and in order to use this formula, it is necessary to introduce the concept of the **correlation coefficient**. This is a measure of the *strength* of a statistical relationship between variables. The correlation coefficient can vary between +1 (a perfect positive relationship) where the return on one instrument always increases in direct proportion to the return on another instrument, through 0 where there is no relationship at all to a relationship of –1 (a perfect negative relationship) where the return on one instrument always increases in direct proportion as the return on another instrument decreases.

An example of positive correlation would be the relationship between the price of an equity of a tyre manufacturing organization and a car manufacturing organization. It would be reasonable to expect that a positive correlation would exist here.

An example of a negative correlation would probably be the price of the equity of a home video rental chain and the price of a satellite TV company's equity, since generally people spend less on home video rental when they have installed a satellite TV facility, which would give access to home movies, among other things.

The formula for the correlation coefficient is as follows:

$$r_{xy} = \frac{\sum_i (x_i - m_x)(y_i - m_y)}{n\delta_x \delta_y}$$

where r_{xy} is the conventional notation for the correlation coefficient of x_i and y_i and where x_i and y_i are the different items in respective tables x and y, that is the two tables across which we are measuring the correlation; m_x and m_y are the means of all the x and y items respectively; and δ_x and δ_y are the standard deviations of the x and y items respectively.

Applying this formula to the data in our example gives a correlation coefficient of 0.25646 or 0.2565 (to four decimal places). Therefore the correlation coefficient is 0.2565, which we can regard as a fairly weak positive correlation.

Going back to the objective of calculating the formula for the standard deviation of two sets of returns, this is as follows:

$$\sigma_{xy} = w_x^2 \cdot \sigma_x^2 + w_y^2 \cdot \sigma_y^2 + 2w_x w_y \times r_{xy} \cdot \sigma_x \cdot \sigma_y$$

where w_x and w_y are the weights of x and y ($\Sigma w_i = 1$); σ_x and σ_y are the standard deviations of x and y respectively; and r_{xy} is the correlation coefficient.

Applying this formula to the data in our example gives a figure of 11.44 for the standard deviation of the two sets of returns.

THE ADVANTAGE OF DIVERSIFICATION

The reason why the standard deviation of the two combined investments has been calculated here is that our example is an illustration of the principle which stands at the heart of quantitative analysis that *risk (standard deviation) can be reduced by diversifying between different investment.* By combining in equal proportions two investments with the same mean return and with risks of 17.57% and 10.83%, Mr Money is able to obtain an overall mean return of 4% and risk of 11.44%, which is much less than the risk of 17.57% that he incurs for the first set of investments.

It can be shown even more clearly how useful diversification is if we take two different potential investments, each of which have the same return and the same risk. Suppose each different investment offers (extrapolated as usual from past experience) a return and risk of 12% and 14% respectively, with correlation between their movements (i.e. the correlation coefficient) of 0.25. Even though this is not a zero or negative correlation, then it still pays to diversify because the mean of the two investments (assuming that we are sharing available funds equally between the two investments) is also 12%, but the standard deviation is 11.07%. *So the risk has been reduced from 14% by the simple process of diversification.*

Generally, and as common sense suggests, the closer that the correlation coefficient is to −1, the more likely it is that risk will be reduced through diversification. However, what is really interesting here is the principle that the risk of holding one instrument can almost always be reduced by diversifying into two instruments (the exception is where both instruments are perfectly positively correlated). Further extensions of the above reasoning show that risk can also be reduced by diversifying to three different investments, unless (which is highly unlikely) the first two investments are perfectly correlated among themselves. Indeed it is possible to draw a most useful general rule, namely that *in a portfolio which consists of n possible investments, then any further investment can at most be fully correlated with one of the existing investments, say, but the first investment is less than fully correlated with all other investments, so any additional investment must be less than fully correlated with them; therefore further diversification is worthwhile.*

The practical results of this conclusion are naturally immensely important for an investment manager who wishes to maximize return and minimize risk. Since risk can always be decreased by diversification, an investment manager who is managing a portfolio containing a certain number of different types of instruments (between, say, 20 and 100) will know that he can always reduce the level of risk of his portfolio by increasing the number of types of instrument in that portfolio.

THE CONCEPT OF THE OPTIMAL PORTFOLIO

So far, the concepts of risk and return have been analysed in a relatively theoretical manner which has none the less revealed important conclusions about how risk within a portfolio can be reduced by diversification of that portfolio. Two important and related questions now arise, the solution of which takes the analysis further into the real world of investment management. These questions are as follows:

1. How does an investment manager decide which particular level of risk and return he ought to take on board?
2. To what extent should an investment manager practising quantitative analysis diversify risk from his portfolio?

These questions can be answered as follows.

(1) How does an investment manager decide which particular level of risk and return he ought to take on board?
Quantitative analysis, above all, provides powerful methods of *understanding* the nature of risk and return, and the relationship between them. It does not necessarily provide tools for specifying to the investment manager precisely what levels of risk and return he ought to take on board within his portfolio, for the very good reason that individual investment managers will differ in their particular requirements of risk and return. The task undertaken by **proprietary quantitative analysis systems** lies much closer to the actual specification of return–risk configurations, although even here the responsible investment manager who uses a proprietary system will always ensure that the return–risk profile of the portfolio that he is constructing should conform to what he and his clients want rather than what the supplier of the proprietary quantitative analysis system wants to sell.

Proprietary quantitative analysis systems all have one thing in common: they make use of computers in their operation. Understanding why this should be so provides an important insight into the nature of return and risk within a multi-instrument portfolio.

The material that has already featured in this chapter will allow an investment manager to know – based on previous historic returns of two investments – what his overall return and risk is likely to be if the two investments are combined. However, in real life what an investment manager will usually want to do is to select – as far as the principle of predicting future return and risk from historic performance allows – a return and risk profile that suits his requirements.

Evaluating the *return* on a multi-instrument portfolio is relatively simply and is based upon the following formula:

$$E(R_p) = \sum_{i=1}^{n} w_i E(R_i)$$

where $E(R_p)$ is the expected return on a portfolio; w_i the weights of the n investments and $E(R_i)$ are the mean expected returns of the n investments.

So, for example, if a portfolio contains five investments, all of which are equally weighted within the portfolio (i.e. the individual weightings are 0.2, and the individual

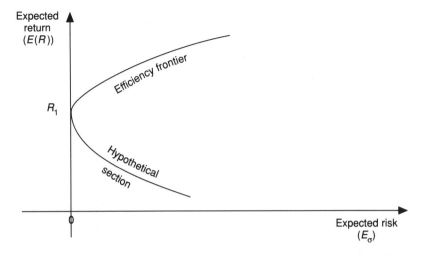

Fig. 2.2   Return plotted against risk where riskless investments are available.

mean returns are 3%, 5%, 6%, 10% and 20%), then the mean return of the portfolio will be 8.8%. Although this calculation is relatively straightforward, it can readily be imagined that a computer, programmed with the formula, could carry out the job far more quickly and more efficiently.

Where we wish to evaluate the *risk* of a multi-instrument portfolio, the calculation is extremely complex, and involves matrix algebra, which may be unfamiliar to many readers. In practice, it is extremely unlikely that an investment manager, no matter how experienced, will be involved in a manual calculation of the risk for a multi-instrument portfolio. What is far more likely is that he will have access to a screen-based decision support system which incorporates this formula. But even though the formula involves lengthy and complex calculations, the principle underlying the relationship between return and risk in a multi-instrument portfolio is fairly straightforward, and it is this principle which must be clearly understood.

Figures 2.2 and 2.3 show the principle in action. In Fig. 2.2 the investment manager has access to riskless investments as part of the possible return–risk profile of the portfolio. Although in theory no investment can be said to be entirely without risk, in practice government bonds issued by nations with the highest credit ratings (e.g. Switzerland, the USA, Japan, Germany, France and the UK) can be said to be riskless. In Fig. 2.3 the investment manager does not have access to riskless investments.

In both figures return (the vertical axis) is plotted against risk (the horizontal axis) for an entire portfolio, that is the curve of the graph describes the possible combinations of return and risk for the entire portfolio.

Plotting return against risk for an entire portfolio always produces a curve of the nature shown in both figures, although the specific slope of the curve will of course depend upon the nature of the relationship between the return and risk for the particular portfolio. Two extremely important points arise with reference to Figs 2.2 and 2.3, as follows:

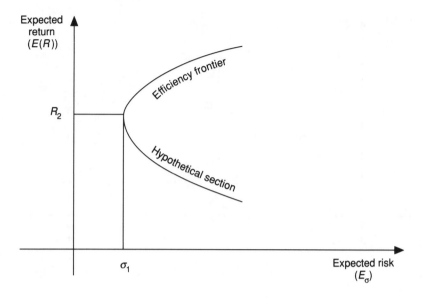

Fig. 2.3 Return plotted against risk where no riskless investments are available.

1. Only the top section of the curve (i.e. the section of the curve above the 'turn', which indicates where return starts to increase as risk increases) will be of interest to the investment manager as showing possible configurations of return and risk *because, below the turn, the investment manager can always obtain a higher return for less risk*. As a result, it is conventional to call the section of the curve above the 'turn' the **efficiency frontier** since only those return–risk allocations on this part of the curve will be of interest.

2. In Fig. 2.2 where riskless investments are available, the investment manager has a 'zero risk' option giving return R_1, whereas in Fig. 2.3 which provides no zero risk option, the lowest degree of risk (σ) gives a return of R_2. However, *in both cases the investment manager can only obtain a higher return at the expense of accepting higher risk*.

Common sense suggests that there must always be a trade-off between return and risk, which is exactly what mathematical analysis of return and risk proves. Nevertheless, some suppliers of proprietary quantitative analysis systems still try to suggest, in their marketing literature, that their systems are able to provide increased returns hand-in-hand with decreased risk. While it is by no means unlikely that a good quantitative analysis system can give an investment manager higher returns and a lower risk than he is currently obtaining from a portfolio constructed according to some other means, *it is nonsense for any quantitative analysis organization to claim that its system routinely provides higher returns and reduced risk. There must always be a trade-off.* Let us move now to question 2.

(2) *To what extent should an investment manager practising quantitative analysis diversify risk from his portfolio?*

As we have already seen, unless a successive investment is perfectly correlated

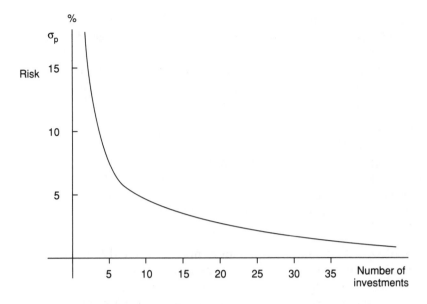

Fig. 2.4 The pattern of decreasing risk with various sizes of portfolio.

with an existing investment, diversifying a portfolio among a larger number of investments (i.e. investment instruments) will always reduce risk. Figure 2.4 shows the typical relationship between risk and the number of instruments in a portfolio.

We can see from the figure that as the number of instruments in the portfolio increases, risk first drops off rather quickly and then the incremental reductions in risk start to decrease, so that when the portfolio is very large indeed, the incremental gains by further diversification are very small. Again, this is what we should expect.

The question that naturally arises here is whether it is possible to avoid *all* risk (i.e. reduce risk to zero) by further diversification. After all, if two investments are perfectly *negatively* correlated, then in theory there should be a proportion of investment between the two that would result in zero risk. Perfect negative correlation is in fact a theoretical abstraction that does not arise in the real world. However, since the risk in portfolio reduces the greater the number of investments in the portfolio, it might reasonably be expected that continuing to diversify a portfolio will eventually result in the risk of that portfolio being zero.

However, this is not the case, and it is not difficult to show why. In real life, an investment manager can invest across very many investments within a market. Indeed there is no reason why he should not invest in all the different investments available on a market (e.g. all the equities on an equity market), and while for a large stock exchange such as the London Stock Exchange or New York Stock Exchange this would mean buying into many thousands of equities, it is important to remember that many of the world's stock exchanges trade only a few hundred – or even only a few dozen – equities, in which case full diversification is easily possible.

It should be easy to see that where full diversification is being practised, the risk to the investor will be the risk to the whole economy. And since the risk of an entire economy cannot possibly ever be zero, *so it is never possible to avoid all risk, even by full diversification.* Risk is concerned with the likelihood of increase and decrease in the market price and the stream of income arising from holding assets, and just as the fortunes of the individual investment change, so do the fortunes of whole economies.

Factors that affect economies include:

1. world trade prospects generally;
2. the trade cycle;
3. the changing competitiveness of other nations;
4. innovation in whole industries or particular products;
5. changing patterns of protectionism;
6. natural factors (such as droughts and famines);
7. wars.

So even the widest diversification cannot completely avoid risk. Indeed, even if the diversification were worldwide, many of the factors listed above would still mean that there was a 'world risk' inherent in the portfolio that was not zero.

In real life, the pattern that is found of risk within a market is that shown in Fig. 2.4. Risk will reduce steeply as the number of investments within a portfolio increases to around 20–50, but will reduce much more slowly after that. However, unlike the case of Fig. 2.4, the risk will not usually go much below about 30% (0.3), with the exact figure for practical minimization of risk depending on which 'total' set of investments is being considered – the usual benchmark is one of the indices that represents a major market such as the London Stock Exchange or the New York Stock Exchange. *By diversifying, risk can be reduced, but there comes a point at which risk cannot for practical purposes be reduced any further.* This is because the investment manager confronts the risk of the market, known as **market risk**, or alternatively **systematic risk**, because it is the risk of the total economic system.

An individual investment will also have its own risk, but much of this (up to about 70%, using the figure of 30% for systematic risk) can be diversified away. This means that, *for all practical purposes*, this part of the investment's risk is irrelevant. The difference between the total risk of the investment and the systematic risk is called the **unique risk**, or more usually **unsystematic risk**. The importance of this concept for quantitative analysis is that whereas the implication so far has been that the two most important parameters for an investment manager undertaking quantitative analysis are return and risk, it is now necessary to acknowledge that the two most important parameters are return and **systematic risk.** Systematic risk is a stumbling-block that cannot be avoided; unsystematic risk can, if required, be diversified away. Figure 2.5 illustrates the concepts of systematic and unsystematic risk.

THE CAPITAL MARKET LINE

In the real world, an investment manager has the opportunity to invest in both risky and risk-free investment instruments. This being the case, what is needed is

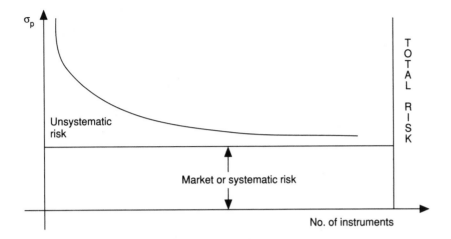

Fig. 2.5 Systematic and unsystematic risk.

an indication of the best balance between return and systematic risk, *given that the portfolio can be composed of both risky and risk-free investments*. The **capital market line** (CML) provides this indication (Fig. 2.6). This is, in essence, an aggregate of Figs 2.2 and 2.3.

The risk-free rate offered on, say, short-dated government securities is shown as R_f. An investor is free to divide his funds between an investment in the set of risky assets represented by point M on the efficiency frontier, and the risk-free stock R_f. This gives a linear combination of the form:

$$w_m M + (1 - w_m)B$$

where M represents a parameter of the risky investments, B a parameter of the risk-free investments and w_m the proportion placed in the risky investments.

So, for example, if the expected return on risky investment is 20%, the return on risk-free investment is 12% and the proportion invested in the risky investments is 60%, then the expected return of the portfolio is the linear combination:

$$0.6 \times 20\% + (1 - 0.6) \times 12\% = 16.8\%$$

All points that represent such combinations of risky and risk-free investments must, since we have a linear combination, lie on the straight line that joins R_f to M. If the investor prefers less risk, the position will be nearer to R_f; if he prefers more risk, the position will be nearer M.

Quantitative analysis theory holds, furthermore, that the points along the capital market line maximize return and minimize risk, with the investor's own preferences deciding which particular point along the line should be adopted. Any portfolio constructed along the capital market line can be regarded as an **optimal portfolio**.

According to quantitative analysis theory, the optimal portfolio (market portfolio) gives the highest return for the lowest risk, and therefore all rational participants in the market should favour it. The fact that in real life they do not all do this, thereby giving quantitative analysts who do hold optimal portfolios a clear

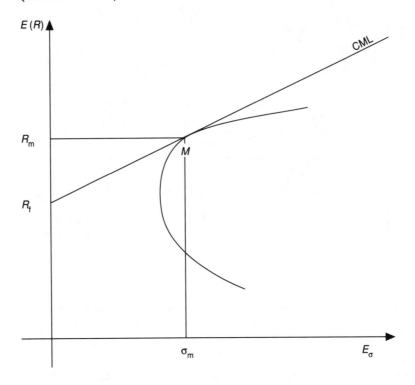

Fig. 2.6 The capital market line.

advantage, is another important reason why quantitative analysis is becoming increasingly popular worldwide.

SUMMARY OF THE BASIC PRINCIPLES OF QUANTITATIVE ANALYSIS

Before proceeding to the final part of this chapter, it is useful to summarize here the material that has been discussed so far, as follows:

1. Returns are not certain for most investments. Some way of dealing with the risk involved is consequently required.
2. All investors can, if they wish, make their decisions based on two parameters: the returns they expect, and the chances of receiving those returns (i.e. the risk).
3. Return and risk can be conveniently measured through the statistical criteria of mean and standard deviation respectively. These two statistics become the basis for financial decisions.
4. Risk can almost always be reduced by diversifying among a number of investments rather than restricting choice to one or a few. This is because investments are rarely perfectly positively correlated; hence, though the return to be

received will be the arithmetic average of the returns of the individual investments, the risk will be less than that average.

5. For a set of risky investments, there will be an efficiency frontier that represents the most efficient combinations in terms of the maximum return for the minimum risk. An investor will therefore choose a selection that is on the efficiency frontier.

6. Risk can never be diversified away completely, as systematic risk remains no matter to what extent diversification has been practised.

7. Since risk-free investments are available, the best portfolio available is composed of risky and also risk-free investments. The resulting set of best investments is known as the capital market line. Any portfolio which provides a return and risk at points along this line can be regarded as an optimal portfolio.

FURTHER APPLICATIONS OF THE PRINCIPLES OF QUANTITATIVE ANALYSIS

Enough of the principles of quantitative analysis has already been shown for useful applications of these principles to be made in a real-life investment management scenario. If markets are efficient, and the efficient markets hypothesis (EMH) holds, then an investment manager who diversifies his risks over a reasonably wide portfolio can reasonably expect to produce a better performance, in the medium to long term, than an investment manager who does not practise this diversification. Similarly, an investment manager who puts the principles of quantitative analysis into action can reasonably expect to produce a more sustained, consistent level of performance than an investment manager who does not practise this diversification. A portfolio managed according to quantitative principles might not produce such a good short-term performance as one which is managed according to more traditional techniques of choosing stocks according to fundamental factors, and where the stocks that have been selected exhibit a high growth rate; but the EMH suggests that in the long term lucky gains will be offset by losses.

Of course, if all the participants in the market practised quantitative analysis and put these procedures into action, then individual investment managers who used these methods could not really expect to outperform their rivals to any great extent, but as long as most participants in the market continue *not* to manage according to quantitative principles, the advantages of quantitative management should be available. Furthermore, these gains should be available even where a portfolio is diversified around a smaller number of stocks (say, up to approx. 50) than would be required for full diversification.

Proprietary quantitative analysis theories and systems based on these theories try to go further than the relatively simple principle of diversifying a portfolio for consistent, long-term returns. These proprietary theories aim to give one quantitative manager an advantage over another by looking more deeply at the nature of systematic and unsystematic risk and trying to maximize returns and minimize risk on an incremental basis. It must be acknowledged that some of these systems have a large number of satisfied clients worldwide and are responsible for managing many billions of dollars of funds. It is interesting to look at examples of these systems and consider the basic principles that underlie their operation. Before doing this, there is one further principal concept in quantitative analysis which must be examined.

THE CONCEPT OF BETA VALUE

We have now seen how an investor ought to behave within a market that contains opportunities to invest both in risky and risk-free investment instruments. We have seen how the investor should best mix risky assets with risk-free assets in order to obtain a position on the capital market line (CML) that would be efficient, as it would give the best risk–return relationship for that investor's own particular risk preference.

Now, as we have already seen, in practice it is very difficult to calculate the risk of a portfolio composed of numerous instruments. Although a computer can do this, once the number of instruments gets much above 20, the calculation is rather lengthy, even for a powerful computer. There is, however, a way out of this problem: it involves relating the individual investments *to the market as a whole instead of to each other*. It also involves one assumption: that the relationship between each investment and the market as a whole is linear. Once that assumption has been made, each share can be regressed (i.e. analysed in terms of how its risk relates to another instrument) on to the market instead of to each other. For 20 investments, then this means 20 regressions, and so on.

Any linear regression is of the form:

$$y = a + bx + e$$

where y is the dependent variable; x is the independent variable; a is a constant term that is independent of x; b is the coefficient of x representing the slope of the curve; and e is a residual error term.

When this linear regression is mapped, it gives a straight line with a as the intercept with the vertical y-axis and b as the slope of the line. In the case examined here, the independent variable line will be the return obtained by investing in the market for a given period, in this model a single period. The dependent variable is the return on any share: we shall call it share j. We can then create a graph with the market return on the horizontal axis, and the share's return on the vertical axis.

If we then proceed with the assumption that the share's return is just a function of the market's return, we get a straight line with α as the intercept and β as the slope of the line. The linear equation then becomes:

$$R_j = \alpha_j + \beta_j R_m + e_j$$

If this ideal model works, we then find this line which is known as the **characteristic line**, as in Fig. 2.7.

A part of the equation that is particularly interesting is the coefficient of R_m. Here this has been expressed as β_j, and beta has become a part of the natural

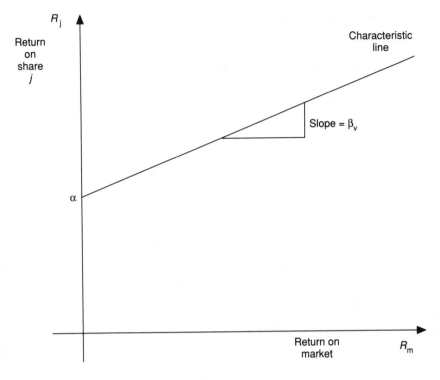

Fig. 2.7   The characteristic line.

language of finance. The reason why this is so is that the assumption which led to the linear equation has been found to hold good, although in the real world plotting the return on a share against the market is likely to produce a 'scatter' diagram that approximates to the linear equation rather than a clearly defined line. None the less, the assumption is sufficiently valid for its implications to play a crucial role in quantitative analysis.

Beta refers to the relationship between the returns on an individual share and returns on the market: *the beta value indicates to what extent, on average, the returns on an individual share fluctuate when the market fluctuates.* This means that beta is really a measure of risk: the risk of a particular stock compared to the risk held within the market. In mathematical terms, beta is the slope (or regression coefficient) of the regression line drawn on a variety of points, where the regression line measures the performance of an instrument against that of the market.

Market fluctuation is usually measured against the index of the market; that is, a hypothetical benchmark which is either produced by assessing the fluctuations of all the instruments within the market (as, for example, in the Financial Times All-Share Index) or a representative sample of those instruments. Since the composition of different indices on the same market varies, each of these indices will result in different betas for the instrument under consideration. However, the beta values will remain sufficiently constant for this analysis to be useful.

Since the relationship between a share price and the market index can in theory be any proportion, there are no restrictions on the possible values of beta (as, for example, there are on the values of the correlation coefficient, which can only vary from −1 to +1). Where beta is +1, it means that the price of an individual stock varies in exact proportion as the market varies. If the market index increases by 5%, the price of the stock would be expected to increase by 5%. Similarly, where beta is −1 the price of the stock increases in direct proportion to a decrease in the market index. If the market index falls by 5%, the price of the stock would be expected to increase by 5%. In practice, beta is not often negative, and beta values tend to vary from about +0.5 upwards.

There are two extremely important points to make about beta:

1. Because it measures the sensitivity of a security to the change in the market as a whole, beta is a highly significant measure of the relevant risk of an investment *in terms of the economy more generally.*
2. Beta can be applied to a portfolio as well as to individual investment instruments.

This second point explains why beta analysis has become a primary focus – some sources would argue *the* primary focus – of quantitative analysts' efforts to construct portfolios that produce a consistently good performance. If the beta values for all the individual instruments in a portfolio are known, the beta for the portfolio itself can be worked out. These two measurements – individual instrument beta and portfolio beta – are very powerful tools for constructing portfolios that reflect with a high degree of accuracy the preferences of a particular investor for holding a particular level of risk relative to the risk of the market as a whole. Since, as we have already seen, systematic risk (i.e. market risk) can never be diversified away completely, *the investor is compelled to take some position regarding how the risk of his own portfolio relates to the risk of the market as a whole.* Beta provides the means by which this position can be modulated with a relatively high degree of accuracy, *given that beta is a measurement based on previous returns, and when a portfolio is managed we are concerned with obtaining maximized returns in the unknown future.*

Measuring beta for an individual instrument

It is useful to be able to measure beta from sets of data relating the change in the price of a stock relative to the change in the market index. Note that the more time-periods the measurement of beta includes, the more reliable the measurement may be taken to be. A beta value based on one or two time-periods would be very unlikely to be useful.

The raw data of beta measurement is obtained by looking at how the price of the instrument in question changes over the time-period in question, compared to how the market index changes over the same time. A typical time-period would be one month, and we can show how beta value can be calculated by measuring how price has changed relative to stock over the past year for the 12 separate historical monthly time-periods. Note, however, that most quantitative analysts would want to measure beta over at least 60 monthly time-periods, and that proprietary computer systems for measuring beta base their measurements on 15 years of historical monthly time-periods.

We consider here the price of Stock A – an S&P500 corporation – against changes in the S&P500 index (the following measurements are of course hypothetical):

Month 1
Day 1: Stock price stood at $100
Last day of month: Stock price stood at $110
(Stock price has increased 10%)

Day 1: Index stood at 300
Last day of month: Index stood at 315
(Index has increased 5%)

Month 2
Day 1: Stock price stood at $110
Last day of month: Stock price stood at $126.50
(Stock price has increased 15%)

Day 1: Index stood at 315
Last day of month: Index stood at 330.75
(Index has increased 5%)

A similar procedure is followed for each of the other ten months, allowing the following compilation:

	% change in stock price	*% change in index*
1	10 (up)	5 (up)
2	15 (up)	5 (up)
3	12 (up)	6 (up)
4	20 (up)	8 (up)
5	5 (up)	7 (up)
6	1 (down)	1 (down)
7	10 (down)	3 (up)
8	5 (down)	3 (down)
9	20 (down)	15 (down)
10	3 (up)	2 (up)
11	10 (up)	6 (up)
12	13 (up)	7 (up)

Plotting these results on a graph gives Fig. 2.8. Note:

1. In the graph, 'up' values are represented as positive values, and 'down' values as negative values.
2. The mean of the changes in stock prices is 52/12 = 4.3
    The mean of the changes in the market index is 30/12 = 2.5
    ('Up' values are seen as positive, 'down' values as negative, as before.)

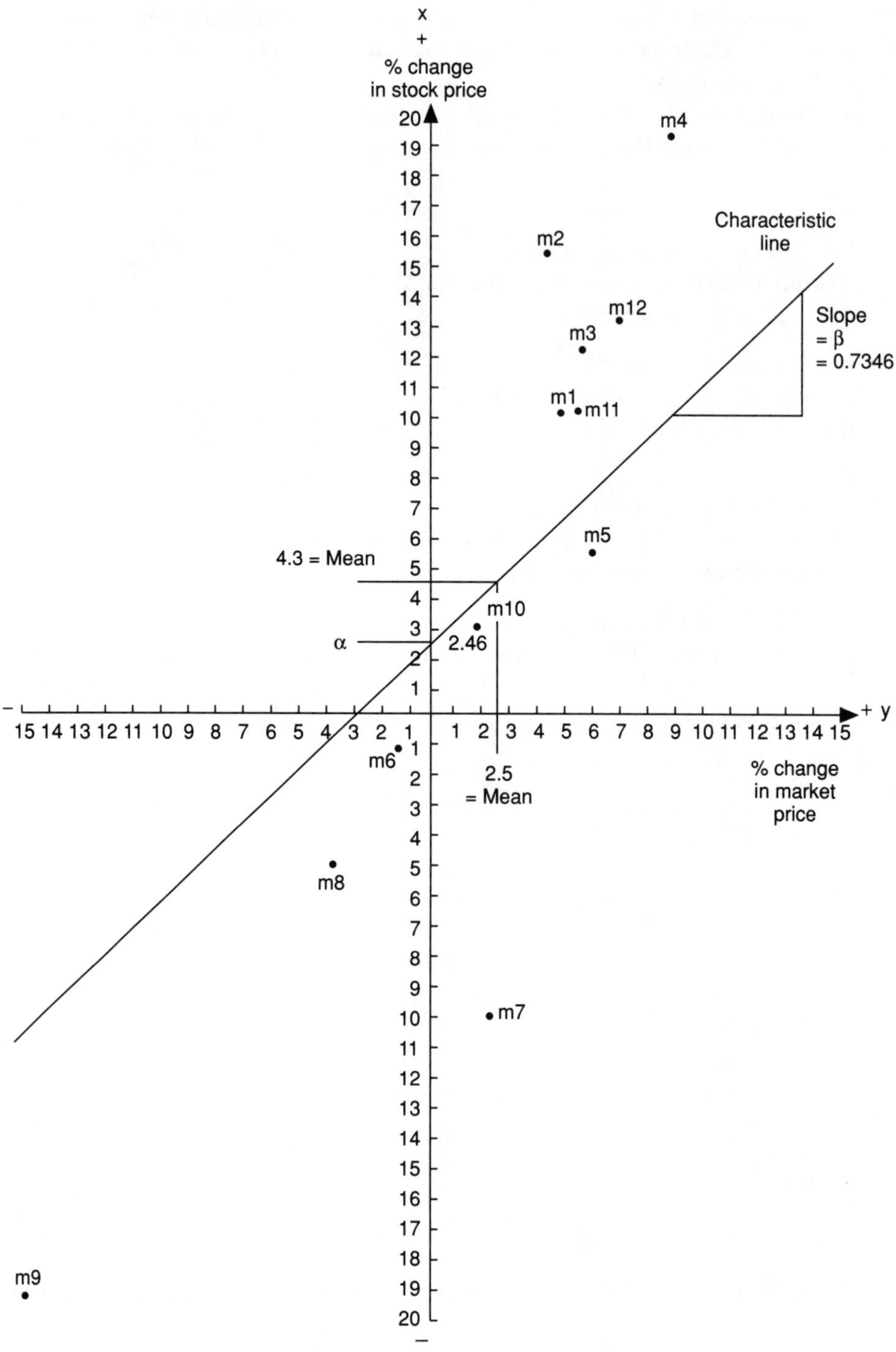

Fig. 2.8   Scatter of stock against index. (m1 = month 1, m2 = month 2, etc.)

Using the above data, we can calculate the regression coefficient by using the following formula:

$$b_{yx} = \frac{\sum_i x_i y_i - n M_x M_y}{\sum x_i^2 - n M_x^2}$$

where x_i = stock price changes; and y_i = index changes.

Applying this formula to our data gives the following calculation:

$[(10 \times 5) - 12 \times 4.3 \times 2.5] + [(15 \times 5) - 12 \times 4.3 \times 2.5] + [(12 \times 6) - 12 \times 4.3 \times 2.5]$
$+ [(20 \times 8) - 12 \times 4.3 \times 2.5] + [(5 \times 7) - 12 \times 4.3 \times 2.5]$
$+ [(-1 \times -1) - 12 \times 4.3 \times 2.5] + [(-10 \times 3) - 12 \times 4.3 \times 2.5]$
$+ [(-5 \times -3) - 12 \times 4.3 \times 2.5] + [(-20 \times -15) - 12 \times 4.3 \times 2.5]$
$+ [(3 \times 2) - 12 \times 4.3 \times 2.5] + [(10 \times 6) - 12 \times 4.3 \times 2.5]$
$+ [(13 \times 7) - 12 \times 4.3 \times 2.5]$
$= (50 - 129) + (75 - 129) + (72 - 129) + (160 - 129) + (35 - 129)$
$\quad + (1 - 129) + (-30 - 129) + (15 - 129) + (300 - 129) + (6 - 129)$
$\quad + (60 - 129) + (91 - 129)$
$= -79 + -54 + -57 + 31 + -94 + -128 + -159 + -114$
$\quad + 171 + -123 + -69 + -38$
$= -713$ (the top of the dividing line)

$[(10)^2 - 12(4.3)^2] + [(15)^2 - 12(4.3)^2] + [(12)^2 - 12(4.3)^2] + [(20)^2 - 12(4.3)^2]$
$+ [(5)^2 - 12(4.3)^2] + [(-1)^2 - 12(4.3)^2] + [(-10)^2 - 12(4.3)^2] + [(-5)^2 - 12(4.3)^2]$
$+ [(-20)^2 - 12(4.3)^2] + [(3)^2 - 12(4.3)^2] + [(10)^2 - 12(4.3)^2] + [(13)^2 - 12(4.3)^2]$
$= (100 - 221.88) + (225 - 221.88) + (144 - 221.88) + (400 - 221.88) + (25 - 221.88)$
$\quad + (1 - 221.88) + (100 - 221.88) + (25 - 221.88) + (400 - 221.88) + (9 - 221.88)$
$\quad + (100 - 221.88) + (169 - 221.88)$
$= -121.88 + 3.12 + -83.88 + 178.12 + -196.88 + -220.88 + -121.88 + -196.88 + 178.12$
$\quad + -212.88 + -121.88 + -52.88$
$= -970.56$

So the regression coefficient is:

$-713/-970.56 = 0.7346$ (This is beta for the stock under investigation)

In order to draw the line, we need to know the intercept (α); the formula for this is as follows:

$$\alpha = M_x - \beta(M_y)$$

So, in our example,

$\alpha = 4.3 - (0.7346)(2.5)$
$\alpha = 4.3 - 1.84$
$\alpha = 2.46$

This value has been indicated in Fig. 2.8. The characteristic line has been plotted by the simple expedient of making another point by intersecting the mean of the stock price changes (4.3) with the mean of the changes in the market index (2.5) and plotting the line by joining this intersect with the intercept (α). The beta coefficient – the slope of the line – is also indicated.

Measuring beta for an entire portfolio

Once the beta for all the instruments in a portfolio is known, the beta for the portfolio can be worked out by the simple procedure of averaging the weighted betas according to the following formula:

$$\beta_p = \sum_{i=1}^{n} w_i \beta_i$$

where β_p is the beta for the portfolio as a whole; w_i are the weights of the individual betas; and β_i are the betas of the individual instruments. Note that this is analogous to the formula for evaluating the return on a multi-instrument portfolio.

So, for example, if we have a portfolio composed of 10 instruments with the following betas:

$$1, 1.5, 1.2, -0.5, 2, -0.25, 1.1, 1, 1.8, 0.5$$

and the first five instruments all receive 2/15 of the funds available while the last five instruments all receive 1/15 of the funds available, then the beta value for the entire portfolio can be calculated, as follows:

β_p = (0.133 × 1) + (0.133 × 1.5) + (0.133 × 1.2) + (0.133 × −0.5) + (0.133 × 2)
    + (0.067 × −0.25) + (0.067 × 1.1) + (0.067 × 1) + (0.067 × 1.8) + (0.067 × 0.5)

Note that since the fractions 2/15 and 1/15 do not make exact percentages, the approximations 0.133 and 0.067 have been used respectively:

β_p = (0.133) + (0.1995) + (0.1596) + (−0.0067) + (0.266) + (−0.0168) + (0.0737)
    + (0.067) + (0.1206) + (0.0335)
β_p = 1.0294
β_p = 1.03 (as beta is usually expressed to two decimal places)

Again, the relative complexity of this calculation shows (as with most areas of quantitative analysis) how computers have an essential role to play in carrying out calculations quickly and giving investment managers rapid access to data used in making quantitative judgements.

THE ULTIMATE USEFULNESS OF QUANTITATIVE ANALYSIS

In this chapter we have seen the basic principles that guide quantitative analysis and it has been suggested how the tools of this form of analysis can be powerful methods of meeting a particular investor's objectives for return and risk, and with a high degree of accuracy, given that no matter how refined the tools, the unknown future is extrapolated from the known past.

Of all the three main forms of analysis (i.e. fundamental analysis, technical analysis and quantitative analysis), it is quantitative analysis which is the area where most research is currently undertaken, particularly in the USA. Numerous specialized books on the field are published each year in the USA and UK, and readers wishing to find out more regarding quantitative analysis may refer to *Financial Management: Method and Meaning* by A.G. Puxty and J.C. Dodds (Chapman & Hall: 1991).

3 INDEXATION

DEFINITION

Indexation, *which is also known as* **indexing** *and* **passive investment**, *involves an investment manager basing an investment portfolio on either an official index or on a customized index which has been designed to meet certain specific investment requirements of the client on whose behalf the funds are managed. As with quantitative investment, technology plays an essential role in facilitating indexation.*

INDEX FUNDS

Index funds are investment funds which are constructed and maintained in order to imitate an index such that the actual return on the fund will be as close as possible to the hypothetical return on the index. An index fund will be constructed to have the same exposure to significant characteristics, such as company size, industrial sector and foreign companies, as the index itself. Because of this, the return on an indexed portfolio should be very close to the rate of return on the index. Experience has found that this is roughly the case over whatever time-periods are surveyed. *An index fund gives approximately the same return as the index on a consistent basis.*

One way of looking at indexation is to regard it as the process of initially establishing the index fund, and running the fund such that it will continue to represent the given target index. Running an index fund is a highly complex process, although it has been rendered practicable by the use of computers. A considerable degree of accuracy is required, as small errors in the composition of the index fund can have a disproportionate effect on the performance of the fund.

Indexation can be applied to most types of financial markets, especially equity markets and bond (fixed-interest) markets. In today's investment management industry, by far the most important indices upon which index funds are based are equity indices. The principal criterion when assessing whether or not an index fund can be constructed is whether a suitable target index is available.

CONSTRUCTING AN INDEX FUND

There are two alternatives facing investment managers who wish to create an equity index fund.

1. *The fund can include all the stocks which comprise the index.*
This is known as a **fully replicated fund**. Fully replicated funds have the advantage that they provide a completely accurate replication of the fund, but have the serious drawback that if the index comprises a large number of instruments (say, more than about 300), then the transaction costs associated with creating and maintaining the index fund will probably be high enough to place in jeopardy the benefits of running the indexed fund.
2. *The fund can be made up of a sample of stocks which is designed to replicate the index as accurately as possible.*
Funds that are constructed in this way are usually known as **sampled funds**. Sampled funds contain fewer instruments than fully replicated funds, and are consequently almost always less expensive to set up and operate.

Although it is clear that setting up and maintaining a sampled fund will cost less than creating and operating a fully replicated fund, the cost advantage here is to some extent offset by a factor known as the **tracking error**. This statistic indicates the expected divergence of the return of the fund from that of the index. For example, a fund with a tracking error of 0.50% will be expected to perform within half a percentage point of the index two-thirds of the time and within one percentage point of the index 95% of the time. The tracking error for a particular fund is calculated according to the following procedure:

1. Details of the return of the index for a number of different time-periods are obtained; these time-periods are typically one month. In practice, organizations such as the Edinburgh-based investment management performance measurement organization, the WM Company, calculate tracking error based on either 36 or 60 different monthly calculations. Evaluating the tracking error from such a large quantity of data (assuming that the data is available) gives a highly accurate figure for tracking error, but it requires a computer to perform the calculation.
2. Details of the return of the index fund for the same number of different time-periods are also obtained.
3. Lists are compiled giving the percentage changes in the returns on the index and the returns of the indexed fund for the relevant time-periods.
4. The differences between the percentage changes in the returns on the index and the returns on the indexed fund are calculated and placed in a third table.
5. The tracking error is the standard deviation of these differences.

It is important to realize that the greater the number of stocks in a sampled index fund, the less will be the tracking error. This is of course what we should expect since the more instruments in the sampled fund, the closer this portfolio will be to a fully indexed fund.

THE RATIONALE FOR INDEXATION

Supporters of the principle of indexation usually group their arguments in favour of this technique into four specific categories, as follows.

The theoretical argument

The theoretical arguments for indexation are based on the notion that in the medium to long term no investment manager can hope to obtain exceptionally good sustained performance by the expedient of selecting stocks using such techniques as fundamental analysis. This notion argues that attempts to obtain exceptional performance on a sustained basis will not succeed because it is only possible to obtain exceptional performance where markets are 'imperfect', that is where some participants have access to better information than others. The theory says that leaving aside **insider information** (i.e. illegal access to information which the recipient obtains by virtue of some special relationship which he has with the information source), financial markets generally exhibit little imperfection, with all the prices of the instruments on that market fairly accurately reflecting all the information that is known about the instruments. This theory does not suggest that financial markets never exhibit certain 'pockets' of imperfection which may give some participants the opportunity to gain exceptional performance by virtue, for example, of some special, detailed research which they have undertaken, but that financial markets do not contain sufficient imperfections for this exceptional performance to be sustainable.

This theory is known as the **efficient markets hypothesis** (EMH) which has gained ground in the USA, and is becoming increasingly widely accepted in other countries, and holds that while it is impractical to suggest that markets are perfect (because some participants will at any one time have information which may give them the opportunity to gain a short-lived edge over other participants), the *prices in the market will none the less reflect all relevant available information*.

The notion of the EMH has extremely important implications for investment managers. If the EMH is valid, then the notion that unusual profits can be *consistently* made on a stock exchange is revealed as nothing more than superstition. Someone might be lucky enough to make unusual profits, on occasion, but this only indicates good fortune. There are no real opportunities for consistent profits within stock exchanges because all opportunities evaporate through the pricing mechanism, which 'absorbs' and rapidly evens out the portions of imperfection which have given one participant the opportunity to make abnormal profits.

Although it is not possible to prove the validity or otherwise of the EMH, the theory is gaining increasing currency among academics and many market participants as *probably* the best available explanation of how financial markets behave. The supporters of the EMH would agree that selecting stocks by fundamental analysis or by following 'hunches' is likely to produce as many losses as gains. Supporters of the EMH argue that the only way to obtain consistent returns from a market that is efficient is to diversify assets according to certain principles which indicate – principally by mathematical means – how return and risk might be maximized for a given asset allocation.

The EMH is a backbone of the theory of quantitative analysis. This is a form of analysis of investment instruments which is based primarily on the expected return and risk accruing from the different investment instruments within a diversified portfolio. Indexation might well be described as a subset of quantitative analysis.

Another principle of quantitative analysis that is extremely important in connection with the theoretical justification for indexation is the idea that if an investor takes on additional risk, he should in effect be compensated for carrying that risk by receiving a higher return. Therefore, if the EMH holds, then any strategy which is geared to gaining higher returns by careful stock selection will also involve higher risks; and if the strategy does not gain these higher returns, then the investor will be carrying risk for which he is not being compensated. There is in fact considerable empirical evidence that investors who select stocks by whatever means are indeed carrying additional risk and are not being sufficiently compensated for it by achieving higher returns. Incidentally, it is possible to see this as evidence that the EMH may hold.

The performance argument

The performance argument says, simply, that indexation appears to work. Since the 1970s, when US academics first began to suggest that a more effective way for an investment manager to achieve a consistently good (rather than consistently exceptional) level of fund performance might be to base a fund around a market index, rather than employ traditional stock selection methods, considerable effort has been expended by economists and financial market analysts around the world to investigate whether indexation is effective as an investment management technique. There is no longer any doubt that in almost all financial markets *the majority* of actively managed funds fail to produce as good a level of return as the market index.

Part of the reason for this is that a real-life portfolio into which investment instruments are bought, and from which instruments are sold, incurs transaction costs which a market index does not incur. However, this is only a partial explanation of why a market index usually outperforms an actively managed portfolio. The main reason why this should be the case appears to be that a market index is able to avoid excess risk and obtain consistent returns because it represents, in effect, a *diversification* across a fairly wide range of instruments. One major tenet of quantitative analysis theory is that diversification can reduce the risk in a portfolio of holding particular instruments, until the point is reached where the only risk held by the investment manager is the **market risk** (known as **systematic risk**), which is the unavoidable risk held within the market and a consequence of a wide variety of economic factors. With this in mind, we should not be surprised that a market index will over a period produce (generally, the longer the period, the more this principle holds) a level of performance that is better than that gained by a portfolio which embodies less diversification.

In practice, the appeal of indexation to those investment managers who practise it is the high likelihood which it offers that the indexed fund will not only perform with low volatility, but also produce a return that is very close to that of the index.

The strategic argument

There is also what might be termed a 'strategic' argument in favour of indexation. This maintains that indexation provides a complete investment strategy which not only offers the investment manager the likelihood of obtaining good, consistent performance, but also represents a more efficient use of investment resources than active management, which appears to involve the carrying of risks that are not likely to be fully compensated in terms of higher returns.

The economic argument

The economic argument for indexation is an extension of the performance argument and the strategic argument. The economic argument which, if valid, is very powerful maintains that indexation is not only in the long run a less expensive investment management technique than active management, but also likely to produce a better performance. The argument says that this being the case, indexation is economically desirable, as it is an efficient means for maximizing returns to investors, and where a fund (such as a pension fund) with many contributors is involved, it helps to minimize contributions for a particular level of eventual return.

THE ARGUMENTS OPPOSING INDEXATION

The arguments in favour of indexation are unquestionably powerful. However, the reader might well ask why, if these arguments are all valid, active investment management has not long been abandoned in favour of indexation. The following arguments – some of which appear to be more valid than others – suggest why this is not the case.

The performance argument

Just as there is a performance argument in favour of indexation, there is also a performance argument opposed to indexation. This performance argument is usually voiced by investment managers practising one of two types of analysis, fundamental analysis and quantitative analysis.

- *Managers practising fundamental analysis*: investment managers practising fundamental analysis, while conceding that indexation is an effective technique, would argue that none the less truly effective fundamental analysis should be able to turn in a performance that beats the index. It is of course hardly surprising that fundamental analysis think in this way. In the City of London, as in all major financial centres, the day-to-day analysis of stocks by stockbrokers and research houses according to fundamental principles is an industry which employs thousands of people earning in aggregate hundreds of millions of pounds every year. In the same way that one would hardly expect turkeys to vote for an early Christmas, one would hardly expect that all these people would give too much approval to an investment management technique which in effect argues that they are unnecessary! Besides, some of them must be right in claiming that they will be able to beat the index. Not even the staunchest advocate of indexation would argue that fundamental analysis can never beat the market index. However, in the long term it is almost certainly a reliable rule that the instances when fundamental analysis beats the market index are at least balanced by – and possibly outweighed by – the number of times when fundamental analysis fails to beat the index.

Unfortunately, it is less easy to prove whether or not investment management companies practising fundamental analysis can consistently beat the index more than might be expected. Performance measurement companies have a strict policy of only providing fund performance comparison information to their investment management company subscribers and – not surprisingly – these companies only make this information public when it paints a favourable picture of them. Useful as it would be to have access to, for example, details of the top performing fund managers practising fundamental analysis for each of the past ten years, and then see whether this information suggests that any of these companies can *consistently* outperform the index, this information is not readily available. However, observations within the investment management industry suggest that there are very few firms practising fundamental analysis which manage consistently to outperform the index.

• *Managers practising quantitative analysis*: the claims of some investment management companies that practise quantitative analysis to be able consistently to beat the index appears to deserve serious consideration. Far from opposing the basic concept of indexation, quantitative analysts welcome it, but maintain that nevertheless by careful assessment of risk and return for different stocks, and by trying to identify areas where they believe the market is inefficient in terms of how it values one instrument compared to another, they can produce a more efficient risk and return profile than would even be provided by an indexed portfolio.

Empirical evidence suggests that the best quantitative managers are on balance able to outperform the index more often than they fail to beat it. US organizations like BARRA and Rosenberg Institutional Equity Management (both founded by former US academic Barr Rosenberg) have turned the attempt to beat market indices by using quantitative techniques into a reasonably exact science, and the substantial funds which these organizations manage worldwide suggests that their clients are happy with their approach.

The market equilibrium argument

This argument sounds rather more like 'sour grapes' than a logical argument against indexation. Some active managers suggest that it would be detrimental to the market if a large proportion of its market capitalization were locked into a strategy which was highly predictable and static. This argument suggests that if this was the case, the market would actually cease to be efficient since the state of efficiency is maintained by the frequent and continuing movements of investment funds into and out of different securities, after fundamental research by analysts to identify undervalued stocks.

This argument does not really hold water. Much of the academic research into market efficiency was carried out in the USA during the 1960s, long before institutional fund managers became so influential within financial markets. The markets were efficient enough then, which rather contradicts the idea that market efficiency depends on the action of the stockmarket analyst.

The capital allocation argument

This is really another 'sour grapes' argument, which says that one of the principal functions of a stockmarket is to provide capital to industry, and that if the concentration on indexed funds persists, then the only companies which will be able to raise capital will be those listed in the major stock market indices. The smaller companies would be unable to raise capital until they graduate to the big indices, and they will be unable to graduate until they raise capital.

Although there is doubtless some truth in the argument that a market where most of the assets were invested in indexed funds would not be economically desirable, this argument hardly gainsays the principle of indexation. In any event, growth industries can be supported by venture capital, more of which is usually available for suitable investments than there are suitable investments to receive it. In any case, there is absolutely no reason why an investment manager who wishes to use indexation should not construct specialized indices based on smaller companies.

Conclusion to arguments for and against indexation

From looking at the above arguments, it is difficult to conclude anything other than that indexation is a perfectly valid (even advantageous) investment management technique. Even those active managers who reject it will readily accept the usefulness of having a market index against which to manage the performance of their actively managed funds. Since information with which to make comparisons with other active managers' performance is not always available, an active manager who was reporting to a client or pitching to a new client would not easily be able to show off his investment expertise unless there were a market index against which to measure performance.

Instead of producing arguments against indexation, a good active manager should rather be aware of the opportunities that it offers. There is no reason, for example, why an active manager should not create funds that are closely based on an index – thereby obtaining the expected advantages of consistent returns and low risk – while retaining the opportunity to take a considered and well-researched view over a particular stock and to hope (with some reason) for an advantage over managers who take a purely passive approach to managing their indexed fund.

Another important area of opportunity is where a new security is going to enter the index; indexers practising indexation will all be buying into that stock in order to ensure that their portfolios continue to match the index. Since the imminent arrival of a new stock in an index is public knowledge, active managers can often take advantage of the forthcoming demand for that stock from indexers and make a profit here, although indexers will usually do their best to protect themselves by such methods as buying an option on the stocks that will be coming into the index.

TECHNOLOGY'S ROLE IN INDEXATION

Had it not been for the rapid development of computers during the past 20 years, the principle that a fund based on a market index could achieve a consistently good performance would never have achieved practical realization. It is theoretically possible to construct and operate manually an index fund, but the laboriousness of the operation and the high associated labour costs would certainly remove the financial benefits of investing with an index fund.

However, the development of extremely powerful, compact and relatively inexpensive computers, particularly since the early 1980s, has provided tools which can easily handle the most complex demands of an indexed fund, given that the computer is programmed with a comprehensive and effective computer program (software).

None the less, the computing resources necessary to run an index fund cost money, and mean that while the ongoing costs of operating an index fund will probably be fairly low, the entry costs of indexation – the costs of setting up the index fund – will be high, although many investment management organizations may be able to modify existing software in order to handle the requirements of an index fund. If this is not possible, the would-be index fund manager will need either to commission customized software for the index fund management or else buy in an existing package from a software house or information technology consultancy and arrange for any necessary customizations to be made. Note that basing index fund management software on a bought-in package will usually be far less expensive than designing the software from scratch. Overall, the cost of the software will be directly proportional to the degree of customization that is involved.

The software will need to be able to perform the following functions.

- *Portfolio design*: this involves the initial construction of the index fund according to the principles that the index fund manager has chosen.
- *Monitoring the index*: this involves monitoring the index to ensure that the index fund remains an accurate full or sampled replication of the index. Any changes in the composition of the index against which the match is being made must be acted upon as soon as they become official.
- *Process transactions*: all transactions made by the index fund should be processed within the software, with the system ideally relaying details of transactions to counterparties and the appropriate official settlement authorities.
- *Provide performance comparisons against the index*: this function allows the index fund manager to keep closely in touch with how the index fund is performing relative to the index.
- *Provide performance comparisons against customized benchmarks*: as well as knowing how the index fund is performing against the index that it is tracking, the index fund manager will also want to know how it is performing against customized benchmarks that the index fund manager will have selected. For example, one benchmark might be the performance of an actively managed portfolio. Such a procedure would allow a client to compare the performance of an index fund and

an actively managed fund, with a view to increasing the allocation of funds to the best-performing fund.

• *Monitor dividends*: as with any actively managed fund, dividends will accrue from holdings in an index fund. The software should hold details of days when corporations are likely to declare dividends, store information relating to the extent of those dividends, and allocate dividends to different clients in proportion to the clients' holdings within the index fund.

• *Process commission charges*: all transactions on the index fund will, as with an actively managed fund, incur commission charges. The software should be able to record these charges and accommodate them in calculations of monetary return from investing in the index fund.

• *Monitoring and controlling cash flow*: it is said by many commentators that one important means by which index fund managers can establish competitive advantages over each other is by the efficiency with which they monitor and control cash flow into and out of the fund. Just because a fund manager has opted for an investment strategy that is essentially passive does not, of course, reduce the need to run the fund efficiently, and keep himself, his colleagues and clients in contact with information relating to the operation of the index fund, and its cash flows.

If the wide range of the above functions suggests that today's index fund managers rely very heavily on technology in order to manage their funds accurately and efficiently, this is indeed the case. No matter how skilled and experienced the index fund manager, if his organization's technology is poorly programmed and weak in functionality, the fund manager's skills will not be properly utilized.

The cost of technology

It is important to bear in mind that technology for index fund management offers very substantial opportunities for the index fund manager to benefit from economies of scale. This is because it would make very little difference to the systems' requirements whether the fund manager was responsible for managing £10 million, £100 million or even £1 billion in the indexed fund. It follows that once an index fund manager has obtained funds to manage in order to cover his costs, he can afford to be very competitive on fees.

As might be expected from the above, it is the largest index fund managers who are defining pricing policy for the entire indexation industry. Confronted by this pricing situation, smaller index fund management companies inevitably tend to be less profitable than larger organizations.

PRACTICAL ASPECTS OF CREATING AND OPERATING AN INDEX FUND

Creating the fund with a basket trade

Although it is perfectly possible to create an index fund from scratch by buying up the different stocks, this will in most cases be more expensive than establishing the index fund by means of a **basket trade** (otherwise known as a 'package' or 'program trade'). Program trading received an undeservedly bad name following the 1987 world stock market crash, in which it was blamed for causing undesirable volatility within the major US financial markets. However, basket trades are simply trades that involve a 'basket' of securities. Where a fund manager is seeking to create an index fund, he will make this requirement known to the market maker who, if he has something suitable for sale, will give the fund manager a good idea of what instruments the basket will contain, but he will expect the fund manager to bid for the basket *without necessarily knowing which specific instruments it contains*. This is possible because what will be attractive to the fund manager is the stability of risk (gained through diversification), which the basket represents, rather than the short-term attractions of some of the instruments.

Where an index manager who is already managing an index fund wishes to manage the fund according to different underlying criteria, or in order to match another index, the fund manager will often wish to sell the index fund in its entirety. He will usually choose to do this through a basket trade since even the gradual release of the large blocks of instruments to the market is likely to have a detrimental effect on their price. Again, the fund manager will sell the basket fund without informing potential customers of the precise composition of the fund.

Adjusting the composition of the index fund

There are two reasons why an index fund manager would wish to change the composition of the index fund. The first and most likely reason would simply be that the composition of the index itself had changed and the manager wishes to ensure that his index fund remains a close match to the index.

The second reason is that the underlying criteria by which the index fund is matched to the index (assuming that full replication is not taking place) have altered, usually because the index fund manager wants to provide a closer replication to the index.

In both cases, it is advisable for the index fund manager first to explore the possibility of buying or selling the required instruments in house, to any other managers who are practising active management within his organization.

Minimizing the cost of trading securities

Index fund managers must always be on their guard against unnecessarily increasing the costs of securities transactions. Basket trades are certainly one way of doing this when an index fund is being created since the fund manager will almost certainly be able to buy the instruments in a basket less expensively than if he had purchased them all individually. However, a major problem that always arises when an index fund is being managed is how the fund manager disposes of a single large block of securities without depressing the price of the securities, which would happen if the stocks were all unloaded on to the market-place together.

An index fund manager faced with the need to unload a large block of a single security can choose to sell the block slowly, perhaps over a period of two weeks, in order to minimize the likelihood of the sale having a detrimental effect on the price. Alternatively, the fund manager can take a **placing broker** into his confidence, who will seek to place the stock among his contacts and clients with the minimum disruption to the price of the security. It is in being acquainted with the most appropriate placing brokers for different types of stock that an important part of an index fund manager's expertise consists.

Finding the right staff

Indexation is a highly specialized task and requires a wide range of skills, including expertise in computer modelling, database management, financial indices, general investment management knowledge and specific knowledge regarding how to trade securities at minimum cost.

Staff recruitment may be a problem, with too few people possessing the right level of expertise available on the employment market. Many index fund managers avoid this problem by training staff in house, but this (as always) has the drawback that the trained staff may go and work for a rival organization.

Client reporting

One of the most time-consuming, and for some managers, tedious, aspects of active investment management is the need to report back to clients on performance. Many index fund managers find that once the index fund is in place and running satisfactorily, the client is happy to receive more formalized and less in-depth types of report, and may also be content to meet with the index fund manager less often than the client may have wished to meet with an active manager. Consequently, index fund managers may frequently have more time available for product development and marketing-related activities than do their active managing counterparts.

Marketing the index fund

As with other areas of the financial services business, not even the best index fund will sell itself in the market-place, and marketing both the general concept of index funds and any particular index fund requires a high priority on any index fund manager's agenda.

The most usual method of marketing an index is via advertisements that discuss (in positive terms of course) the fund's performance, and the (probably) lower costs to clients of having an index fund manager rather than an active fund. Another important marketing technique for index funds, and one not greatly explored to date by many index fund managers, is for the fund manager to seek to generate coverage in the financial press, which in the UK includes the *Financial Times*, the business pages of the quality national dailies and a surprisingly large number of specialized financial journals and newssheets.

THE LATEST THINKING IN INDEXATION

The high potential rewards of successful indexation, and the sheer intellectual interest of the subject, means that some of the best brains in the international investment management community have devoted themselves to the theory and practice of indexation. Most financial journals in the USA, UK and many other countries publish regular features on indexation, and readers will find these useful for gaining up-to-date information regarding developments in this area.

The following is a brief summary of some of the most important subjects on which the latest thinking on indexation focuses.

* *Customized benchmarks*: these are becoming increasingly popular throughout the indexation community. They can be used at one level to measure the performance of an active or passive investment strategy that sets out to fulfil certain specific preferences held by the client such as avoiding what the client perceives as unethical investments. Similarly, customized benchmarks can be used as the basis for index funds which are constructed in accordance with certain client preferences.

In order for customized benchmarks to be constructed and maintained, it is important that the client's preferences are objective and hence translatable into computer instructions. Furthermore, by using computers to construct customized portfolios the index fund manager has rapid access to reliable information detailing the extent to which the switch to a customized benchmark has affected performance.

The ability to make comparisons between different customized benchmarks is particularly developed in the USA, where some specialized investment management advisory organizations operate investment strategies that involve regular switching between different customized benchmarks in order to gain an edge over a principal market index.

* *Tilt funds*: these, as the name suggests, are funds – usually index funds – operated rather as a combination of straight index fund and actively managed fund. A tilt fund will be based on a particular index, but is biased towards certain factors which the index fund manager believes will give the tilt fund a performance advantage over a standard index fund. Examples of factors which govern the tilt are high-yield stocks, stocks of a particular country (in the case of an international index) or stocks in companies of relatively small size. In other words, the tilt fund manager is seeking to obtain the best of both the active and passive investment worlds. There appears to be much scope for further research into tilt funds.

* *Using indexation in conjunction with other quantitative investment management techniques*: this is perhaps the most interesting current development within indexation. Since indexation is a subset of quantitative analysis, it seems likely that applying other principles of quantitative analysis in conjunction with an indexation strategy could constitute a powerful investment strategy. For example, an index

fund manager practising this strategy – which might be seen as a sophisticated form of tilt fund management – bases his investment activity upon a particular index, but applies quantitative analysis to identify areas within the market-place where stocks are undervalued in terms of the returns they provide for a certain level of risk. Such a strategy, if implemented systematically and efficiently, might well be a fairly reliable means of outperforming the index on a consistent basis.

4 CUSTODY

THE NATURE OF CUSTODY

Investment managers make use of custody services and so discharge in an efficient and timely manner a wide variety of administrative requirements relating to the securities that they hold. The hub of the custody service involves the safekeeping and custody of certificates proving the ownership of securities. However, the custody service also includes a widening range of services that develops in accordance with individual investors' requirements.

Today technology plays an extremely important role in custody services, both in terms of the communications link between the investment manager and the custodian and in the way in which screen-based custody information is configured and distributed on screens within the investment manager's office.

There are two distinct types of custody:

1. *Domestic custody* – involves the provision of custody services relating to an investment management organization's domestic holdings.
2. *Global custody* – involves the provision of custody services relating to an investment management organization's foreign holdings.

Further, the Geneva-based International Society of Securities Administrators (ISSA), an influential international association which promotes progress in securities administration, defines the activities of a global custodian as follows: *A global custodian provides clients with multi-currency custody, settlement and reporting services which extend beyond the global custodians' and clients' base region and currency; and encompass all classes of financial instrument.*

For investment managers, the main area of complexity in the custody arena lies in the area of global custody. Domestic custody will in many cases be handled by the investment management organization's own bankers, or even by a separate department of the investment management organization itself. However, where an investment manager has holdings in numerous countries, the efficient liaison with one or more global custodians becomes of prime importance to the investment manager's efficient and profitable operation.

THE ROLE OF CUSTODY TECHNOLOGY

Today's custody industry is inextricably connected with the technology that is used to deliver the custody service. Custody technology is used to provide computerized support in all areas of custody-related activity.

Investment managers use technology to communicate with their custodians and receive screen-based information from them. Although not all investment management organizations use technology for the communications process, for example, smaller companies may still rely on receiving information via a facsimile machine or even through the post, the vast majority of medium to large investment management organizations prefer to communicate with their custodian primarily through a computer screen and a communications system.

Screen-based communications between custodians and investment management organizations fall into two distinct categories; these are:

1. *Batch-processed communications*: here the information is held within the custodian's or investment management organization's computer system until the time when the information is relayed from the custodian to the client, or vice versa. Batch-processed communications are typically relayed during the night, both because there are not likely to be any incoming transactions to alter the position while the relaying takes place, and also because sending messages at night is usually much less expensive than sending messages during the day.
2. *Real-time (on-line) communications*: here the message is relayed from one party to another, to all intents, instantaneously. The expression 'real time' relates to the fact that the system is in effect operating to the same 'real' timetable as used by the investment management, custodian or other interested parties.

If technology is used by an investment management organization for the purposes of communicating with its custodian, the custodian will arrange for the organization to receive all the information that it requires via the system. This may include information on all of the different elements of the overall custody service that the custodian is providing to the investment management organization. Where a screen-based service is being provided, the investment manager should as a minimum expect the custodian to supply the following types of information:

*   details of the day-to-day contents of all portfolios under management;
*   a daily transmission of bargains struck;
*   information about transactions that are cleared and settled, and those that are still outstanding;
*   detailed information relating to banking movements and balances available;
*   portfolio valuations (multi-currency, if necessary);
*   information necessary for the preparation of client reports;
*   relevant information about regulation and compliance.

The point of contact at the investment management organization

There is a trend within the custody industry for all investment managers to have direct screen-based access to custody information coming straight from the custodian. However, in practice most investment management organizations prefer to delegate the task of direct liaison with the custodian to one or more administrative officers, typically located in the organization's back office (i.e. administrative department). Unlike the investment managers themselves, who are likely only to want a particular item of custody-related information at any one time, the back office will need all custody information, all the time.

Communications between a back office and investment managers can often take place via the organization's local area network (LAN). However, even in the largest organizations, paper-based transactions are relied upon to a surprising extent for back-office/investment manager communications. For example, the investment manager will pass paper order forms to the back office and receive paper transaction slips in return. Details of the transactions, however, are likely to be relayed by the back office to the custodian via the screen.

THE NATURE OF CUSTODY TECHNOLOGY

The specification and implementation of the technology with which an investment management organization communicates with a custodian is a specialized task. For a medium to large investment management organization, the task will usually be carried out by the organization's specialized information technology (IT) division. For a smaller organization, the task will probably be carried out by an external systems house or information technology consultancy.

Custody systems of the 1990s are almost invariably designed either to be run on mainframe computers (e.g. IBM mainframes) or minicomputers (e.g. IBM AS/400 system). In addition, some global custody software packages run on IBM (or compatible) PCs.

Where electronic communications between custodians and their clients are being used, the method of communications is either via leased telephone lines or proprietary lines. The communications process will typically involve the following parties:

- the lead custodian (i.e. the principal custodian in any custodian and sub-custodian network);
- the investment manager;
- the sub-custodian(s) (i.e. any subcontracted custodian or agent bank);
- the depository (where appropriate).

CASE STUDY: A LEADING NETHERLANDS INVESTMENT MANAGEMENT ORGANIZATION AND ITS USE OF CUSTODY TECHNOLOGY

This company is one of the largest investment management organizations in the Netherlands. It is a subsidiary of a major Dutch bank, which handles the subsidiary's custody requirements. Although in the UK and USA regulatory protocols prevent custodians from acting for investment managers within their group, no such restrictions exist in continental Europe.

The investment management organization holds the equivalent of $3 billion under management, of which approx. 50% consists of individually managed pension funds, approx. 20% in private investors' funds and approx. 30% in mutual funds. Most of the managed assets are held in equities and bonds, although money market instruments also feature in the mix.

The custodian is already a highly automated bank and the investment management company can hook up to the bank's central computer system, which is powered by a Unisys mainframe. The system provides the subsidiary's investment managers with a full range of information about the state of particular portfolios and customer accounts, as well as price information from a variety of data vendors. The system, which also allows an on-line link to the custodian and its investment management subsidiary, is a PC-based system connected to the bank's mainframe. A director of the investment management organization says that the system already meets the vast majority of the screen-based information requirements of the investment managers. The director is, however, constantly examining ways of improving the system, and he is looking at possibilities for implementing a performance measurement module which will provide the investment management organization's clients with a performance measurement service for individual and aggregate portfolios against a variety of benchmarks, including client-constructed benchmarks.

The director has said that he sees the ability of an investment management company to have access to screen-based on-line links as a prime weapon in the battle for competitive supremacy.

The director also believes that in future the trend for investment managers to make more use of derivative instruments could only result in a situation where custodians will need to follow this trend very carefully, to ensure that the operational and technological structures are in place to keep a custodian fully in tune with the increased use of derivatives by investment managers.

CLEARANCE AND SETTLEMENT

Clearance and settlement have a great importance within the custody process. The efficiency of national clearance and settlement procedures has received particular attention within the international custody industry, for even the most efficient custodian is restricted in how it handles clearing and settlement by the different clearance and settlement procedures of the financial markets in the countries where it operates. Technology plays an increasingly important role in clearance and settlement since it gives national exchanges and regulatory authorities the opportunity to deploy technological infrastructures which allow clearance and settlement to take place electronically.

There is an increasing impetus within the financial communities of the world for greater standardization of clearance and settlement procedures. This impetus was initiated after the 1987 world stock market crash, which featured unprecedented trading volumes in most of the world's financial markets. During the months following the crash, approx. 40% of all international securities transactions failed to settle on the value date.

Prior to the crash, there had been intermittent concern within the international securities trading community at the inefficiency of many national clearance and settlement infrastructures, and particularly at the lack of standardization of clearance and settlement procedures for cross-border transactions. The years since the crash have seen the first ever concerted international effort to create a national and cross-border securities trading environment which conforms to internationally accepted standards. There is a general consensus throughout the world's financial markets that the creation and implementation of such standards is in everybody's interest. Speedier clearance and settlement of transactions should result in a less complex, more efficient investment and trading scenario that will reduce the time taken to clear and settle transactions, and the cost of doing this; and with consequent benefits for the investing and trading public at large, institutional investors, global custodians and sub-custodians.

An important consequence of an improved national and international clearance and settlement environment would be an increased willingness on the part of investment managers in general, and institutional investors in particularly, to invest overseas. Since increased overseas investment is regarded as economically desirable, other things being equal, the steps taken towards the standardization of international clearance and settlement are seen as carrying important economic benefits.

This direct connection between the health of the world economy and the efficiency of national clearance and settlement procedures has come about because of the interdependence of world financial markets.

Links between world financial markets

Over the past few years, a number of key factors have led to the increasing interdependence of the international financial markets; these factors include:

- increasing international trade;
- a generally heightened interest within the world's financial community in cross-border trading and investment;
- a great expansion in the role that technology plays in relaying market information around the world;
- the international proliferation of trading and investment strategies which exploit technology's ability to relay this information rapidly to all relevant parties.

This interlinking of the world's financial markets has resulted in a situation where events and transactions, and even changes in attitude many thousands of miles away, can influence the behaviour of a market at home, or close to home.

It is usually agreed that the benefits which interdependent markets bring in terms of increased liquidity far outweigh the possible danger that, in a widespread crash, interdependence can sometimes lead to more volatility than is desirable. Many practitioners within the world's securities markets believe that the full benefits of the international linking of financial markets will only be gained when coordinated international policy on relevant financial issues creates the 'fast lanes' along which cross-border transactions can travel at top speed.

These financial issues range from complex economic matters, such as the international money supply, to more fundamental issues, such as clearance and settlement of securities trades, and the creation of a standardized system for the numbering of securities in different markets. Above all, what matters is that the process of coordination of policy on these issues moves ahead, worldwide, on a broad wavefront.

THE GROUP OF THIRTY

One group of practitioners, policy-makers and theoreticians which has set out to try to understand what holds the global economy together, and to make recommendations for the smoother functioning of different aspects of the world economy, is the Group of Thirty. This has proved itself to be a powerful force for change within the world's custody industry.

The Group of Thirty was set up in 1978 by Dr Johannes Witteveen, after his retirement as managing director of the International Monetary Fund. Witteveen gathered together an international group of private bankers, central bankers and economists in the belief that there were certain key international issues that no official body could tackle effectively, and that there were other issues which could be furthered by an independent, non-partisan viewpoint being added to the debate. Many of the 30 founding members – all leaders in the financial community, senior academics or top policy-makers – were economists by background with an interest in issues of public policy and private practice within the international financial and economic sector. Members came from all over the world. The composition of the Group's members has been such that the focus on international economic and financial issues is maintained and that all of the major industrial countries, and several smaller countries besides, are well represented.

The Group of Thirty's recommendations carry no statutory force, and the Group has no power to enforce its recommendations. However, many of the recommendations do carry very considerable weight among the international banking industry. This is partly because of the experience, expertise and authority of the members of the Group of Thirty, and also because the practitioners to whom the recommendations are directed have in the case of custodians and investment managers come to realize the importance of the recommendations for streamlining their particular industry.

Recommendations are communicated to all interested persons. Within the custody industry this would include the management of investment management organizations, lead custodians and sub-custodians. The Group of Thirty has usually been accorded considerable press coverage. It communicates its recommendations principally by means of publications, although seminars and conferences for industry participants are also a means by which it presents its thoughts. To date, the only area of its activities which affects the custody industry is the Group's work on clearance and settlement systems.

The Group of Thirty's recommendations on clearance and settlement

The Group of Thirty has issued nine technical recommendations for moving national clearance and settlement procedures towards a standardized protocol. Central to these recommendations is the introduction of settlement of transactions within three days following the transaction date, and the introduction of national clearance systems, which would usually be operated by a particular country's leading financial market or stock exchange, so that all participants can easily determine exactly what counterparties owe, and what they are due to receive, on settlement date. The Group believes that the introduction of national clearance systems will allow money to change hands in the most efficient and accurate manner for all participants, both national and foreign. The national clearance system will also manage the process of settlement, thereby completing the securities transaction.

Another prime function of a national clearance and settlement system would be to act as an intermediary. In this type of situation, the risk of any one member's default is shared by all members of the system.

Many leading industrialized nations are without a central clearance and settlement system. The Group of Thirty is determined to urge the introduction of such systems worldwide. As the Group says: 'Ownership of securities cannot function in an expeditious, riskless manner without a central clearing and settlement system.'

On the specific nature of the ideal clearance system, the Group says:

> It is essential that the clearing entity discharging obligations and payments has significant financial strength in the form of reserves or collateral – and the ability to receive additional assistance quickly from members and other financial institutions. This can be accomplished either through drawing rights against members or lines of credit at banks. To facilitate the settlement of large volumes of securities transactions, a clearance system should minimise the movement of both cash and securities. To do this, many clearing systems incorporate some form of netting of securities and/or funds. This process reduces trades in securities of the same issue between and among counterparties to the minimum number of deliveries and funds transfers, respectively.

CASE STUDY: THE LONDON STOCK EXCHANGE'S TAURUS SYSTEM

In order to move towards a standardized clearance and settlement scenario for the world's securities markets, and thereby to comply with the Group of Thirty's recommendations, the central financial markets in most of the world's industrialized nations are involved in streamlining their clearance and settlement procedures, in many cases by introducing (if this has not already been done) a national central securities depository to facilitate clearance and settlement.

It is often the financial markets in the world's leading economic nations which have the most to do if they are to comply with the Group of Thirty's recommendations. The reason for this is simply that financial markets in the world's leading nations have had longer to go their own way and to pursue non-standardized tracks.

For example, in the UK, USA and Japan the leading stock exchanges have much to do in terms of Group of Thirty compliance, while in countries such as Switzerland, with a much smaller population and geographical area, full compliance with Group of Thirty recommendations may be less expensive.

The London Stock Exchange is in the process of deploying an electronic share transfer and registration system to be known as TAURUS (Transfer and Automated Registration of Uncertificated Stock). TAURUS represents the UK's first major initiative to dematerialize stock.

TAURUS has been subject to a number of delays, caused according to the London Stock Exchange by technical problems. However, TAURUS is expected to be operational by the end of 1992, when it will provide a consistent settlement period of ten days after the transaction day (in abbreviated form, T + 10). It is planned that by the end of 1993, TAURUS will offer settlement three days after the transaction day (T + 3), in line with the Group of Thirty's recommendations.

The London Stock Exchange lists the benefits of TAURUS to the UK financial markets as being the following:

- compatibility with internationally accepted standards;
- reduction of risk;
- a platform for the future development of electronic share trading and confirmation systems;
- communication of shareholders' names to the stock-issuing company more quickly than at present.

The Stock Exchange says that, if TAURUS were not deployed, the following problems would eventually arise:

- the UK's reputation for having an archaic share registration system would be perpetuated;
- major investors would be tempted to migrate to financial centres which guarantee more efficient registration and settlement;
- the quality of the UK capital market would be jeopardized and the ease with which companies raise capital would be affected.

Although TAURUS is being deployed several years after the 'Big Bang' of 1986, which led to the UK financial markets moving off the floor of the Stock Exchange and the creation of electronic markets based around the Stock Exchange Automated Quotations (SEAQ) service, the need for an electronic transfer and registration system was foreseen by the Stock Exchange in 1986. Plans to build TAURUS were afoot at the same time as SEAQ was being planned. (Part Two of this Handbook contains a detailed article on TAURUS by the London Stock Exchange.)

PART TWO

An industry forum

5 ARBITRAGE PRICING TECHNIQUE AND PORTFOLIO MANAGEMENT

Roberto Wessels

Managing Director, Arcas–Wessels Roll Ross, Rotterdam, The Netherlands

INTRODUCTION

In order to be successful, a fund manager needs to understand why different assets have different returns. More than 30 years of academic research have shown that risk is by far the most important determinant of return. In recent years, a good deal of progress has been made both in refining the concept of risk and in developing the tools necessary to control it. Here the purpose is to summarize the most advanced theory in this area, **arbitrage pricing theory** (APT), and to illustrate it with an application from the field of portfolio management.

THE BACKGROUND

All theories about risk and return share a number of simple principles. First, return is the reward for bearing risk. If an investor can invest in an asset with a certain return such as a Treasury bill, then he or she will demand a risk premium as an inducement to investing in an asset with an uncertain or risky return. A risk premium is defined as: *the return in excess of the return on a riskless asset.* The riskier the expected return, the larger the required risk premium.

Secondly, the risk of a portfolio of different assets is lower than the sum of the risk of the individual assets going into the portfolio. Diversification reduces risk. The risk that remains after a portfolio has been fully diversified is called 'systematic' because it has a predictable effect on the return of the portfolio.

Thirdly, not all forms of risk can command a risk premium. The reason is that portfolio diversification is relatively cheap to do. Cost considerations will therefore not force anyone to bear unsystematic risk. One should therefore not expect to be rewarded for bearing the risk of an undiversified portfolio. In other words, only undiversifiable or systematic risk contributes to expected return.

Finally, assets which have the same risk should also have the same return, and vice versa. These conditions must hold in order to prevent riskless arbitrage. If two assets are seen to have the same risk but provide a different return, then investors are better off by selling the asset with the smaller return and buying the one with the larger return. Of course buying and selling will put pressure on prices, a process which will continue until investors cannot be made better off by rebalancing their holdings. This will obviously be the case when the returns of the two assets are equal.

MEASURING SYSTEMATIC RISK: CAPM AND APT

Although there is a broad agreement among practioners and academics that systematic risk has a predictable effect on expected returns, there is much less agreement on how systematic risk is to be measured.

The **capital asset pricing model** (CAPM) is probably the best-known model in this area. The CAPM was developed in the early 1960s, and provided the theoretical underpinning for the portfolio management technique known as 'indexing'; that is, managing portfolios of securities which closely replicate the risk and return characteristics of an index such as the S&P500 or the Financial Times-All Shares.

Increasingly however, textbooks and finance courses at leading business schools are adopting the arbitrage pricing theory (APT) as the standard model to explain the relation between risk and return. The APT was first proposed by Stephen Ross of Yale University; together with Richard Roll of UCLA, Ross subsequently developed APT into a portfolio management technique. The technique has been used to manage portfolios since 1986 and has performed successfully in different countries over several market cycles.

In the CAPM exposure to systematic risk is measured by an asset's **beta coefficient**, or simply beta. Beta is the sensitivity of the return of an asset to the return of the market portfolio (what we mean by the market portfolio is explained below).

The expected returns of an asset with a beta equal to one move perfectly in unison with the return on the market, and the asset has the same risk as the market portfolio. Assets with betas less than one are less sensitive to market movements and thus less risky. The opposite applies to assets with betas greater than one. By virtue of its simplicity, this description of the risk–return trade-off has considerable appeal. Still, a number of problems limit the application of the CAPM.

First, beta measures exposure relative to a reference portfolio or benchmark. In the CAPM, the **market portfolio** acts as the benchmark. The problem is that the market portfolio of the CAPM is a theoretical concept meant to include all available investment opportunities. This portfolio is of course not observable; one can construct indexes for particular markets or asset classes, but there is no way of knowing whether these indexes represent the true 'market' portfolio.

This creates a potentially serious problem as the measure of beta depends on the particular index chosen to represent the market portfolio. Different indexes may well produce different betas and thus seriously influence the outcome of the portfolio selection process.

A second problem is that beta tries to summarize how different economic forces affect stock returns by means of a single number. If there are different sources of systematic risk and assets have different exposures to these risks, then summarizing the risk–return trade-off by means of one number can be misleading. To illustrate the relevance of this point a small digression is perhaps necessary.

Suppose one creates two well-diversified portfolios of stocks. One portfolio consists of stocks selected from the capital goods sector; the other is selected from the food and beverages sector. Given that the portfolios are well diversified, they are exposed only to systematic risk. But the expected returns on these portfolios will be different. The reason for this is that the capital goods sector is more exposed to the business cycle, while the food and beverages sector is more exposed to inflation shocks. To a certain extent, inflation shocks are independent of the business cycle. Exposure to these two economic factors then represent separate risks, each of which can command its own risk premium.

If systematic risk (as this example suggests) comes from many sources, then a more general framework than the CAPM is needed to analyse the risk–return trade-off. This is what the development of the arbitrage pricing technique has accomplished. It attributes risk to different sources and determines how these different risks are to be priced (i.e. what the risk premiums are), in order that the returns be consistent.

RISK AND RETURN IN THE APT

According to APT, the expected return on an asset depends on just two variables. The first is the exposure to systematic risk, and the second is the risk premium for bearing systematic risk. The product of these two variables determines expected return. If there are many sources of systematic risk, expected return $E(R)$ can be written as follows:

$$E(R) = b_1 RP_1 + b_2 RP_2 + \ldots + b_k RP_k \qquad (5.1)$$

where b_i measures exposure to the ith source of systematic risk and RP_i is the risk premium for the ith source of systematic risk.

What investors expect, and what actually comes to pass, are generally quite different things. In fact, given the nature of risk, it would be very surprising if expected returns and observed returns were ever closely matched.

The difference between realized returns and observed returns is attributable to unexpected changes in the sources of systematic risk, i.e. economic factors. This difference can be written:

$$R - E(R) = b_1 F_1 + b_2 F_2 + \ldots + b_k F_k + e \qquad (5.2)$$

where b_i are the same measures of exposure as in equation (5.1), F_1 and F_2 are the unexpected changes in the sources of systematic risk and e is the return associated with exposure to unsystematic risk. How one goes about measuring the exposures and risk premiums is explained below.

The sources of systematic risk are unexpected changes in the fundamental economic factors. Although the theory does not specifically identify these factors, one can easily see that the factors must be related to variables that investors think are important in valuing assets: expected cash flows and discount rates. A great deal of fundamental research has confirmed intuition and identified five factors which can account for 95% or more of the variation in returns; these economic factors are:

1. Investor confidence.
2. Interest rates.
3. Business cycles.
4. Long-term inflation.
5. Short-term inflation.

In Fig. 5.1 the exposure of two portfolios to these sources of systematic risk is shown. What is interesting to note is that these portfolios have the same exposure to the benchmark, that is a 'market' beta of one, but that they have very different exposures to the economic factors. Thus, even though the two portfolios can be expected to track the benchmark quite closely, the returns of the portfolios will be different when, for instance, there are unexpected changes in interest rates.

MANAGING FUNDS USING APT

APT can be applied to manage portfolios with a wide variety of objectives in mind. One interesting application is to use APT to outperform a benchmark. The example below uses stocks, but APT can be used to manage bonds equally well.

Suppose a fund manager is given a brief to create a portfolio with the same level of risk as the S&P500 but which will outperform by 2% a year. How can this objective be achieved?

First, note that the S&P500 is a portfolio in which the largest 500 stocks quoted on the New York Stock Exchange are included according to their market capitalization. The return on this portfolio is therefore a value-weighted average return of the constituent stocks.

Using capitalization as a criterion for stock selection, however, does not necessarily lead to an efficient portfolio; that is, a portfolio which has the highest possible expected return given its level of risk.

Research shows that value-weighted portfolios, such as the S&P500, are rarely efficient and that one can form other portfolios which have the same level of risk but a higher expected return. These other portfolios are obviously more desirable from the investor's point of view. How does one go about finding these more efficient portfolios? There are two approaches.

The first is to construct a portfolio with 'undervalued' stocks, that is a portfolio consisting of stocks which have an expected rate of return that is higher than the rate of return of stocks with a comparable level of risk. The big problem in this

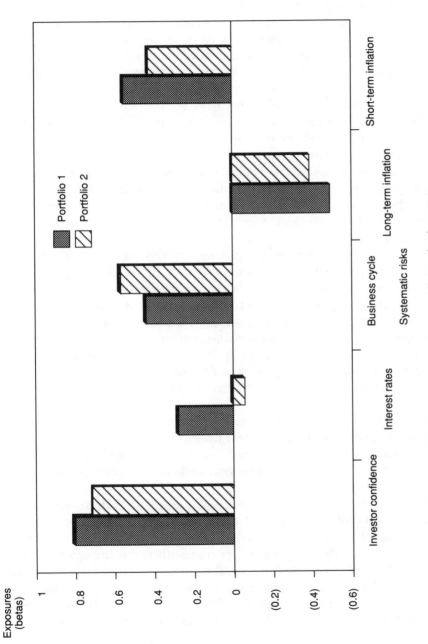

Fig. 5.1 Exposure to systematic risks (market beta = 1).

approach is how to decide that a stock is 'undervalued'. Styles of investment management (and fads) abound. Some fund managers, for example, place emphasis on firm size or on price to earnings ratios or on book to price ratios in their portfolio selection. The problem is that, given enough data, computer resources and patience, one can uncover correlations between returns, price–earnings ratios, size and myriad other factors as well. What is missing is a cogent and testable explanation as to why these factors help to select undervalued stocks. The upshot is that the search for undervalued stocks seldom produces consistent results.

A totally different approach is to recognize that although markets are by and large efficient, benchmark portfolios need not be. Instead of looking for undervalued stocks, the alternative is to construct a portfolio with a pattern of risk exposures which will provide a more efficient risk–return trade-off than the pattern of risk exposures of the benchmark.

Briefly, this approach involves, first, measuring the exposures of the S&P500 to the underlying risk factors, then determining what the premium is for bearing the risk of each factor and, finally, selecting a more efficient portfolio by overweighting exposures to relatively attractive risks – i.e. exposures to factors with a high ratio of expected return to risk.

These three steps involve the use of comparatively advanced numerical and statistical techniques, but the basic elements involved are easily explained. The main building-block is to form a number of well-diversified portfolios which are exposed to one (and only one) source of systematic risk. The return on each portfolio is, by definition, then equal to the risk premium investors receive for bearing the risk of just one economic factor, for instance the risk of unexpected inflation shocks. By tracking the return on these portfolios over time, one can also measure the volatility of the risk premiums. The ratio of the premium to its volatility can then be used to rank the attractiveness of exposures to different economic factors.

The exposure of asset returns to unexpected changes in economic factors can be measured in two ways. One can either use one's judgement to determine what economic factors are important and apply regression analysis to measure exposure or use a technique known as **factor analysis** to determine simultaneously the exposures and the relevant factors.

In general, factor analysis is preferable because it is difficult to find adequate data to represent economic factors. Moreover, even if the data can be found, it is never available at the necessary notice. On the other hand, the big drawback of factor analysis is that the estimated factors are statistical constructs, which are not identified in terms of observable variables. Thus, though one can identify the sources of risk in statistical terms, the analysis does not label these risks with familiar terms such as 'business cycle risk', 'interest rate risk' or 'inflation risk'. In contrast, if one predetermines the factors, then the interpretation of the exposures is intuitively clear.

What is therefore done in practice is a two-step procedure which combines the advantages of the two methods. In the first step, factor analysis is used to measure exposures to (unnamed) statistical factors, then as many portfolios as there are factors are formed. Each portfolio has exposure to just one factor. Finally, a regression of the return on each of these factor portfolios is run using as explanatory variables the observable economic factors that one thinks are relevant. These regression coefficients can then be used to describe the statistical factors as combinations of observable economic factors; that is, the exposure to a statistical factor can be expressed as a combination of exposures to observable economic factors, thus providing the link between statistical factors and observable economic factors.

SUMMARY

A great deal of research has shown that risk is the most important determinant of return. Portfolio theories such as the capital asset pricing model and arbitrage pricing theory try to explain how risk and return are related by carefully defining what risk is.

APT explains the risk–return trade-off by focusing on the exposure of asset returns to multiple sources of systematic risk. Exposure to risk is rewarded by a risk premium. APT derives how exposures and risk premiums must be related in order for returns in the market to be consistent.

APT has been adapted to be used as a technique for portfolio optimization. One application for this technique is to construct portfolios which will outperform a given benchmark by improving its efficiency. The APT technique produces what are known as 'core plus' or 'tracker plus' portfolios, that is portfolios which closely track the index but offer an additional return.

6 THE USE OF QUANTITATIVE TECHNIQUES TO BEAT THE INDEX

Jennie R. Paterson

Managing Director/Director of Marketing, Barr Rosenberg European Management, London

Ever since the investment management industry was 'created' in the post-war years, everyone has been searching for a winning formula: something that will generate better returns, not just for one or two years, but consistently. Before George Ross–Goobey encouraged everyone into equities in the late 1950s and early 1960s, performance considerations were not regarded as very important. Once they began to be seen as important, a whole new environment was created, one that has supported not only many careers, but also the financial infrastructure of industry. As one would expect, the pension funds that provided this liquidity became concerned about the effectiveness of their investments, and the performance measurement industry was born.

Reasonably enough, it soon became unacceptable to claim to have performed better than 50% of the managers while, at the same time, underperforming the index of the particular asset class. Plan sponsors rapidly realized that the combination of modern computing power and electronic databases meant that it was possible to produce a portfolio that generated index returns on a consistent basis, and as indexation became a commodity product, for much lower fees. While we have seen the proportion of assets managed on a passive basis climb considerably in most countries, a large number of plans still seek that elusive goal of actually beating the index.

To achieve this zenith many funds still put their faith in human subjective judgement. Others, and I would suggest an increasing number, are looking to the 'quant' houses to not just match, but beat, the index. So the second generation of quant houses was born, the active quants!

Before getting too enmeshed in the detail, it is appropriate to explain the differences between a quantified approach to investment management, and a traditional approach. It would be possible to devote a whole chapter to this subject alone, but a useful working definition should suffice: *a quantitative investment firm has three key characteristics, namely an explicit quantified investment objective; a complete reliance upon quantified data as the basis for decision-making; and a computer program which serves as the basis for decision-making.*

So, having established why active quantitative houses were founded and took up the challenge of beating the index, it seems logical to examine both how they went about it and what they have done and achieved.

A good starting-point is to consider the relevance of quantitative techniques to active management, and what such techniques have to offer over the traditional approach. Conventional wisdom relates the use of quantitative techniques in investment management to the advent of **modern portfolio theory** in the 1950s. Harry Markowitz is generally attributed with laying the groundwork for this theory, in a 1952 paper. The significance of this work was that it provided a common frame of reference for investors seeking to create portfolios that optimized the risk–reward trade-off. The major contribution was to break risk down into two types: **diversifiable or residual risk**, that is the risk associated with an individual stock, and the **non-diversifiable or market risk**.

The first application of this analysis was the creation of index funds. However, it was only a short time before these insights were applied to active management. In some ways the most obvious development was to construct an index fund and then overlay a simple tilt. This development utilized the **capital asset pricing model**: essentially, having broken risk or return down into market return or stock specific return, this model further subdivided the risk–return into a series of fundamental factors such as industry effects, the effect on the market of the size of the holding, or a variety of other financial or economic factors. This 'factor' analysis enabled managers to create a portfolio, which while neutral against the benchmark in respect of most of the factors, emphasized, or was tilted towards, one or more factors.

Practioners often distinguish between two generations of factor models, those described as **simple tilt models** and those thought of as **multi-factor models**. The former essentially seeks to overlay a tilt on an index fund, having identified the factor that is currently producing the outperformance. *The weakness of this approach, which those offering multi-factor models were quick to exploit, was that no one factor generates outperformance consistently; as the stages of the market cycle come and go, so does the efficiency of any factor.*

The simple tilt approach rapidly became replaced by the multi-factor models. The challenge here was to identify a series of factors that together accounted for the returns of the specific index. Each model is of course unique not only in terms of the precise number of factors that it uses (some look at as many as 50, others as few as eight), but also the precise definition of the factors. The logic behind the approach is fairly self-evident. If, in total, the factors account for the returns of the index, then by definition, some factors would produce outperformance, others underperformance, if emphasized in a portfolio that otherwise replicated the index. The multi-factor models gained popularity on both sides of the Atlantic and, given the performance achieved by some of the acknowledged market leaders, this is not surprising.

The advantage that the multi-factor models have over their simple tilt rivals is ironically quoted by their detractors as their source of weakness. By monitoring on a consistent and continued basis the contribution of all the factors in their model, the multi-factor practitioners overcome the major negative of the simple tilt approach, namely *the charge that when the efficiency of the particular tilt began to weaken, there was no alternative strategy in place.* Clearly, such a charge cannot be levelled at the multi-factor approach. Their problem is more subtle, namely when the factor(s) that they are currently emphasizing begins to weaken, they (the professionals responsible for running the model) will be able to distinguish between a genuine weakening of the factor and a short-term statistical aberration. By definition, the fund therefore will be subject to a period of underperformance while the distinction is drawn. Furthermore, such models are dependent on human intervention to identify the replacement factor. There is of course an ongoing check on the robustness of the model as constructed, namely the requirement that all factors continue to explain the returns of the index.

A lot of the development work in the creation of the multi-factor models was, and in many cases still is, based on the **BARRA risk model**. Originally founded by the US academic Barr Rosenberg, who subsequently severed his relationship with the BARRA organization when he set up his own fund management company, the BARRA model has applications for both portfolio construction and performance attribution. Indeed it has enabled quantitative techniques to infiltrate even the most qualitative operations. Traditional active managers are, by definition, taking bets; however, *the diverse nature of most corporations makes it very difficult for these managers to be sure that they are actually taking the bets they want to.* An oft-quoted example is P & O. A manager would typically select this on the basis that he was buying a shipping and transport stock, in reality he would also be exposing the portfolio to the UK's largest house builder! Multiply this confusion over the total stockholding of a portfolio, and clearly the end-product could look very different from the original intention. So a check that enables the manager to be sure that a portfolio does correctly reflect the bets he wishes to take in order to outperform is of obvious benefit. Consequently, in the goal of outperforming the index, quant techniques have even made inroads into some of the most traditional operations.

Another area where quantitative techniques have been applied successfully to beat an index is at completely the other end of the spectrum, when it comes to taking bets. As we have seen, having successfully established BARRA as an international consultancy, Barr Rosenberg set himself the ultimate challenge in setting up his own fund management company. The Rosenberg approach uses a factor model purely to control risk, not to add value. Instead it uses quantitative techniques, in the form of a proprietary valuation model and quadratic optimizer, to analyse publicly available fundamental data and identify a portfolio of undervalued stocks that closely replicates the benchmark, in respect of a whole series of risk factors. In other words, an expert system is used to identify modest misvaluations by the market, then create broadly diversified portfolios that have very tightly controlled exposure to diversifiable risk. Originally, in 1985, this approach was applied to the US market, then through a joint venture with the Nomura Group the model was successfully adapted to the Japanese market in 1989. As I write, the finishing touches are being put to the European model, which will facilitate a truly global approach.

What many plan sponsors find reassuring about this approach over, say, a factor model is that it actually seeks to replicate the thought processes of a traditional analyst or fund manager, utilizing modern technology to do it much more rapidly and efficiently than the human mind can. Likewise, because there are essentially no bets involved, human judgement plays no part beyond the original design phase.

So is the market share of the active quant houses likely to increase? The answer has to be 'yes'. When all is said and done, when consistently good performance is the aim, quants – active or not – have a real advantage over traditional managers. Put at its simplest, their performance is much less vulnerable to the vagaries of human judgement, or indeed the retention of key staff. As funds become more mature and focus more on their liabilities as well as their assets, there is a tendency to set quantified benchmarks, with both an outperformance objective and a downside risk. Not only are the quants better placed to provide such products, they can do so with greater precision and therefore greater conviction. Logically, replacing clerical power with computing power has considerable attractions. Likewise, taking the emotion out of stock selection is extremely beneficial. Indeed it is interesting to note that as the large mainland European funds increase their exposure to equities, they are tending to go straight to the active quant approach, as being the most logical methology, and bypassing both the traditional stockpickers and the indexers. The trend is obviously set to continue and funds will increasingly turn to quantitative houses to beat the index.

7 NORMAL PORTFOLIOS AND MANAGER STYLES: THE MONEY MANAGER'S PERSPECTIVE

Edward Baker

Director of Marketing, BARRA, Berkeley, California, USA

A **normal portfolio** is a customized index, or benchmark, used to represent an investment manager's style. It should be viewed as an index of his or her style that could be purchased passively. In other words, its pattern of returns should be reproducible through a process of passive replication, optimizations or other sampling methodology.

In the USA investment styles are often classified into distinct groupings. Among the descriptions of style groups used by pension consultants in the USA are: value, yield-oriented, cyclical, contrarian, growth, quality growth, momentum, large cap, small cap, medium cap, core, tactical allocator, thematic, sector specific and concentrator. These style classification schemes vary from consultant to consultant, but they all have a value group, a growth group and make some differentiation across the size dimension. Value and growth are thus seen to be well-defined and distinct styles.

A more careful analysis, however, shows that these styles are not really so easily defined, nor so clearly differentiated. First, there are different ways of measuring these style concepts. Value can be measured in terms of high earnings to price, book to price, yield, and so on. Growth can be measured in terms of low payout, high growth in earnings, low earnings to price, and so on. Size, on the other hand, is a much less ambiguous dimension of style; it is usually measured by market capitalization. But even this fails occasionally; some companies with considerable assets have very little float available for investors.

Secondly, managers for whom these styles seem appropriate differ along other style dimensions. Growth managers differ according to momentum, for example, some growth managers tend to buy and hold stocks with strong price momentum, while others do not. Similarly, some managers will avoid leveraged stocks, while others tend towards them. Some will like steady growth and others variability in growth, etc.

Several style indices are available in the USA to proxy for manager styles. These are primarily of three kinds: value, growth and size. Managers often use these indices as style representations or normal portfolios. The ones I will discuss here are the Russell 1000, Russell Price Driven, Russell Earnings Growth, Russell 2000, BARRA Big, BARRA Big Growth, BARRA Big Value, BARRA Small, BARRA Small Growth and BARRA Small Value. Though these indices are designed to represent similar styles, they are defined quite differently and can have very different performance characteristics.

The Russell 1000 is the largest 1000 stocks in the USA, and the Russell 2000 is the next largest 2000. The Russell 1000 is broken into the Russell Price Driven (value) and the Russell Earnings Growth (growth) based on the book to price ratios of the stocks. The book to price cutoff is chosen such that each sub-index contains half of the total market capitalization. The Russell 2000 is not further divided into growth and value sub-indices.

The BARRA indices, on the other hand, are designed explicitly to account for institutional interest. They only include stocks followed by an analyst, as tracked by the IBES[1] database.

The BARRA Big Index consists of all stocks above a level of capitalization indexed to the S&P500 that are followed by at least eight analysts. It contains approx. 1000 stocks. It is divided into the BARRA Big Growth and the BARRA Big Value indices based on the median predicted five-year earnings growth rate for each company as tracked by IBES.[2] The cutoff is selected to allocate roughly half of the total capitalization to both the growth and value sub-indexes. The BARRA Small Index contains companies too small to be in the BARRA Big Index, but that are followed by at least one analyst, which have a capitalization above $10 million[3] and are priced above $5 per share. The Small Index is divided into the BARRA Small Growth and BARRA Small Value, using the same criteria as the BARRA Big Index.

Table 7.1 contrasts these indices' returns: note that the returns for indices designed to capture the performance of the same style can be quite different. For example, in 1991, a growth year, the BARRA Big Growth index was up 44.78%, while the Russell Earnings Growth index was only up 41.16%. However, they both seem to capture some element of the growth stock effect as they both significantly outperformed the S&P500's return of 30.55%, although the BARRA index captured more of this effect. Clearly these supposed style indices are capturing different

---

1. IBES is the Institutional Broker's Estimation System database. It is a database of earnings forecasts made by sell-side analysts in the USA. Over 80 brokerage firms offer their estimates and the database includes about 3000 securities.
2. If the predicted first-year earnings growth is not available, we use the historical five-year growth rate. If this is also unavailable, we use the book–price ratio.
3. The minimum capitalization level was $10 million as of 1 January 1991 and is indexed to the level of the S&P500.

Table 7.1 Annual returns

	From 8207 1982	1983	1984	1985	1986	1987	1988	1989	1990	1991
Big	14.636	21.286	5.672	32.072	17.123	3.221	17.066	30.190	-4.399	33.358
S&P500	14.721	22.174	6.083	31.443	18.075	5.152	16.479	31.314	-3.167	30.554
FR1000	15.117	22.130	4.750	32.267	17.871	2.941	17.231	30.418	-4.160	33.028
Big Growth	15.928	16.671	0.107	31.464	11.755	3.461	15.446	30.752	-1.161	44.779
FR Earnings Growth	16.634	15.983	-0.952	32.854	15.363	5.305	11.267	35.923	-0.260	41.163
Big Value	13.196	26.261	11.610	32.567	22.252	3.183	18.598	29.645	-7.666	22.411
FR Price Driven	13.629	28.285	10.098	31.514	19.980	0.499	23.160	25.178	-8.082	24.605
Small	17.004	30.070	-0.141	32.499	11.170	-8.198	21.062	18.035	-20.047	43.877
FR2000	19.777	29.131	-7.307	31.052	5.682	-8.769	24.894	16.243	-19.508	46.052
Small Growth	18.654	28.878	-4.525	29.245	9.029	-7.667	20.733	20.666	-18.386	50.352
Small Value	15.302	30.808	4.329	35.668	13.251	-8.743	21.415	15.393	-21.848	37.443

elements of their respective styles and this brings into question their role as representations of manager styles.

Another problem with using these indices to represent manager styles is that they are all market capitalization weighted. In contrast, most managers tend to equal-dollar weight their portfolios. As a result, managers tend to hold a greater proportion of their portfolios in smaller stocks, relative to the index, and thus appear to have a bias towards smallness.

At BARRA, we further characterize manager styles using a linear multi-factor risk model. We have developed these models for many different equity markets, including those in the USA, UK, Canada, France, Germany, Australia, Switzerland and Japan. Each model consists of a number of indices of risk, or style characteristics, and industry groups. Table 7.2 shows the components of each model in detail.

We have consistently observed the importance of value, growth and size, even though these characteristics are represented differently in different markets. This should come as no surprise, as value and growth are the primary determinants of stock price in any fundamental valuation approach. The simple **constant growth dividend discount model**, for example, expresses a stock's expected return in terms of its dividend yield (value), plus its growth rate (growth). Since virtually every other fundamental valuation model is a modification of this simple case, the value and growth dichotomy will obtain in every one.

A multi-factor risk model characterizing manager styles allows style to be both unique and multidimensional. For example, the BARRA US Equity Model has a momentum characteristic called Success. While all growth managers will have a positive exposure to the Growth factor, the momentum managers will also have a positive exposure to Success. Those who are not momentum managers will not.

Although we use the dimensions of our multi-factor model to characterize a manager's style, we actually build a portfolio to serve as the manager's normal. We evaluate the manager's characteristics historically to determine, along with the manager, the key elements of his or her style. We then use a screening methodology to cull out a universe of assets appropriate for the manager's style. We weight this universe in a manner consistent with the manager's size, or capitalization policy, to give us a normal portfolio that uniquely proxies for the manager's style characteristics.

We have performed this exercise for well over 100 managers in the USA and have found, surprisingly, that managers have a strong tendency towards a fixed set (subset) of style characteristics. Less surprisingly, we find that growth, value and size can be used as generic categories to characterize more broadly manager styles. But we have also found that yield is an additional, independent dimension and that there is an additional group of 'core' managers who tend to keep their characteristics in line with the market – i.e. they show the same style structure as the broad market.

It is worth mentioning that some managers are capable of operating within a variety of style dimensions. These are typically quantitative managers who use a valuation approach with both growth and value elements. They can then set the parameters of their model to reflect either a growth or value bias. Often they use

Table 7.2 Factor characteristics chart

US	US Small Cap	UK	Canada	Australia	Germany	Japan	GEM (Global Equity Model)
Variability in Markets (VIM)[1]	Volatility	VIM	VIM	VIM	VIM	Systematic variability Specific variability	VIM
Success	Momentum	Success	Momentum	Success	Success	Success Relative price momentum	Success
Size	Size	Size	Size	Size	Size	Size	Size
Trading activity	Liquidity	Trading activity	Liquidity	Trading activity		Trading activity	
Growth	Growth	Growth	Growth	Growth		Growth	
Earnings–price	Operating value	Value–price	Profitability	Value	Value	Value–price	
Book–price	Fundamental value		Value			Sales–price	

Earnings variability	Financial stability	Earnings variability			Extraordinary earnings		
Financial leverage		Financial leverage	Financial leverage		Financial leverage	Financial leverage	
Foreign income		Foreign exposure	US sensitivity		Foreign income	Export revenue	
Labour intensity		Labour intensity			Labour intensity		
Yield	Interest rate sensitivity	Yield	Yield	Interest rate sensitivity	Yield	Yield	Yield
LOCAP[2]	LARGECAP[3] low price	Non-FTA[4]	Non-TSE300	Non-ALLORDS[5]	Non-estimation universe		
+55 Industry groups	+44 Industry groups	+34 Industry groups	+46 Industry groups	+23 Industry groups	+17 Industry groups	+30 Industry groups	+36 Industry groups
							+24 Country factors

Notes:
1. 'Variability in Markets' is a proprietary term used to denote the volatility of an asset within a particular market.
2. LOCAP comprises US corporations which are not within the top 1400 largest US corporations.
3. LARGECAP comprises the 1400 largest US corporations.
4. FTA is the Financial Times All Share (Actuaries) Index.
5. ALLORDS is the Australian All Ordinaries Index.

optimization techniques to select their investment proportions. This allows them to pick their asset weights in the context of various style benchmarks.

Value, growth and size characteristics predominate for most managers. Still, there is considerable heterogeneity within these groups. This heterogeneity is especially pronounced in the small cap area; small cap value and growth managers are much less alike than large cap value and growth managers. Perhaps there is less agreement as to what value and growth are among small capitalization stocks.

ARE NORMAL PORTFOLIOS USEFUL?

A manager should find that a normal portfolio which clearly expresses his style is very useful when communicating with his or her clients. Normals are an explicit, succinct and convenient way to establish investment objectives with a client.

We often see the client take responsibility for developing the manager's normal. This is clearly not in the manager's best interest; only the manager can accurately define his own style. This is especially important where the normal is being used to determine performance fees.

For example, a manager who tends to equal-weight his portfolio should not want to be measured and compensated relative to a capitalization-weighted benchmark, as the choice of benchmark weighting can significantly affect investment performance. In 1990, for example, the equal-weighted S&P500 was down 12.5%, while the capitalization-weighted version was only down 3.2%. An equal-weighted manager being compensated on the basis of a one-year fulcrum fee relative to the capitalization-weighted S&P500 would surely have had a sad Christmas based on these results. Note that, in this case, the performance differential was due only to weighting the stocks differently.

The manager should also control the development of the normal to insure that a long-term bet is not reflected in the normal as a style bias. The manager might very well have a bet on growth, value or size that lasts several years. In the USA investors earned an extraordinary return from a value bias for most of the decade of the 1980s. The astute manager who held such an active bet over this time-period would only be credited for it if it were *not* reflected in the normal. Otherwise the performance of the normal would be credited for it.

Despite its usefulness, there is a danger in taking the normal too seriously. While the normal reflects the manager's area of specialization, it should ordinarily not influence his investment decisions. The manager should behave the same regardless of the benchmark used to evaluate his performance.

The manager may have a problem if performance varies due to the benchmark used. Clients and their consultants do not like to see disparity in investment results across a manager's accounts. An obvious exception is the manager who can operate with a variety of normals. In this case, the client might actually come to the manager with a normal in hand and the manager will then adapt his process to reflect this normal.

Typically, however, the manager's style is determined by fundamental elements of his approach to investing which are, in a sense, immutable. A manager's investment philosophy is the expression of his beliefs about investment opportunity, while the investment process is the set of methods used to implement the philosophy. Investment processes are adaptable – philosophies generally are not.

A value manager will fundamentally feel that the best investment opportunities are found in companies where some accounting or economic feature of the firm is underpriced. A growth manager will look for opportunities where growth rates are not being properly evaluated and priced. Investment process influences style, but philosophy is the foundation upon which it rests. A manager's normal is a direct outgrowth of his investment philosophy. It should be viewed as a reflection of his philosophy and not as an influence on it. The manager may adapt his process due to the normal, but this should be done with great care.

8 USING KEY RATE DURATIONS TO REPLICATE A TREASURY INDEX*

William F. McCoy

Global Advanced Technology Corporation, New York, USA

RESEARCH OVERVIEW

In structuring a fixed-income portfolio relative to a benchmark, one looks for the most accurate method of matching that portfolio's behaviour. The purpose of Bill's research was to compare the accuracy of **key rate durations** to effective duration in replicating an index portfolio. He looked at the behaviour of the portfolio replicated with effective duration and with two alternative key rate duration measures.

For the basis of his research, Bill used GAT's Treasury index. He calculated effective and key rate durations for the non-parallel shifts in the monthly spot curves. Then he used the durations as input for three optimizations in order to replicate the index. The results show the tracking error to be much less for the key rate duration portfolios than for the effective duration portfolio. These results imply increased accuracy can be achieved when using key rate durations as part of a portfolio management strategy.

INTRODUCTION

Key rate durations identify a portfolio's sensitivity to non-parallel yield curve movements. Thus, should all of the key rate durations (KRDs) be matched relative to a target, the replicating portfolio should generate the same returns as the target, given small shifts in interest rates. Clearly the ability to control against non-parallel interest rate risk has a wide variety of applications. Asset/liability immunization

* The author would like to thank Bob Lally of Metropolitan Life for his valuable assistance in the preparation of this study.

could achieve greater control with such a technique. Index replication could also be enhanced.

In particular, I tested the ability of KRDs to match the Treasury index over 1990. With monthly rebalancing, there was a 62% reduction in the monthly tracking error using four key rate durations vs effective durations, and a 33% reduction in the monthly tracking error using 11 key rate durations vs four key rate durations. This chapter reports that study. The first part is a brief review of the theory of key rate durations. The second part covers the construction of the portfolios. The third part presents the results of the analysis.

KEY RATE DURATIONS[1]

Before the idea of key rate durations is developed, it might be useful to take a moment to review the idea of **effective duration**. If interest rates change instantaneously, how will the price of the security change? Effective duration is a commonly used measure of interest rate risk exposure. The computation of effective duration is easy to describe. The computer shifts the spot curve a like amount up and down. It then recomputes the price of the security after each of these shifts. Because the computer generates each of the yield shifts and has calculated the price change, effective duration is calculated as the ratio between the proportional change in the security value to a parallel shift of the spot curve.

However, the spot curve rarely moves in a parallel fashion. Investors are aware that the spot curve is capable of any number of gyrations. The price change experienced during a non-parallel spot curve shift could be radically different than that predicted by effective duration. Thus effective duration is not a complete measure of interest rate risk.

Key rate duration is a more complete measure of interest rate risk. The key rates are the interest rates of certain points on the spot curve. The **integrative bond system** (IBS) uses 11 points, from three months to 30 years. Thus key rate duration is a duration vector representing the price sensitivity of a security to each key rate change. Since effective duration is the total risk exposure to parallel moves, the key rate durations are the component parts of the effective duration when all of the key rates move in parallel.

The mechanics of computing a key rate duration are similar to those of effective duration. However, instead of shifting the entire curve in parallel, only that point on the spot curve is shifted. The first key rate shift is x basis points up to the first key rate, and then linearly declines to zero at the second key rate and zero beyond. All other key rate shifts are zero up to the $n - 1$ key rate, linearly increase to x basis points at the nth key rate, linearly decrease to zero at the $n + 1$ key rate, and are zero beyond. Similarly to effective duration, the spot curve is shifted, as defined, by a like amount up and down, the price of the security is recomputed based

1. A more complete reference is Thomas Ho, *Key Rate Durations: A Measure of Interest Rate Risks Exposure*, NYU Salomon Brothers Center Working Paper series, May 1990.

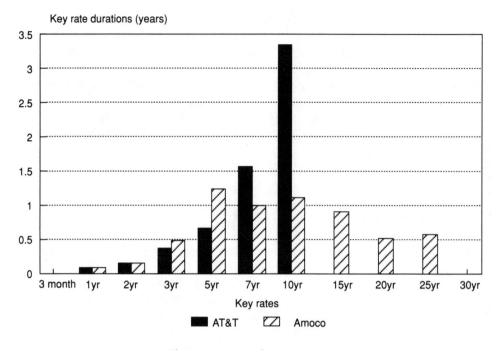

Key rate durations (years)

Fig 8.1 Key rate durations.

on these shifts, and the key rate duration is the proportional change in security value based on this particular change in the spot rate.

Figure 8.1 is a graph of the key rate durations of two bonds. Both bonds have the same effective duration. However, they have very different key rate duration profiles. The AT&T bond has much greater sensitivity to changes in the seven- to ten-year area than does the Amoco bond. However, the Amoco bond is sensitive to movements in the 15-year area, while the AT&T bond is completely insensitive. Clearly, should the seven-year rate decline relative to the 15-year rate, the AT&T bond would outperform the Amoco bond. This sort of anticipation is not available by using effective duration.

Key rate durations have several useful properties. As we have already noted, a shift of similar magnitude in each of the key rates simultaneously is the effective duration. Secondly, because only a portion of the curve is moved each time, each key rate duration is a way of identifying the price sensitivity of a security to a change in that area of the spot curve. Moreover, while specific points are targeted, key rate durations can be added to measure the sensitivity to interest rate movements along sections of the curve. Thirdly, the key rate durations of individual securities can be market value weighted to determine the key rate durations of a portfolio.

Key rate durations have many applications in portfolio management. A replicating portfolio with the same key rate durations as its target index should provide a better match than a replicating portfolio constructed with effective duration. This chapter is a particular application of key rate duration to replicate the returns of a Treasury index. Managing vs an index, particularly a Treasury index, is similar to that of managing vs a liability. Using key rate duration as the basis of the immunization should provide a better match than effective duration alone. Clearly the uses of key rate duration are not limited to asset–liability management or index replication. Any stream of cash flows over time, even with embedded options, have key rate durations. Once these key rate durations are determined, they can be matched and interest rate risk can be controlled.

There are other ways to control against non-parallel interest rate moves. One way of describing non-parallel interest rate risk is through a statistical analysis of rate moves over time. Factor analysis describes three types of moves. The first is a parallel move. The second is a 'pure' short rate move, where the full movement is at the short end of the curve, declining to zero at the long end. The third is a 'pure' intermediate move, with the full movement at the middle of the curve, and near zero at both ends. Key rate durations is an improvement in two directions. First, these moves can be described as a key rate vector; that is, given the magnitude of each key rate in the proposed shift, the change in portfolio market value is the sum of the changes implied by each key rate. Thus the information on portfolio interest rate sensitivity provided by factor analysis is a subset of the information provided by key rate durations. Secondly, the factor analysis approach provides a model but no underlying intuition or financial insight. The model proposes an intermediate rate shift, but neglects to discuss its origin or method of propagation.

METHODOLOGY

GAT's Treasury index was used as the basis for the studies. In general, there are over 200 Treasury issues in the index. These are all of the publicly traded coupon issues with greater than a year to maturity. On the last business day of every month, from December 1989 to November 1990, the replicating portfolios were created. Over the test period, the spot curve exhibited non-parallel movements. During this period, the two-year rate moved from 7.90% to 9.10% and back to 7.30%, while the 30-year moved from 7.60% to 8.90% and back to 8.00%. Spot rate volatility ranged from 6% to 13%.

On the last business day of every month the characteristics of the index were determined using GAT's Integrative Bond System. These characteristics could be divided into two groups of constraints. The first group was based on the effective and key rate durations. Four and 11 key rate durations were used. The 11 key rate durations are based on the 3-month and 1-, 2-, 3-, 5-, 7-, 10-, 15-, 20-, 25- and 30-year spot curve rates. The four key rates are based on the 3-month to 2-year, 3-year to 7-year, 10 to 20-year and 25 to 30-year spot curve rates. The second group was constrained on the following characteristics: convexity, average price, average cheap/rich, yield to worst and percentage of callable securities. All characteristics are based on observed prices.

Three separate optimizations were run. For each optimization, the same set of non-interest rate sensitive characteristics were matched. The interest rate sensitive characteristics were varied as follows. The first replication was based on matching effective duration. The second replication was based on matching the four key rate durations. As we have already mentioned, the four key rate durations are sums of

Table 8.1 Treasury replicating portfolio performance

	Treasury index		Eff duration only		KRD1-4		KRD1-11	
	1 month	3 month	1 month	3 month	1 month	3 month	1 month	3 month
Dec. 89	-1.42	-1.31	-1.12	-1.24	-1.40	-1.14	-1.39	-1.24
Jan. 90	0.07	-0.82	0.15	-0.59	0.14	-0.68	0.10	-0.71
Feb. 90	0.04	1.85	0.23	1.95	0.10	1.86	0.04	1.83
Mar. 90	-0.93	3.41	-0.89	3.28	-0.93	3.30	-0.95	3.34
Apr. 90	2.76	5.72	2.77	5.62	2.73	5.69	2.78	5.69
May 90	1.58	1.35	1.61	1.34	1.61	1.39	1.58	1.37
Jun. 90	1.28	0.75	1.20	0.53	1.24	0.62	1.27	0.74
Jul. 90	-1.49	1.12	-1.41	1.08	-1.45	1.03	-1.45	1.05
Aug. 90	0.98	4.90	0.95	4.82	0.95	4.86	1.01	4.89
Sept. 90	1.65	5.56	1.68	5.41	1.63	5.42	1.64	5.46
Oct. 90	2.20	4.93	2.23	4.83	2.23	4.84	2.20	4.88
Nov. 90	1.61	3.23	1.58	3.28	1.57	3.20	1.59	3.24
Dec. 90	1.04	2.05	1.10	2.28	1.04	2.12	1.05	2.09
Cum. Ret	9.67		10.45		9.77		9.78	
Average absolute error			0.08	0.12	0.03	0.08	0.02	0.05
Worst absolute error			0.30	0.23	0.07	0.17	0.04	0.11

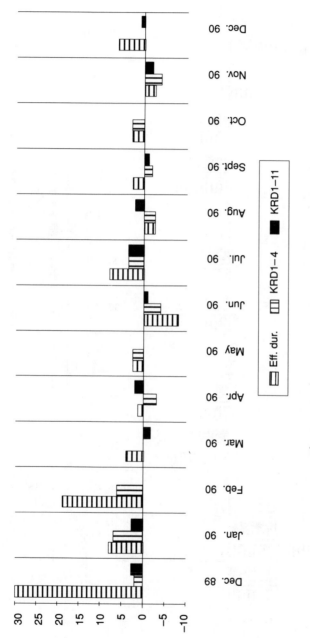

Fig. 8.2 Tracking error vs Treasury index one-month horizon.

Legend: Eff. dur.   KRD1–4   KRD1–11

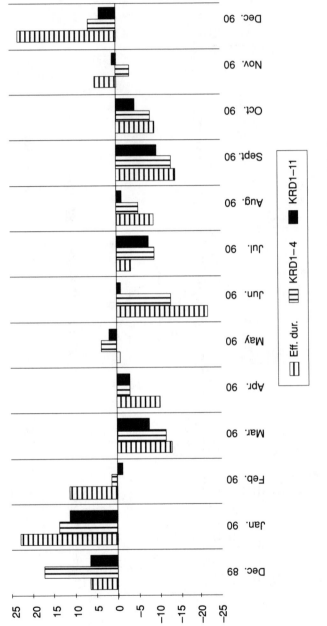

Fig. 8.3 Tracking error vs Treasury index three-month horizon.

the 11 key rate durations. The third replication was based on matching the 11 key rate durations. The optimization then picked a set of bonds from the Treasury index that matched the characteristics of each replication. Between 5 and 20 bonds were used to replicate the index.

The crucial point to note is that the three optimizations were constructed by the same process. The only varying element in each of the portfolios is the set of duration constraints. Thus the difference in the returns should be due only to the interest rate sensitivity.

Each portfolio was held for one and three months and compared to the returns of a Treasury index over a similar time-period. Because the composition of the Treasury index changes every month and does not hold cash, the tracking error, or deviation from the index returns, of the three-month replicating portfolios should be worse than that of the one-month replicating portfolios. No transaction costs were assumed.

RESULTS

Table 8.1 contains the Treasury and replicating portfolio returns for the one- and three-month horizons. The summary statistics at the bottom demonstrate the effectiveness of key rate duration in controlling interest rate risk. In addition to cumulative return, average absolute tracking error and single worst error are included. Average absolute error is an important statistic in portfolio replication because it is as bad to be over as it is under the target. Graphs of the tracking error over time are shown in Figs 8.2. and 8.3.

The cumulative return for the Treasury index over the period was 9.67%. For the effective duration portfolio, the tracking error was 78 basis points. The key rate duration portfolios had tracking errors of 10 and 11 basis points.

For the one-month horizon, the average absolute error is eight basis points for the effective duration portfolio, three basis points for the four key rate duration portfolio and two basis points for the 11 key rate duration portfolio. When examining the worst error, the effective duration was off by 30 basis points in a single month. The four key rate duration portfolio was substantially less, at seven basis points in a single month. The 11 key rate duration portfolio was off by only four basis points in its worst month. The results are more dramatic for the three-month horizon.

Although this was not an exhaustive study of the topic, we are confident that it is representative of the power of key rate durations. Had a longer test period been used, we are certain that key rate duration would continue to demonstrate its effectiveness as a robust measure of interest rate sensitivity.

9 REGULATION OF THE INVESTMENT MANAGEMENT INDUSTRY: FUTURE DIRECTIONS

George Nissen

Former Chairman Investment Management Regulatory Organization (IMRO), London

It may seem strange after the various upsets of the past two years for anyone to say that the first need of financial regulation is 'leave it alone', but it remains a fact that nothing that has happened so far shows that the basic structure of financial services regulation in the UK – which is centred upon this premise – is fundamentally wrong. There is, as always, room for improvement and reform – in some areas, substantial reform – but that is largely concerned with reform of rules and practices, not of the basic regulatory infrastructure. In regulatory terms, the structure is still relatively young, and a great deal of time has been spent in writing and rewriting rulebooks and working out supervisory practices to enforce them. It may be difficult for politicians, the press and the general public to accept, but it is a fact of life that getting a regulatory structure up and running from scratch is a very long job, and after six years any such structure is still adolescent. The UK regulatory system is providing an adequate level of investor protection but now needs time to settle down, mature and strengthen.

Having recently implemented the SIB's New Settlement and IMRO's revised Rulebook, the grand strategy now for investment management regulation is to make the system work, taking into account any market or commercial changes, and resultant regulatory changes, which have an impact on investors, practitioners and regulators alike.

At the time of writing, the most evident large issue is the outcome of the Clucas Report, which addresses the future structure of the UK's regulatory system for the financial services industry. It is not for an SRO to claim that the conclusions and recommendations of that report are right or wrong. IMRO, perhaps rather more than some other SROs, believes that it is the common will of the membership of an SRO which makes it function effectively in the provision of investor protection.

An unwilling member of an SRO, coerced into membership, is almost by definition an unsuitable member of that SRO. It is unlikely that investors will feel confident that their interests are best protected by an SRO which does not enjoy the willing support and commitment of its members. To this extent, any coercion of members would only weaken regulation and the benefits it brings to investors. That is why IMRO, in its own submission to Sir Kenneth Clucas, laid emphasis on the notion of 'functional best fit' to identify the scope of proper membership of an SRO. IMRO, as presently constituted, is a good example of just such a 'best fit'. Fund managers, whatever the status of their various clients, are fundamentally performing a similar set of functions, and it would be difficult to find a practising fund manager who agreed with the Clucas Report proposition that fund management for a private client was in any way essentially different from fund management for an institutional client: fund management is fund management. Those engaging in fund management activity deploy the same range of skills and expertise on their clients' behalf, whatever the nature of the client. To restructure regulation on the basis of client type is to create artificial divisions, both in the regulatory system and the business of members.

However, that is certainly not to say that IMRO would in any way seek to retain in membership any fund manager – or indeed any other kind of investment business – which wished to belong to another competent SRO. We exist by the wish of our members, and their continuing commitment to our regulatory regime and culture. Our belief that practitioners should not be coerced into joining an SRO is matched by our belief that they should not be coerced into staying if their regulatory needs can best be met elsewhere, either by the SIB or by another SRO. This simple principle will continue to govern our contribution to the implementation of the Clucas Report, or any agreed modification of it. In discussing such implementation, we are bound to take note of the fact that the proposed new SRO is recommended to have the ability to offer 'one-stop regulation' to a variety of investment businesses, while IMRO does not, at present, have such wide scope. We certainly do not wish to upset discussions on the creation of the new SRO, whose existence we shall welcome, but it is unlikely our existing members would welcome a preferential distinction which might be prejudicial to their interests. For many members, one-stop regulation by IMRO would be both desirable and effective – in terms of investor protection, cost and resource effectiveness and best fit for their business. They should not be denied this opportunity.

Linked with the question of the Clucas Report, and indeed largely responsible for its initiation, is the question of investor compensation. The inability of the members of FIMBRA to meet their obligations under the Investor Compensation Scheme has been the root cause of the organizational instability among SROs for a considerable time. The merger of FIMBRA and LAUTRO seems highly desirable in order to inject the financial stability of the LAUTRO membership into a weak area of the regulatory system in which they have a direct interest. Sir Kenneth Clucas was asked, in preparing his report, to pay particular regard to the following:

- the continued delivery of high standards of investor protection;
- the continued availability to consumers of a wide choice of financial advice;

- the importance of self-regulation, that is, of those who are regulated having sufficient responsibility for, and commitment to, the development and implementation of regulation;
- the importance of cost-effective regulation.

IMRO wholeheartedly supports the formation of the new SRO and will do all it can to assist, particularly in key areas (e.g. rule harmonization) which are of major concern to all practitioners and regulators. There are inevitably consequences for the balance of influence within the new SRO, but we believe that they are soluble in a practical way without disturbing the essential stability and effectiveness of the rest of the self-regulatory system.

Any discussion of investment management is bound to raise the issue of the management of the assets of occupational pension funds. IMRO can obviously make no claim to have got this area of supervision right. We have substantial lessons to learn, and we are studying them with care. But what went wrong in the Maxwell affair was far from being just a simple matter of SRO supervision or the ability of the FSA to deal with occupational pension schemes. As we pointed out to the Select Committee (and as we have previously pointed out to the government), the whole system is a muddle, not just that small corner of it which is covered by the Financial Services Act. In IMRO's view, everyone concerned with the Maxwell collapse – actuaries, trustees, financial institutions, regulators and the government – has cause to review their role and responsibilities and the way in which they fulfilled, or failed to fulfil, their responsibilities to those affected. A particularly worrying aspect of the affair is that those who were closest to it, namely people in the Maxwell companies, particularly at a senior level, and trustees and auditors, never thought to utter a word of warning to the regulator.

The strength of a chain is its weakest link; in so far as the investment of pension fund assets is governed by the Financial Services Act, there is a sizeable chain of allegedly knowledgeable and responsible people, and yet, conspicuously, the chain broke. One must hope that future changes to the OPS system include clarifying the roles and responsibilities of those involved, as well as producing a system which can be clearly understood by the individuals concerned. One alarming feature of this affair was the belief by some of the individuals who were trustees of the funds that the FSA somehow prevented or precluded them from carrying out their duties. The consequences of this misconception, coupled with the omissions and mistakes of others, will be with us for some time to come.

IMRO's submission to the Select Committee contained a section of recommendations for future action on the governance of pension funds, including the following:

- a compulsory separation of function between trustees and investment managers;
- the requirement for a strong custodianship function in relation to pension funds, with the custodian being independent of manager and trustee alike;
- the requirements for audit, and audit report to some appropriate external authority, to be reviewed;
- improving the lot of beneficiaries by automatically providing all beneficiaries

with information concerning the scheme, including trustees, auditors and actuarial reports;

- applying prudential limits to the contents of pension scheme portfolios which would prevent an imbalance in assets held and requiring regular reports on the composition of portfolios;
- strengthening the trustee function by ensuring that trustees were independent of the employer company, understood their role and had the necessary knowledge, training and expertise to perform their duties in a suitable manner.

We were glad to see that a number of our recommendations have been accepted and adopted by the Select Committee.

Of smaller interest to IMRO particularly, but obviously of large interest to financial services in general, are the SIB's proposals for retail regulation. So far, these are in the realm of consultation, and it appears that only a relatively small part of IMRO's membership is likely to be directly affected. For example, Investment Trust Savings Schemes seem likely to be subject to the polarization regime for the first time, and that will be a matter of considerable concern in the organization of their retail structure. It is of course too early to predict the outcome of the SIB's large-scale consultative process.

Above and behind all these considerations lies the increasing influence of European developments. All regulatory policy increasingly needs to take account of the fact that legislative authority is inexorably moving towards Brussels. The imminent implementation of the Second Banking Directive, and the expectation of a Capital Adequacy Directive and, at some time, of an Investment Services Directive mean that the entire regulatory system must look increasingly towards European contacts, European exchanges of information and common European standards of rule-making, supervision and enforcement. The City of London is exceptionally well placed, particularly in its investment management capacity, to take advantage of the new freedoms that are becoming offered. It is vital for the operators of the UK regulatory structure to ensure that unnecessary bureaucratic obstacles are not placed in the way of London's ability to take advantage of these new freedoms which offer the prospect of great benefit both to the economy at large and to investors in that economy.

There are too many Jonahs about; there are also too many amateurs with screwdrivers, dashing about poking into the machinery. Despite them, and despite black spots, self-regulation is alive, well and effective for both investors and practitioners.

10 TAURUS AND BEYOND

Tony Preece

Head of TAURUS Business Development, London Stock Exchange, London

The year 1993 marks the beginning of the end of the familiar share certificate. It will make its exit along with the stock transfer form. These two pieces of paper, which have been vital documentation in the share ownership process for over a century, will step aside to make way for the computerized statement.

This statement is an integral feature of the London Stock Exchange's TAURUS system, designed to introduce the electronic recording and transfer of shares. TAURUS has required a significant change to UK company law, and will have implications for all those who are in any way involved with handling or owning UK securities. Once operational, a more efficient and less risk-prone settlement process for both professional and private investors will become a reality.

The concept of a paperless settlement system is nothing new. The disadvantages of copious amounts of paper were accentuated during a period of heavy trading in 1987. Two years later, the Group of Thirty set out recommendations for improving settlement worldwide. With the ultimate aim of retaining its already acknowledged position as the dominant financial market in Europe, London is now striving to surpass settlement developments in other markets, some of which already have a form of paperless settlement.

An outline design was agreed in January 1990, and TAURUS is now on target to become operational in 1993. Over two years major milestones have been reached, and a number of hurdles have had to be cleared. But no more than could reasonably be expected from a project of such magnitude – arguably one of the largest technological developments currently taking place in Europe. To put this into context, the Stock Exchange will be the central TAURUS operator but there will eventually be some 300 interlinked systems. Only one-third of the total development is directly under the Stock Exchange's control. Central to the design of TAURUS was the need to reflect the existing market structure. It includes the registration of investors' shares – an important factor for companies – and will also allow institutions both to control their investment portfolios and their settlement.

A major milestone was reached in February 1992 when the House of Lords approved regulations to permit dematerialized settlement. This legislation gives UK quoted companies the reassurance they need to pass resolutions to move their securities on to the TAURUS system. Those companies which pass resolutions at AGMs in 1992 will be in a position to join TAURUS in 1993. In order to do so, they will need to seek a 75% majority vote. All shareholders in companies proposing to vote will receive notification and full details well in advance. Information packs have been sent to the chairmen and company secretaries of all UK quoted companies advising them of the necessary procedures for transferring their stock into TAURUS, notices have appeared in the national press and the Stock Exchange is currently liaising closely with those companies who have expressed their intention to pass a vote in the near future.

If any one message needs to be understood by everyone it must surely be that there is not going to be an overnight revolution. The intention is for some half-dozen companies to join the system as quickly as possible, but only when they and their registrars are ready. The process will be managed such that companies join up gradually once a full system dress rehearsal has been staged. Ideally the FTSE 100 stocks will join during the first year and the remainder will be in by end-1994. There will obviously be a period when investors will hold certificates for some securities and statements for the remainder. During that time market participants and registrars will also be required to handle stock in two forms. This transitional state will, hopefully, be shortlived as the benefits of moving on to TAURUS quickly become evident.

Inevitably, a few companies will be reluctant to convert their securities to TAURUS. The Stock Exchange will not be able to insist that they convert, but pressure from institutional shareholders unhappy with the inconvenience of paper transfers, and from registrars unhappy with the cost of running two systems, is likely to influence their decision. Furthermore, it is unlikely that the Stock Exchange will be willing to continue operating the TALISMAN system, once TAURUS is firmly established.

The day when the first companies move into TAURUS will be significant, in that it will be the first visible indication to many people that things are moving. It is important, however, that it is only seen as the first of a series of initiatives being taken to update settlement in the UK.

Following Taurus and in line with the Group of Thirty recommendations, delivery vs payment and a rolling settlement period will be introduced to replace the current two-weekly account settlement period. The objective is to reduce risk by minimizing the delay between trade and settlement. Rolling settlement will be introduced on a ten-day basis as soon as the majority of the trading volume is being settled electronically. Once 90% of the volume is being settled through TAURUS, some six months after the introduction of ten-day rolling settlement, the settlement period will be reduced to three days. It is expected that this stage will be reached by the end of 1994.

Like all changes to established practices, the impact of rolling settlement will vary. Institutions will appreciate reduced risk and the ability to employ investment practices which mirror those in other markets. On the other hand, if smaller private client brokers need to operate a short settlement cycle, they are faced with the difficulty of having good funds available from purchasing clients on settlement day. Inevitably, many clients pay by cheque, making a short cycle difficult to achieve. Already many retail brokers are planning either to maintain cash deposit accounts for their clients or to make arrangements with a local bank or building society. Such measures will effectively minimize the impact on cash flow resulting from rolling settlement. The Stock Exchange's focus is on flexibility, allowing both the three-day and ten-day settlement periods to co-exist for as long as they are both needed.

At the time of introducing rolling settlement, it is intended to introduce delivery vs payment (DVP) – a key element in the settlement infrastructure. The current payment facilities available to the securities industry in the UK are impressive by global standards since they allow stock and money to move on the same day with the money transfer in 'same-day' cleared funds. TAURUS will progress this further by guaranteeing buyers entitlement to stock and those sellers linked to the central system, good money on the day.

The essence of the Stock Exchange's DVP scheme will be a bank's guarantee of its customer's settlement risk. Although the details are still being confirmed, the banks have already agreed in principle.

While work on settlement is forging ahead, considerable progress is being made on related services such as rapid trade agreement. This will enable all comparisons of trades between participants to be achieved on the day of the trade. Such a service will allow institutions and their agents to use existing links with the Stock Exchange for agreeing their trade with the UK market on a same-day basis. In early 1992, a representative institutional user group selected SEQUAL as one of the systems to be developed as an industry standard. While effectively handling trade confirmation for national trades, SEQUAL will also establish openings for the matching of cross-border business. Continuing on the international front, the UK is one of the first countries to have adopted ISIN codes intended to create universally standardized identification numbers for securities. This initiative will encourage a cost-effective system for the immediate identification of international securities and will improve worldwide access to information.

The plans for settlement over the next two years are clear. What has sometimes been dismissed as a straightforward system enhancement is in fact a total infrastructure change.

What will begin with the demise of the share certificate must be recognized as a vital investment in the future of London as a financial centre. The early introduction of TAURUS is essential if London is to establish Europe's most efficient and secure settlement system. The second-phase developments demonstrate commitment to the Group of Thirty recommendations and will go a long way towards a cost-effective system for global settlement. In a fast-changing world it is unlikely that London will ever be in a position to stand still. What is more certain is that as a financial centre it is well placed to maintain its competitive edge in Europe and meet the changing demands of major organizations throughout the 1990s and beyond.

11 HOW SCOTTISH WIDOWS MADE SCOTTISH WIDOWS BEAUTIFUL

Fiona Tunstall

Communications Co-ordinator, Scottish Widows, Edinburgh, Scotland

HISTORY

From 1815 till the present day, Scottish Widows has developed in a variety of ways. It has not only grown in size and product range, it has also gradually emerged from being a traditional life assurance company to being a high-profile investment house, with a strong reputation for astute fund management.

In the Victorian era there was less emphasis on marketing, a relatively narrow product range and little or nothing in the way of mass communications, though Scottish Widows has always played a significant role in the life and pensions market. Much of the development of life assurance may have been due to the thriving mercantile environment in nineteenth-century Scotland. From these modest but intrinsically sound beginnings, the growing impact of communications – culminating in today's mass communications – led the company to recognize the need to establish and maintain its leading position by gradually developing systems to promote and target products. Overall, making Scottish Widows beautiful has been achieved by raising public awareness, through advertising and increased press and public relations. These are the three strands that have contributed to increased company profile and public awareness, particularly over the past few years.

The growing size and diversity of the company required an explanation to the general public of the name 'Scottish Widows'. Of course this could be achieved through marketing literature, but a greater impact on public awareness through advertising was identified as a means of increased exposure for the company and its distinctive name.

Scottish Widows was founded at the time of the Napoleonic Wars in 1815. It was described as 'A general fund, for securing provision to widows, sisters and other females'. This seems to have had in mind female relations of deceased clergymen, schoolmasters, and the like, and was designed as a safety net should they be left, as was not uncommon at the time, indigent. The original prospectus promoted a plan for establishing a general fund in Scotland for the purpose of insuring capital sums on lives. It was to be called the Scottish Widows' Fund and Equitable Assurance Society. The prospectus reads:

> The beneficial effects of the establishment for making provision to Widows of the clergy of the church of Scotland have long been felt and acknowledged, and have given rise to similar institutions, which have also been attended with the most salutory consequences to particular districts, societies, and corporations. It has occurred to some Gentlemen in Edinburgh, to propose the formation of a General Society, with similar but more enlarged views, the benefit of which may be extended to all parts of the United Kingdom.
>
> The principle of the proposed Institution is, to take from contributors no more than what, according to the most approved calculations, is sufficient, by careful accumulation of the funds, to afford annuities contracted for, excluding any idea of proprietorship or advantage to particular individuals; and it will be a fundamental rule, that the whole business of the Society shall be managed by persons deriving their appointments from the free choice of the members themselves.

Modern PR techniques require that communications are succinct and easy to absorb. The verbosity of the above message would not fit well with current requirements. Another factor is that over the years the need to communicate more widely has become increasingly more important – in the words of Marshall McLuhan, 'the new electronic interdependence recreates the world in the image of a global village' – indicating the incredible rapidity at which information circulates via electronic mass communications. An enhanced company image has been developed by defining the corporate philosophy and embodied by the new logotype.

The Oliver and Boyd's *New Edinburgh Almanac* (1878) claimed that Scottish Widows' Fund Society offered 'Special Advantages': 'The society, besides offering to its members the most ample security, combines with the advantages of Life Assurance a Very Profitable Investment.' This strong message has remained with the company throughout. It is from this firm footing that the future growth of the company began to take root. In the early stages it was weighted towards life cover, but investment now takes a large role.

INVESTMENT STRENGTH

Scottish Widows has a defined mission statement, which says that it will invest clients' funds to achieve investment returns in the upper quartile compared with competitor portfolios, over a medium-term time-scale of between three and five years. In deciding in which individual shares to invest a large number of factors are taken into consideration. These include financial strength, potential sales growth and management strength of the particular company. It is important to recognize that longer-term results inevitably comprise periods of over- and underperformance, though medium-term results in the last five years have been very satisfactory. In comparison to returns from building society accounts, Scottish Widows has consistently outperformed over the medium to long term.

In the past 20 years, Scottish Widows has been transformed from a typical life assurance company with just a few funds into a major force in the investment management business, with over £15 billion of funds under management. The investment philosophy followed by Scottish Widows has been a continuing quest to obtain the best value between differing asset classes. Continuity of investment personnel and confidence in our own analytical ability have enabled us to make the right decisions when it matters most. This sometimes means taking positions against market consensus in the short term, with beneficial results in the longer term.

Despite the recession, 1991 was a good year for most investment markets. The FT Actuaries World Equity Index rose 14% in local terms, while UK equities and UK conventional gilts produced returns of around 20%. Against this, yields on property and rental income have fallen for the second year running. Funds under Scottish Widows management are heavily weighted towards equities with correspondingly low exposure to the direct property market.

Scottish Widows' premier position in the managed pension fund market-place is built on excellent long-term results. In 1991, new business was at record levels with the addition of over 200 new corporate clients. The segregated pension fund area, which we only entered in 1984, continues to make significant progress. At present, there is a total of £1400 million in pension funds under management, comprising 22 pension funds with both corporate and local authority clients.

The long-term results of our unit-linked funds remain very competitive. Thirteen out of fourteen funds have produced above-average results over five years and from their inception over 10 years ago, eight are in the upper quartile. 1991 also saw very good results from our European and UK Special Situations Unit Trusts, with both funds achieving top-quartile status within their respective sectors.

Scottish Widows' reputation in the investment industry, and the location of our Head Office in Edinburgh, has helped to attract some of the best investment managers available. This includes several foreign nationals who have brought local insight/expertise into some of the key overseas investment areas. The turnover rate of managers has remained one of the lowest in the industry.

Scottish Widows' expertise is reflected in:

- first-class investment returns;
- strong reserves relative to competitors;
- continuity of senior investment management.

BRANDING SCOTTISH WIDOWS

The unusual company name proved to be an asset, in that a strong brand position could be achieved by focusing on the actual name. In 1971, Dewe Rogerson (a London-based advertising and public relations agency) developed the name of the company into a 'living logo'. The visual representation of the society was developed creatively into an enigmatic 'Scottish Widow'. Dressed in black, her appearance provides instant recognition of the name in a way that gives a recall advantage over other competitors. Instantly recognizable, the general public are unlikely to confuse her or attribute her to any competitor.

The persona of the enigmatic lady in the Scottish Widows television advertising campaigns is one which is used with great care. She is not a 'real' woman, rather the personification of all that Scottish Widows is about. She never speaks, she is more of a living trade-mark, embodying undertones of the classic, well-informed and independent. The most recent commercial makes the claim that the company possesses top-notch investment managers who have consistently used their expertise to give investors a very competitive return on their investments.

Research showed that investment expertise was something for which Scottish Widows was particularly well known. Consumers stated that in assessing insurance companies, perceptions of such expertise played an important part in their choice of whom to use for their investments. Further, it appeared that the feelings of confidence conveyed by such acknowledged expertise spilled over into other products supplied by Scottish Widows. In addition, pre-testing with consumer groups revealed that the television advertisement was felt to be particularly relevant in today's economic conditions.

CONCLUSION

So, what of the future? As with the entire financial services industry, formidable challenges lie ahead. In an unpredictable age when success or failure is measured by how well future trends are forecast, investment expertise can help ensure that Scottish Widows will be one of the major players in the twenty-first century. In addition, we are dedicated to making ourselves user-friendly. High levels of customer service are of vital importance to our continued success. Customer service is to do with a new positive look at the people who do business with us; we have no God-given right to this business, customers have a wide choice when it comes to the provision of financial services. Scottish Widows believes that, in making itself beautiful (i.e. accessible, responsive and empathetic), it must give out positive signals. It must look after investors, cherish them and make them feel 'beautiful' too.

12 IMPROVING THE EFFECTIVENESS OF PERFORMANCE MEASUREMENT

Pat Harkin

Marketing Department, The WM Company, Edinburgh

Investment **performance measurement** has been with us now for some 30 years, and its role in the management and stewardship of invested assets is no longer questioned.

At the outset, performance measurement was regarded as something rather specialist and complex (like some variants of quantitative management today). Nowadays every trustee and plan sponsor is aware of his or her duty to understand the performance of the assets entrusted to their guardianship. Every investment management house looks to performance measurement to persuade existing clients of a job well done and new clients of a similar outcome.

Thus the question is no longer one of persuading the investment industry to accept performance measurement; that task has largely been completed. The role of the performance measurers now is to ensure that their profession adheres to the highest standards of methodology and presentation within an increasingly complex investment environment.

THE BOUNDARIES OF PERFORMANCE MEASUREMENT

The investment environment is indeed complex and constantly changing. There are many differences between practice in the USA and the UK; further practical and cultural differences exist between the Anglo-Saxon and European approaches; and the Pacific Basin is different again.

Yet there are similarities. In the investment process, wherever enacted, there are a number of agents. The chain starts with the owner of the assets or the owner's representatives – i.e. trustees or plan sponsor. The owner is often advised on asset allocation and manager selection by consultants. One or more investment management houses will manage the assets on the owner's behalf. A bank will handle the custody of the assets and handle the movements of cash and other assets into, out of and within the investment fund.

This scenario is typical for a UK pension fund. Of course there are variants to these arrangements, both in the pension fund industry and in the investment environment generally, but the principles remain the same.

The key point is that the investment chain consists of a number of bodies, each of which affects the overall performance of the investment fund. Traditionally, performance measurement has been regarded as being relevant only to the investment manager's activities. This may have been valid when the investment manager was a merchant bank or stockbroking firm with total responsibility for the fund. It is not valid in the modern environment, and performance measurement cannot be fully effective unless it is attributed fairly and accurately to each link in the chain.

PERFORMANCE MEASUREMENT STANDARDS

Having established the boundaries of performance measurement, we must next look to the standards governing its practice. Without standards, there is no consistency: without consistency, credibility and acceptance are reduced and, along with them, effectiveness.

When people talk of performance measurement standards, they are usually referring to standards imposed on investment managers of pension funds. This is understandable where the investment manager is the source of all the performance; however, as measurement extends to the wider group of organizations, mentioned above, so standards will need to apply to everyone in that wider group.

Most commentators on standards place methodology high on their list; under this heading, measurers are encouraged to compute total returns and time-weighted returns. The emphasis should be on long-term, rather than short-term, returns. Portfolios should be valued at middle-market prices, derivatives should be based on market exposure, and so on.

There is little argument that sound methodology is important: without that, the results are not likely to be taken seriously. However, methodology needs to be complemented by accurate underlying data, and we will return to this point later.

Following on from methodology, universe (or composite) construction is of great importance, particularly when used by an investment management house to demonstrate track record. It is, in the long run, crucial to the good name of performance measurement that the investment management industry employs the highest standards of ethics and intellectual honesty in this area.

Measuring an investment house's performance over a period of time should include failures, as well as successes. The chances are that, at any particular juncture, only the successes will be in evidence – the failures having gone away to find more successful managers. The correct approach here is to chain-link the weighted average returns of the house's universe for each period within the required time-frame.

(This is one extremely important reason why the weighted average is a more satisfactory statistic than the median: chain-linking medians is statistically unsound.)

One further aspect to this particular standard is the issue of how many of a manager's funds should be included in the universe. The number should be large enough to ensure a proper representation of all his funds. Opinions vary, but The WM Company insist on 50% of an organization's portfolios by number and by value. Further, the portfolios must of course be nominated at the beginning of each time-period (normally each year).

The universe has for many years been regarded as the appropriate benchmark against which to compare the individual investment fund. It is still very relevant for, say, a pension fund to compare itself to a universe of like pension funds.

There are, however, an increasing number of investment funds and portfolios with objectives so specific that a proper universe of peer funds for portfolios does not exist. In these cases, more customized benchmarks will be needed. Here two criteria will improve the quality of results. First, those who request the performance measurement must be very careful to define clear objectives for the fund. Secondly, those who provide the performance measurement must have a service flexible enough to construct benchmarks which truly reflect the objectives.

Finally, in this consideration of standards, we should mention presentation. After all, it does not take much reflection to conclude that bad presentation will undo any amount of good work in methodology or computation.

Presentation of performance data should be concise, precise, relevant and user-friendly. Gone are the days (if indeed they ever existed) when investment managers and owners were prepared to put up with a battery of statistics resembling a world airline's timetable. Successful presentation combines creative design and skilled interpretation.

The design challenge is in some ways becoming easier with technological advances in desktop publishing, printing hardware and PC-based application software. The quality today of screen and paper output in terms of definition, colour and formating of graphics and text is at a level unthinkable ten or even five years ago.

However, no performance report can, of itself, convey the whole story. A whole array of history, market events and investment background underpin and make up the report. It requires skill and experience to separate the significant from the irrelevant. Looking at a balance sheet or a cathedral or a baseball match is enhanced by informed commentary: so it is with performance measurement.

THE UNDERLYING DATA

Performance measurement has always been hampered by the difficulty in obtaining accurate data. The more summarized the data provided, the greater has been this problem.

Ideally, the measurer should receive data at the lowest possible level of data. This entails maintaining for each portfolio a list of individual assets and recording all capital and income transactions.

This approach presents two benefits. First, consistency between all portfolios is assured. With the advent of real-time prices, exchange rates and indices, and the increasing use of ever more complex investment instruments, it is desirable to achieve uniformity of treatment, as far as possible, across portfolios.

Secondly, data at this level of detail makes available a great deal of valuable and accurate analysis. One would not necessarily want acres of such information on a regular basis, but a 'cascade' approach is facilitated.

The cascade approach simply means being able to step down to increasingly greater levels of detail. Ideally, one would use a PC or workstation. A simple downward route might entail the following succession of enquiries:

- Returns at total portfolio level and related benchmark.
- Returns for a particular country or industry sector within the portfolio.
- Individual security characteristics within the industry sector.
- Timing impact of trade x on each of the above returns; and so on.

The advantage of this approach is that it focuses quickly on the exceptional items, and this by-exception information represents genuine management information.

THE ROLE OF TECHNOLOGY

This, then, is a framework for the development of more effective performance measurement. It is all made more possible by modern hardware and software tools. The ideas put forward in this chapter involve the movement and processing of large amounts of portfolio and market data. Much of this data, once processed, may not again be directly accessed, but it underpins a very extensive range of management information.

The WM Company, a leading performance measurement company, constantly strives to extend the effectiveness of performance measurement, and we believe that technology is the key.

13 FUTURE DIRECTIONS IN CUSTODY TECHNOLOGY FOR INVESTMENT MANAGERS

Deborah Seal

Vice-President, Marketing, Vista Concepts Inc., New York, USA

INTRODUCTION

Technology will continue significantly to impact all phases of the international investment community throughout the 1990s and beyond. While growing technological functionality automated much of the industry during the 1970s and 1980s, the business was often held captive by the available technology and the people able to use it. An evolutionary corner is being turned. We are now entering a period where specific business requirements, coupled with technological advancements, are driving the use of computer systems.

It is increasingly difficult to cost-justify technology expenditures outside of a financial organization's core business. Even core business expenditures must be carefully analysed for optimum return on investment. This chapter examines key trends facing the global investment community and the emerging **custody technology** supporting these trends. The following topics are discussed:

- Global business environment.
- Investment management industry trends and technology advances.
- Emerging strategies and system architecture.

GLOBAL BUSINESS ENVIRONMENT

The investment community operates within a **global business environment**. Several important factors are impacting the use of information technologies; these are shown below:

Global business forces
- Information society
- Industrial development
- Personal computer and client/server technology
- Integrated solutions
- Industry-specific solutions
- Networks
- International standards

Both developed and developing countries recognize the use of information to be competitive in the modern world. Costs of leveraging information technology continue to decline as information increasingly becomes a commodity in developed countries. Privatization and the allocation of greater proportions of national budgets to technology are indicators of the recognition of the value of information technology to national development. However, many countries are unable to make significant use of technology. It is widely accepted that an industrial base is necessary to make maximum use of information technology.

Advances in low-cost, high-power computers, as well as LANs and client/servers, will provide significant opportunities for increased information utilization. Integrated and industry-specific solutions which meet targeted business requirements are in growing demand. Network-based systems and services are developing as a primary means of information delivery and interorganization communications. Worldwide networks are becoming critical for maximizing international information delivery.

Information industry forces combined with the movement towards international standards are significantly impacting the information industry. Progress towards the creation and adoption of worldwide information technology standards is increasing steadily. Standards allow the end-user to assess return on information technology investment – a cost justification trend becoming increasingly more important.

INVESTMENT MANAGEMENT INDUSTRY TRENDS AND TECHNOLOGY ADVANCES

Specific trends within the **investment industry** are also impacting the use of information technology; these are shown below:

Investment industry trends
- Globalization
- Removal of middle-level players
- Institutionalization/consolidation
- Competition
- Product development/diversification
- Technology applications

International investment is growing markedly. Overcapacity and mergers have tremendously impacted both the US and European banking industries. In the USA consolidation has given rise to a new class of super-regional banks built through mergers and acquisition. In Europe banks have set up cross-border ventures to allow entry to other national markets without the expense of setting up branch networks. As a result of industry forces, increased competition is being felt by the entire banking industry.

Advances in technology allow for increased product development opportunities for banks while, concurrently, allowing investment managers to take on more technology applications themselves. This growing trend can remove the middle-level player, sometimes called **disintermediation**.

Several investment management technology advancements are evident. Transaction processing is becoming a commodity as the information itself is the value-added product. Downsizing staff and computer platform size to reduce costs and improve efficiencies is being analysed and implemented by financial organizations striving to maintain profitability in an increasingly global and complex investment market. Downsizing is being made possible by client/server technologies, increased use of relational databases and more powerful open-systems workstation technology.

Systems which add value to investment transaction processing are more in demand. These systems provide decision support capabilities which help financial institutions and their clients make use of the increased flow of investment management information. Cost reduction and increased efficiencies will continue to drive evaluation of the technological investment.

EMERGING STRATEGIES AND SYSTEM ARCHITECTURE

Banks and financial institutions are reacting to industry forces through significant cost control and reduction strategies. Downsizing, expense examination and the increased use of outsourcing (everything from facility management to application development to training) are evident. Diversification of products and services, in addition to improved customer service and strengthened distribution channels, help to distinguish investment processing service providers. Investment managers as a group are becoming more global and technologically sophisticated. They are demanding increased products and services from their regional and global custodians. To serve an increasingly knowledgeable client base custodians must provide extremely complex technological services through a global network on a routine basis.

At a minimum, the **global custodian** must provide the functionality shown below:

Custody system architecture
- Fully integrated (information, trading, settlement and accounting)
- Real-time, on-line, 24-hour access
- Multi-currency, multi-lingual, multi-firm, multi-branch
- Interface to depositories and others
- Extremely flexible – handle variety of transactions
- Direct customer access and use
- Effective network communications

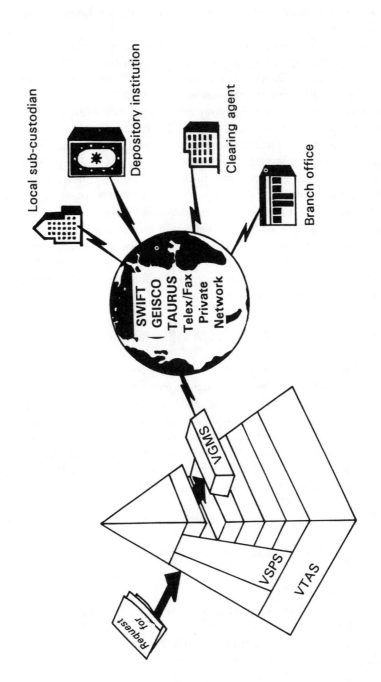

Fig. 13.1 Global message capability.

In addition to the critical areas of functionality described above, investment managers are requesting additional capabilities, including portfolio management, performance measurement, use of relational databases, securities lending and the increasing diversity of investment instruments. Current technological changes are also being driven by the international recommendations set forth by the Group of Thirty. Two key recommendations, settlement of trades by T + 3 and use of same-day funds, are spearheading rapid changes throughout the international investment community.

Communication networks are increasingly more important to support the globalization of international trading and settlement. SWIFT is rapidly becoming the *de facto* financial investment communications network through use of common message types and emphasis on worldwide training and standardization. Network participation, however, must expand to include fund managers in order to maximize this important trend. Proprietary networks and other network options will remain viable for specific users but the emphasis will continue to be on network automation based upon worldwide standards.

FUTURE DIRECTIONS IN CUSTODY TECHNOLOGY FOR INVESTMENT MANAGERS

Vista Concepts strives to meet industry standards and demands for increased functionality through its integrated product line. The heart of the product line is the Vista Securities Processing System (VSPS) which provides real-time, on-line securities movement and control. The Vista Trust Accounting System provides comprehensive multi-currency cash management. There are also several subsystems which provide remote customer access, global message switching and other key areas of functionality. The fully integrated Vista Concepts product line provides the comprehensive global custody system architecture, described above.

Figure 13.1 illustrates the integrated product line and highlights the Vista Global Message Switch subsystem which provides access to SWIFT and other networks. The company has major banking and financial clients in the USA, Canada, Europe and the Pacific Rim.

SUMMARY

Global custody technology is emerging as an integral part of a global or international banking system. Rather than remain a series of separate systems for discrete banking functions, such as securities processing and trust accounting, there is significant movement towards the integration of a diverse set of banking systems. This is particularly true for banks with substantial international investment business and those which plan to compete in an increasingly complex financial environment. Business and economic forces continue to drive advances in investment technology. As the twenty-first century approaches, the investment technology itself must provide comprehensive business solutions with proven productivity gains to support successfully the growing demands of worldwide financial institutions.

Investment management around the world

INTRODUCTION

The national surveys that form Part Three of this Handbook provide the following information:

1. The address and telephone number of the country's principal stock exchange(s).
2. The country's principal regulatory authority for the securities industry.
3. The prevailing national time difference from Greenwich Mean Time (GMT).
4. The forms and types of securities issued within the country.
5. The structure and regulation of the financial markets in the country.
6. Information about the country's leading custodian banks.

Here the aim has been to include details of each leading national financial institution which is able to provide domestic or global custody services. Please note, however, that information about particular custodians is supplied for the purposes of guidance only, and inclusion in the list should not be taken to imply a recommendation from either the author or the publishers. Similarly, non-inclusion within the listings does not imply failure on the part of any non-included custodian to reach a satisfactory level of performance. The custody industry is constantly expanding, and it is consequently impossible to provide a list of custodians that is definitive and unchanging. However, custodians who would like to be included in further editions of this book should contact the author via the publishers.

A large proportion of the information in this part of the Handbook is reproduced by kind permission of the Secretariat of the International Society of Securities Administrators (ISSA). The ISSA was founded in 1975; it is an independent body with the following principal objectives:

1. to promote progress in securities administration;
2. to contribute to a common language among, and to open up communications channels between, securities administrators;
3. to develop personal contacts among securities administrators;
4. to enlarge the professional knowledge of securities administrators.

Readers seeking detailed information, on a country-by-country basis, regarding securities administration should refer to the excellent and highly informative *ISSA Handbook* (2 vols), which is regularly updated by the ISSA. The handbook is available from:

ISSA Secretariat
Union Bank of Switzerland
Att: WLGB/WLSO
PO Box 645
8021 Zurich
Switzerland

Tel: (41) 1 235 7421 or 234 1111
Telex: 813811 ubs ch
Fax: (41) 1 235 6214

14 AUSTRALIA

1 PRINCIPAL STOCK EXCHANGE

Australian Associated Stock Exchanges
9th floor
Plaza Building
Australia Square
Sydney
NSW 2000
Australia

Tel: (612) 227 0400
Telex: 24628 STOCKEX

2 PRINCIPAL REGULATORY AUTHORITY

Australian Securities Commission
31 Queen Street, 17th floor
GPO Box 5179 AA
Melbourne
Australia

Tel: (613) 616 1811
Telex: (71) 37764 (NCSC AA)
Fax: (613) 614 2856

3 TIME DIFFERENCE FROM GMT: +10 HOURS

4 FORMS AND TYPES OF SECURITIES

4.1 Forms of securities

Registered certificate Equity shares are issued in registered form with a certificate despatched to the shareholder after registration. At January 1991, 63 listed companies were participating in the extended FAST pilot scheme.

Shareholders can elect to hold shares in uncertificated mode (see 'Uncertificated securities', below).

Jumbo certificate Australian companies are not restricted to issuing certificates in marketable parcels. Companies will permit consolidation of individual certificates into a jumbo certificate or, alternatively, splitting into smaller certificates.

Inscribed stock Australian government and semi-government securities can be held as inscribed stock permitting a book entry system to be operated by the issuer. Australian government issues prior to July 1984 are available in bearer form, as well as inscribed stock.

Uncertificated securities At January 1991 the 63 Australian Stock Exchange (ASX) listed companies participating in the Flexible Accelerated Security Transfer (FAST) pilot scheme have been able to issue shares in either certificated or uncertificated mode, depending upon the requirements of individual shareholders. The FAST concept does not encompass a central clearing house or securities depository. Transfer of legal ownership will continue to be effected by issuing companies' registries in response to physical lodging of transfer documents with the registries. Participation in FAST is either as an ASX-accepted institution or broker-sponsored individual.

4.2 Types of securities

Equities and options

Ordinary share This is the most common form of share and forms the basis of most companies' issued capital. In Australia ordinary shares must be registered securities. An ordinary share usually confers upon its holder one vote.

Preference share Share with preferential rights over ordinary shares as to claims on assets, earnings and dividends, but ranking below creditors and debentureholders in the event of liquidation. Preference shares usually have a fixed dividend rate.

Contributing share An ordinary share that is party paid – i.e. the par value is not fully paid. Most commonly, contributing shares are issued by no liability (NL) companies. Companies issuing contributing shares do not ask for immediate payment of all the capital and premium (if any), but call for further payments in the future. There is no legal obligation on a holder to pay a call in an NL company. Non-payment of a call will result in the security being forfeited. A holder of a contributing share in a limited liability company does have a legal obligation to pay a call.

Deferred delivery Shares quoted as 'deferred delivery' are the result of a new share issue or a reconstruction of a company's share capital (requiring shareholders to surrender old certificates) and for which the company has not yet issued new scrip. These shares often sell for slightly less than the existing shares to compensate for a delay in delivery.

Deferred dividend share   A company raising capital for a project which is not likely to be profitable for several years may choose to issue deferred dividend shares. These shares do not rank for dividends until a specified date, so that the company will not have to service the shares until the project is likely to be profitable. Deferred dividend shares normally trade for less than ordinary shares to reflect the dividend difference. Similar securities called 'capital units' are also common for Property Trusts.

Cumulative preference share   A preference share which carries an entitlement to receive arrears of preference dividends before a dividend payment to ordinary shareholders.

Option   A method of raising capital, often used by exploration companies. An option may be exercised to take up shares on or before a specified expiry date for a fixed price. Options not exercised by that date expire. The terms of some option issues allow early exercise at specified periods during the currency of the option.

Right   Shareholders are offered the right to subscribe for an allotted entitlement to new shares or other securities. In most cases, a proportional allotment will be made (e.g. one new share and one option for every four shares held). The new shares will usually be offered at a discount to the prevailing market price. There are two types of issues: renounceable and non-renounceable. In a renounceable issue a choice of two timetables is available to companies: normal and short trading. Short trading issues, where rights are not quoted for the full term of the issue, are increasing in number. A right not taken up, or sold, from a short trading issue is usually lapsed. Rights from non-renounceable issues are not quoted on the ASX. Rights lapse if they are not applied for by the issue closing date. The allotment will usually be securities in the existing company.

Warrants   Equity warrants are long-dated, institution-issued options over specific securities. The terms of any one issue may vary from 15 months to five years. Each warrant will constitute a right to one share, unless the terms of issue allow for adjustments since the initial issue, at a contracted price. Warrants may be issued as either call warrants or put warrants. It is the originating institution that maintains the obligations attached to the warrant. Delivery or acceptance of the underlying securities is not enforceable by the ASX. The first warrant issue was made in uncertificated form, and it is expected that subsequent issues will be handled similarly.

Debt instruments

Debenture   A security with a fixed interest rate issued for a fixed period. May be issued in secured or unsecured form; if secured, the debenture will have a charge over the issuer's assets. Debenture certificates are issued in registered form only.

Convertible note A security issued at a fixed interest rate usually with the right to be either redeemed for cash or converted into ordinary shares before or at a predeterminated date. Some note issues are not redeemable for cash. Security entitlements accruing to convertible notes vary according to the terms of the issue, some participate fully in cash issues offered to ordinary shareholders and some only partially. Participation in bonus issues is usually only consummated on conversion of notes to shares; if the notes are not converted, the underlying bonus accrual lapses.

Commonwealth bond Security issued by the Commonwealth of Australia. Issues prior to July 1984 are available in inscribed or bearer form. Issues since July 1984 are available only in inscribed (registered) form.

Semi-government bond Security issued by the semi-government bodies and guaranteed by the federal or state government.

Discount bond A limited number of institutions raise funds by issuing bonds at a discount on redemption value. This type of bond carries a low or zero interest rate.

Money market instruments

Negotiable certificate of deposit Certificate issued by a bank at a fixed rate of interest, transferable by endorsement.

Commercial bill Bill of exchange offered at a discount usually by a money market institution, an authorized money market dealer, finance company or bank. It may be a trade bill or a finance bill. The rate of discount depends upon the credit standing of the parties and occasionally upon the goods.

Bank endorsed bill A discount security endorsed by a bank. The rate of discount depends upon the credit standing of the issuing corporation.

Promissory note Short-term security issued by banks, corporations or semi-government bodies usually at a fixed rate of interest. In the case of notes issued by semi-government bodies, they are guaranteed by the government concerned.

Treasury note Short-term discount security issued by the Commonwealth of Australia, usually for 90 or 180 days. Has the same standing as a Commonwealth bond.

Investment trust units

Unit trust units Part of an open-ended fund which pools and invests the money subscribed by investors.

Stock exchange traded options

Exchange traded option   Put and call options on the ordinary shares of some 27 of the major ASX-listed companies. The normal contract parcel is 1000 shares, but this may change to reflect capital issues or reconstructions during the currency of the option. Exchange traded options have a maximum life of nine months, with maturities spaced three months apart. More liquid issues also have additional option series with 'spot month' maturities.

Futures

90-day bank-accepted bill   Contract unit: AUD 500 000 face value of 90-day bank-accepted bills of exchange. Quotation is an index derived by deducting the percentage yield, to two decimal places, from 100.

Ten-year Commonwealth Treasury bond   Contract unit: Commonwealth Treasury bond with a face value of AUD 100 000, a coupon rate of 12% per annum and a term to maturity of ten years, no tax rebate allowed. Quotation is an index derived by deducting the percentage yield, to two decimal places, from 100.

Three-year Commonwealth Treasury bond   Contract unit: Commonwealth Treasury bonds with a face value of AUD 100 000, a coupon rate of 12% per annum and a term to maturity of three years, no tax rebate allowed. Quotation is an index derived by deducting the percentage yield, to two decimal places, from 100.

Five-year semi-government stock   Contract unit: semi-government inscribed stock with a face value of AUD 100 000, a coupon rate of 12% per annum and a term of five years. A minimum of AUD 200 million to be outstanding four months prior to contract expiry date. Quotation is an index derived by deducting the percentage yield, to two decimal places, from 100.

All Ordinaries Share Price Index   Contract unit: a sum of money equal to 100 times the ASX All Ordinaries Share Price Index expressed as Australian dollars; quotation is in the same form as the ASXs All Ordinaries Share Price Index expressed to one decimal place.

Australian dollar   Contract unit: AUD 100 000; quotation is in US dollars per Australian dollars in multiples of 0.0001 US dollars.

Wool   Contract unit: 2500 kg (22 μm) clean weight of combing wool; quotation is in cents per kilogram.

Live cattle   Contract unit: 10 000 kg live weight of cattle; quotation is in cents per kilogram live weight.

Call options on futures contracts

– All Ordinaries Share Price Index
– Ten-year Commonwealth Treasury bonds

- Three-year Commonwealth Treasury bonds
- Five-year semi-government stock
- 90-day bank bills
- Australian dollar.

Put options on futures contracts

- All Ordinaries Share Price Index
- Ten-year Commonwealth Treasury bonds
- Three-year Commonwealth Treasury bonds
- Five-year semi-government stock
- 90-day bank bills
- Australian dollar.

Equities futures   Parcels of 10 000 shares in ten major ASX-listed companies (ANZ, BHP, Coles Myer, CRA, CSR, Fosters Brewing, National Australia Bank, Santos, Western Mining and Westpac Bank). Contracts are either three- or six-month terms. Contracts are non-deliverable. Settlement is by cash only.

4.3   Securities identification code

There is no uniform numbering system used for securities identification in Australia. However, each market organizer has a coding system for the securities traded on that market. The ASX identifies securities with the six-character ASX security code. This is an alphabetic code comprising a three-character code identifying the issuer, combined with a code of up to three characters identifying a particular class of security for that issuer.

4.4   Transfer of ownership

Transfer of bearer securities

Ownership is transferred by the handing over or delivery of the bearer document of title from the seller to the buyer, without entry in any register. When the securities are held by a custodian on behalf of the seller, title to the securities is transferred by debiting the securities account of the seller and crediting the securities account of the buyer.

Transfer of registered securities

Ownership is transferred by completing a transfer form which is recognized by the company register. The company register records the change of ownership in the register of members, register of debentureholders, etc., of the company and, in the case of a certificated security, issues a new certificate for the buyer. In the case of an uncertified shareholder under the FAST system, a confirmation is issued upon first joining the company's register, and subsequently in the form of statements of transactions. Transaction statements will be routinely issued four times per year at no cost to the shareholder. Additional statements may be obtained, but the company has the right to charge for these. In Australia it is not necessary for the transferee (buyer) to sign an ASX market transfer document. Since the middle of 1989, it is also no longer necessary for the seller to sign a market transfer.

Transactions dealt in outside the ASX give rise to 'off market' transfers which cannot be registered into the buyer's name until such time as both the seller and the buyer (transferee) sign the transfer, usually a Standard Transfer Form. Stamp duty consistent with the laws of the state of registration must be accounted for before an off-market transfer can be accepted for registration.

Commonwealth government securities, which are referred to as 'inscribed stock' when in registered form, are transferrable by signing a transfer form. The transfer is lodged with the Registrar of Inscribed Stock (Department of the Reserve Bank) in one of the major cities.

5   STRUCTURE AND REGULATION OF FINANCIAL MARKETS

5.1   Structure of financial activities

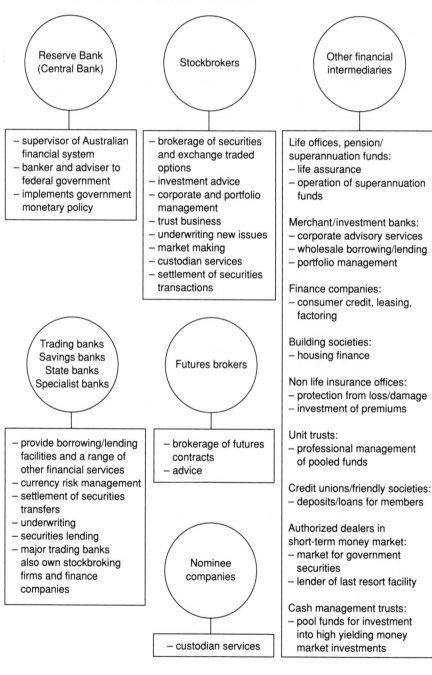

Reserve Bank (Central Bank)

– supervisor of Australian financial system
– banker and adviser to federal government
– implements government monetary policy

Stockbrokers

– brokerage of securities and exchange traded options
– investment advice
– corporate and portfolio management
– trust business
– underwriting new issues
– market making
– custodian services
– settlement of securities transactions

Trading banks
Savings banks
State banks
Specialist banks

– provide borrowing/lending facilities and a range of other financial services
– currency risk management
– settlement of securities transfers
– underwriting
– securities lending
– major trading banks also own stockbroking firms and finance companies

Futures brokers

– brokerage of futures contracts
– advice

Nominee companies

– custodian services

Other financial intermediaries

Life offices, pension/ superannuation funds:
– life assurance
– operation of superannuation funds

Merchant/investment banks:
– corporate advisory services
– wholesale borrowing/lending
– portfolio management

Finance companies:
– consumer credit, leasing, factoring

Building societies:
– housing finance

Non life insurance offices:
– protection from loss/damage
– investment of premiums

Unit trusts:
– professional management of pooled funds

Credit unions/friendly societies:
– deposits/loans for members

Authorized dealers in short-term money market:
– market for government securities
– lender of last resort facility

Cash management trusts:
– pool funds for investment into high yielding money market investments

5.2 Regulatory structure

Overview

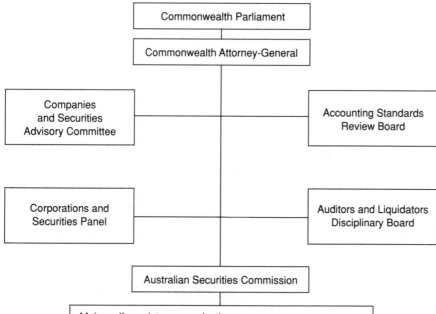

Major self-regulatory organizations:

– Australian Stock Exchange Limited
– The Sydney Futures Exchange Limited
– Australian Society of Accountants
– Institute of Chartered Accountants in Australia
– Law institutes, societies
– Numerous industry associations, e.g.:
  • Australian Investment Planners Association
  • International Financial Planners Association
  • Securities Institute of Australia
  • Australian Merchant Bankers' Association
  • Council of Authorised Money Market Dealers
  • Life Insurance Federation of Australia
  • Association of Superannuation Funds Australia
  • Australian Bankers' Association
  • Australian Finance Conference
  • Trustee Companies Association of Australia & New Zealand
  • National Insurance Brokers Association of Australia

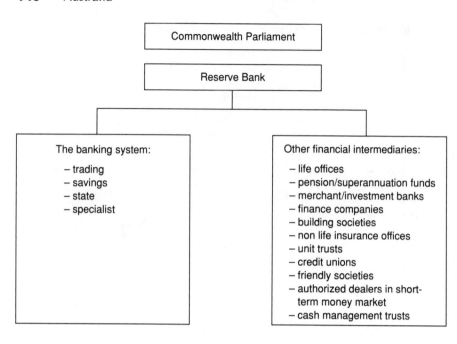

Responsibilities of regulatory bodies

Major government regulatory authorities

Regulatory body	Legal basis	Responsibilities
Australian Securities Commission	Corporations Act 1989 Australian Securities Commission Act 1989	Legislative power: – ASC policy statements – notices – practice notes – commentaries – general bulletins Adjudicatory power: – regulatory oversight over companies, brokers, dealers, investment advisers and managers, stock exchanges, futures exchanges and investors – imposing administrative and disciplinary sanctions Power of enforcement: – investigation of potential violations – prosecution

Regulatory body	Legal basis	Responsibilities
Reserve Bank of Australia	Reserve Bank Act 1959 Banking Act 1959 Bank (Shareholdings) Act 1972 Financial Corporations Act 1974 (part proclaimed)	Regulatory oversight of banks, building societies, credit unions, merchant banks, authorized dealers, pastoral finance companies, general financiers (which are not significant borrowers), retailers engaging in financing on a significant scale and intragroup financiers
Foreign Investment Review Board	Foreign Takeovers Act 1975	Foreign investments in Australia
Office of the Insurance Commissioner	Insurance Act 1973 Insurance (Agents and Brokers) Act 1984 Insurance Contracts Act 1984 Insurance (Deposits) Act 1984	General insurance companies
Office of the Life Insurance Commissioner	Life Insurance Act 1945 Insurance (Agents and Brokers) Act 1984 Insurance Contracts Act 1984	Life insurance companies and superannuation funds
Trade Practices Commissions	Trade Practices Act 1974	All industries
Consumer Affairs Bureau	Various State and Territory Consumer Affairs Acts Various Small Claim Tribunals Acts Various Credit Acts Motor car traders, residential tenancies	All industries
Registrar of: – co-operatives housing societies – co-operative societies – permanent building societies – friendly societies	Various state and territory Acts	Regulation of member financial intermediaries

Regulatory body	Legal basis	Responsibilities
Stamp duties offices and state taxation	Various stamp duties	All industries
Registrars of finance brokers, auctioneers and money lenders	Various money lenders Acts	Finance brokers, auctioneers and money lenders

Self-regulatory organizations (SROs)

Regulatory body	Legal basis	Responsibilities
Stock exchanges	Corporations Act 1989 Business rules Listing rules	Regulatory oversight over brokers and listed companies: – investigation – disciplinary proceedings – administration
Futures exchanges	Corporations Act 1989 Futures Exchanges Business Rules Trading Etiquette Manual Clearing house regulations	Regulatory oversight over futures brokers – investigation – disciplinary proceedings – administration
Accounting standards	Corporations Act 1989	Undertake and sponsor research and conduct hearings in order to develop accounting standards
Australian Society of Accountants		Member accountants
Institute of Chartered Accountants in Australia		Regulatory oversight over member accountants: – investigation – disciplinary proceedings – administration
Law institutes/ societies		Regulatory oversight over legal practitioners: – investigation – disciplinary proceedings – administration
Unit Trust Association		Unit trusts

Regulatory body	Legal basis	Responsibilities
Australian Investment Planners Association		Investment planners
Australian Bankers' Association		Trading banks
Australian Merchant Bankers' Association		Merchant banks
International Financial Planners		Financial planners
Securities Institute of Australia		Education of securities industry participants
Council of Authorized Money Market Dealers		Authorized money market dealers
Life Insurance Federation of Australia		Life insurance industry
Association of Superannuation Funds of Australia		Superannuation funds
Australian Finance Conference		Banking/financial intermediaries
Trustee Companies Association of Australia and New Zealand		Trustee companies
National Insurance Brokers Association of Australia		Insurance brokers

Supervision of stock exchanges

The Corporations Law came into operation in all states and territories of Australia on 1 January 1991. The Corporations Law restructures the previous companies and securities regulatory regime, by introducing national legislation regulating companies, the securities industry, the futures industry and takeovers. The Australian Securities Commission (ASC) was established under the Australian Securities Commission Act 1989 to administer on a national basis the Corporations Law. The ASC replaced the NCSC and the Corporate Affairs Offices of each state and territory.

Since the introduction of securities industry legislation in the early 1970s, the Australian model for stock market regulation has been one of co-regulation (i.e. combination of statutory and self-regulation). The minister is required to approve the establishment of a new stock exchange and has the power to disallow amendments to the stock exchange business or listing rules. Under the Corporations Law, the ASC has considerable responsibility to ensure the proper working of stock exchanges, although there are provisions which allow for self-regulation. The Corporations Law gives the ASC the power to give notice to a stock exchange requesting it to prohibit trading in certain securities or to direct the stock exchange to do so if it fails to act.

The ASC recognizes that the primary role in regulating stock markets is left to the stock exchanges, with the ASC having the power to intervene where it is not satisfied that an exchange is discharging its responsibilities adequately.

Supervision of settlement and clearing houses

The Australian Stock Exchange operates a clearing house for settlement of equities transactions between its member brokers, and an options clearing house for settlement of transactions in exchange traded options.

Australia does not have a central depository for the immobilization of certificates representing title to equity securities and for settlement of transactions between participants. In the modernization of the equity settlement system Australia has adopted a policy of 'dematerialization' rather than immobilization of certificates in a central depository. These developments are evolving towards a central clearing entity which will settle transactions between direct market participants (brokers), and between brokers and indirect market participants (custodians and institutional investors).

ICCH currently operates the clearing house for settlement of transactions on the Sydney Futures Exchange. However, it is planned that clearing operations will transfer to the Sydney Futures Exchange Clearing House from December 1991.

Supervision of broker/dealers and custodian banks

Securities industry participants are regulated by a licensing system operating under the new Corporations Law. The new law introduced a number of significant changes to the previous licensing system which have added considerable bite to the self-regulatory aspect of the legislation.

Other sections of the Corporations Law and ASX business rules govern the activities and conduct of brokers and dealers. The licensing provisions are currently supervised by the ASC, although the new Corporations Law places the onus on dealers and investment advisers to ensure that those dealing or advising on their behalf are properly authorized. Licensees have more than a passing interest in this as they now assume legal responsibility for the acts of their representatives under statute (in addition to any liability under general law principles).

The most significant changes to the licensing provisions were in respect of representatives of dealers and investment advisers. Under the Corporations Law, it is no longer necessary for a person who acts as a representative of a licenceholder (dealer's representatives and investment adviser's representatives) to obtain a separate licence. The dealers and investment advisers are now required to issue 'proper authorities' to their representatives. Dealers and investment advisers are required to properly supervise representatives and to give them adequate training and education. Statutory liability is imposed on dealers and investment advisers for certain conduct of their representatives, which liability cannot be excluded and the licensed dealers and investment advisers are required to maintain a public register of their representatives. The grounds on which the ASC may revoke a licence have been extended and the ASC has been given the power to issue 'banning orders' against individuals prohibiting them from acting as a representative of a dealer or investment adviser.

Futures brokers are required to be licensed by the ASC, and their employees/representatives are required to hold a proper authority from their principal. In addition, anyone who deals in or advises on a futures contract is required to be registered with the Sydney Futures Exchange (SFE) or the much smaller Australian Financial Futures Market (AFFM).

The SFE is a self-regulatory organization which supervises the market and its participants using the SFE Articles and By-Laws and the Corporations Law.

Dealers are similarly required to be licensed by the ASC and the employees/representatives must hold a proper authority from the dealer.

The Corporations Law imposes stringent requirements on brokers and dealers to ensure that they are responsible for the activities of those persons holding proper authorities. As the representatives are no longer licenced by the government regulator, the ASC may issue a banning order against any individual to preclude him from operating in the industry.

Where a dealer is also a member of the Stock Exchange, they are also regulated by Australian Stock Exchange Limited (ASX) via their Articles and Business Rules. ASX is a self-regulatory organization which is also responsible for monitoring market activity and regulating dealers and companies to provide an efficient and fair market.

6 CUSTODIANS

ANZ Nominees
30 Elizabeth Street
Melbourne
Victoria 3001
Australia

Tel: 61 3 658 2100
Fax: 61 3 614 1877

Bank of New Zealand
9th floor
BNZ House
333–339 George Street
Sydney
NSW 2000
Australia

Tel: 61 2 290 6666
Fax: 61 2 290 3414

Citicorp Nominees Pty
Level 14
35 Collins Street
Melbourne
Victoria 3000
Australia

Tel: 61 3 239 9447
Fax: 61 3 239 5741

Indosuez Australia
13th floor
303 Collins Street
Melbourne
Victoria 3000
Australia

Tel: 61 3 602 5100
Fax: 61 3 629 4506

National Australia Bank
Investment Services Department
271 Collins Street
Melbourne
Victoria
Australia

Tel: 61 3 605 3500
Fax: 61 3 602 3459

Westpac Banking Corporation
10th floor
50 Pitt Street
Sydney
NSW 2000
Australia

Tel: 61 2 226 3311
Fax: 61 2 231 2661

15 AUSTRIA

1 PRINCIPAL STOCK EXCHANGE

Vienna Stock Exchange
Wiener Borsekammer
Wipplingerstrasse 34
A-1011 Vienna
Austria

Tel: 43222 534 990
Telex: 132447 WBKA
Fax: 43222 535 6857

2 PRINCIPAL REGULATORY AUTHORITY

Vienna Stock Exchange
contact details as above

3 TIME DIFFERENCE FROM GMT: +1 HOUR

4 FORMS AND TYPES OF SECURITIES

4.1 Forms of securities

Bearer certificate **(Inhaberurkunde)** Common form for equity and debt instruments with coupons representing dividends, interest, subscription rights, etc.

Registered certificate **(Namenspapier)** Relatively rare; by law, partially paid-up shares must be in registered form.

Book entry securities **(Sammelverwahrfähige Wertpapiere)** Certificated (immobilized) or uncertificated securities which may be transferred by book entry from one safe-custody account to another on the books of the Central Securities Depository (Wertpapiersammelbank).

Depository receipt (certificates for foreign shares) **[Zertifikat-Sammelurkunde (Zert. SU)]**   Certificates issued by Austrian bank on the basis of shares held with a foreign custodian.

Global certificate **(Sammelurkunde)**   Security deposited with the Central Securities Depository and representing an entire issue. Distinction possible between: temporary and permanent global certificate; 90% of all outstanding domestic bonds are represented by global certificates.

Temporary global certificate **(Zwischensammelurkunde)**   Basis for book transfers through Central Securities Depository until such time as definitive certificates are available.

Permanent global certificate **(Dauernde Sammelurkunde)**   Permanent global certificates represent an entire issue of bonds in accordance with the terms and conditions of the issue. This applies to debt instruments and investment certificates only.

Jumbo certificate **(Globalurkunde)**   Certificate representing a large number of shares or fixed-interest securities.

4.2   Types of securities

Equities and warrants

Ordinary share **(Stammaktie)**   A share represents membership rights in a public limited company and also represents a portion in the capital of a company. The holder is entitled to vote at the shareholders' meetings, to participate in rights issues, to receive dividends and to receive his portion in the liquidation proceeds. Minimum par value ATS 100,-. (Issued in bearer or registered form.)

Preferred share **(Vorzugsaktie)**   Preferred shares usually carry preferential rights as to dividends in contrast to ordinary shares. Preferred shares are usually non-voting and, by definition, cumulative. (Issued in bearer form.)

Participation certificate **(Partizipationsschein)**   Securities incorporating the right to participate in the profit and the liquidation proceeds of a company. The holder has no membership rights, in particular no right to subscribe for new shares and no voting right in shareholders' meetings. Participation certificates are issued for the purpose of raising capital, and its nominal value is part of the equity of the company. (Issued in bearer form.)

Profit participation certificate **(Genussschein aus Beteiligungsfonds)**   Grants the right to a fixed portion of the net profit of a fund investing its money (received by public offering of the certificates) for ten years as equity into companies. It does not represent a participation in the company, although the holder bears the financial risk of a company's default. (Issued in bearer form.)

Warrant (**Optionsschein**)   A warrant is a certificated marketable option, tradable like a share. It entitles the holder to subscribe for a specific amount of shares (or, as the case may be, bonds) at a set price during a prescribed period, usually several years. (Issued in bearer form.)

Debt instruments

Straight bond (**Anleihe; festverzinsliches Wertpapier**)   Interest-bearing instrument with a fixed date of maturity, without conversion right or other features. (Issued in bearer form.)

Public bond (**Anleihe der öffentlichen Hand**)   Issued by the government, the federal provinces, the municipalities and companies owned by the state (Sondergesellschaften). (Issued in bearer form.)

Convertible bond (**Wandelanleihe**)   Convertible bonds may be exchanged for shares at the bondholder's option on certain conditions. (Issued in bearer form.)

Zero bond (**Nullkuponanleihe**)   Zero bonds pay no interest during the lifetime of the bond; they are sold at a discount to reflect earnings. At maturity, the bondholders will be paid the full face value. (Issued in bearer form.)

Warrant issue (**Optionsanleihe**)   An issue that combines the features of a bond with those of a warrant. The warrant is usually a detachable, separate certificate and may be exercised in accordance with the terms and conditions of the issue. (Issued in bearer form.)

Floating rate note [**Variabel verzinsliche Anleihe ('Floater')**]   Interest-bearing instrument subject to change of the interest rate at set intervals (e.g. three months, six months). Changes based on defined market indicators. (Issued in bearer form.)

Medium-term note (**Kassenobligation**)   Issued by banks on an ongoing basis with maturities of up to five years. (May be held in book entry form.)

Mortgage bond (**Pfandbrief**)   Issued by private and public sector mortgage banks for long-term finance and secured by first mortgages. (Issued in bearer form, may be held as global or jumbo certificate or in book entry form).

Municipal bond (**Kommunalobligation**)   Issued by private and public sector mortgage banks to provide finance for communities and municipalities, as well as private commercial investments under public guarantee. (Issued in bearer form.)

Corporate bond (**Industrieanleihe**)   Issued by private corporations; a specific authorization by the Ministry of Finance is required by law if issued in form of bearer bonds. (Issued in bearer form, may be held as global or jumbo certificate.)

Unit trust certificate

Unit trust certificate (Investmentzertifikat)   Certificate representing part ownership in a professionally managed investment portfolio. (Issued in bearer form, may be held as jumbo certificate.)

4.3   Securities identification code

Code, name and structure

The Austrian Securities Identification Number consists of a six-digit figure:

Wertpapierkenn-Nummer:	Securities Identification Number:
No. 001 000 – 059 999	Bonds
No. 060 000 – 099 500	Shares, warrants and unit trusts

Name and address of organization responsible for the Securities Identification System

Oesterreichische Kontrollbank
Aktiengesellschaft
Am Hof 4
A-1010 Vienna
Austria

Tel: (222) 53127 207
Telex: 132 771
Fax: 53127 407

4.4   Transfer of ownership

Transfer of bearer issues

The value of these securities is embodied in the relative document or certificate. The transfer of ownership can be effected by physical delivery of the certificate to the buyer or the transfer can be effected by mere book entry (debit and credit of respective securities accounts).

Transfer of registered issues

The transfer of ownership of registered securities may be effected by means of an endorsement. When endorsed in blank, such endorsable securities can be transferred like bearer securities.

   The share registers are maintained by the companies themselves. In some cases, transfer of registered shares is subject to certain conditions.

5   STRUCTURE AND REGULATION OF FINANCIAL MARKETS

5.1   Structure of financial activities

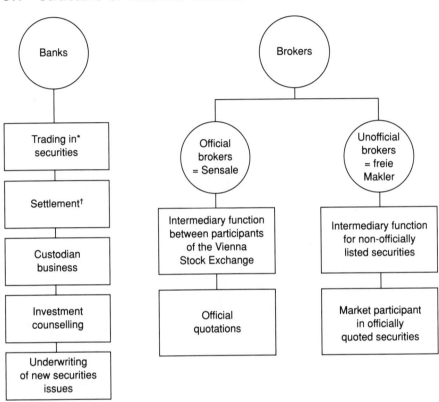

Note:
* Commission business for private and institutional clients;
  Nostro-trading (trading for own account).
† Most deals are settled by the clearing agency of the Vienna Stock Exchange, i.e. the
  Arrangementbureau operated by Oesterreichische Kontrollbank.
The Banking Act of 1979 and 1986 authorizes Austrian banks to engage in all types of
banking business.

5.2 Regulatory structure

Overview

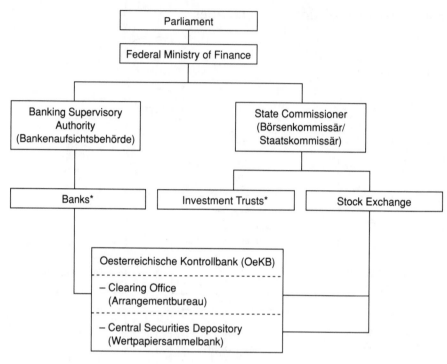

* Supervision is partly through independent public accountants.

Responsibilities of regulatory bodies

Name of body	Tasks/responsibilities
Banking Supervisory Authority (Bankenaufsichtsbehörde)	This body is a part of the Federal Ministry of Finance. Its main task is to prevent abuses in the banking industry. The Authority acts either through independent accountants (annual audit, including audit of custodian business, i.e. Depotprüfung) or directly.
State Commissioner	(a) to the Stock Exchange: permanent supervision of trading and official quotation (b) to the Investment Trust: permanent supervision of legal requirements

Supervision of Stock Exchange

Council of the Vienna Stock Exchange (Wiener Börsekammer) and State Commissioner (Börsenkommissär) As an independent corporation under public law (Körperschaft öffentlichen Rechts), the stock exchange operates through the Council of the Vienna Stock Exchange which has permanent supervision over all relevant activities in the market.

Supervision of Clearing and Central Securities Depository Organization

State Commissioner(s) (Staatskommissär/Börsenkommissär) Oesterreichische Kontrollbank acts as central securities depository and is supervised by its state commissioner and an independent public accountant.

As clearing and settlement system (Arrangementbureau), OeKB is assisting the Stock Exchange and is in this case supervised by the Stock Exchange State Commissioner.

Supervision of broker/dealers and custodian banks

State Commissioner He supervises the activity of the official brokers (Sensale) according to § 19, Stock Exchange Law 1989.

6 CUSTODIANS

Citibank Austria AG
Lothringerstrasse 7
1010 Vienna
Austria

Tel: 1 71717
Fax: 1 713 9206

Creditanstalt Bankverein
Schottengasse 6
1010 Vienna
Austria

Tel: 43 1 53131
Fax: 43 1 5359859

Girozentrale Vienna
Schubertring 5
1011 Vienna
Austria

Tel: 1 711940
Fax: 1 713 7032

Oesterreische Landerbank
Amhof 2
1010 Vienna
Austria

Tel: 1 53124
Fax: 1 531 2452

Schoeller & Co.
Renngasse 1–3
1010 Vienna
Austria

Tel: 43 1 534710
Fax: 43 1 533 4390

16 BELGIUM

☞ ### 1 PRINCIPAL STOCK EXCHANGE

Commission de la Bourse de Bruxelles
Palais de la Bourse
1000 Brussels
Belgium

Tel: 322 509 1211
Telex: 21 374 BOURS B
Fax: 322 511 9500

☞ ### 2 PRINCIPAL REGULATORY AUTHORITY

Commission Bancaire
99 Avenue Louise
1050 Brussels
Belgium

Tel: 32 2 535 2211
Telex: 46 62107 (CEBECE-B)
Fax: 32 2 535 2323

3 TIME DIFFERENCE FROM GMT: +1 HOUR

4 FORMS AND TYPES OF SECURITIES

4.1 Forms of securities

Bearer certificate **(Au porteur; Aan Toonder)**   Security on which the name
of the owner is not mentioned. Such certificates are freely and easily transferable. Most securities traded in Belgium are in bearer form.

Note: Terms are given in English, French and Dutch, respectively, followed by comments.

Registered certificate (**Nominatif; Op Naam**)   Security of which the owner-ship is established by registration in the register of the issuing company and confirmed to the owner by the issuance of a certificate. Registered certificates are governed by articles 42, 43 and 43 bis of the Lois Coordonnées sur les Sociétés Commerciales (LCSC) with regard to shares, and article 89 of the LCSC with regard to bonds.

Global certificate CIK certificate (**Titre global; Globaal Effekt**)   Used ex-clusively by CIK, the central depository (see 4.1.2). Issued in addition to the usual bearer securities for the part of the issue which is deposited by banks with CIK (e.g. representing registered shares for institutional investors, printed without coupon sheets). It never represents the total amount of the issue.

Depository receipt (**Certificat représentatif; Certificaat vertegenwoordiging**)   Bearer certificate issued in order to facilitate the trading and possession of foreign registered securities.

Book entry (**Obligations linéaires; Lineaire Obligaties**)   Linear bonds (since May 1989):

– issued by tender
– fungible
– dematerialized

4.2   Types of securities

Equities and warrants

Ordinary share (**Action ordinaire, Action de capital; Gewoon aandeel**)   Most shares traded in Belgium are in bearer form (titre au porteur); registered form (titre nominatif) is rare; with or without par value. In permitting no-par-value stocks, Belgium is an exception among European countries.

AFV share (**Action AFV; AFV aandeel**)   Share issued in 1982 or 1983, with fiscal advantages for residents, granted by the Royal Decrees Nos 15 and 150 of 1982: the holder is entitled to eventual superdividends representing cor-porate tax relief up to 1992; withholding tax 20% instead of 25%; exemption from legacy duties.

Preference share (**Action privilégiée, Action de préférence; Bevoorrecht Aandeel**)   Share with preference rights regarding dividend payments and distribution of assets on liquidation; issued with or without par value.

Jouissance share, dividend – right certificate (**Action de jouissance; Dividendaandeel**)   Share which does not confer any ownership rights, but grants the right to participate in the net profit of the company; issued without par value.

Founder's share (**Part bénéficiaire, Part de fondateur; Winstdeelbewijs, Oprichtersaandeel**)   Has no ownership rights, but entitles to participate in the net profit; mostly former founder's shares; issued without par value.

Subscription right **(Droit de souscription; Inschrijvingsrecht)**   Right attached to shares to subscribe to an issue of shares in the case of a capital increase. The right is usually represented by a coupon designated for this purpose.

Warrant **(Warrant; Warrant)**   Right to purchase shares under certain predetermined conditions.

Bonus **(Droit d'attribution; Toewijzingsrecht)**   Right to obtain new shares for free. The right is represented by a coupon in the case of bearer shares.

Real estate certificate **(Certificats immobiliers; Vastgoedcertificaat)**   Security, generally in bearer form, concerning a right to a portion of the income and the asset at liquidation of specified real estate.

Mutual investment trust fund part (Mutual fund) **(Part de fonds communs de placement; Deelbewijs gemeenschappelijk beleggingsfonds)**   Certificate conferring a right in a mutual investment trust fund; mostly in bearer and rarely in registered form.

Capitalization fund **(SICAV-SICAF; BVEK-BEVAK)**   Security of an investment fund with possibility of capitalization of dividends.

Debt instruments

Straight bond **(Obligation; Obligatie)**   Long-term loan issued by the government, local authorities, public institutions or private companies, normally in bearer form, though registered form is possible.

Cash bond **(Bon de caisse; Kasbon)**   Bond issued for short- or medium-term (maximum five years) by public or private financial institutions according to their needs, normally in bearer form. Maturities differ according to the following types:

– Classical (up to five years): cash bond for which interest is paid on a regular basis (monthly, quarterly, etc.).
– Capitalization (up to 12 years): a cash bond for which interest is capitalized until reimbursement date. For 12-year bonds, intermediate maturities can fall after four and eight years.
– Mixed (three to five years): a cash bond for which the holder has the possibility of capitalizing its interest:
– Bons de croissance (Groeibons): interest is capitalized until a coupon is paid which induces the payment of all subsequent coupons.
– Multibons: the holder may freely collect each coupon; the interest is capitalized only if the coupon remains invested until the final maturity.

Convertible bond **(Obligation convertible en actions; In aandelen converteerbare obligatie)**   Bond which may be converted by the holder into stocks; usually in bearer form, although the registered form is possible.

Lottery bond **(Obligation à lot; Lotenobligatie)**   Long-term bond which is, in the course of reimbursement, entitled to participate in a lottery and to receive a complementary amount (= lot).

Participating bond **(Obligation participante; Participerende obligatie)**   Bond which, in addition to the normal interest, is entitled to participate in the net profit of the issuing company.

Certificate of conversion **(Certificat de conversion; Conversie-certificaat)**   Bond that must be converted by the holder into stocks by the end of the conversion period.

Money market instruments

Treasury bill **(Certificat de Trésorerie; Schatkist-certificaat)**   Issued by the government with maturities of three months (auctioned every Tuesday) or 12 months (auctioned on Tuesday, every fourth week). Treasury bills are held only in book entry form in the National Bank.

4.3   Securities Identification Numbers

Code name and structure

Belgian securities are identified by the SVM Code (Secrétariat des Valeurs Mobilières) which consists of six digits for the security number and two additional digits as 'check digits':

Structure:	1 2 3 4 5 4 6 – 1 2 –	1 2
	Code Check	Modification of dividend or
	digit	interest entitlement

Example: 003012–05 (Générale Bank, ordinary share)

Name and address of organization responsible for the securities identification system

The system is maintained by:

Secrétariat des Valeurs Mobilières (SVM)
Secretariat voor Roerende Waarden (SRW)
Bd Bisschoffsheim 15
B-1000 Brussels

Tel: 516 33 72
Fax: 516 43 29

4.4   Transfer of ownership

Transfer requirements of bearer securities

The transfer is effected by handing over the securities. No special formalities are required.

For the professionals affiliated to CIK (Central Depository), transfer by book entry is possible.

Transfer requirements of registered securities

In addition to physical delivery, one of the following is necessary:

- a transfer declaration signed by the two parties to the register of the issuer; or
- the notification of the cession to the issuer by a legal document (signification par exploit d'huissier); or
- any document or correspondence indicating the agreement between the parties to the issuer.

In all these cases, a new certificate is issued after the transfer is registered and the old certificate is invalidated.

5 STRUCTURE AND REGULATION OF FINANCIAL MARKETS

5.1 Structure of financial activities

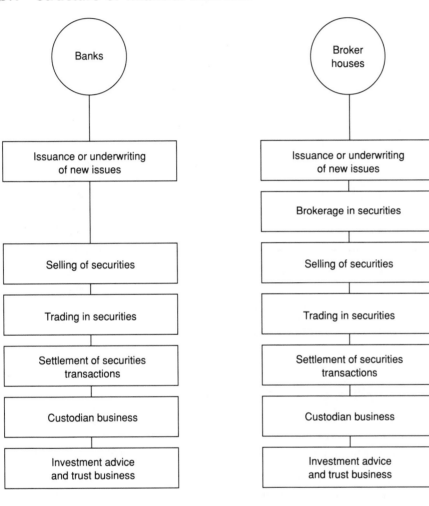

5.2 **Regulatory structure**

Overview

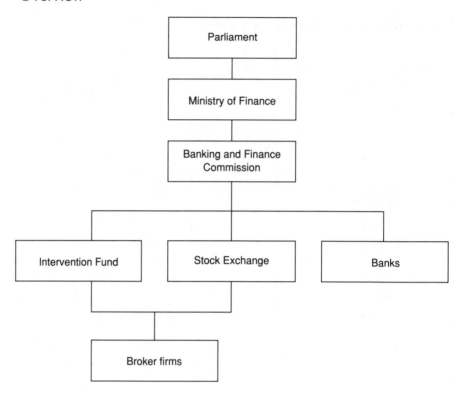

Responsibilities of regulatory bodies

Parliament   The Parliament has no direct responsibilities or link as far as the financial business is concerned. Indirectly it may have some responsibilities via the laws that it approves and the control over the government and hence over the Ministry of Finance.

Ministry of Finance   The Ministry of Finance is responsible for the public issue or admission to the Stock Exchange of non-Belgian securities.

Banking and Finance Commission   Public institution in charge of the supervision of banks' legal status and organization, and of compliance with the rules regarding the issuance and public offer of Belgian securities and public takeovers. Since the issue of the law of 4 December 1990, the Banking and Finance Commission has also a supervisory function on broker firms.

Comité de la Cote Noteringscomité   The Listing Committee consists of 12 members (seven brokers and five representatives of the principal financial institutions). The government commissioner is notified of meetings and generally attends them. The Committee decides on the admission of securities to the Stock Exchange, and their removal (will be absorbed by the Stock Exchange by the end of 1992).

Commission de la Bourse/Beurscommissie The functions of the Stock Exchange Committee are as follows:

– is the directory board of the Stock Exchange
– decides on the listing and the delisting of stocks
– decides on the suspension of listing
– organizes public sales of non-listed securities
– admission of broker firms
– ensures the organization, functioning and control of the securities markets
– monitors and controls compliance with the rules
– settles disputes between broker firms
– ensures the transparency of the market by informing the public.

Caisse d'Intervention des Sociétés de Bourses/Interventiefonds von de beursvennootschap

– ensures totally or partly fufilment of the professional duties of stock broker firms
– controls the broker firms.

Supervision of the Stock Exchange

The Stock Exchange Committee is supervised by the Banking and Finance Commission and also by the Intervention Fund.

Supervision of clearing and central securities depository organizations

Central Securities Depository: Caisse Interprofessionelle de Dépôt et de Virement de Titres (CIK)

A semi-public organization, supervised by its Board of Directors and a government commissioner representing the Minister of Finance. The latter has a veto right, if decisions contravene existing Belgian laws, legal rules and regulations of the company or public interest.

As a limited company, it is subject to all laws applying to commercial companies and to the supervision of statutory bank auditors.

Clearing organization

Settlement Institution of the Forward Market: The Coopérative de Liquidation des Opérations à Terme is a private company but still subject to supervision by the government commissioner. Two members are responsible for the control of the operations.

Euroclear

Private company.

Supervision of broker/dealers

The Intervention Fund checks if the brokers and counterparty brokers fulfil their obligations, both to each other and with regard to other parties.

The Stock Exchange Commission settles professional differences between brokers and can impose sanctions against them.

Supervision of custodian banks

Supervision by the Banking and Finance Commission.

6   CUSTODIANS

Banque Bruxelles Lambert
24 Avenue Marnix
1050 Brussels
Belgium

Tel: 32 2 517 2111
Fax: 32 2 517 3844

Euroclear
Rue de la Regence
1000 Brussels

Tel: 32 2 519 1211
Fax: 32 2 519 1287

Générale de Banque
Montagne du Park 3
1000 Brussels
Belgium

Tel: 32 2 518 3685
Fax: 32 2 518 3623

Kredietbank
Arenbergstraat 7
1000 Brussels
Belgium

Tel: 32 2 517 4111
Fax: 32 2 517 5385

Morgan Guaranty Trust
Avenue des Arts 35
1040 Brussels
Belgium

Tel: 32 2 508 8210
Fax: call telephone number for fax

17 CANADA

1 PRINCIPAL STOCK EXCHANGES

The Toronto Stock Exchange
The Exchange Tower
2 First Canadian Place
Toronto
Ontario
M5X 1J2
Canada

Tel: 416 947 4700
Telex: 062 17759

Bourse de Montreal
CP 61
Tour de la Bourse
800 Victoria Square
Montreal
Quebec
H4Z 1A9
Canada

Tel: (514) 871 2424
Telex: 055 60686

2 PRINCIPAL REGULATORY AUTHORITY

Securities regulation in Canada is carried out on a federal basis. Three of the most important federal regulators are as follows:

Commission des Valeurs
Mobilières du Québec
800 Square Victoria
17 étage
Montreal
Quebec
H4Z 1G3
Canada

Tel: 514 873 5326
Fax: 514 873 3090

Ontario Securities Commission
20 Queen Street West
Suite 1800
Box 55
Toronto
Ontario
N5H 3S8
Canada

Tel: 416 593 8200
Fax: 416 593 8240

British Columbia Securities
Commission
1200 865 Hornby Street
Vancouver
British Columbia
V6Z 2H4
Canada

Tel: 604 660 4881
Fax: 604 660 2688

3 TIME DIFFERENCE FROM GMT: −5 HOURS

4 FORMS AND TYPES OF SECURITIES

4.1 Forms of securities

Registered certificate A certificate with the holder's name imprinted on it and recorded in the security register maintained by the transfer agent. Transfer of the certificate requires the assignment section be endorsed by the registered holder and the holder's signature guaranteed by a member of the Canadian financial community. Registered certificates are available for equities, bonds and warrants. All ownership entitlements (proxies, income, etc.) are delivered to the registered holder.

Bearer certificate A certificate for which no register of holders is maintained. Transfer of the certificates is accomplished by delivery of the certificates. Coupons are attached to income certificates which are detached and presented to the paying agent when due.

Depository receipt Registered certificates representing the deposit of underlying assets (precious metals) or securities (e.g. foreign securities, coupons) with a custodian.

Jumbo certificate Large-denomination certificates representing holdings of a large amount of a securities issue. These certificates result in the reduction of printing and storage costs.

Permanent global certificate A single certificate representing the holding of an entire securities issue.

Book entry security The issue is represented by a permanent global certificate held by a custodian or depository. All transfers are recorded on the books of the custodian or depository and certificates are not available to the holders. This method is used primarily for stripped bonds and coupons. (*See also*: Electronic security.)

Electronic security (book-based security) This issue exists only in electronic form with no certificate in any form available. This method is used for some mutual fund securities, traded options and notes of some financial institutions; this issue is also known as book entry security.

4.2 Types of securities

Equities and warrants

Common share Represents ownership in a corporation and holds voting rights. (Issued in registered form; may be held as a jumbo certificate, depository receipt or in book entry form.)

CLASS share These securities carry a numeric or alpha designation (e.g. CLASS A, B, etc., or CLASS 1, 2, etc.). They represent ownership in a corporation. However, there is no consistency from corporation to corporation for similar classes of securities. The terms of each issue must be read. (Issued in registered form; may be held as jumbo certificate.)

Restricted share   This security contains a variety of restrictions. The terms must be read to determine the restrictions. The most common forms are non-voting, or limited voting (e.g. 1 share = 1/100 vote). (Issued in registered form; may be held as jumbo certificate.)

Preferred share   Share representing ownership in a company to the limit of its stated or par value which normally contains a designated dividend rate usually expressed as a fixed amount or percentage of par value. This share has a prior claim over common shares upon the earnings of the company to the extent of the dividend payment. In the case of liquidation, they usually have a claim on the assets prior to the common shares. Normally voting rights do not exist. Many preferred shares contain special privileges. The terms of each issue must be read. (Issued in registered form; may be held as jumbo certificate.)

Cumulative preferred share   This preferred share retains its right to earnings to the limit of the dividend rate until paid, the amount accumulating each year if not paid. (Issued in registered form; may be held as jumbo certificate.)

Participating preferred share   This share obtains the right to share equally in dividends with the common shares after payment of specified amounts on the preferred and common shares. The participation in earnings is normally limited to dividend payments. (Issued in registered form; may be held as jumbo certificate.)

Convertible preferred share   This share is convertible into other securities, usually common shares, at a designated rate. The conversion may be for a limited duration or for the life of preferred shares. (Issued in registered form; may be held as a jumbo certificate.)

Retractable preferred share   This share permits the holder at specified dates to choose to have the share redeemed at a price usually the par value. (Issued in registered form; may be held as jumbo certificate.)

Redeemable preferred share   This share can be called in by the issuer usually after a specified date in the future for a price usually the par value. (Issued in registered form; may be held as jumbo certificate.)

Unit of participation   Represents an undivided interest in a pool of assets most commonly used for investment funds. Usually has voting rights. (Issued in registered form; may be held as jumbo certificate, depository receipt or in book entry form.)

Warrant   A security which entitles the holder to purchase another security, usually common shares, at a specified price until a date in the future when the right to purchase expires. At the time of issuance of the warrant, the price specified for purchasing the security is above the current market value. (Issued in registered and bearer form; may be held as jumbo certificate.)

Right A security usually issued to a holder of common shares which permits the holder to purchase common shares at a specified price until a date when the right to purchase expires. At the time of issuance of the right, the price specified for purchasing the common shares is less than current market value of the common shares. (Issued in bearer form; may be held as jumbo certificate.)

Unit A combination of more than one equity issue sold and traded as a package, usually a combination of common shares and warrants. The package can be separated after a specified date, usually shortly after the issue of the units. (Issued in bearer or registered form; may be held as jumbo certificate.)

Debt instruments

Bond A fixed-income interest bearing debt security secured by a specific asset or assets. Issued in bearer form with coupons attached or in registered form with no coupons. The coupons represent the interest payments and are detached on due date and presented for payment. (Issued in registered or bearer form; may be held as jumbo certificate.)

Debenture A fixed-income interest bearing debt security secured by the creditworthiness and a general charge against the assets of the issuer. (Issued in bearer or registered form; may be held as jumbo certificate.)

Straight bond or debenture An issue containing no special clauses or privileges and with a stated interest rate payable on stated dates. (Issued in bearer or registered form; may be held as jumbo certificate.)

Convertible bond or debenture An issue which can be exchanged into another security, usually common shares at a prescribed rate and for a specific period. (Issued in bearer or registered form; may be held as jumbo certificate.)

Variable rate bond or debenture An issue whose interest rate is adjusted at regular intervals according to a formula set out in the terms of the issue. (Issued in registered form; may be held as jumbo certificate.)

Federal bond Debt security backed by the full faith and credit of the government of Canada. (Issued in bearer or registered form; may be held as jumbo certificate.)

Provincial and municipal bond or debenture Debt security backed by the full faith and credit of the government. Provincial issues are normally available in either registered or bearer form. (Most municipal issues are available only in bearer form; may be held as jumbo certificate.)

Government guaranteed Issue of Crown corporations guaranteed by a governmental body, usually federal or provincial. (Issued in bearer or registered form; may be held as jumbo certificate.)

Mortgage backed security An issue which represents an interest in a pool of mortgages and which provides a repayment of interest and principal on a regular basis. Most common are NHA (National Housing Act) mortgage backed which pay monthly and are guaranteed by the Central Mortgage and Housing Corporation, a Crown corporation of the government of Canada. (Issued in registered form; may be held as jumbo certificate or in book entry form.)

Residual The principal portion of a bond or debenture from which the interest portion is removed. This security trades as a discount note. (Issued in bearer form; may be held as jumbo certificate or in book entry form.)

Stripped coupon The interest amount due on a bond or debenture for a specific date and which has been separated from the principal portion of the issue. This security trades as a discount note. (Issued in bearer form; may be held in book entry form.)

Units A combination of a debt issue and another security, usually warrants, which are packaged together at the time of issue. The unit can be separated after a specified date usually shortly after issue. (Issued in bearer or registered form; may be held as jumbo certificate.)

Money market instruments

Treasury bill (federal) Short-term obligation of the Canadian federal government. Treasury bills are sold at a discount and are issued with maturities of one year or less with a minimum denomination of CAD 1000. (Issued in bearer form; may be held as jumbo certificate.)

Treasury bill (provincial) Short-term obligation of a Canadian provincial government sold at a discount with a term of three months or less. Denomination of not less than CAD 25 000. (Issued in bearer form; may be held as jumbo certificate.)

Bankers' Acceptance (BA) Bill of exchange accepted by Canadian banks. BAs are discount instruments and bear interest for periods of seven days or longer. They constitute an irrevocable primary obligation of the acceptor banks and a contingent obligation of the drawer and of any endorsers whose names appear upon them. The minimum amount accepted is CAD 100 000; BAs primarily serve to finance imports and exports. (Issued in bearer form.)

Commercial paper Short-term, unsecured promissory note issued by large, creditworthy financial institutions. Interest bearing or on a discount basis. Term is for one day or longer. The minimum amount is CAD 50 000. (Issued in bearer form.)

Certificate of deposit (CD) A negotiable certificate issued against funds deposited in a chartered bank for a definite period of time, earning a specified rate of return. Normally available for periods of one to five months. Minimum amount CAD 10 000. (Issued in bearer form.)

Guaranteed investment certificate Instrument issued and guaranteed by a chartered bank or trust company with a term of one month to five years. The certificate is interest bearing with a principal amount of not less than CAD 1000. (Issued in bearer or registered form.)

Traded options

Equity based Equity-based options, puts and calls, are traded on a standard basis on the Montreal Exchange, the Toronto Stock Exchange and Vancouver Stock Exchange. Expiry dates, exercise, price and terms of trading are established for listed options.

In addition, puts and calls can be traded over-the-counter. These transactions are negotiated case by case as to expiry date, exercise price and quality. There is normally no secondary market.

Index based Options based on the Toronto Stock Exchange 35 Index.

Interest based Options based on issues of Canada Bonds. Expiry dates, exercise price and forms of trading are established by the exchanges.

Commodity based Options based on silver, gold and platinum are traded on the Montreal Exchange and Vancouver Stock Exchange. These options are also traded in Sydney and Amsterdam under IOCC.

Futures

Commodity based Futures contracts on grains are traded on the Winnipeg Commodity Exchange. The contracts are for 20 metric tonnes. The grains traded are wheat, oats, barley, flaxseed and rapeseed. (Issued in book entry form.)

Index based A futures contract on the Toronto Stock Exchange 35 Index is traded on the Toronto Futures Exchange.

Interest rate based A futures contract on Bankers' Acceptances is traded on the Montreal Exchange. The contract size is CAD 1 million.

Others

Precious metal certificate Certificate representing gold, silver or platinum may be purchased and sold. This certificate represents the quantity of precious metal held by the issuing financial institution and can be converted to the metal on demand. (Issued in registered form; can be held as jumbo certificate.)

4.3   Securities Identification Code

Code name and structure

The securities identification system used in Canada is the CUSIP numbering system used in the USA. The CUSIP Service Bureau assigns numbers to most Canadian securities. The exceptions are those issues only of interest to Canadians, primarily municipal debt securities. For these securities, numbers compatible with the CUSIP numbering system are assigned by the Canadian Depository for Securities Ltd.

The number is nine digits, alpha numeric, and is permanently assigned to a single issue. The first six digits represent the issuer, the next two digits represent the issue and the last digit is a check digit.

Example: 077855-10-4 = Bell (CUSIP)

Name and address of organization responsible for the Securities Identification System

The Securities Identification Numbering System for Canada is the responsibility of:

The Canadian Depository for Securities Limited
85 Richmond Street West
Toronto, Ontario M5H 2C9
Canada

4.4   Transfer of ownership

Transfer of bearer securities

Bearer securities payable to bearer or registered securities (endorsed in blank) have no transfer requirements. They are transferred upon voluntary delivery.

Transfer of registered securities

A bona fide purchaser upon delivery of a security obtains all rights in the security free from any adverse claim. The security must be rendered negotiable through endorsement to the purchaser or endorsement in blank.

For securities held in a depository, transfer occurs when the depository reduces the position held in the ledger of the deliverer and increases the position held in the ledger of the receiver.

To effect a transfer of a certificate it must be rendered negotiable and delivered to the transfer agent. The transfer agent will then cancel the certificate and issue a new certificate according to the registration instructions received. The name of the new holder will be recorded on the register. The certificates will be delivered to the new holder or his agent in accordance with the instructions given to the transfer agent.

All ownership rights, including interest or dividend payments, are sent to the new holder who may exercise all the rights and powers of an owner of the security.

5 STRUCTURE AND REGULATION OF FINANCIAL MARKETS

5.1 Structure of financial activities

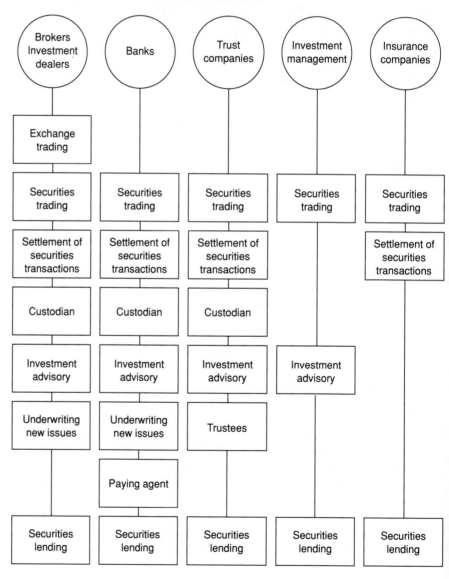

Banks, trust companies and insurance companies may own outright or have a majority interest in other financial institutions.

Currently all major Canadian banks have majority control or outright ownership of a major Canadian investment dealer.

5.2 Regulatory structure

Overview

(a) Federal structure

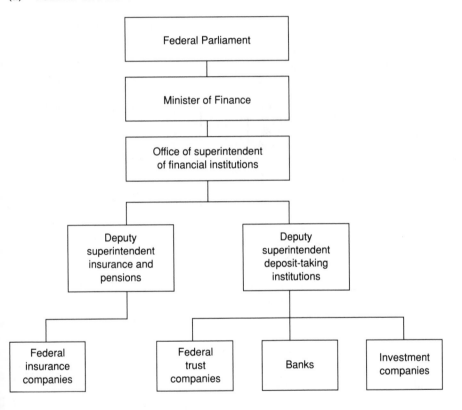

(b) Provincial structure

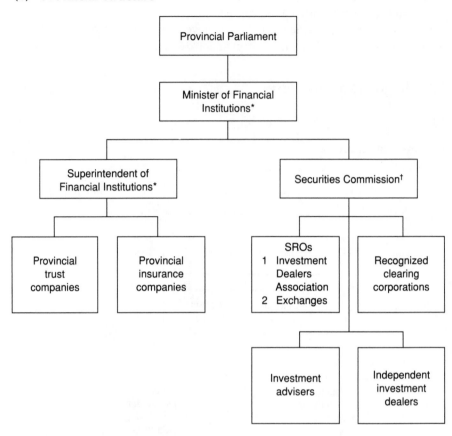

* Title will vary from province to province.
† The provincial securities commissions meet regularly to try to maintain harmonization in the regulations among all provinces.

Responsibility of regulatory bodies

Name of body	Responsibilities	Legal basis
Office of the Superintendent of Financial Institutions (OSFI) (government agency)	Powers by legislation	Financial Institutions and Deposit Insurance Amendment Act of 2 July 1987
	Adjudicatory powers: – regulatory oversight over chartered banks, federally incorporated trust and loan companies, federally incorporated insurance companies, investment companies	

Name of body	Responsibilities	Legal basis
	Powers of enforcement: – investigation of possible violations – compliance orders – prosecutions	
Provincial Securities Commission (government agency)	Powers by: – National policies – Uniform Act policies – Commission policies Adjudicatory powers: – regulatory oversight over Stock Exchange, provincial district of the Investment Dealers Association, clearing agencies, securities dealers, investment advisers – imposing of administrative disciplinary sanctions Powers of enforcement: – investigations of possible violations – prosecutions – compliance orders	Ontario: Securities Act 1987 Quebec: Securities Act 1987 British Columbia: Securities Act 1985 Manitoba: Securities Act 1988 Alberta: Securities Act 1988
Stock exchanges (SROs*): – Toronto Stock Exchange – Montreal Exchange – Vancouver Stock Exchange – Calgary Stock Exchange – Winnipeg Stock Exchange	Powers by: – constitution – by-laws Adjudicatory powers: – regulatory oversight over members and their employees Powers of enforcement: – investigation of possible violations – compliance orders – reprimands, fines, suspensions, expulsions	Recognition by Provincial Securities Commission
Futures exchanges (SROs): – Toronto Futures Exchange – Winnipeg Commodity Exchange	Powers by: – constitution – by-laws	Recognition by Provincial Securities Commission

Name of body	Responsibilities	Legal basis
Investment Dealers Association (SRO)	Adjudicatory powers: – regulatory oversight over members and their employees Powers of enforcement: – investigation of possible violations – compliance orders – reprimands, fines, suspensions, expulsions	Recognition by Provincial Securities Commission

* SRO = self-regulatory organization.

Supervision of stock exchanges

Stock exchanges	Regulator
Toronto	Ontario Securities Commission
Montreal	Quebec Securities Commission
Vancouver	British Columbia Securities Commission
Alberta	Alberta Securities Commission
Winnipeg	Manitoba Securities Commission

Supervision of clearing and central securities depository organizations

Name	Regulator
Canadian Depository for Securities Limited	Ontario Securities Commission Quebec Securities Commission Alberta Securities Commission
West Canada Depository Trust Company	British Columbia Superintendent of Financial Institutions
West Canada Clearing Corporation	British Columbia Securities Commission Alberta Securities Commission
Trans Canada Options	Quebec Securities Commission Ontario Securities Commission British Columbia Securities Commission
Winnipeg Commodity	Canadian Grain Commission monitors but does not regulate

International Options
Clearing Corporation

Quebec Securities Commission
British Columbia Securities Commission

Supervision of broker/dealers and custodian banks

Institution	*Regulator*
Broker/dealers	Stock exchanges Investment Dealers Association Provincial Securities Commissions
Custodian banks	Office of the Superintendent of Financial Institutions

6 CUSTODIANS

Bank of Montreal
PO Box 6002
Place d'Armes
Montreal
Quebec
H2Y 3S8
Canada

Tel: 514 877 7110
Fax: call telephone number for fax

Scotiabank
44 King Street West
Toronto
Ontario
M5H 1H1
Canada

Tel: 416 866 7701
Fax: 416 866 7703

Canada Trust Company
320 Bay Street
Toronto
Ontario
M5J 2T2
Canada

Tel: 416 361 8188
Fax: 416 361 8669

Canadian Imperial Bank of
  Commerce
Commerce Court East
11th floor
Toronto
Ontario
M5L 1A2
Canada

Tel: 416 980 2211
Fax: 416 360 3824

Citibank
123 Front Street West
Toronto
Ontario
M5J 2M3
Canada

Tel: 416 947 5843
Fax: call telephone number for fax

Montreal Trust Company
1800 McGill College Avenue
Montreal
Quebec
H3A 3K9
Canada

Tel: 514 982 7000
Fax: call telephone number for fax

National Bank of Canada
Security Department
150 York Street
Toronto
Ontario
M5H 3A9
Canada

Tel: 416 864 7576
Fax: 416 864 7543

Royal Bank of Canada
12th floor
South Tower
Royal Bank Plaza
Toronto
Ontario
M5J 2J5
Canada

Tel: 416 974 5501
Fax: 416 974 8542

Royal Trust Bank
Royal Trust Tower
Toronto
Ontario
M5W 1P9
Canada

Tel: 416 981 7000
Fax: 416 864 9021

The Toronto-Dominion Bank
PO Box 1
Toronto Dominion Centre
Toronto
Ontario
MSK 1A2
Canada

Tel: 416 982 2302
Fax: 416 982 6041

18 DENMARK

1 PRINCIPAL STOCK EXCHANGE

Kobenhavns Fondsbors
Nikolaj Plads 6
Post Box 1040
DK-1007 Copenhagen
Denmark

Tel: 4533 993 33 66
Telex: 16496 COSTEX DK

2 PRINCIPAL REGULATORY AUTHORITY

The Danish Supervisory Authority of Financial Affairs
Gl. Kongevej 74A
1850 Frederiksberg C
Denmark

Tel: 5 31 231 188
Telex: 55 19457 (TILSYN DK)
Fax: 5 31 230 441

3 TIME DIFFERENCE FROM GMT: +1 HOUR

4 FORMS AND TYPES OF SECURITIES

4.1 Forms of securities

Book entry security (**Edb-registreret vaerdipapir**)   Security that is not represented by a certificate (dematerialized security). The title-holder of the rights
incorporated in the security is evidenced by a mere record in an accounting
system. Transfer of dematerialized securities is effected by debits and credits,
without physical movement of certificates. Today, all Danish shares, bonds
and investment certificates listed on the Copenhagen Stock Exchange, except

a few foreign securities listed in Copenhagen and premium bonds, are registered electronically at the Danish Securities Centre Vaerdipapircentralen (VP). Generally, Danish Stock Exchange listed shares are issued to bearer but a company's Articles of Association may require registration. A shareholder can always arrange for registration of his shares. This is done through the bank where he maintains his account and is effected via the system of the Danish Securities Centre. Danish listed bonds are bearer securities.

4.2 Types of securities

Equities and warrants

Share (**Aktie**) Security representing a participation in a company. Shares issued by a certain company may differ with respect to the voting right – e.g. the voting right attached to a preference share or B-share may be only one-tenth of the voting right of the ordinary share, which is the maximum difference allowed by law. (However, issue of bonus shares in existing series originally issued without voting right is allowed.)

Bearer share (**Ihaendehaver Aktie**) Most of the shares quoted on the Copenhagen Stock Exchange are issued as bearer shares. In order to vote, however, the shares must be registered in the holder's name. The name of the holder of the share is registered through VP (the Danish Securities Centre) and transmitted to the company's register of shareholders.

Registered share (**Navne-aktie**) A few companies issue registered shares only.

Preference share (**Praeference Aktie**) The preference attached to these shares may vary from company to company, and may e.g. consist in the right to receive dividends prior to other shareholders, possibly on a cumulative basis. In the event of a winding up, holders of preference shares may also have the right to receive cover prior to the holders of ordinary shares. Holders of preference shares, however, may have no or only a reduced voting right.

B-share (**B-aktie**) A B-share usually carries only one-tenth of the votes conferred by an A-share of the same nominal value. B-shares are widely used, for instance, in connection with share capital increases associated with stock exchange listings.

Trust unit (**Investeringsbevis**) There are two types of open-end investment companies:

- the accumulating unit trusts employ the profit realized (after taxation)
- the dividend-paying unit trusts pay out the dividends, interest earned and net realized gains on shares owned less than three years.

The first type is subject to a 50% tax on its profits. The second is exempt from taxation.

Subscription and bonus right (**Tegningsret or Aktieret**)   Right of a share-holder to subscribe for or receive new shares when a company increases its capital. The number of shares to which a shareholder is entitled depends on his holding at the time of increase of the capital. Rights can normally be traded on the stock exchange during the subscription period, normally a period of approximately 14 days, and trading is commenced three business days before the subscription period starts.

The nominal value of a subscription right or a bonus right does not ne-cessarily correspond to the nominal amount of shares to be subscribed for or received free of charge. If, for example, the share capital is increased by 25% with preferential subscription right to the shareholders, a shareholder with a subscription right of nominal DKK 4000 is entitled to subscribe for nominal DKK 1000 new shares.

Warrants (**Warrants**)   The Danish warrants market has grown rapidly over the past few years. In many cases, foreign banks have issued warrants on both Danish and foreign shares on the Copenhagen Stock Exchange. At present, warrants are available on the following Danish shares: Danisco, Novo-Nordisk B, Hafnia Holding, Accumulator Invest, the EAC and a basket of shares consisting of Novo Nordisk B, ISS B, J. Lauritzen Holding B and Hafnia Holding B. In addition, a warrant has just been introduced on the German DAX index. The bulk of these warrants are so-called 'covered warrants' or warrants with financial settlement, and so differ from conventional warrants. All warrants are subject to settlement and redemption rules specific to indi-vidual papers.

Debt instruments

Bond (**Obligation**)   Fixed-income, interest-bearing securities. By far the greater part of the bonds are issued by the Danish government and by a number of mortgage credit institutions which operate under the supervision of the Supervision of Mortgage Credit Institutions, which is a part of the Danish Supervisory Authority of Financial Affairs, an independent body under the Ministry of Industry. Nearly all bonds are issued as tap issues on a dis-count basis.

Government bond (**Statsobligation**)   Danish government bonds are issued either as fixed loans or serial loans with maturities of five to 20 years, mainly with maturities up to ten years. The government issues bonds with both fixed and floating interest rates. Interest on the fixed-rate bonds is paid annually, while interest on the floating-rate bonds is paid four times a year. Govern-ment loans issued as serial loans with a period of grace are redeemed at par in groups of equal size, and the cash flow is therefore predictable. Normally, drawing of a group for redemption takes place once a year three months before payment date.

The fixed government loans are bullet loans redeemable at par.

The issuance of floating rate bonds began in 1984. The coupon rate is computed on the basis of the average yield on government bills and bonds with a remaining maturity of more than three months and less than three years. The average yield is calculated based on a period running from six months and ten days before the coupon date to three months and ten days before the coupon date. The floating rate bonds are issued with maturities of five and ten years.

Mortgage bond (**Realkreditobligation**)   Up to 1971 the greater part of the mortgage bonds were issued by some 25 mortgage institutions. Following mergers, there are now three major institutions which offer mortgages on residential as well as agricultural, commercial and industrial property.

The three major institutions are:

• BRFkredit A/S, formerly Byggeriets Realkreditfond – The Housing Mortgage Fund
• Kreditforeningen Danmark – The Mortgage Credit Association Denmark
• Nykredit – The New Danish Credit Association.

The Mortgage Credit Association Denmark and Nykredit, the Danish Mortgage Credit Association, are organized as associations of those borrowers who have obtained a mortgage from these institutions. BRFkredit A/S, on the other hand, is a limited liability company. The lending activities of the mortgage credit institutions are strictly regulated by law and supervised by the Supervision of Mortgage Credit Institutions. The Mortgage Credit Act with supplementary ministerial decrees lays down provisions for the maximum amount and the currency of the mortgages. The activities of the mortgage institutions are to take mortgage charges on property, to receive interest and instalments from owners of mortgaged property, to issue bonds for an amount corresponding to that of the mortgages, and to pay interest and instalments to bondholders. The institutions do not accept deposits. Annual outgoing payments must not exceed ingoing payments by more than 1% of the institution's funds.

The bonds are issued at market prices in series kept open from one to three years. The closing of a series means that no more bonds are issued in that particular series. This, however, does not affect the trade or liquidity in the series provided the outstanding amount is sufficiently large. The market for daily quoted bonds comprised more than 2000 series at the end of 1990. They differ from one another with respect to issuer, coupon and maturity.

In addition to mortgage on property (up to 80% of the value), the mortgage institutions also have substantial reserve funds in support of the circulating bonds.

Overall, Danish mortgage bonds enjoy a high credit rating. So far, no series has been in default.

With a few exceptions, the bonds are issued to maturities of 10, 20 or 30 years and the coupons are payable two or four times a year. The majority of mortgage credit bonds are callable at par value. Due to cost of carry calls are not, in practice, made until prices exceed 102%. With a very few exceptions, bonds are redeemed at par value. Payments under bond loans are effected by drawing bonds to a nominal value corresponding to payments due from the debtors. Bond loans are issued as annuity or serial loans.

Four specialized institutions issue bonds based on mortgages on specific types of assets: ships, municipal property, industrial and agricultural property. These institutions are:

(1)   Danmarks Skibskreditfond (Ship Credit Fund of Denmark)
This institution grants loans against ship mortgages on terms agreed upon among OECD countries. A guarantee capital has been subscribed by the Danish Central Bank, private banks, insurance companies and others. The activities of the Fund are supervised by the Ministry of Industry. The bonds are issued in series to mature after one to 14 years. Each series is fully redeemed on 1 December in the year given as its maturity year. Thus the cash flow and yield from a portfolio of ship credit bonds are fully predictable. Semi-annual payments of coupons.

Danish owners ordering ships from Danish yards may be granted index-linked loans with a coupon of 2.5% or 4% per annum.

(2)   Kreditforeningen af Kommuner i Danmark (Credit Association of Local Authorities in Denmark)
This Association mainly offers loans to municipalities against such security as is based on the municipalities' authority to levy taxes. These bonds are issued as serial loans – i.e. with equal semi-annual instalments within each series, or as annuity loans. The Association issues index-linked bonds to a limited extent.

(3)   Dansk Landbrugs Realkreditfond (Mortgage Credit Fund of Danish Agriculture)
This mortgage credit institution issues bonds against secondary mortgages on agricultural property. The bonds are further secured by a guarantee capital subscribed by the Danish Central Bank, private banks and others. The activities of the institution are supervised by the Ministry of Agriculture. The bonds are usually uncallable serial loans with fixed semi-annual coupons. Index-linked bonds are also issued.

(4)   IRF Industrifinansiering A/S, formerly Industriens Realkreditfond (Industrial Mortgage Credit Fund)
This institution issues bonds against mortgages on industrial property. The bonds are further secured by a guarantee capital subscribed by the Danish Central Bank, private banks and others. The activities of the Industrial Mortgage Credit Fund are supervised by the Supervision of Mortgage Credit Institutions.

It should be pointed out that the volume and turnover of bonds of a number of closed series of the specialized institutions may be very limited. Even small deals may affect the prices considerably.

Index-linked bonds   The major issuers are the mortgage credit institutions and the Ship Credit Fund of Denmark. Index-linked bonds carry interest of

2.5% or 4% per annum payable semi-annually. The amount outstanding is adjusted twice a year in step with the price index. The life of ship credit index-linked bonds is 14 years, and the bonds are redeemed as serial loans after a grace period of four years. The life of index-linked mortgage credit bonds is up to 35 years in the case of an annual inflation rate exceeding 17% and can be as short as 21 years at zero inflation rate.

Private mortgage deed (**Pantebrev**)   Financing real property can be done through a Mortgage Credit Institution. Owner dwellings must be financed by a mixture of annuity and serial loans of up to 80% of the value of the property. The rest is provided partly through the down payment, and partly through mortgage deeds secured upon the property, issued by the buyer to the seller, who may either keep or sell them. These securities are unlisted, but there exists a well-organized market for private mortgage deeds. Bank loans secured on real property are an additional possibility.

Convertible bond (**Konvertibel Obligation**)   Bonds that may be exchanged for shares in accordance with the terms of the issue.

Premium bond (**Praemieobligation**)   A fixed loan on which no interest is paid to the bond owners. Instead the interest is paid into a pool, split up into premiums the amount of which varies a good deal, and the pool is then distributed by lottery among the bond owners. At maturity the bonds are redeemed at par.

Money market instruments

Treasury note (**Statsgaeldsbevis**)   Treasury notes are issued on a tap basis for periods of two years and are traded on a discount basis. Treasury notes are the most liquid form of short-term investments.

Certificate of deposit (**Indlansbevis**)   Negotiable claim issued by a bank in return for a short- to medium-term deposit, usually one to twelve months. These instruments exist to a limited extent, but there is no secondary market.

Treasury bill (**Skatkammerbevis**)   Treasury bills are discount securities sold at a price below par and redeemed at par at maturity. Treasury bills with maturities of three and six months are issued. Treasury bills are sold by auction. The Ministry of Finance may, however, sell additional Treasury bills to the Central Bank for resale to the market. Treasury bills are negotiable securities and are listed on the Copenhagen Stock Exchange. The bills are quoted on the basis of the price per DKK 1 million.

Futures and options

The Danish futures and options market has been growing steadily over past years and is still expanding. The Guarantee Fund for Danish Options and Futures carries the day-to-day responsibility for the organized futures and option market in Denmark and provides a guarantee for all contracts registered by the member companies (all important broker companies). A fee is charged by the Fund to register a contract, and a margin is required for all futures contracts and all sold option contracts.

All the instruments are financial, i.e. there is no physical delivery of the underlying assets, and all settlements are cash settlements.

(a) Futures

At present, three futures contracts are traded in the Danish market: futures on 9% mortgage bond 2006; futures on 9% state bullet bond 2000; and futures on the KFX stock index.

Futures on 9% mortgage bullet bond 2006 are issued with three, six and nine months of maturity with expiration dates on the first business day in January, April, July and October. The individual contracts are for DKK 1 million. The initial margin payment is 4%.

Futures on 9% state bullet bond 2000 are currently issued with three and six months of maturity, with the possibility of a later opening for contracts with a maturity of nine months. The expiration dates are the third business day in March, June, September and December. The individual contracts are for DKK 1 million and the initial margin payment is 4%.

Futures on the KFX index are futures on a stock index composed of the 25 most traded shares on the Danish stock market – excluding the shares of companies whose primary purpose is to hold shares. The index is updated every quarter on the same date as the contracts expire. One month before the expiration date of a contract, the new index will be announced by the Copenhagen Stock Exchange. In the period of one year before the announcement of a new composition of the index, the 40 most traded shares will be listed daily by the Copenhagen Stock Exchange. The 25 shares which have figured most frequently on the list during the period will become the new KFX index. The settlement index price will be corrected in the case of new issues in the underlying securities, mergers, etc. during the lifetime of a contract – the only exception is in case of dividend payments. One contract is for DKK 100 000 and the initial margin payment is 10%.

(b) Options

Only options of the European type are traded on the Copenhagen Stock Exchange.

Call and put options are traded on the bond futures and the stock index futures. The sizes of the contracts and the expiration dates are the same as for the underlying futures. Selling options requires both an initial and a maintenance margin.

It is further possible to trade options on individual shares in the Danish market. At present, it is possible to trade in options on shares in Den Danske Bank, Unidanmark, the East Asiatic Company, Danisco, Novo Nordisk and Hafnia Holding. The maturities of the options are currently three and six months, with the possibility of opening for contracts with a maturity of nine months. The expiration dates are the first business days in March, June, September and December.

4.3 Securities Identification Code

Code name and structure

Denmark uses a uniform securities code (Fondskode) consisting of seven digits.

Example: 093 1203   Kreditforeningen Danmark 9% 2006
          100 0020   Share of Den Danske Bank

The first digit indicates the type of security:

0 = bond
1 = equity
2 = future/option

Digits two to six form a serial number (digits two and three are used to identify the bond issuers). Digit seven is a check-digit.

The ISIN numbering system was introduced into the VP system on a stepwise basis, starting in August 1991. The first step will include assignment and publication of ISIN for all securities. ISIN will be published on equal terms with NSIN in the Danish lists of security identification numbers.

Numbering agency

The organization responsible for the Securities Identification System is:

Vaerdipapircentralen
(The Danish Securities Centre)
Helgeshoj Alle 61
DK-2630 Taastrup

Tel: 45 42 999 666

Each stock exchange listed security has been assigned a seven-digit number along the lines above. The numbering system is maintained in cooperation with the Danish Securities Centre by the Copenhagen Stock Exchange:

Kobenhavns Fondsbors
Nikolaj Plads 6
Postbox 1040
DK-1007 Kobenhavn K

Tel: 45 33 93 33 66

Unlisted shares and bonds may also be assigned a seven-digit number, the system being maintained by the Danish Securities Centre (for address see above).

4.4 Transfer of ownership

Transfer of bearer issues

Since quoted physical securities no longer exist, except for foreign companies listed in Copenhagen, transfers are effected by means of electronic registrations in the Danish Securities Centre (VP) – i.e. through a transfer from seller's to buyer's VP-account. Bonds exist solely as 'bearer issues'.

Transfer of registered issues

The transfer message to VP is marked to the effect that the company's registrar is advised automatically that the seller is no longer the owner of the registered holding and indicates the buyer's identity.

5   STRUCTURE AND REGULATION OF FINANCIAL MARKETS

5.1   Structure of financial activities

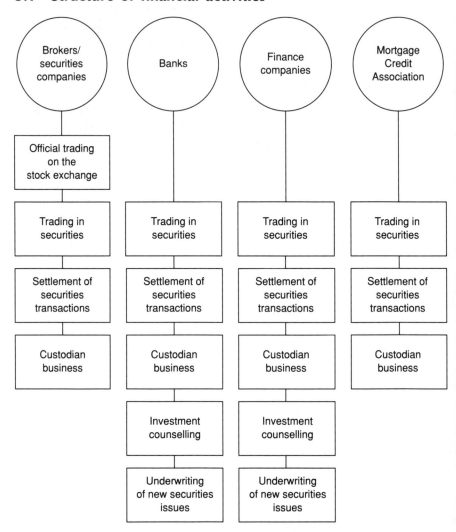

In 1987 an electronic trading system was introduced on the Copenhagen Stock Exchange and the 28 authorized broking firms lost their sole right to trade at the beginning of 1989. Denmark's larger banks and savings banks have bought existing broking firms or set up their own subsidiaries. The new firms' (Boersmaeglerselskaber) activities comprise brokerage of securities, investment advising and issue of securities.

Trading in guaranteed options and futures contracts quoted on the stock exchange was introduced in September 1988. The Guarantee Fund for Danish Options and Futures was set up to guarantee contracts entered into.

5.2 Regulatory structure of financial markets

Overview

(a) Ordinary banking business

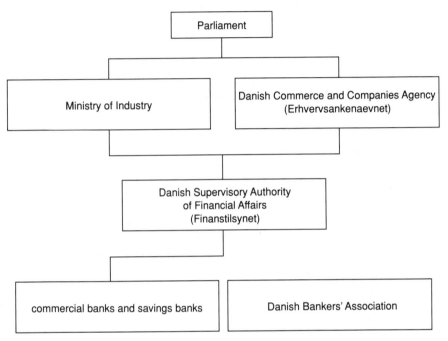

(b) Monetary and foreign exchange operations

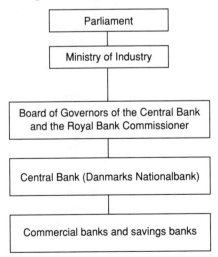

(c)   Stock exchange/stockbroking companies

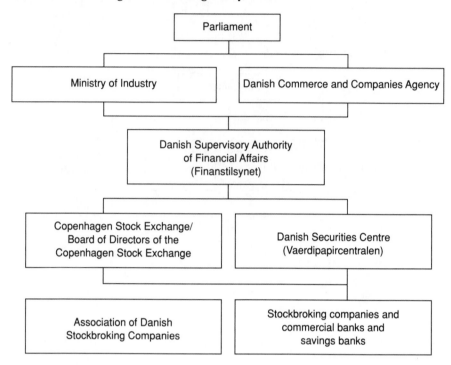

Responsibility of regulatory bodies

(a)   Ordinary banking business

Name of body	Tasks/responsibilities
Parliament	Setting out the legislative basis (i.e. the rules set forth in): (a) the Commercial Bank and Savings Banks Act of 2 April 1974 as last amended in May 1990 (the Bank Act); (b) the Companies Act of 13 June 1973 as last amended April 1991; and (c) the Commerce and Companies Act of 23 December 1987
Ministry of Industry	Administration of the Bank and the Companies Act and the Commerce and Companies Agency Act. Holds legislative initiative
Danish Commerce and Companies Agency (Erhvervsankenaevnet)	Independent public institution. Acts on complaints of the administrative decisions of the Danish Supervisory Authority of Financial Affairs and tries these independently according to the Bank and Companies Act

Name of body	Tasks/responsibilities
Danish Supervisory Authority of Financial Affairs (Finanstilsynet)	Enforcing the Bank and Companies Act concerning banks and savings banks mainly through the following instruments: (a) supervision of the capital requirements of banks and saving banks as set out in the Bank Act; (b) approval of the business of banks and savings banks; (c) supervision of management and owner representation of banks and savings banks; and (d) approval of the annual yearly accounts of banks and savings banks
Danish Bankers' Association	Independent private organization with no formal legal status acting in a professional capacity concerning new legislation and other regulatory Acts
Commercial banks and savings banks	According to the Banking Act, only banks and savings banks can conduct banking business, such business being defined as: 'Banking institution activities are understood as being the performance of functions relating to transactions of money, instruments of money, instruments of credit and securities and the services involved and the participation in reconstruction of commercial business enterprises. Business banks and savings banks are allowed to conduct insurance activities and offer credit secured by mortgage on real property in subsidiary companies.'

(b) Monetary and foreign exchange operations

Name of body	Tasks/responsibilities
Parliament	Setting out legislative basis – i.e. (a) Central Bank Act of 13 April 1938 with subsequent amendments; and (b) Foreign Exchange Transactions Act of 11 April 1988
Ministry of Industry	Administration of the Central Bank Act and the Foreign Exchange Transactions Act. Enforcement of these Acts by separate regulations. May regulate the import and export of goods and payments

Name of body	Tasks/responsibilities
Board of Governors/the Royal Bank Commissioner	The Central Bank is an independent institution and responsible for ensuring a sound financial system and the orderly supply of credit. Important decisions on monetary policy are made after consultation with the Board of Governors of the Central Bank and the Royal Bank Commissioner. The Central Bank exercises a continuous control over the banks' compliance with the foreign exchange regulations. In addition, it holds the gold and foreign currency reserves of the Kingdom of Denmark
Central Bank (Danmarks Nationalbank)	The most important instruments of monetary policy available to the Central Bank are (a) the official discount rate, (b) open market operations, (c) voluntary agreements with the financial institutions, (d) the borrowing rate on certificates of deposit, (e) the interest rate paid on special deposits of the financial institutions with the Central Bank and (f) intervention in the money market
Commercial banks and savings banks	The regulatory powers of the Central Bank involve stand-by measures which can be implemented if lending and bond purchases by the banks and savings banks grow too sharply. The system stipulates marginal reserve requirements related to bank liabilities

(c) Stock exchange and stockbroking companies

Name of body	Tasks/responsibilities
Parliament	Setting out the legislative basis – i.e. (a) Stock Exchange Act of 8 September 1988; (b) Securities Centre Act of 16 January 1991; and (c) Commerce and Companies Agency Act of 23 August 1987
Ministry of Industry	Administration of Stock Exchange Act and Danish Securities Centre Act. Holds legislative initiative. Enforcement of the Stock Exchange Act with regulations of (a) the organization and activities of the

Name of body	Tasks/responsibilities
	Stock Exchange; (b) the rights, obligations and capital requirements of the stockbroking companies; and (c) the terms of trade on the stock exchange
Danish Commerce and Companies Agency	Independent public institution. Acts on complaints and tries the administrative decisions of the Danish Supervisory Authority of Financial Affairs, the Board of Directors of Copenhagen Stock Exchange, the Copenhagen Stock Exchange and the Danish Securities Centre independently according to the relevant Acts mentioned above
Danish Supervisory Authority of Financial Affairs	Supervision of the activities of the Copenhagen Stock Exchange, the Securities Centre, the banks and the Stock Broking Companies Act according to the relevant acts mentioned above
Copenhagen Stock Exchange	The Copenhagen Stock Exchange is an independent institution and holds a monopoly on (a) matching bids and sales offers on securities to public trade and quotations; (b) operating the necessary trade systems; (c) operating a public information system and publishing the quotations and transactions; and (d) issuing regulations
Board of Directors of the Copenhagen Stock Exchange	The members of the Board of Directors of the Copenhagen Stock Exchange are nominated by various financial organizations and are appointed by the Minister of Industry, and the Board holds the overall responsibility of the activities of the Copenhagen Stock Exchange
Guarantee Fund for Danish Options and Futures	Non-profit-making, private-owned fund with the primary objectives to guarantee, clear and settle futures and options listed on the Copenhagen Stock Exchange
Board of Directors of the Guarantee Fund for Danish Options and Futures	The Minister of Industry appoints the chairman. Danmarks Nationalbank (the Danish Central Bank) and the Copenhagen Stock Exchange appoint

Name of body	Tasks/responsibilities
	one member each. The Danish Bankers' Association and the Association of Danish Stockbroking Companies appoint two members each. The Danish Securities Centre appoints one observer
Danish Securities Centre (Vaerdipapircentralen)	Independent clearing institution with the primary task of registering trades of the securities which are quoted on the Copenhagen Stock Exchange. The registration constitutes the legal transfer of title. The computerized registration of securities has to a great extent replaced the existence of physical certificates as bearer of rights and obligations of the registered securities
Association of Danish Stockbroking Companies	Independent private organization with no formal legal status acting in a professional capacity concerning new legislation and other regulatory Acts
Stockbroking companies	The stockbroking companies and the Central Bank have the exclusive right to participate in deals on the Copenhagen Stock Exchange. Stockbroking companies are only authorized to perform ordinary stock exchange transactions, which besides stock exchange dealings mainly consist of the management of securities portfolios, the undertaking of stock exchange introductions and investment advising
	Stockbroking companies must not have subsidiaries. However, it is permitted that a company be established as a subsidiary where the parent company is e.g. a bank or another financial institution with a special authorization from the Danish Supervisory Authority of Financial Affairs

Supervision of ordinary banking business

Independent public institution: Danish Commerce and Companies Agency (complaints of the Financial Supervisory Authority).

Government body: Danish Supervisory Authority of Financial Affairs (day-to-day operations).

Supervision of monetary and foreign exchange transactions

Independent institution:
(a) Board of Governors and the Royal Bank Commissioner (policy and principal matters).
(b) Central Bank (Danmarks Nationalbank) (day-to-day operations).

Supervision of Copenhagen Stock Exchange

Independent public institution: Danish Commerce and Companies Agency.

Government body: Danish Supervisory Authority of Financial Affairs (day-to-day operations).

6   CUSTODIANS

Christiania Bank og Kreditkasse
Studiestraede 38
1455
Copenhagen K
Denmark

Tel: 1 93 60 02
Fax: call telephone number for fax

Den Danske Bank
2–12 Holmens Kanal
1092 Copenhagen K
Denmark

Tel: 1 33 44 00 00
Fax: 1 42 29 01 46

Unibank
Safe Custody Services
1786 Copenhagen V
Denmark

Tel: 1 33 33 33 33
Fax: 1 33 13 53 45

19 EIRE (REPUBLIC OF IRELAND)

☞ ## 1 PRINCIPAL STOCK EXCHANGE

Irish Stock Exchange
28 Anglesea Street
Dublin 2
Eire

Tel: 353 1 77 88 08
Telex: 93437

Note: The Irish Stock Exchange is part of the International Stock Exchange of the United Kingdom and the Republic of Ireland.

☞ ## 2 PRINCIPAL REGULATORY AUTHORITY

The regulation of the Irish securities industry is currently in a process of change. At the end of 1991 the Irish government finalized a proposal for a new regulatory framework for the securities industry. This proposal will involve the Central Bank of Ireland acting as the principal regulator for the investment sector and securities trading sector. It is likely that this new regulatory framework will be in place by the end of 1992.

Contact details for the Central Bank of Ireland are as follows:

Central Bank of Ireland
Dame Street
Dublin 2
Eire

Tel: 353 1 716666
Telex: 31041
Fax: 353 1 716561

3 TIME DIFFERENCE FROM GMT: NONE (BUT, AS IN THE UK, CLOCKS GO FORWARD 1 HOUR IN THE SPRING AND BACK 1 HOUR IN THE AUTUMN FOR SUMMER TIME).

4   FORMS AND TYPES OF SECURITIES

[*see United Kingdom*]

Note: As a constituent element of the International Stock Exchange, the Irish Stock Exchange shares all its systems and services with the UK's International Stock Exchange.

However, the Irish Stock Exchange operates its own gilts market and a gilts CSD in the form of the Irish Gilts Settlement Office.

5   STRUCTURE AND REGULATION OF FINANCIAL MARKETS

[*see United Kingdom*]

6   CUSTODIANS

AIB Custodial Services Limited
AIB International Centre
IFSC
Dublin 1
Eire

Tel: 353 1 740222
Fax: 353 1 741975

Bank of Ireland
Lower Baggot Street
Dublin 2
Eire

Tel: 353 1 615933
Fax: 353 1 762402

20 FINLAND

☞ ## 1   PRINCIPAL STOCK EXCHANGE

Helsinki Stock Exchange
Fabianinkatu 14
PO Box 361
SF-00131 Helsinki
Finland

Tel: 358 0 173301
Telex: 123460 HESE SF

☞ ## 2   PRINCIPAL REGULATORY AUTHORITY

Banking Supervision of Finland
Ratapihantie 9
00520 Helsinki
Finland

Tel: 358 0 159 931
Fax: 358 0 159 3681

🕐 ## 3   TIME DIFFERENCE FROM GMT: +2 HOURS

4   FORMS AND TYPES OF SECURITIES

4.1   Forms of securities

Bearer certificate **(Haltijapaperi)**   Negotiable security entitling the bearer to all its rights (*see also*: 'Equities and Warrants').

Registered certificate **(Rekisteröity)**   The name of the owner of the security is registered in the company's register (*see also*: 'Debt instruments').

Depository receipt **(Talletustodistus)**   Receipt issued by a bank in the form of a certificate representing and based on underlying original securities.

Book entry security A security that has been dematerialized (i.e. that is in book entry form). All rights, for example subscription rights, dividend and interest rate coupons, related to book entry securities are also dematerialized.

4.2 Types of securities

Equities and warrants

Equities **(Osake)** In Finland shares are issued in registered form. All shares carry a nominal value. A share certificate comprises one or more shares, dividend coupons and share issue coupons. Share certificates are usually for one, five, ten, 100, 500, 1000, 10 000 or 100 000 shares. On a liquidation all shares rank *pari passu* in any surplus of assets unless otherwise specifically provided in the Articles of Association of the company concerned. Most companies have two or several share series. Share series differ from one another in respect of voting power but may also carry different rights to dividend. Shares carrying less voting power may carry preference rights to a minimum dividend before shares carrying maximum voting power. All share series of a listed company are not necessarily quoted on the Helsinki Stock Exchange (HSE) (*see*: 'Transfer of ownership').

Ordinary share **(Kantaosake)** Ordinary shares usually carry greater voting power than preference shares. Under Finnish law no share may carry more than 20 times the voting power of another share. Dividend on ordinary shares is, however, usually paid only after payment of the minimum dividend on preference shares or the dividend paid on ordinary shares differs from that on preference shares.

Preference share **(Etuoikeutettu osake)** Share with preference rights with regard to dividend payment. There are both restricted and non-restricted preference shares. (Issued in registered form.)

Restricted share **(Sidottu osake)** Restricted shares may be purchased by Finnish residents only.

Non-restricted share **(Vapaa osake)** Non-restricted (free) shares may be purchased or transferred to both residents and non-residents. Non-restricted shares may account for a maximum of 40% of a company's share capital and 20% of the votes.

Interim certificate **(Väliaikaistodistus)** An interim certificate is given in a new issue and is exchanged for a share certificate on a specified date. An interim certificate is comparable to a share certificate, except in respect of rights (voting and dividend rights). The interim certificate is negotiable on the HSE, but quoted separately if it does not carry the same rights as the corresponding old shares. It is also transferable. Quotation of such certificates normally ends after the date of payment has expired. (Issued in registered form.)

New share **(Uusi osake)**   Even if an interim certificate has been exchanged for a share certificate, the new share's rights may still differ from those of old shares, usually until the next AGM, and it is therefore quoted separately. (Issued in registered form.)

Subscription right coupons **(Merkintäoikeus)**   Subscription rights are negotiable instruments separately quoted on the HSE during the issue period. Quoting is discontinued five days prior to the end of an issue period. Subscription rights are also simultaneously sold in small amounts over-the-counter in many banks during an issue period. (Issued in bearer form.)

Mutual fund unit **(Sijoitusrahasto-osuus)**   Unit evidencing participation in a mutual fund (unit trust) in which investors pool their capital for joint investment. The assets are held and managed by a special management company in account of the investors. In Finland only open-end mutual funds are allowed. They issue new units continuously and are obliged to redeem shares at net asset value. Fund units sold in Finland may be purchased by only Finnish residents without restriction. This restriction is expected to be abolished in early 1992. (Issued in registered form.)

Closed mutual fund share **(Sijoitusyhtiön osake)**   Share of a fund or company that invests its fixed capital in securities and its units are quoted as shares on the Helsinki Stock Exchange. Their units are instruments with coupons. A closed-end fund is composed largely of equities, bonds, debentures and other domestic securities quoted on the HSE and owned jointly by the persons or institutions which have invested in it. For residents only. This restriction is expected to be abolished. (Issued in registered form.)

Warrant **(Optiotodistus merkintäotio)**   In bonds with equity warrants the promissory note is accompanied by a detachable certificate which entitles the owner to subscribe for the shares of the issuing company during a certain period. (Issued in bearer form.)

Debt instruments

Bond **(Joukkovelkakirjalaina)**   Bonds are issued by the state or private institutions. Bonds and debentures.

Bond loan **(Obligaatio)**   A bond, issued by the state, town, parish, financial institution or company. Issuers other than the state or municipalities are required to put up security. Government bonds are straight or floating-rate bonds. Rates on new issues have been linked to base rate (Bank of Finland) or HELIBOR (Helsinki Inter-bank Offered Rate), the average of the Certificate of Deposit (CD) call prices quoted by the five major banks. The bonds include coupons which entitle the holder to interest. (Issued in bearer form.)

Mortgage bank bond **(Kiinnitys luottolaitoslaina)**   Normally a straight or floating-rate bond issued by privately owned mortgage banks. Similar to government bonds. (Issued in bearer form.)

FIM bond **(Jvk, joukkovelkakirjalaina)**   A bond with annual coupon payment. Denominated in Finnmark (FIM), interest rates, either fixed or floating, being linked to the HELIBOR-rate. The FIM bonds are negotiable bearer instruments. Domestic bonds are kept in vaults with Finnish banks. Most new issues are also accepted by Euroclear or Cedel.

Other bonds **(Muut joukkovelkakirjalainat)**   Other listed bonds are straight of floating rate and comprise corporate, municipal, city, parish and other public issues. Security may be posted for these issues. (Issued in bearer form.)

Debenture **(Debentuuri)**   Subordinated loan (vastuudebentuuri); unsubordinated debenture (luottodebentuuri).

Debentures are unsecured loans. The difference between the two kinds of loan lies in the fact that a subordinated debenture is subordinated to other commitments in the event of the issuer's bankruptcy. Unsubordinated debentures carry the same rights as the issuer's other commitments. (Issued in bearer form.)

Convertible bond **(Vaihtovelkakirjalaina)**   A bond which carries the right to convert part or all of the loan amount into shares of the issuing company. In a convertible bond loan, the loan may not be separated from the conversion right. The loan's rate of interest is frequently below market rate. The redemption sale right, if any, permits the investor to sell the loan back to the issuing company within a specified period and at a specified price. Convertible bonds are quoted on the HSE. (Issued in bearer form.)

Bond with warrant (into equity) **(Optiolaina)**   A bond loan with equity warrants is a bond and subscription right loan issued by a limited company for a specified period. The loan carries warrants allowing the holder to subscribe for shares of the issuing company at a specified price. In addition to interest yield, a bond loan with warrants entitles the holder to subscribe for new shares at the subscription price indicated in the loan terms. The bond and the warrant are separate instruments. They may be quoted separately or jointly.

Money market instruments

Certificate of Deposit (CD) **(Sijoitustodistus)**   A certificate usually with a lifetime of up to 12 months issued by a bank. Quoted daily (on Reuters). A pure discount note with a zero coupon issued in bearer form. Private persons cannot buy CDs. The minimum amount is FIM 1 000 000.

Commercial paper **(Yritystodistus)**   A commercial paper is a negotiable note issued usually by large companies for corporate financing, similar to a certificate of deposit. The company concludes a commercial paper programme with a bank. The maturity is up to 12 months.

Municipal paper (**Kuntatodistus**)   Used for municipal financing, identical with the commercial paper. (Issued in registered form.)

Treasury bill (**VVS, Valtion Velkasitoumus**)   A short-term zero coupon certificate of deposit issued by the government.

Traded options

Option (**Option**)   A right but not an obligation to buy/sell underlying securities under certain conditions.

Index based (**Indeksioptio**)   Put and call options related to a stock index.

Currency based (**Valuuttaoptio**)   Put and call options related to the exchange rate of a currency.

Futures

Futures (**Termiini**)   An agreement to buy/sell underlying securities at a fixed price at a fixed time.

Equity Based (**Osaketermiini**)   Future related to a specific stock series.

Index Based (**Indeksitermiini**)   Future related to a specific stock index.

Currency Based (**Valuuttatermiini**)   Put and call options related to the exchange rate of a currency.

4.3   Securities Identification Code

Code name and structure

The Helsinki Stock Exchange uses the ISIN identification number as securities identification code.
   The ISIN code consists of 12 characters:

characters 1 and 2:   FI for Finland (country code)
characters 3–11:   decided by HSE
character 12:   check digit number

Example of security code:

Security: Enso Gutzeit, serie R, non-restricted
Code: FI009000350

The ISIN-code will be used as identification code in the book entry system.

Authorized ISIN numbering agency in Finland

The Helsinki Stock Exchange
PO Box 361
SF-00131 Helsinki
Finland

4.4 Transfer of ownership

Transfer of bearer securities

Ownership of bearer securities is transferred by physical delivery of the certificate. In the coming book entry system all owners of shares in book entry form will automatically be registered in the list of owners kept by the Central Share Register. These lists of owners are public. Nominee registration will, however, be possible for foreign investors only.

Transfer of registered securities

Registration of shares after change of ownership is not compulsory in Finland. Registration is only necessary if a shareholder wishes to attend and to vote at an AGM or EGM, unless he has otherwise produced evidence of ownership of shares. Registration may also help in the event of theft.

When endorsed, the share becomes a bearer instrument and is transferred by delivery. Interim certificates are also endorsed. Transfer is usually done by blank endorsement by the owner or by a custodian.

5   STRUCTURE AND REGULATION OF FINANCIAL MARKETS

5.1   Structure of financial activities

The universal banking system is prevailing. A bank may combine all functions under one roof – i.e. commercial, savings and investment banking, as well as broker/dealer functions.

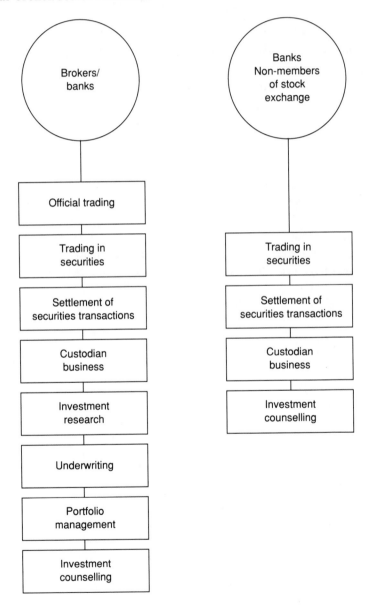

5.2 Regulatory structure

Overview

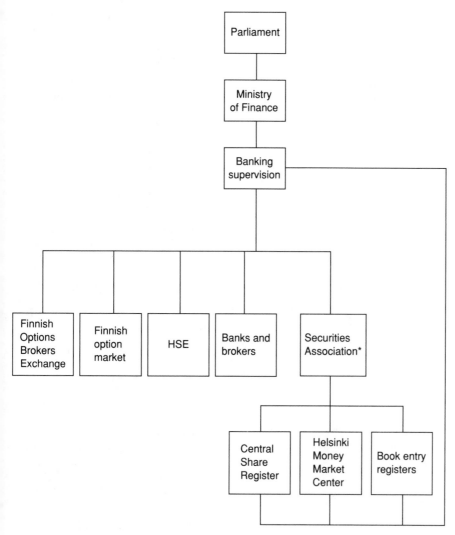

* This applies to the coming book entry system.

Responsibilities of regulatory bodies

Name of body	Tasks/responsibilities/legal basis
Ministry of Finance (Valtiovarainministeriö)	Grants licences for securities and derivative exchanges and stockbrokers. Confirms the self-regulatory rules of organized exchanges
The Banking Supervision (Pankkitarkastusvirasto)	Supervises the banks, stockbrokers, finance companies, securities and derivative markets and compliance with laws. Monitors on a real-time basis trading in the securities and derivative markets by means of a fully automated system. Promulgates directives. Legal basis: Banking Supervision Act and Securities Market Act
Helsinki Stock Exchange Cooperative (Helsingin Arvopaperipörssi Osuuskunta)	The purpose of the HSE is, in order to promote the business of its members, to operate the Exchange for its members by providing the required conditions for securities trading activities. The HSE provides also clearing, data processing and trade guarantee services related to the transfer of securities, as well as training and information services
	The HSE supervises compliance with its own rules (supplementary to the Securities Market Act), legislation, other directives and good trading practices. It monitors also the daily trading and quotations. The HSE decides on admission for listing. It grants and cancels rights to a securities intermediary, to the authorized brokerage firms and their employees to act as brokers. Legal basis: Securities Market Act 1989
OTC-market (OTC-markkinat)	The Finnish Association of Securities Dealers runs the OTC-market and the Brokers' List. The Securities Market Act also applies to OTC-securities. The OTC-market has supplementary rules to the Securities Market Act. The FASD supervises and monitors the OTC-market. OTC-companies must conclude a market-making agreement with a member of the FASD. Legal basis: Securities Market Act

Name of body	Tasks/responsibilities/legal basis
Derivative market	Trading and clearing of the Finnish Options Market and the Finnish Options Exchange is governed by their own Rules and General Conditions. Legal basis: Act on Trading in Standardized Options and Futures 1988

Supervision of stock exchange

Ministry of Finance and Banking Supervision. Legal basis: Securities Market Act 1989 and Rules of the Helsinki Stock Exchange 1990.

Supervision of clearing

The regulations of the clearing of equities and equity-based instruments by the Helsinki Stock Exchange are a part of the Rules of the Helsinki Stock Exchange (supplemented 1991) confirmed by the Ministry of Finance. A working group is drafting the legislation related to clearing and settlement of securities.

Supervision of broker/dealers and custodian banks

Ministry of Finance and Banking Supervision. Custodian Banks are supervised by the Banking Supervision; stockbrokers are monitored by the exchanges as well.

6 CUSTODIANS

Kansallis-Osake-Pankki
Aleksanterinkatu 42
00100 Helsinki
Finland

Tel: 358 0 1631
Fax: 358 0 175117

Postipankki
Unionkatu 20
00100 Helsinki
Finland

Tel: 358 0 1641
Fax: 358 0 164 5503

Union Bank of Finland
Foreign Safe Custody
PO Box 868
00101 Helsinki
Finland

Tel: 358 0 68051
Fax: 358 0 759 2029

21 FRANCE

☞ ## 1 PRINCIPAL STOCK EXCHANGE

Société des Bourses Françaises
4 Place de la Bourse
75080-Paris, Cedex 02
France

Tel: 33 1 40 41 1000
Telex: 230 844 SYNAGEN

☞ ## 2 PRINCIPAL REGULATORY AUTHORITY

Regulatory responsibilities are divided among the three following organizations:

Commission des Operations de
  Bourse
39–43 Quai André-Citroën
75739 Paris, Cedex 15
France

Tel: 33 1 4058 6565/6726
Telex: 42 205 238 (COBPARI)
Fax: 33 1 4058 6500

Conseil des Bourses de Valeurs de
  France
4 Place de la Bourse
75080 Paris
France

Tel: 33 1 4041 1000
Telex: 42 215 561
Fax: 33 1 4026 3140

Conseil du Marche à Terme de
  France
5 Boulevard Montmartre
Bureau 176
Paris 75002
France

Tel: 33 1 4421 3742
Telex: 42 218 362
Fax: 33 1 4221 3741

3 TIME DIFFERENCE FROM GMT: +1 HOUR

4 FORMS AND TYPES OF SECURITIES

4.1 Forms of securities

Bearer and registered securities

Bearer certificate **(Titre au porteur)**   A certificate whose holder is regarded as the legitimate owner.

Identifiable bearer certificate **(Titre au porteur identifiable)**   The Law of 17 June 1987 allows quoted companies, under certain conditions, to ask SICOVAM, the central depository in France, for a list of all its shareholders, as well as their voting rights. The list provided by SICOVAM gives the following information:

– Nationality of the shareholder
– Address of each shareholder
– Number of shares held by each shareholder
– Restrictions
– Special rights attached to the shares.

Registered certificate **(Titre nominatif)**   The owner of registered certificates can decide between two forms of registration: pure registered or administered registered.

Pure registered certificate **(Titre nominatif pur)**   In this case, ownership is recorded by the issuer, who acts as account holder, informing the owner on all matters relating to the security and acting on his behalf.

Administered registered certificate **(Titre nominatif administré)**   As in the preceding case, the ownership of the shares is registered with the issuer, but in addition the securities are registered with an account holder (a financial intermediary chosen by the owner), which means that the registration is duplicated in the accounts of the account holder who will handle the relevant activities for the account of the owner of the shares. Only the obligation to inform remains with the issuing company.

Dematerialized form of securities (law dated 30 December 1981)

All movable assets, whether registered or bearer, may only be represented by entry in an account, in the name of the owner, with either the issuing company or a financial intermediary approved by the Ministry of Finance. Ownership is transferred by debiting and crediting the accounts concerned.

This regulation is valid as of 3 November 1984. Only securities issued by listed or assimilated companies may be in bearer form:

- the securities (shares, bonds, investment certificates, participation certificates, etc.) of companies which are listed officially on the Stock Exchange or on the 'second marché' of the stock exchange
- SICAV shares
- the shares of over-the-counter companies giving the right to detaxation of income invested in shares.

All securities which do not enter into one of these categories must compulsorily be in registered form.
Exceptions: The dematerialization does not apply:

- for bonds issued before 3 November 1984 and redeemable by drawing of specific certificate numbers
- for French securities which circulate abroad and which can be represented by certificates issued by SICOVAM (which are intended exclusively for use abroad).

Regulations for book entry securities accounts:

- securities admitted to SICOVAM: see section on SICOVAM on p. 219
- securities not admitted to SICOVAM.

There is no legislative or regulative disposition which governs the holding of securities accounts. Therefore, the company's by-laws must determine such matters. Companies may refer to the procedures proposed in a document approved by the Treasury Board of the Ministry of Economy and Finance, entitled '*Cahier des charges des émetteurs teneurs de comptes de valeurs mobilières non admises en SICOVAM* (*Regulations affecting issuers who hold accounts for securities which are not admitted to SICOVAM*).

Effective 3 May 1988, all owners of securities who had not complied with the provisions of the law concerning the special (dematerialized) form of domestic securities lost their rights as shareholders and became simple creditors of the issuer, up to his/her proportionate share in the sales proceeds of his/her securities. However, these creditors have the right within a period of 30 years from the aforementioned date, to obtain redemption of the sale proceeds of their securities from the Caisse des Dépôts et Consignations.

4.2   Types of securities

Equities and warrants

Bearer or registered share (**Action au porteur ou nominative**)   With the exception of the shares which, based on the company's by-laws, must be registered, all other shares are negotiated as bearer shares and held in an account with SICOVAM.

Predominantly registered share (**Action essentiellement nominative**)   Certain shares have to be compulsorily in registered form (e.g. shares of companies working for the national defence and of companies where the nominative form is stipulated by its by-laws). Registration has been compulsory since 1 October 1982 for all shares issued in France which are subject to French law and not listed on a stock exchange.

'Mixed' share **(Action mixte)**   Registered share with coupons attached, hardly used in France.

Ordinary share **(Action ordinaire)**   Security which represents an ownership interest in a company. (Bearer or registered issue, held in book entry form.)

Preferred share **(Action à dividende prioritaire)**   Share with preference rights with regard to dividend payments and any distribution of assets on liquidation, without voting rights. A company can only issue preferred shares on the condition that it has made profits (with or without distribution) during the preceding two years.

The minimum priority dividend is fixed by law at a rate of 7.5% of the normal value of the share. It can be partially cumulative or without a time limitation attached.

If preference dividends are not paid in full for the duration of three payment terms, then the voting right is granted until payment of all outstanding dividends. (Bearer or registered issue, held in book entry form.)

Warrant share **(Action à bon de souscription d'action)**   Share accompanied by an option to subscribe to another share and whose price and date of exercise are laid down in the issuing contract. (Bearer or registered issues, held in book entry form.)

Founder's part **(Part de fondateur)**   Share issued to founders of a company as compensation for previously unpaid services, granting certain preferential rights. The issuance of founder's parts has been forbidden in France since 1 April 1967. (Bearer or registered issues, held in book entry form.)

Share from the French-zone **(Action de la zone Franc)**   Share issued by companies located in former French colonies, mostly African ones, which are listed on the Paris Stock Exchange or on a stock exchange in one of the provinces. (Bearer or registered issues, held in book entry form.)

Investment certificate **(Certificat d'investissement or Certificat d'investissement privilégié)**   In the event of an increase in capital or splitting of existing shares, a company can create investment and voting right certificates up to the amount of one quarter of the company's capital. The first certificate is negotiable and represents the pecuniary rights (right to dividends, subscription right, etc.); the second is non-negotiable and in registered form, representing the voting rights which are divided among the shareholders and possibly the holders of former voting right certificates.

However, companies that have issued investment certificates can now request the listing of their voting right certificates on the stock exchange. Voting right certificates can only be acquired by bearers of investment certificates, and the possession of both essentially involves the reconstitution of one share. (Bearer certificates held in book entry form.)

Dividend-right certificate exclusively for circulation outside of France **(Action de jouissance représentatif d'actions en circulation exclusive hors de France)** Common share whose represented capital has been paid back, which does not confer any ownership rights, but grants the holder the right to participate in the net profit and the liquidation proceeds. (Bearer or registered issues, held in book entry form.)

French certificate exclusively for circulation outside France **(Certificat représentatif d'actions en circulation exclusive hors de France)** Security representing shares of a French company listed on the Paris Stock Exchange and at least one foreign place, issued by SICOVAM for circulation only outside of France. (Bearer issue.)

Warrant **(Bon de souscription)** This is a certificate that is detached when the share or bond is first issued allowing the holder to subscribe to new securities according to the originally specified terms (price, date, per value).

Subscription right **(Droit de souscription)** Priority right of participation for a shareholder to a direct or indirect issue of shares against cash payment (subscription to new shares, to bonds convertible into shares and bond-note subscriptions, etc.). The rights are traded during the subscription period. The shareholders may renounce either in whole or in part their priority right of subscription. (Bearer issues, held in book entry form.)

Right of attribution **(Droit d'attribution)** Priority right of participation for a shareholder to an issue of shares from the company's reserves and free allotment of shares. These rights are traded during an indefinite time period, but after a period of three months, the market becomes narrow and makes the closing of such an operation difficult. It is for this reason that the law of 15 December 1985 has granted the issuer the possibility of not listing these rights. The shareholders are compensated for unused fractions of rights. (Bearer issues, held in book entry form.)

Priority right **(Droit de priorité)** A non-negotiable right entitling the owner of securities, for a given period (15 days), to a priority share in the issue of new securities before they are made available to the public. This right is realized through the blocking of the securities until the end of the priority period.

Stock dividend option **(Droit d'option)** In the case of a stock dividend, the holder has the choice during one to three months to collect dividend, either in cash or in the form of stock.

Debt instruments

Only the bonds issued prior to 3 November 1984 may circulate freely in the form of either a bearer or a registered bond. As of 3 November 1984, as is the case with shares, bonds are issued not in paper form, but registered in the account of a financial intermediary chosen by the owner of such bonds, either in a current bearer account with SICOVAM or in an administered registered account. Those securities owners who do not wish to go through a bank or an agent, must compulsorily deal directly with the issuer or his agent who will register the assets in an account in purely nominative form.

Fixed-income bond (G,P,C)* (**Obligation à taux fixe**)   Fixed-income security which is either a bond in registered form or in bearer form.

Straight bond (G,P,C)* (**Obligation classique**)   Bond without clauses granting conversions or warrant privileges. (Bearer or registered issues, held in book entry form.)

Floating-rate bond (G,P,C)* (**Obligation à taux variable**)   Bond with an interest rate which is subject to change, in relation to money market rates or bond market rates. (Bearer or registered issues, held in book entry form.)

Different types of floating-rate bonds
(**TMM or T4M**)   Mean monthly interest rate of the money market. Arithmetic mean of the Weighted Mean Rates (calculated daily) of the month in question. This rate is calculated and published monthly by the Banque de France.

(**TAM**)   Annual money market interest rate. Monthly capitalization of the last 12 mean monthly rates. This rate is calculated and published monthly by the CDC.

[**PIBOR (TIOP)**]   Paris Inter-bank Offered Rate on the French franc for private paper with the following maturities: one, two, three, six, nine and twelve months. This rate is calculated and published by Telerate on behalf of the French Bankers' Association.

(**THB**)   Actuarial interest rate of Treasury bills with a maturity of 13 weeks (weekly publication).

(**TMB**)   Mean monthly interest rate of Treasury bills with a maturity of 13 weeks (arithmetic mean of the actuarial Treasury bill rate of the month).

(**THE**)   Weekly actuarial yield of government bonds with a maturity of more than seven years.

(**TME**)   Monthly actuarial yield of government bonds with a maturity of more than seven years.

(**TMO**)   Monthly actuarial yield of bond loans.

(**TRA**)   Interest rate revisable yearly. It is determined either according to the TMO of the month preceding the redemption period, or it can be calculated in the form of an arithmetic mean of the 12 TMOs preceding this period.

---

* G = government issue; P = public sector issues guaranteed by the government; C = corporate issue.

(TRE)   Rate revisable as a function of the yield of government bonds with a maturity of more than seven years.

(TRO3)   Rate revisable every three years according to the last two TMOs established prior to the revision date.

Government bond (G)* **(Obligation de l'Etat)**   Bond issued by the French government. (Bearer or registered issues, held in book entry form.)

Assimilable French government bond (OAT) (G)* **[Obligation Assimilable du Trésor (OAT)]**   OATs can be fixed or variable rate bonds issued by the French government. The initial maturity can extend from seven to twenty-five years. The particular feature of the OATs lies in the fact that after a first issue the government has the possibility of issuing other bonds which have the same characteristics and can be assimilated.

Renewable government bond (G)* **[Obligation renouvelable du Trésor (ORT)]**   Bond which can be re-issued at maturity. The holder then can either obtain repayment with the total accrued interest from the date of issue, or renew his investment at the new issue date for a new period. (Bearer or registered issues, held in book entry form.)

Redeemable bond (G)* **[Obligation à sorties optionelles (ou à fenêtres)]**   Bond subject to redemption upon demand of either issuer or holder, prior to maturity in accordance with the terms and conditions of the issue. (Bearer or registered issues, held in book entry form.)

Public or semi-public authorities bond (P)* **(Obligation de collectivités publiques ou semi-publiques)**   Bond issued by public and semi-public authorities, such as Credit Foncier de France, Electricité de France, etc. Also called OATs – i.e. Obligations assimilables du Trésor. (Bearer or registered issues, held in book entry form.)

Compensation bond (G)* **(Obligation indemnitaire)**   Registered or bearer bonds issued in 1982 against shares of nationalized French companies with index-linked interest rates (weighted average of interest on returns from non-index government loans with fixed interest rates and having a minimum term of seven years). (Bonds held in book entry form.) (Examples: Caisse Nationale des Banques (CNB), Caisse Nationale de l'Industrie (CNI).)

Convertible bond (C)* **(Obligation convertible)**   Bond which may be converted by the holder into stock. (Bearer or registered issues, held in book entry form.)

Warrant bond (C)* **[Obligation à bon de souscription d'action ou d'obligation (OBSA, OBSO)]**   Bond accompanied by an option to purchase shares of stock or bonds at a subscription price fixed in the terms and conditions of the issue. The period for exercising the subscription rights must not exceed three months after the final redemption date of the debt obligation. (Bearer or registered issues, held in book entry form.)

Bond redeemable in shares (C)* **(Obligation remboursable en action)**   A loan issued by a listed company whose redemption on maturity can only be effected against the remittance of shares according to the originally specified terms. (Bearer or registered issues, held in book entry form.)

Warrant bond redeemable in shares (C)* **(Obligation à bons de souscription remboursable en action)**   This bond is a further development of the two preceding bonds and gives the bondholder the right to acquire shares against the warrant and also to become a shareholder when the bonds are redeemed.

Exchangeable bond (G,P,C)* **(Obligation échangeable)**   A loan issued at a rate of interest which can be exchanged as it matures against another rate of interest (fixed rate against variable rate or vice versa). (Bearer or registered issues, held in book entry form.)

Partly paid up bond (G,P,C)* **(Obligation partiellement libérée à l'émission)**   Bond issued with the possibility to pay on subscription only a part of the price, with the balance being paid in instalments as stipulated in the issuing contract. (Bearer or registered issues, held in book entry form.)

Bond from the French zone (C)* **(Obligation de la Zone Franc)**   Bonds issued by companies or by a government of the former French colonies, mostly African ones, which are listed in Paris or on one of the provincial stock exchanges.

Participating instruments

Participating certificate **(Titre participatif; Titre participatif à bon de souscription; Titre participatif convertible)**   Security issued by a nationalized French company, a public institution or by an agricultural cooperative society. It is negotiable and its duration is not limited, although redemption is possible at the initiative of the company, at the earliest after seven years. There is a minimum distribution, consisting of a fixed and a variable part. Capital is considered as equity, but holders have no voting rights; however, they do benefit from tax regulations concerning bonds. (Bearer or registered issues, held in book entry form.)

Subordinated issue for an indefinite period (TSDI) **[Titres subordonnés à durée indéterminée (TSDI)]**   Bonds having the following characteristics:

- the redemption of the loan only occurs after the other creditors have been paid off in full (except participating certificates)
- the maturity is indefinite
- annual payment of the coupon may be carried forward by resolution of the Board of Directors. However, this clause does not apply to all such issues.

Redeemable subordinated issue (TSR) **[Titre subordonné remboursable (TSR)]**
This bond has very similar characteristics to those of the TSDI. It differs, however, by the fact that it bears a redemption date.

***Subordinated issue with progressive interest (TSIP)* [Titre subordonné à intérêt progressif (TSIP)]**   This bond is similar to the TSDI, the difference being a progressivity clause relating to the interest paid. The TSDIs and TSIPs are considered a part of the equity of the debtor.

Money market instruments

Treasury bills   Negotiable certificates of indebtedness issued by the Treasury with a minimum amount of FRF 1 million and a maturity of 13, 26 or 52 weeks (bills with fixed interest on discount basis, BTF) or a maturity of two or five years (bills with annual interest fixed on normal basis, BTAN). Treasury bills are issued by the government in an auction system. The issue of Treasury bills with a maturity of less than two years is restricted to a specialized agency.

Current account Treasury notes   Current account Treasury notes – which previously were reserved for credit institutions, for non-banking institutions authorized to deal on the money market, for SICAVs and for mutual investment funds – can now be subscribed to also by private persons and firms. The standard amount of these notes is FRF 1 million.

Commercial paper   Issued by companies other than credit institutions which have existed for more than two years.

Term of the notes: between ten days and seven years. Minimum amount: FRF 1 million. Interest rate depends on maturity:

– less than 1 year: fixed income
– more than 1 year: freely negotiable.

Trading is restricted to the issuer, to banks, securities houses and interbank market agents.

***Notes of specialized financial institutions* (IFS = Institutions Financières Spécialisées, such as Crédit National, CEPME, SDR, Crédit Foncier de France, etc.)**   These notes can be issued with a maturity from two to seven years for a minimum amount of FRF 1 million, the only condition being that the resources of the IFS must, on the average, be longer term than their use, so as to avoid all transformation risks.

***Deposit certificate* (Certificat de dépôt)**   Negotiable certificates of indebtedness exclusively issued by a credit institution. Since 1990, they can also be issued in currencies other than FRF.

Minimum amount: FRF 1 million. Maturity: between ten days and seven years. Interest: freely negotiable (fixed if the lifetime of the issue is less than one year).

The issue of certificates of deposit for a period exceeding two years is subject to quotation by a specialized agency.

Bank savings note (**Bon de caisse**)   Issued by a commercial bank and re-deemable at a date fixed at the time of issue. The note can be discounted. (Bearer issues, held in book entry form.)

Other instruments

Mutual investment fund [**Fonds d'investissement (OPCVM)**]   The French financial market has both closed and open-ended mutual investment funds. The first, called Société d'Investissement à capital fermé (SICAF), has a fixed capital which can be modified only after a decision of a special shareholders' meeting. The capital of the open funds (SICAV, Fonds Communs de Place-ment) is variable in relation to the flow of subscriptions and repurchases.

SICAV share (**Action de SICAV**)   Share of a Société d'Investissement à capital variable (Company with a variable share capital) managed by a large bank which invests money in securities. (Bearer or registered issues, held in book entry form.)

Mutual Investment Funds Unit (**Part de Fonds Communs de Placement**) Investment trust fund which sells its parts to the public and whose assets are invested in securities in which the part-holders have an undivided interest proportional to their investment. (Bearer or registered issues, held in book entry form.)

Mutual Fund for Interventions on the Futures Markets (FIMAT) [**Fonds Commun d'Intervention sur les Marchés à Terme (FIMAT)**]   Purely specu-lative fund entitled to invest up to 50% of its assets in futures and options contracts.

Units of Mutual Debt Fund (**Parts de Fonds, Commun de Créances**) Securitization is the mechanism by which a co-ownership called Mutual Debt Fund (FCC) acquires debts held by credit institutions and refinances the acquisition by issuing on the market representative units of the acquired debts. These units are securities that are likely to be admitted for quotation on a stock exchange.

4.3   Securities Identification Code

Code name and structure

For the time being, French banks and brokers use various securities codes (codes alphanumériques), the systems being maintained by:

Code of six digits: DAFSA Documentation
Code of three digits: Ministry of Finance
Code of five digits: SICOVAM

DAFSA has been commissioned to organize a unified service of securities codification in compliance with SICOVAM specifications. Consequently, the Agence Française de Codification (AFC = French Codification Agency) has been created, whose rules and regulations are being developed by the CFONB. The AFC has thus taken the place of the Ministry of Finance, SICOVAM, the Société des Bourses Françaises (Corporation of Brokers) and of DAFSA, all of which were previously engaged in managing their respective areas.

Name and address of organizations responsible for the Security Identification System

DAFSA
Immeuble le Ponant

F-75015 Paris

Agence Française de Codification
4 Cité Paradis

F-75010 Paris

4.4   Transfer of ownership

French securities are usually in bearer form. However, the issuer may make it compulsory to have all shares in registered form.

Unless they belong to the category which must be registered, securities may be changed from one form to the other and vice versa upon the owner's request by changing the entry in the respective accounts. The bearer form guarantees the anonymity of the holder (*see*: 'Forms of securities'). In the case of the registered form, the holder is known to the issuer, which has some advantages (double voting right for the shares in registered form if held for at least two years and if provided for in the articles of association of the company, and direct mailing of company information by the issuer to the registered shareholders).

Transfer of bearer issues

By simple transfer from account to account.

Transfer of predominantly registered issues

The transfer of predominantly registered securities to a new holder necessitates a cession form and must be recorded in the books of the company in the name of the new holder. It may be subject to the approval of the company if this is stipulated in the by-laws.

A transfer between private individuals or transfer between companies can only take place through a stock exchange transaction, except between two companies where the first is the subsidiary of the second.

5   STRUCTURE AND REGULATION OF FINANCIAL MARKETS

5.1   Structure of financial activities

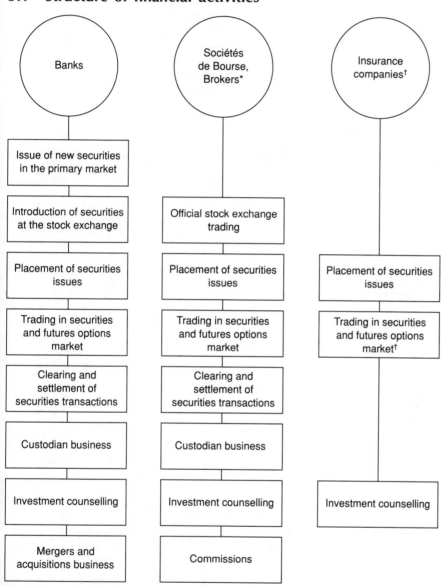

* Brokers' monopolies on transactions will be abolished in 1992.
† The intervention of insurance companies on the markets is limited to buying and selling operations for their own account.

5.2 **Regulatory structure**

Overview

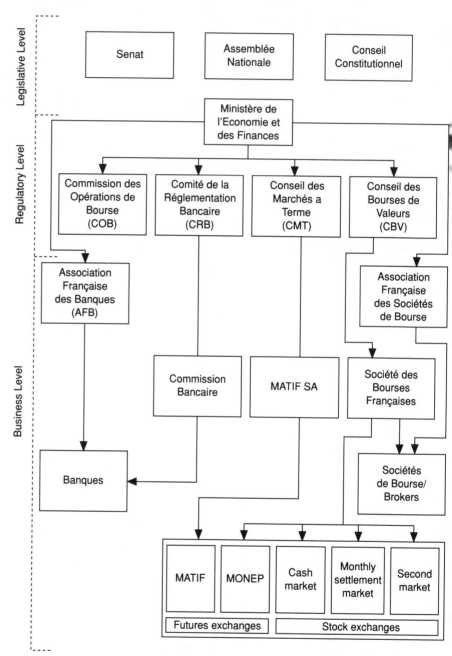

Notes:

SCMC	Société de Compensation des Marchés Conditionnels (MONEP).
MATIF SA	Chambre de Compensation du MATIF.
MATIF	Marché à Terme International de France.
MONEP	Marché des Options Négociables à Paris.
CMT	Conseil de Marché à Terme.

Responsibilities of regulatory bodies

Name of body	Responsibilities
Committee for Stock Exchange Transactions (Commission des Opérations de Bourse, COB)	The Committee for stock exchange transactions (COB = Commission des Opérations de Bourse) consists of a President and eight members chosen by the French government and has, among others, the following functions: – Providing protection for the investor – Ensuring that financial information is circulated and transactions are properly conducted – Protection against insider dealing and price manipulation – Receiving investors' complaints and claims A law passed on 2 August 1989 has considerably strengthened the powers of the COB regarding investigations and has given it the power to impose penalties.
Stock Exchange Council (Le Conseil des Bourses de Valeurs)	The Stock Exchange Council consists of 12 members of whom ten are elected by brokerage firms. Its powers are: – Lays down the general rules of the stock exchange – Decides on the listing or delisting of securities – Fixes the prudential ratios of brokerage firms – Imposes penalties where rules are violated.
Futures Markets Council (CMT) (Conseil des Marchés à Terme)	Consists of one President and 16 members. Its powers are: – Lays down the general rules of the futures markets – Orders the admission or striking out of contracts – Can order disciplinary penalties The CMT is working out the rules applicable to GLOBEX

Supervision of Clearing and Central Securities Depository Organization

SICOVAM (Société Interprofessionelle de Compensation des Valeurs Mobiliéres) is a limited company (*société anonyme*) whose capital is held by the principal operators on the financial market (banks and brokers). The Board of Directors consists of four members chosen from among the shareholders. The operating costs are shared among all the members.

6 CUSTODIANS

Banque Indosuez
96 Boulevard Haussman
75008 Paris
France

Tel: 33 1 45 61 20 20
Fax: 33 1 43 87 58 94

Banque Paribas
3 Rue D'Antin
75078 Paris
France

Tel: 33 1 43 77 13 60
Fax: 33 1 42 98 12 99

Banque Worms
Tour Voltaire
1 Place des Degrés,
Cedex 58
92059 Paris
France

Tel: 33 1 49 07 50 50
Fax: 33 1 49 07 57 05

Barclays Bank
BP 24X, Cedex 10
75460 Paris
France

Tel: 33 1 40 06 85 85
Fax: 33 1 40 06 51 43

Caisse Centrale des
Banques Populaires
115 Rue Montmartre
75002 Paris
France

Tel: 33 1 40 39 39 97
Fax: 33 1 40 13 08 95

Crédit Commercial de France
103 Avenue des Champs-Elysées
75008 Paris
France

Tel: 33 1 40 70 70 40
Fax: 33 1 42 95 31 00

Crédit Lyonnais
19 Boulevard des Italiens
75002 Paris
France

Tel: 33 1 42 95 70 00
Fax: 33 1 42 95 60 22

Morgan Guaranty Trust
Custody Place
14 Place Vendôme
75001 Paris
France

Tel: 33 1 40 15 45 02
Fax: call telephone number for fax

Société Générale
29 Boulevard Haussman
75009 Paris
France

Tel: 33 1 40 98 20 00
Fax: 33 1 40 98 46 33

22 GERMANY

1 PRINCIPAL STOCK EXCHANGE

Frankfurt Stock Exchange
Biebergasse 6–10
6000 Frankfurt am Main 1
Germany

Tel: 49 69 299903–0
Telex: 411412

2 PRINCIPAL REGULATORY AUTHORITY

Federal Ministry of Finance
Graurheindorferstrasse 108
5300 Bonn 1
Germany

Tel: 49 228 682 4372
Telex: 41 228 3735
Fax: 49 228 682 4420

3 TIME DIFFERENCE FROM GMT: +1 HOUR

4 FORMS AND TYPES OF SECURITIES

4.1 Forms of securities

***Bearer certificate* (Inhaberurkunde, Inhaberpapier, Inhaberstück, Inhabertitel)**
Most common form for equity and debt instruments with coupons representing
dividends, interest, subscription rights, etc.

***Registered* certificate* (Namenspapier, Namensstück, Namensurkunde,
Namenstitel)** Relatively rare; insurance company shares and special debt

---

* Insurance company shares may often only be transferred into another shareholder's
name if the company agrees to the transfer (Vinkulierte Namensaktie); see also 'Transfer
of registered issues'.

instruments are in registered form. Shares usually carry coupons for dividends, subscription rights, etc.

***Book-entry security* (Girosammelverwahrfähiges Wertpapier)**   Certificated (immobilized) or uncertificated securities which may be transferred from one safecustody account to another on the books of the central depository, Deutscher Kassenverein AG.

***Uncertificated bond/note* (Wertrechtsanleihe)**   Bonds or notes for which no certificates have been or will be issued. Mostly issued by federal authorities (federation, federal states, post, railways).

***Depository receipt (German certificates of foreign shares)* (Deutsche Zertifikate)**   Certificate issued by Deutscher Auslandskassenverein and deposited with Deutscher Kassenverein AG on the basis of shares held with a foreign custodian. DRs represent ownership of the holder's fraction of DKV's total holding. (Legal title identical to collective custody – Girosammelverwahrung – of Germany securities).

***Global certificate (GC)* [Globalurkunde (or: Sammelurkunde)]**   Security deposited with the central securities depository and representing a large part of or an entire issue. (Distinction possible between the following.)

***Temporary GC* (Interimistische Globalurkunde)**   Basis for book transfers through central securities depository until such time as definitive certificates are available.

***Technical GC* (Technische Globalurkunde)**   Technical GCs frequently represent part of an issue in lieu of definitive certificates. They are usually deposited with the central securities depository.

***Permanent GC* (Dauer-Globalurkunde)**   Permanent GCs represent an entire issue of bonds or a part thereof, in accordance with the terms and conditions of the issue. They apply to debt instruments only, where bondholders may not withdraw physical certificates. They are customary for about 90% of all corporate debt issues. On the other hand, a shareholder's right to demand delivery of physical certificates may not be excluded.

***Jumbo certificate* (Grossurkunde, Grosstück)**   Certificate representing a large number/amount of shares or fixed-interest securities.

4.2   Types of securities

Equities and warrants

***Share (ordinary)* [Aktie (Stamm-)]**   A share represents membership rights in a public limited company. It also represents a portion of the capital of a company.

The holder is entitled:

– to vote at the shareholders' meetings
– to receive rights in a rights issue
– to receive payable dividends
– to receive a portion of the liquidation proceeds.

Minimum par value: DM 50.–. (Issued in registered or bearer form.)

Preferred share (Vorzugsaktie)   Preferred shares usually carry preferential rights as to dividends in contrast to ordinary shares. Preferential shares are usually non-voting and, by definition, cumulative. They may also be ahead of ordinary shares with respect to liquidation proceeds. (Issued in bearer form.)

Profit-sharing certificate (Genussschein)   Usually grants the right to a fixed portion of the net profit of a company, but does not represent a participation in the company. It has the same creditor claims as a bond (*see also*: 'Profit participatory bond').

Warrant (Optionsschein)   A warrant is a certificated marketable option, tradable like a share. It entitles the holder to subscribe to the company for a specific amount of shares (or, as the case may be, bonds or currencies) at a set price during a prescribed period, usually several years. (Issued in bearer form; may be held in book entry form or as global certificate.)

Covered warrant (Gedeckter Optionsschein)   Covered warrants are usually issued by a bank or finance company holding the necessary position in the underlying security which covers the issue. Usually in bearer form.

Interest warrant (Zinsoptionsschein, Zinswarrant)   A warrant entitling the holder to the difference in money between a predetermined exercise price and the fixing price of a particular fixed-interest security on the exercise date. Interest warrants are usually issued by banks or finance companies. Bearer certificates prevail.

Debt instruments

Bond (straight) (Anleihe; festverzinsliches Wertpapier)   Interest-bearing instrument with a fixed date of maturity without conversion right or other features. (Issued in bearer form; may be held in book entry form, as global certificate or as jumbo certificate.)

Public bond (Anleihe der öffentlichen Hand)   Bonds issued by federal or state authorities (federation, railway, post, federal states), usually uncertificated; various maturities. (Book entry only.)

Convertible bond (Wandelanleihe)   CBs may be exchanged for shares at the bondholder's option on certain conditions. (Issued in bearer form; may be held in book entry form, as global certificate or as jumbo certificate.)

Zero bond (**Nullkuponanleihe**)   Zero bonds pay no interest during the life-time of the bond; they are sold at a discount to reflect earnings. At maturity, the bondholders will be paid the full face value. (Issued in bearer form; may be held in book entry form, as global certificate or as jumbo certificate.)

Warrant issue (**Optionsanleihe**)   An issue that combines the features of a bond with that of a warrant. The warrant is usually a detachable, separate certificate and may be exercised in accordance with the terms and conditions of the issue. (Issued in bearer form; may be held in book entry form, as global certificate or as jumbo certificate.)

Floating rate note (**Variabel verzinsliche Anleihe; 'Floater'**)   Interest-bearing instrument subject to change of interest rate at set intervals (e.g. three months, six months). Changes based on defined market indicators (e.g. LIBOR). (Issued in bearer form; may be held in book entry form, as global certificate or as jumbo certificate.)

DEM Euro-Medium Term Note Programme (EMTN)   Following the July 1989 liberalization measure by the Deutsche Bundesbank of the DEM capital market, EMTN programmes are now available in DEM. The arranger/dealer, as well as any other dealer, must be a credit institute domiciled in Germany. This is in accordance with the Bundesbank International DEM bond issuing procedure, and guarantees that the issuance of DEM bonds continues to be based in the domestic market.

Programme: over a long period of time, the programme gives the issuer the right (not the obligation) to issue bearer securities ('notes') in the DEM market at any time (like a tap issue). The notes may be issued in several tranches (minimum DEM 5 million per tranche).

Listing: as a rule, the programme and each individual note are listed on at least one German exchange. At least one German paying agent is mandatory.

Volume: programmes from several DEM 100 million upwards, tranches between DEM 5 million and DEM 25 million.

Maturity: typically from two to five years.

Characteristics: notes may be issued at a fixed-interest rate, floating rate or zero-coupon rate. They may be callable or not callable at issuer's option.

Notes are represented by a global certificate per tranche.

Minimum investment: DEM 80 000 per order in primary transactions. The market segment is aimed at institutions and affluent private investors.

DEM Commercial Paper Programme   Following the abolition of section 795 of the Civil Code, which made the issuance of bearer notes dependent upon state approval, and the abolition of the Stock Exchange Turnover Tax (SETT) as of 1 January 1991, German corporations can now tap the domestic DEM market in a much more flexible manner. A functioning secondary market can develop as a further result of the SETT abolition. As a result of the Bundesbank International DEM bond issuing procedure, foreign corporations can, for the time being, issue CP programmes only through their German subsidiaries or finance companies.

Programme: over a long period of time, the programme gives the issuer the right (not the obligation) to issue notes at any time. The issuer usually enters into a blanket agreement with the selling bank(s). The notes may be issued in several tranches (minimum DEM 5 million).

Listing: since a CP programme is essentially similar to a private placement, the programme and individual tranches will not be listed.

Volume: programme from DEM 100 million upwards; tranches from DEM 5 million upwards.

Maturities: seven days to two years less one day.

Characteristics: interest is always calculated on a discount basis. Notes are represented by a permanent global certificate.

Minimum investment: notes are available in denominations of DEM 500 000. CP programmes are tailored to the requirements of the institutional investor.

Government note **(Bundesobligationen)**   Issued permanently with five-year maturities. Purchase by non-residents only in the secondary market (official quotation). (Book entry only.)

Treasury notes **(Kassenobligationen)**   Issued by federal authorities with maturities of up to six years (regulated market). (Book entry only.)

Mortgage bond **(Pfandbrief)**   Issued by private and public sector mortgage banks for long-term finance and secured by first mortgages. (Issued in bearer or registered form; may be held in book entry form, as global certificate or as jumbo certificate.)

Municipal bond **(Kommunalobligation)**   Issued by private and public sector mortgage banks to provide finance for communities and municipalities as well as private commercial investments under public guarantee. (Issued in bearer form; may be held in book entry form, as global certificate or as jumbo certificate.)

Others

Unit trust certificate **(Investmentzertifikat; Investmentanteilschein)**   Certificates representing part ownership in a professionally managed investment portfolio. Units are sold and redeemed at specified differentials by the company. (Issued in bearer form; may be held in book entry form or as jumbo certificate.)

Certificate of indebtedness (CI) **(Schuldscheindarlehen)**   CIs are marketable instruments. They represent a short, medium or long-term loan for which a loan agreement in writing is signed between the borrower and the lender. The lender normally acts as a fiduciary for third parties who hold parts of the entire loan. Denominations are usually in millions of DEM. However, CIs are not securities (like a bond) in the legal sense and therefore not quoted on stock exchanges. Issuers are usually domestic and foreign public bodies, as well as private and semi-public banks.

Profit participatory bond (PPB) **(Genussschein)**   PPBs usually carry a fixed rate of interest until maturity and entitle the holder to additional revenue payable under certain conditions.

Banks may issue PPBs under relevant clauses of the Banking Act (Kreditwesengesetz):

– minimum five years to maturity
– subject to loss participation
– accepted by supervisory authorities as a form of capital under certain further conditions.

Depending on the terms and conditions of the issue, PPBs are relatively more similar to shares or relatively more similar to bonds.

Profit participatory bond cum warrant **(Optionsgenussschein)**   A profit participatory bond with detachable warrant; in bearer form.

4.3   Securities Identification Code

Code name and structure

The German Securities Identification Number (Wertpapierkennnummer, WKN) is a six-digit numeric figure. It is allocated according to the following rules:

Up to 499 999:   fixed-interest securities
From 500 000:   shares, warrants and unit trusts

Examples: 7% Federal Republic of Germany: WKN 113439
                                                   (85/II 20.06.95)

                   Deutsche Bank AG shares: WKN 804010
                   Dresdner Bank AG shares: WKN 804610

Name and address of organization responsible for the Securities Identification System

Wertpapiermitteilungen
Düsseldorferstrasse 16
D-6000 Frankfurt / M 1
Germany

4.4   Transfer of ownership

Transfer of bearer issues

By simple delivery. (By handing over the certificate or, if applicable by book transfer on the books of the central depository, Deutscher Kassenverein AG.)

Transfer of registered issues

The transfer of registered securities is effected by:

– delivery of the certificate
– transfer from one name into another on the company's shareholders register.

Share assignment forms and registration applications are frequently completed by custodian banks on behalf of the client:

– if the company agrees to the procedure
– if the transfer is necessitated by a sale or delivery against payment.

Transfers of registered shares are frequently subject to approval by the company. Registered shares are not yet eligible for deposit and book entry transfer in the central depository system. As a consequence, share certificates, coupon sheets and transfer forms must be moved physically and separately from payment of the counter-value. This field is being investigated with a view to developing a book entry solution.

5   STRUCTURE AND REGULATION OF FINANCIAL MARKETS

5.1   Structure of financial activities (major market participants)

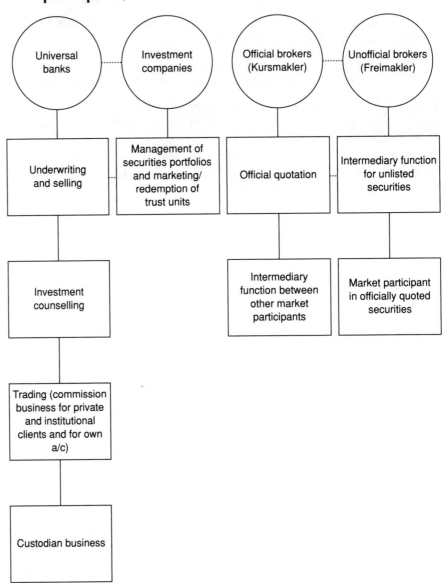

A large portion of transactions in fixed-interest securities, including certificates of indebtedness, are handled directly in interbank trading or between banks and clients.

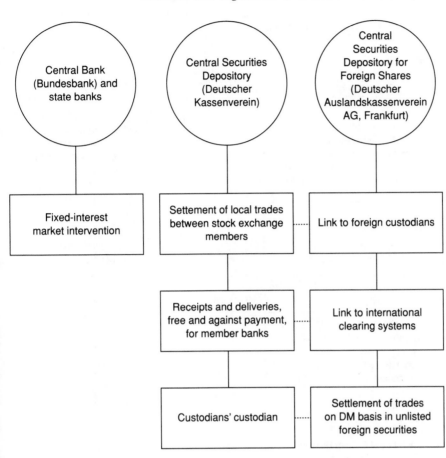

5.2 Regulatory structure

Overview

Stock exchanges	Banking
Government of Federal States (Länderregierungen)	**Federal Banking Supervisory Authority (Bundesaufsichtsamt für das Kreditwesen, Berlin) Deutsche Bundesbank**
State Ministries of Economics or Finance (Länderministerien)	
State Commissioner (Staatskommissar)	**Independent public accountants**
Board of Governors (Börsenvorstand)	
Supervisory Committee (Börsenaufsichtsausschuss)	
Admission Board (Zulassungsstelle)	
Chamber of Official Brokers (Kursmaklerkammer)	
Arbitration Committee (Schiedsgericht)	
Recognized stock exchanges (Börsen) – Berlin – Bremen – Düsseldorf – Frankfurt – Hamburg – Hannover – Munich – Stuttgart – DTB – IBIS	Member banks of the stock exchanges Recognized central depository: – Deutscher Kassenverein AG, with branches at all exchanges except Bremen – Deutscher Auslandskassenverein AG, Frankfurt
Investigation Committee for Insider – Rules (Insider – Prüfungskommission)	

Responsibility of regulatory bodies

***Federal Banking Supervisory Authority* (Bundesaufsichtsamt für das Kreditwesen)**   The Federal Banking Supervisory Authority forms part of the Finance Ministry's sphere of activities. Its main task is the supervision of banks in order to prevent abuses in the banking industry which would endanger the safety of valuables entrusted to banks and which would adversely affect the regular conduct of the banking business or bring about major disadvantages for the economy. The Bundesaufsichtsamt may impose fines of up to DEM 100 000.– in its own right. More serious matters are handled by the courts under the penal code.

The authority usually acts in an indirect way through independent accountants. Main areas of supervision are the annual audit of safekeeping accounts and compliance with other custodial duties as well as bookkeeping practices in respect of trading. (Supervision within the context of the securities business.)

***State Commissioner* (Staatskommissar)**   Permanent supervision of trading and official price quotation.

***Stock Exchange Supervisory Committee* (Börsenaufsichtsausschuss)**   Permanent supervision of trading and official price quotation.

***Chamber of Official Brokers (and Disciplinary Committee)* (Kursmaklerkammer and Disziplinarausschuss)**   Supervision of Official Brokers.

Supervision of stock exchanges

Example of the Frankfurt Stock Exchange (Frankfurter Wertpapierbörse): 'In accordance with the Standing Orders of the Government of the State of Hesse, the Minister mentioned therein shall exercise the supervisory powers' (Börsenaufsichtsbehörde under section 1,2(1) of the Stock Exchanges Act; see also section 3 of the Rules and Regulations of the Frankfurt Stock Exchange.)

Supervision of clearing and central securities depository organizations

Federal Banking Supervisory Authority (Bundesaufsichtsamt für das Kreditwesen) and independent accountants acting on its behalf.

Supervision of broker/dealers and custodian banks

Example of the Frankfurt Stock Exchange:

Official brokers
- Supervision by State Commissioner and Supervisory Committee (daily supervision) in respect of correct trading and price quotation.

- Supervision by the Chamber of Official Brokers in respect of sufficient financial means under section 33(1)1 of the Rules and Regulations of the Frankfurt Stock Exchange.
- Supervision by the Board of Governors in respect of reporting requirements on turnover (section 35, Stock Exchange).

Unofficial brokers
- Supervision by the Board of Governors of the Stock Exchange.

Banks
- Supervision of Stock Exchange dealings within a similar framework as above.
- Supervision by the Federal Banking Supervisory Authority (through independent accountants):

  • Compliance with relevant sections of the Banking Act [Kreditwesengesetz (KWG)], mainly custody auditing.
  • Compliance with the relevant sections of the Investment Companies Act (Kapitalanlagegesellschaften-Gesetz) in respect of duties as custodian for investment companies.
  • Compliance with relevant sections of Public Limited Companies Act (Aktiengesetz) in respect of voting and voting by proxy.

6 CUSTODIANS

Bayerische Vereinsbank AG
Sederanger 5
8000 Munich 22
Germany

Tel: 49 89 3884 3363
Fax: 49 89 3884 8978

Berliner Handels und Frankfurter
  Bank
Bockenheimer Landstrasse 10
6000 Frankfurt 1
Germany

Tel: 49 69 718 3721
Fax: 49 69 718 3017

Citibank AG
Neue Mainzer Strasse 75
Postfache 110333
6000 Frankfurt
Germany

Tel: 49 69 136 6455
Fax: call telephone number for fax

Commerzbank
Breite Strasse 25
4000 Dusseldorf
Germany

Tel: 49 211 827 2297
Fax: 49 211 827 692

Deustsche Bank
Taunusanlage 12
Postfach 100601
6000 Frankfurt
Germany

Tel: 49 69 7150
Fax: call telephone number for fax

Dresdner Bank
Juergen-Ponto-Platz 1
6000 Frankfurt 1
Germany

Tel: 49 69 263 4482
Fax: 49 69 263 2818

J.P. Morgan GmbH
Mainzer Landstrasse 46
6000 Frankfurt
Germany

Tel: 49 69 712 4418
Fax: call telephone number for fax

Trinkhaus & Burkhardt
Koenigsalle 21–23
4000 Dusseldorf
Germany

Tel: 49 211 831 2428
Fax: 49 211 831 2691

Vereins-und-Westbank
Alter Wall 12
2000 Hamburg
Germany

Tel: 49 40 3692 2112
Fax: 49 40 3692 2190

23 HONG KONG

☞ 1 PRINCIPAL STOCK EXCHANGE

The Stock Exchange of Hong Kong Limited
1st Floor
One & Two Exchange Square Central
Hong Kong

Tel: 852 522 11 22
Telex: 86839 STOEX HX

☞ 2 PRINCIPAL REGULATORY AUTHORITY

Securities and Futures Commission
38th floor
Two Exchange Square
8 Connaught Place
Hong Kong

Tel: 852 840 9222
Telex: 802 61919 (SECUR HX)
Fax: 852 521 7836

🕐 3 TIME DIFFERENCE FROM GMT: +8 HOURS

4 FORMS AND TYPES OF SECURITIES

4.1 Forms of securities

Registered share A share which is issued in registered form, with each shareholder appearing as a member in the books of the issuing company. All listed shares in Hong Kong are registered shares.

Allotment letter In the case for the issue of new shares through a rights issue to existing shareholders, the rights are distributed in the form of allotment letters.

Jumbo certificate A certificate comprising more shares than the normal trading board lot. Only used to facilitate physical settlement by special agreement between the buyer and seller.

Depository receipt A certificate which represents the underlying securities held with a recognized depository. Normally used for trading of securities in a foreign market.

Bearer security A security issued in bearer form, where title is demonstrated by possession of the instrument.

4.2 Types of securities

Shares

Ordinary share The class of share representing equity ownership in a company. (Issued in registered form.)

Preference share Share with preference rights with regard to (usually) dividend payments, where the holder is entitled to payments prior to holders of ordinary shares and at a specified rate and any distribution of assets on liquidation. (Issued in registered form.)

Cumulative preference share A form of preference share where the fixed dividend is carried forward to subsequent years until paid in the event of the company not being able to pay dividends when they originally fall due. (Issued in registered form.)

Preferred ordinary share Share with a right to a fixed dividend after the claims of the preference shareholders have been met. (Issued in registered form.)

Warrants

Warrants entitle the bearer to subscribe to new shares or bonds on specified conditions in terms of time limit and subscription price. (Issued in registered or bearer form.)

Debt securities

Loan stock A fixed income security without any clauses granting conversion or warrant privileges. (Issued in registered form.)

Government bond Securities backed by Hong Kong government. Bearer bonds issued at fixed rate with coupons attached. Usually with five-year maturity. (Issued in bearer form.)

Corporate bond Securities issued by local corporations. Bearer bonds issued at fixed rate with coupons attached. Usually with ten-year maturity. (Issued in bearer form.)

Index-linked bond A bond of which the redemption amount is linked to an index. (Issued in bearer form.)

Investment trust investments

Unit trust unit Unit of a unit trust, an open-end fund governed by a trust deed with specific investment objectives. (Issued in registered form.)

Investment trust participation Pro rata interest in the holdings of an investment company. Investment companies open accounts for individual customers, the minimum amount varying from company to company. (Issued in registered form.)

Money market instruments

Certificate of Deposit A negotiable certificate issued against funds deposited with a commercial bank or deposit taking company for a definite period of time, earning a fixed or floating rate of return. Normally available for periods of one month to five years.

Commercial Paper Short-term debt securities usually traded on a discount basis (no interest paid on maturity). The running period normally does not exceed 270 days.

Futures

Hibor futures Futures based on the Hong Kong interbank offered rate (Hibor).

Hang Seng Index future A traded futures contract based on the Hang Seng Index with maturities of two, four or six months. Settlement occurs in even months.

Commodity-based future A traded futures contract based on the price of sugar and beans.

Precious metal future A traded futures contract based on the price of gold.

All futures contracts are traded on the Hong Kong Futures Exchange.

4.3 Securities identification codes

There is no uniform securities numbering system in Hong Kong. The Stock Exchange of Hong Kong maintains a numbering system for listed securities. These numbers are sometimes re-used and therefore not unique. In addition, custodians and brokers may use a separate numbering system for their own internal use.

4.4   Transfer of ownership

Transfer requirements of bearer securities

The value of these securities is embodied in the document or certificate. As no registration is necessary for bearer securities, the title to the security is transferred simply by physical delivery of the certificate(s). Stamp duty at 3% is payable on issue of the securities, except in the case of securities denominated otherwise than in Hong Kong dollars, or loan stock.

Transfer requirements of registered securities

The transfer of registered securities to a new holder requires the issue of contract notes by the buyer and the seller which are each subject to stamp duty at the rate of 0.25% payable by the buyer and the seller respectively. The buyer and the seller must then execute a transfer deed in the prescribed form which must be endorsed to evidence payment of stamp duty. A duty of HKD 5.– is payable on each transfer deed. Registration of transfer usually takes three to four weeks before the new certificates are issued. During this period, shares lodged for registration cannot be sold. Thus, where shares are purchased for quick resale, specific instructions must be issued to the custodian to retain the shares in 'street name', and not to forward them for registration.

A purchaser of registered securities is not regarded as eligible to the rights which are attached to those securities until his name has been entered in the company's register of members.

5   STRUCTURE AND REGULATION OF FINANCIAL MARKETS

5.1   Structure of financial activities

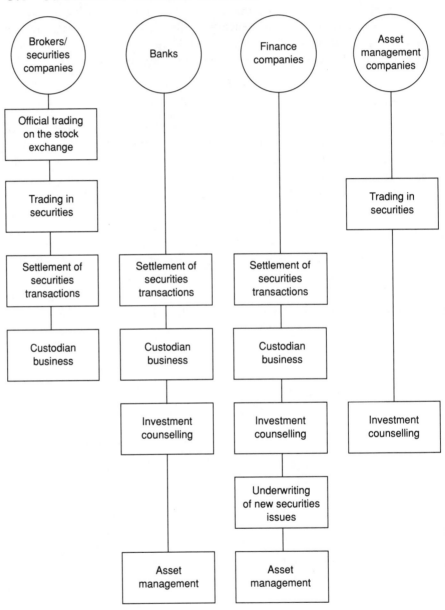

5.2 Regulatory structure

Overview

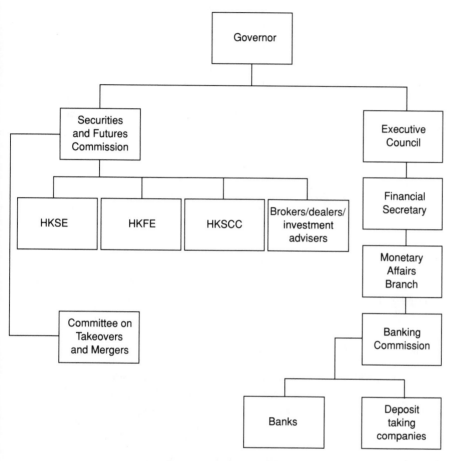

Note:
HKSE: Stock Exchange of Hong Kong Limited
HKFE: Hong Kong Futures Exchange Limited
HKSCC: Hong Kong Securities Clearing Company

Responsibility of regulatory bodies

Name of body	Responsibilities	Legal basis
The Securities and Futures Commission (SFC) (self-regulatory body)	Regulatory oversight over brokers, dealers, investment advisers, exchanges and clearing agencies	Securities and Futures Commission Ordinance
	Imposing administrative disciplinary sanctions	

Name of body	Responsibilities	Legal basis
	Power of enforcement:	
	– investigation of potential violations	
	– prosecution function	
Banking Commission (BC) (governmental agency)	Regulatory oversight over banks and deposit-taking companies, and licensing	Banking Ordinance
	Power of enforcement:	
	– compliance audits	
	– investigation of potential violations	
	– prosecution function	

Supervision of stock exchange

The Stock Exchange is under the supervision of the Securities and Futures Commission.

Supervision of Securities Clearing Company

It is a function of the Securities and Futures Commission to supervise the operation of the Securities Clearing Company in Hong Kong, which has been established and is jointly owned by the Stock Exchange and a group of banks.

Supervision of broker/dealers and custodians

Broker/dealers are under the supervision of the Securities and Futures Commission. Banks and deposit-taking companies who offer custodial services are under the supervision of the Banking Commission.

6   CUSTODIANS

Bank of East Asia
10 Des Voeux Road Central
Hong Kong

Tel: 852 842 3200
Fax: 852 740 836

Barclays Bank
1st floor
St George's Building
Chater Road
Hong Kong

Tel: 852 266 255

Chase Manhattan
One Exchange Square
8 Connaught Place
Hong Kong

Tel: 852 841 4245
Fax: call telephone number for fax

Citibank
35th floor
Citicorp Centre
18 Whitfield Road
Causeway Bay
Hong Kong

Tel: 852 807 6502
Fax: call telephone number for fax

Hongkong & Shanghai Bank
1 Queens Road Central
Hong Kong

Tel: 852 822 3694
Fax: 852 868 1646

Security Pacific Asian Bank
Room 1814–1816 Swire House
9 Chater Road
Hong Kong

Tel: 852 524 4456
Fax: 852 521 2313

Standard Chartered Bank
Edinburgh Tower
The Landmark
Hong Kong

Tel: 852 842 2333
Fax: 852 810 0651

24 ITALY

☞ ## 1 PRINCIPAL STOCK EXCHANGE

Unione dei Comitati Direttivi delle
Borse Valori Italiane
Via Camperio 4
20123 Milan
Italy

Tel: 39 2 805 76 74
Telex: 321430 MICOMB-1

☞ ## 2 PRINCIPAL REGULATORY AUTHORITY

Commissione Nazionale per le Società e la Borsa
Via Isonzo 19/D
00198 Roma
Italy

Tel: 396 84771
Telex: 43 612 434 (CONSOB)
      43 625 302
Fax: 39 6 841 6703

3 TIME DIFFERENCE FROM GMT: +1 HOUR

4 FORMS AND TYPES OF SECURITIES

4.1 Forms of securities

Bearer certificate (**Titolo al portatore**)   State securities, bonds and savings shares are normally issued in bearer form.

Registered certificate (**Titolo nominativo**)   All Italian shares, with the exception of savings shares, are by law in registered form – i.e. the name of the holder must be recorded in the register of the issuer. Bondholders may also apply for name registration as well as holders of savings shares, even though for these two types of securities only bearer certificates are good for delivery in stock exchange transactions.

Jumbo certificate (**Certificato di grosso taglio**)   Issued in connection with the activity of the central depository system. The certificates represent a large portion of the issue. The company or body (Monte Titoli or Banca d'Italia Gestione Centralizzata) holding the certificates are acting as custodian, e.g. for account of a bank, or sub-custodian, on behalf of a bank's client or a stockbroker's client (the latter only in the case of Monte Titoli).

Depository receipt (**Ricevuta di deposito**)   Certificates representing the deposit of an equivalent amount of foreign shares. At present, there is only one issue of Italian Depository Receipts representing Electrolux ordinary shares.

Temporary global certificate (**Certificato globale provvisorio**)   Provisional certificate delivered to the lead-manager when a bond is issued.

4.2   Types of securities

Equities and warrants

Ordinary share (**Azione ordinaria**)   Shares that represent participations in corporations and carry the right to attend the general meetings and to vote on resolutions: one vote per share. Ordinary shares carry the right to share in the distribution of company assets in the event of the company being wound up, once all creditors' claims have been met. (Issued in registered form.)

Participating preferred share (**Azione privilegiata**)   Shares carrying a preference over ordinary shares in the distribution of dividends but normally with a restricted voting power. Such shareholders are not allowed to vote on issues which are concerned with the carrying on of ordinary business, but only in the case of modifications in the company's Articles of Association. Participating preferred shares carry the right to share in the distribution of company assets in the event of the company being wound up, once all creditors' claims have been met. (Issued in registered form.)

Savings share (**Azione di risparmio**)   Shares with no voting rights, but priority rights (compared with preferred or ordinary shares) regarding the distribution of dividends (at least 5% of nominal value) and in the case of the company being wound up. By law, savings shares can only be issued by companies whose ordinary shares are listed on a Stock Exchange. Savings shares may be in bearer form and enjoy also a favourable taxation. Should the company be wound up, savings shares take precedence over ordinary or participating preferred shares in repayment of capital up to their full par value. (Issued in registered and bearer form.)

Warrant (**Warrant or 'buono facoltà di acquisito'**)   Warrants entitle the bearer to subscribe to new shares or bonds under specific conditions. They may be issued together with the so-called warrant bond issues or in relation to capital increases. (Issued in registered and bearer form.)

Debt instruments

Treasury credit certificate [Certificato di Credito del Tesoro (CCT)]   Floating-rate state securities, with annual or semi-annual coupons indexed on Treasury bill yields, issued almost every month. At present, outstanding securities have a remaining life to maturity of up to seven years. (Issued in registered and bearer form.)

Treasury bond [Buono del Tesoro poliennale (BTP)]   Fixed rate state securities, bearing semi-annual coupons. At present, outstanding securities have a remaining life to maturity of up to ten years. (Issued in registered and bearer form.)

Treasury certificate in ECU (European Currency Units) [Certificato del Tesoro in ECU (CTE)]   Fixed-rate state securities denominated in ECU. At present, outstanding securities have a remaining life of a up to five years; a 20-year CTE was issued abroad. (Issued in registered and bearer form.)

Treasury bond in ECU [Buono del Tesoro in ECU (BTE)]   Issued with a maturity of up to one year in registered or bearer form.

Treasury certificate with option [Certificato del Tesoro con opzione (CTO)]   Fixed-rate state securities with a remaining life to maturity of up to six years; holders entitled to apply for advance redemption after three years. (Issued in registered and bearer form.)

Public agency bond (Obbligazione emessa da ente pubblico)   Bonds issued by state-controlled agencies and backed by the full faith and credit of the Italian government. Main issuers: Ferrovie dello Stato (National Railways); ENEL – Ente Nazionale Energia Elettrica (National Electricity) – issuing floating-rate, fixed-rate and zero-coupon bonds; IRI – Istituto per la Ricostruzione Industriale (Industrial Reconstruction Institute) – and ENI – Ente Nazionale Idrocarburi (National Hydrocarbons) – issuing also warrant bonds. (Issued in registered and bearer form.)

Medium–long term credit institutions bond (Obbligazione emessa da Istituti di Credito Speciale)   Main issuers: CCOP – Consorzio di Credito Opere Pubbliche – and IMI – Istituto Mobiliare Italiano – issuing chiefly floating-rate bonds and recently Certificates of Deposit having zero-coupon or semi-annual floating-rate interest. (Issued in registered and bearer form.)

Company bond (Obbligazione societaria)   Companies generally issue convertible bonds or bonds with warrant(s) having a maturity of five to seven years. These bonds are not much traded. (Issued in registered and bearer form.)

Mortgage bond (Cartella fondiaria)   Issued by mortgage banks for the purpose of long-term financing of loans backed by mortgages; there are fixed- and floating-rate bonds. (Issued in registered and bearer form.)

Convertible bond **(Obbligazione convertibile)** Bonds which may be converted by the owner into stocks in accordance with the terms of the issue. (Issued in registered and bearer form.)

Cum warrant bond **(Obbligazione cum warrant)** Bonds accompanied by a warrant to purchase a given quantity of securities at a price according to the terms of the issue. (Issued in registered and bearer form.)

Money market instruments

The money market concerns securities with a term of maximum 18 months.

Treasury bills certificate **[Buono ordinario del Tesoro (BOT)]** BOTs are issued with maturities of three, six and 12 months. They are sold at a discount and have no coupons attached.

Treasury bonds in ECU **(Buoni del Tesoro in ECU)** Issued with maturities of around 370 days bearing one fixed-rate coupon and denominated in ECU.

Certificates of deposit **(Certificati di deposito)** Issued as bearer certificates with a minimum denomination and a term of, at most, 60 months.

Banker's acceptance **(Accettazione bancaria)** Draft with which a company orders a bank to pay a certain amount of money on a given date (as a rule from one to three months). By virtue of a preliminary agreement, the bank affixes its acceptance signature on the certificate thus becoming the main obligator.

Commercial paper **(Polizza di credito commerciale)** Note with which a company that is granted a loan (borrower) acknowledges its debt with the lender. The loan is reimbursable on a given date (from three to 12 months). The note is backed by a guarantee of a bank in favour of the party financing the loan or in favour of whoever becomes transferee of the same credit.

Mutual fund **(Fondi comune d'investimento)** Mutual funds (open end funds) were introduced in Italy by law in March 1983. A unit is evidence of a participation in a mutual fund in which investors pool their capital for joint investment. The assets are managed by the mutual fund's management company for the account of the investors.

4.3   Securities Identification Code

Code name and structure

Italian banks use uniform securities codes (codice UIC). The UIC code is formed by six-digit numbers. However, each bank uses also an internal code.

   Example: 6002 ALIVAR shares

Name and address of organization responsible for the Security Identification System

Ufficio Italiano Cambi
Via delle 4 Fontane 123
00184 Rome
Italy

Tel: 06 46 431
Fax: 06 46 63 47 34

4.4 Transfer of ownership

In Italy bonds may be either in registered or in bearer form, the latter being the most usual one. Under an Act of 1941, shares issued by companies must be, with the exception of savings shares, introduced in 1974, in registered form.

Transfer of bearer issues

The transfer of ownership can be effected either by delivering the certificate physically to the buyer or by book entry.

Transfer of registered issues

Transfer of ownership of registered shares is effected either by registration on the part of the issuing company of the new owner's name in the company's Register of Shareholders and the issue of a certificate in the name of the new owner, or by endorsement on the back of the certificate. Such endorsement must contain:

– Name, place and date of birth, domicile and nationality of the endorsee (in the case of individuals);
– Company name, registered office, domicile and nationality of the endorsee (in the case of an organization having corporate status).

The endorsement must be dated and signed by the endorser, and certified by a public notary or stockbroker or by a bank. Italian banks may themselves sign the endorsement by proxy; this is the most customary procedure, as it allows transfers to be effected smoothly and more rapidly.

The transfer of registered shares by endorsement is fully valid and has full effect towards third parties, even if the relative entry in the company's Register has not been made.

In the case of negotiation abroad between non-residents or Italians resident abroad, of Italian shares legally circulating abroad, transfer is effected by endorsement on the securities, showing the same details as above. The endorsement must be dated and signed by the endorser and certified by a

Consulate or by officials of an Italian bank located abroad authorized for the purpose.

Share registers are maintained by the companies themselves.

The transfer of ownership of registered securities within the Monte Titoli system is done through depositors (Chapter 4) taking part in the centralized administration system and does not involve any physical movement of securities. According to section 2 of article 4 of the Monte Titoli Law, 19 June 1986, No. 289, such transfer has all the effects typical of the transfer envisaged by the rules governing securities circulation in Italy. Depositors inform issuers of the names of the actual owners when the rights attached to securities are exercised (e.g. to attend shareholder's meetings, to cash dividends, to subscribe capital increases, etc.).

5   STRUCTURE AND REGULATION OF FINANCIAL MARKETS

5.1   Structure of financial activities

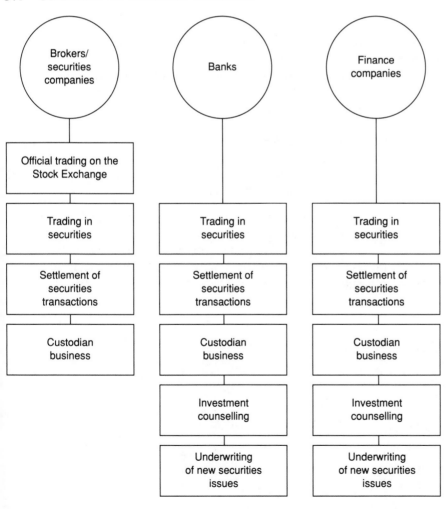

By law the only persons allowed to trade on the floor of the Stock Exchanges are the brokers (agenti di cambio).

Stockbrokers enjoy an exclusive monopoly over fixing the daily prices in bonds and shares on the Stock Exchange floor. Banks may not deal on the Exchange, but have to pass their orders to the stockbrokers. However, banks and stock trading companies (commissionarie) as well as the brokers are allowed to match orders of their clients. The remuneration for the work carried out by the agenti di cambio on behalf of clients is the brokerage commission.

In January 1991, the Parliament approved the new law regulating brokerage activities in the securities market covering the constitution of SIMs (società di intermediazione mobiliare), i.e. Securities Intermediation Companies.

SIMs will be supervised by:

- CONSOB, as to the line of conduct in relation with customers, so that the transparency of prices and the protection of customers' interests be guaranteed;
- the Bank of Italy, as to their assets and risk management requirements.

Article 1 of the law defines the brokerage business as follows:

- negotiation of securities, either for its own account or on behalf of third parties;
- placement and distribution of securities, with or without previous subscription or assumption of warranties in favour of the issuer;
- assets management through transactions in securities;
- collection of purchase or sale orders of securities;
- advice on securities matters;
- solicitation of public savings promoted or transacted in places other than registered or administrative offices of the issuer, the subject proposing the investment or proceeding to the placement.

The implementation regulations, which will set the actual guidelines for the market participants, will be approved by end of June 1991.

Interim provisions set out by article 18 of the law allow any entity carrying on brokerage activities as of the date on which the law was enacted to continue such business for the term of 12 months.

5.2 Regulatory structure

Overview

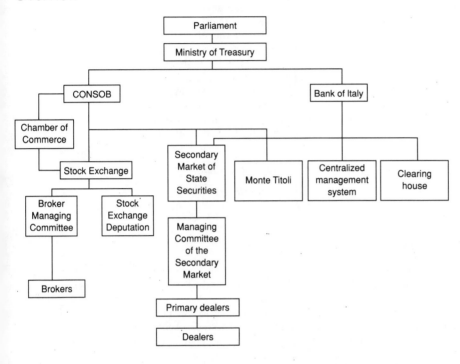

The secondary market of state securities was introduced by a Ministerial Decree in February 1988 and became operative on 16 May 1988. The market is based on a telematic circuit and the primary dealers commit themselves to make bid and offer prices which are binding for them towards other member dealers of the system.

Responsibility of regulatory bodies

Name of body	Task/responsibilities	Legal basis
Ministry of Treasury	Highest authority, politically responsible to Parliament for exchange matters	RDL No. 815 30 June 1932
CONSOB (1 president and 4 members)	Legislative power by: – CONSOB circulars – CONSOB communications – CONSOB recommendations	Law No. 216 7 June 1974 and Law No. 281 4 June 1985

Name of body	Task/responsibilities	Legal basis
	Adjudicatory power: CONSOB has the absolute authority and discretion regarding the organization of the stock exchange and the operations carried out by individuals or companies operating on the stock exchange or engaging in intermediation activity including the right to introduce and remove shares to and from the official listing Power of enforcement: – investigation of potential violations	

Supervision of stock exchange

Name of body	Task/responsibilities	Legal basis
The Chamber of Commerce (Camera di Commercio)	It is responsible for locally controlling the stock exchanges, providing the necessary premises and funds for operations	DPR No. 138 31 March 1975
Broker Managing Committee (appointed by the agenti di cambio)	It is responsible for declaring prices and for compiling the official list published by the Chamber of Commerce	DLL No. 250 18 September 1944
The Stock Exchange Deputation (Deputazione di Borsa), appointed each year by the Ministry of Treasury	It is entrusted with the task of enforcing the laws and regulations of the stock exchange	Law No. 272 20 March 1913
Managing Committee of the Secondary Market of State Securities (formed by seven members)	It has the function of a self-regulatory body and singles out the securities to be traded	DM No. 62 7 February 1988

Supervision of clearing and central securities depository organizations

The clearing house is managed by the Bank of Italy as well as the centralized management operating as central depository for state securities, whereas Monte Titoli is supervised by the Bank of Italy and by CONSOB.

Supervision of broker/dealers and custodian banks

Stockbrokers are appointed by a Presidential Decree and their activity is supervised by CONSOB and by the Broker Managing Committee, as well as by the Stock Exchange Deputation.

The supervision of banks is assigned to the Bank of Italy and for their activity in the securities field they have to comply with CONSOB rules.

The new law on SIMs defined that a Stock Exchange Council (Consiglio di Borsa) will be appointed for a period of three years through a Decree issued by the Ministry of Treasury and it will be formed by 14 members. As from the date on which the Consiglio di Borsa will became operative, the Broker Managing Committee and the Stock Exchange Deputation will be abolished.

6   CUSTODIANS

Banca di Roma
Piazza Tommaso Edison 1
1–20123 Milan
Italy

Tel: 2 88631
Fax: 2 88632 449

Banca Commerciale Italiana
Piazza de la Scala 6
20121 Milan
Italy

Tel: 2 88501
Fax: 2 8850 3026

Barclays Bank
Via della Moscova 18
20121 Milan
Italy

Tel: 2 63721
Fax: 2 637 22180

Chase Manhattan Bank
Piazza Meda 1
20121 Milan
Italy

Tel: 2 8895 2559
Fax: call telephone number for fax

Citibank
Foro Buonaparte 16
20121 Milan
Italy

Tel: 2 854-2554
Fax: call telephone number for fax

Banca Popolare Commercio e
  Industria
Via della Moscova 33
20121 Milan
Italy

Tel: 2 62751
Fax: 2 6599-072

Credito Italiano
Securities Department
Piazza Cordusio 2
20122 Milan
Italy

Tel: 2 8862 2348
Fax: 2 8862 2818

Istituto Bancario San Paulo Torino
Via Broletto 9
20121 Milan
Italy

Tel: 2 5551
Fax: call telephone number for fax

Morgan Guaranty Trust
Corso Venezia 54
20121 Milan
Italy

Tel: 2 774 4242
Fax: call telephone number for fax

Banco Ambrosiano Veneto
Piazza Paulo Ferrari 10
20121 Milan
Italy

Tel: 2 8594 7253
Fax: call telephone number for fax

25 JAPAN

1 PRINCIPAL STOCK EXCHANGES

Tokyo Stock Exchange
2-1 Nihombashi-Kabuto-cho
Chuo-ku
Tokyo 103
Japan

Tel: 81 3 6660141
Telex: TKOSE 'J' 2522759

Osaka Securities Exchange
8–16 Kitahama 1-chome
Chuo-ku
Osaka 541
Japan

Tel: 81 6 229 86 37
Telex: OSKE 'J' 522 2215

2 PRINCIPAL REGULATORY AUTHORITY

Ministry of Finance – Securities Bureau
3-1-1 Kasumigaseki
Chiyoda-ku
Tokyo
Japan

Tel: 81 33 581 3505
Telex: 72 24980
Fax: 81 33 581 6594

3 TIME DIFFERENCE FROM GMT: +9 HOURS

4 FORMS AND TYPES OF SECURITIES

4.1 Forms of securities

***Bearer bond* (Genbutsusai or Honken)**   Bond not registered on the books of
the issuer and payable to the party possessing the bond certificate. Ownership is transferred by delivery of the certificates. Interest and principal are
paid by the paying agent bank against presentation of coupons and bond
certificates respectively on their due dates.

Registered bond (**Tourokusai**)   Bond that is registered in the name of the holder on the books of the issuer or issuer's registrar. Certificates are not necessary for registered bonds and in fact not issued in most cases. The registration agent sends to the holder a receipt form for interest and principal prior to their due dates. The form has to be completed and returned by the holder to the registration agent for payment. Ownership is transferred by filing a completed application form for name registration to the agent who keeps all necessary records of changes in ownership.

Registered share (**Kimei Kabushiki**)   Shares with the holder's name on the books of the issuer as well as on the share certificates. Shares should in principle, under Japanese commercial law, be registered shares. Ownership can be transferred by delivery of the certificates, but various rights on shares such as receipt of dividends and liquidation of assets, as well as voting rights, are not transferred without registration of a holder's name on the books of the issuer. Almost all shares in Japan are registered shares.

Bearer share (**Mukimei Kabushiki**)   Shares which are not registered in the holder's name. These shares are exceptional from the point of view of the commercial law and can only be issued according to the conditions in the Articles of Incorporation of the issuing company. Execution of shareholder's rights requires deposit of the certificates with the issuer.

Uncertificated registered share (inscribed stock) (**Touroku Kabu**)   Shares in lots less than a set trading unit and with no corresponding certificates available. These odd lot shares are registered on the books of the issuing company or its agents and are not transferable to others. Disposal of these shares is only possible by demanding their purchase by the issuing company.

Stock certificate (**Kabuken or Honken**)   Certificate representing a shareholder's ownership in a corporation. The certificate is issued only for shares in multiples of the trading unit number, generally 1000. Ownership of shares is transferred by delivery of the certificate(s), the same as with a bearer bond. However, registration of the (new) holder's name on the books of the issuer or its agent is necessary for the (transfer of the) entitlement to dividends, bonus shares, right issues, etc. (*see also*: 'Inscribed share' and 'Registered share').

Jumbo certificate   Certificates in denominations larger than the trading unit. They are issued for convenience of delivery and safekeeping.

4.2   Types of securities

Equities and warrants

Ordinary share (**Futsu Kabushiki**)   Shares representing equal ownership in a corporation with such rights as the receipt of dividends, bonus shares, rights issues and the liquidation of assets, including the voting rights. Almost all stocks belong to this category in Japan.

Preferred share **(Yuusen Kabushiki)**   Shares that have preference over common stock in the payment of dividends and the liquidation of assets.

Deferred share **[Kouhai (Retsugo or Atodori) Kabushiki]**   Shares of a nature opposite to that of preferred shares, which are subordinate to ordinary shares in the entitlement to dividends and the liquidation of assets.

Mixed share **(Kongou Kabushiki)**   Shares which have the qualities of both preferred shares and deferred shares. These shares can have preference in dividend payments over common shares and have subordinate position to common shares, or vice versa, in the payment of liquidated assets.

Redeemable share **(Shoukan Kabushiki)**   Shares to be redeemed out of the profits of a corporation. Redemption is mostly applied to preferred shares and rarely to ordinary shares.

Convertible share **(Tenkan Kabushiki)**   Shares that can be converted into other types of share. Preferred, deferred, mixed or redeemable shares can be issued with a conversion right attached by a corporation. Conditions of conversion should be clarified in the company's Articles of Incorporation. Generally conversion is possible from preferred shares into ordinary shares.

Non-voting share **(Mugiketsuken Kabushiki)**   Shares without voting rights. Applies only to preferred shares and only to an extent not exceeding a quarter of the entire issued share capital. Voting rights must be restored when no dividends are paid.

Par value share **(Gakumen Kabushiki)**   Shares whose par value is set by the issuing company in its Articles of Incorporation. Since the revision of the commercial law in 1982, the par value can be any amount above yen 50 000. For many corporations organized before 1982, the par value of their shares is either yen 50 or yen 500.

Non-par value share **(Mugakumen Kabushiki)**   Shares that do not have par value. Non-par value shares are equal to par value shares in their various rights and therefore interchangeable. Issuers can choose either or both types. Conversion from one type of shares to the other does not affect the capital of the corporation.

Warrant **(Shinkabu Hikiuke Shosho)**   Certificate representing the right to subscribe to shares of a new issue of common stock. This certificate should be issued based on the approval of the board of directors or the Articles of Incorporation of the issuing company. Certificates are in bearer form and are traded in the market prior to the beginning of (and during) the subscription period.

Debt instruments

(a) Types according to interest payments
Coupon bond **(Ritsuki Sai)**   Bonds issued with detachable coupons that must be presented to a paying agent or the issuer periodically for interest payment. These bonds are in bearer form.

Discount bond (**Waribiki Sai**) Bonds without coupons, issued and traded below their redemption value. (Issued in bearer or registered form; may be held in book entry form or as jumbo certificate.)

Floating-rate bond (**Hendou Ritsuki Sai**) Bonds with a variable interest rate. There are several such bond issues of the Japanese government, having maturities of 15 years. (Issued in bearer form; may be held as jumbo certificate.)

(b) Types according to maturity
Long-term bond (**Chouki Sai**) Bonds with maturities exceeding five years. (Issued in bearer or registered form; may be held in book entry form or as jumbo certificate.)

Medium-term bond (**Chyuki Sai**) Bonds with maturities exceeding one year up to five years. (Issued in bearer or registered form; may be held in book entry form or as jumbo certificate.)

Short-term bond (**Tanki Sai**) Bonds with maturities less than one year. (Issued in bearer or registered form; may be held in book entry form or as jumbo certificate.)

(c) Types according to borrower
Public bond (**Kou Sai or Koukyou Sai**) Bonds issued by the government, local government or governmental organizations. (Issued in bearer or registered form; may be held in book entry form or as jumbo certificate.)

Government bond (**Koku Sai**) Bonds issued by the Japanese government. (Issued in bearer or registered form; may be held in book entry form or as jumbo certificate.

Municipal bond (**Chihou Sai**) Bonds issued by a municipality. (Issued in bearer or registered form; may be held in book entry form or as jumbo certificate.)

Bank debenture (**Kinyu Sai**) Mid-term debentures issued by any one of six authorized banks with maturities of one, three and five years. (Issued in bearer or registered form; may be held in book entry form or as jumbo certificate.)

Corporate bond (**Sha Sai**) Bonds issued by private corporation. (Issued in bearer or registered form; may be held in book entry form or as jumbo certificate.)

Electric power company bond (**Denryoku Sai**) Bonds issued by electric power companies. This is a specific type of corporate bond. (Issued in bearer or registered form; may be held in book entry form or as jumbo certificate.)

Foreign bond in yen currency (Samurai bond) (**Yen Date Gai Sai**) Straight bond denominated in Japanese yen and issued by foreign institution on the Japanese capital market. (Issued in bearer or registered form; may be held in book entry form or as jumbo certificate.)

Foreign bond in foreign currency (Shogun bond) **(Gaika Date Gaisai)**
Straight bond denominated in a foreign currency and issued by foreign institution on the Japanese capital market. (Issued in bearer or registered form; may be held in book entry form or as jumbo certificate.)

(d)   Types according to convertibility
Straight bond **(Futsu Sha Sai)**   Bond without any clauses granting conversion or warrant privileges. (Issued in bearer or registered form; may be held in book entry form or as jumbo certificate.)

Convertible bond **(Tenkan Sha Sai)**   Bond which may be converted by the holder into shares in accordance with the terms of the issue. (Issued in bearer or registered form; may be held in book entry form or as jumbo certificate.)

Bond with warrant **(Shinkabu Hikiukeken Tsuki Shasai)**   Bond issued with warrant(s) that entitle the holder to buy a proportionate amount of common stock at a specified price during a specified period. There are both detachable and undetachable warrants. Usually issued in bearer form; may be held in book entry form or as jumbo certificate.

(e)   Types according to the currency of the face value
Yen bond **(Yen Date Sai)**   Bonds denominated in Japanese yen. (Issued in bearer or registered form; may be held in book entry form or as jumbo certificate.)

Foreign currency bond **(Gaika Date Sai)**   Bonds denominated in a foreign currency. (Issued in bearer or registered form; may be held in book entry form or as jumbo certificate.)

Dual currency bond **(Dual currency Sai)**   Bonds denominated in two different currencies for the principal amount and the interest respectively. (Issued in bearer or registered form; may be held in book entry form or as jumbo certificate.)

(f)   Other types
Government guaranteed bond **(Seifu Hosho Sai)**   Bonds issued by public institution affiliated with the Japanese government and guaranteed by the government. (Issued in bearer or registered form; may be held in book entry form or as jumbo certificate.)

Money market instruments

The Japanese money market is made up of two segments, the interbank money market and the open money market.

Secured call money market, unsecured call money market, Tokyo dollar call market and bill discount market are the constituents of the interbank money market, where financial institutions borrow or lend short-term funds inter-institutionally. The Bank of Japan regulates money supply and other monetary policies mainly through the interbank money market.

Unlike the interbank market, participants are not limited to financial institutions in the open money market. With the increasing number of market instruments, the volume and the share of the open money market transactions have increased rapidly to account for almost half of the total money market transactions. The following instruments are available on the present open money market:

Treasury bill **(Tanki Kokusai)**   Short-term securities with maturities of one year or less issued in denominations of yen 10 million or more at a discount from face value. Three-month bills and six-month bills are issued at present. (Book entry.)

Financing bill **(Seifu Tanki Shoken)**   Short-term securities with maturity of two months issued in denominations of yen 100 million or more at a discount from face value. (Book entry.)

Banker's acceptance **(Banker's acceptance)**   The banker's acceptance market was newly established in June 1985. Yen-denominated bills of lading with a maturity of less than about six months are eligible for trading. The minimum amount to be traded is yen 100 million. Banker's acceptances can be dealt in by securities houses, as well as by banks. The BA market is very inactive with almost nil balance in circulation. (Registered.)

Certificate of deposit **(Certificate of deposit)**   Maturities range from two weeks to two years. Withholding tax applies to interest payments, but no securities transaction tax is levied. Investors can purchase certificates of deposit from banks directly in minimum allotments of yen 50 million. Banks and securities houses can deal in certificates of deposit. (Registered.)

Commercial paper **(Commercial paper)**   Short-term obligations with maturities ranging from two weeks to nine months issued by creditworthy corporations. Commercial papers are underwritten by banks or securities houses and sold to institutional investors. Certificates should be in denominations larger than yen 100 million and, due to stamp duty requirements, are often issued in denominations as large as yen 5 billion. Commercial papers are issued at a discount, and there is no withholding tax on the interest income. (Registered.)

Gensaki **(Gensaki)**   An agreement between a seller and a buyer of Japan government bonds and other securities, whereby the seller agrees to repurchase the securities at an agreed-on price at a stated future date. Although Gensaki is a sale/purchase transaction of securities, its actual function is a short-term money market instrument using the securities as collateral. Government, municipal and corporate bonds are the principal instruments for Gensaki transactions; CDs, CPs and Treasury bills are also eligible for the transaction. The maximum transaction period is 12 months under the MoF's guideline. Transactions of one month to three months are most widely transacted. (Book entry.)

Investment Trust Fund

Investment trust (**Toushishintaku**) A pooled fund of public investors managed by a licensed investment trust management company with specific investment objectives. Unlike the US mutual fund, a Japanese investment trust fund does not form an investment company. Instead it is operated under a trust deed by which an investment trust management company acts as grantor and a bank acts as trustee to administer the fund. The legal status of the Japanese investment trust fund is similar to that of a unit trust in the UK. In general, ownership of the fund is evidenced by a beneficiary certificate issued in bearer form which can be changed to registered form on demand.

Unit-type investment trust (**Tanigata Toushishintaku**) An investment fund unique to Japan. Money paid in by investors forms one unit of the investment fund which is placed in trust and managed for a predetermined period, independently from other funds. No additional issue is made after the original issue. Redemption may be made prematurely on demand at net asset value. (Bearer form or registered form.)

Open-type investment trust (**Tsuikagata Toushishintaku**) An investment trust which is open to subsequent additions to the original fund. The fund runs for an indefinite period in general and the beneficiary certificate can be purchased at market value. (Bearer form or registered form.)

Bond investment trust (**Kaushasai Toushishintaku**) An investment trust whose investments are exclusively limited to bonds, bills and other fixed-income debt instruments. Income derived from a bond investment trust is treated as interest. (Bearer form or registered form.)

Stock investment trust (**Kabushiki Toushishintaku**) An investment trust whose investment mediums include equity shares as well as bonds. Income derived from a stock investment trust is treated as dividend. (Bearer form or registered form.)

Traded options

Stock price index options (**TOPIX Option**) Call or put options based on the Tokyo Stock Price Index (TOPIX) and listed on the Tokyo Stock Exchange.

Nikkei stock average options (**Nikkei Heikin Options**) Call or put options based on the Nikkei Stock Average, and listed on the Osaka Stock Exchange.

Nagoya 25 Index option (**Meisho Option 25**) Call or put options based on the Nagoya 25 Stock Price Index and listed on the Nagoya Stock Exchange.

Bond options (**Saiken Options**) Call or put options based on long-term Japan government bonds and traded on OTC basis.

JGB futures options **(Saiken Sakimono Options)**   Call or put options based on Japan government bond futures, and listed on the Tokyo Stock Exchange.

Futures

Future on bonds **(Saiken Sakimono)**   Japanese government bond (JGB) futures are listed on the Tokyo Stock Exchange.

Commodity and precious metal future **(Shouhin Sakimono)**   There are 16 exchanges in Japan where various commodity futures and precious metals futures are traded. Contract months for these futures are March, June, September and December. Mentioned below are the three exchanges in Tokyo and the corresponding commodities traded on each exchange:

- Tokyo Commodity Exchange (gold, silver, platinum, natural rubber, cotton yarn and woollen yarn)
- Tokyo Grain Exchange (soyabean and adzuki bean)
- Tokyo Sugar Exchange (raw sugar and refined sugar).

Interest future on Japanese yen **(Euroyen Kinri Sakimono)**   Three months Euroyen basis.

Interest future on US dollar **(Eurodollar Kinri Sakimono)**   Three months Eurodollar basis.

US currency future **(Tsuuka Sakimono)**   Japanese yen against US dollars at Tokyo market.

Interest futures and currency futures are listed on the Tokyo International Financial Futures Exchange.

Stock future **(Kabushiki Sakimono)**   There are three listed stock futures:

- Topix listed on the Tokyo Stock Exchange.
- Nikkei Stock Average listed on the Osaka Stock Exchange
- Osaka Stock Future 50 (OSF) listed on the Osaka Stock Exchange.

4.3   Securities Identification Code

Code name and structure

The TSE Code is the standard numbering system utilized for the identification of Japanese securities. The Code consists of five digits for equities and nine digits for bonds. The Stock Code is commonly adopted and used by market participants. However, the Bond Code is not so common as the Stock code due to its insufficient coding capacity under the existing coding rule.

The SICC (Securities Identification Code Conference) is working on a new coding system for Japanese securities, with its introduction planned for 1992. This SICC Code is a 12-digit alphanumeric code based on ISIN standards and is expected to help standardized computer handling of Japanese securities.

Name and address of organization responsible for the Securities Identification System

Securities Identification Code Conference (SICC)
c/o Tokyo Stock Exchange
2-1 Nihonbashi Kabuto-cho
Chuo-ku
Tokyo 103
Japan

Tel: 03 3666 0141
Telex: 0252 2759

4.4 Transfer of ownership

Transfer of bearer securities

The transfer of ownership of bearer securities is effected by physical delivery. In practice, all shares are in registered form, and bearer securities are almost entirely comprised of bonds, although theoretically bearer shares could exist.

Transfer of registered securities

(a) Registered bonds
The transfer of bonds is effected by the transferee presenting an application for registration to the transfer agent. The name transfer process lasts a few days for government bonds and about two weeks for other bonds. Upon completion of the registration of the name transfer, the registration office has to deliver a registration certificate to the applicant. Since this certificate is only a notification of the completion of the name transfer, it cannot be traded or used as collateral. Requests for name transfer registration will not be accepted within three weeks for corporate bonds, and within two weeks for government bonds prior to the coupon payment date or redemption date.

(b) Registered shares
The transfer of ownership of registered shares is usually effected in the same manner as for bearer securities – i.e. by physical delivery. Excepted are shares transferred within JSCC, which provides clearing by book entry to the member brokers.

However, registration of the shares is required for the owner to secure various rights attached to the shares such as dividends, bonus issues, etc.

Less-than-unit shares are not transferable. As an alternative, requests are made to the issuing company to buy back the shares, and the proceeds are paid to the opposite party. Another solution may be to wait until the shares can be consolidated into a unit share as a result of bonus issues, etc.

5 STRUCTURE AND REGULATION OF FINANCIAL MARKETS

5.1 Structure of financial market

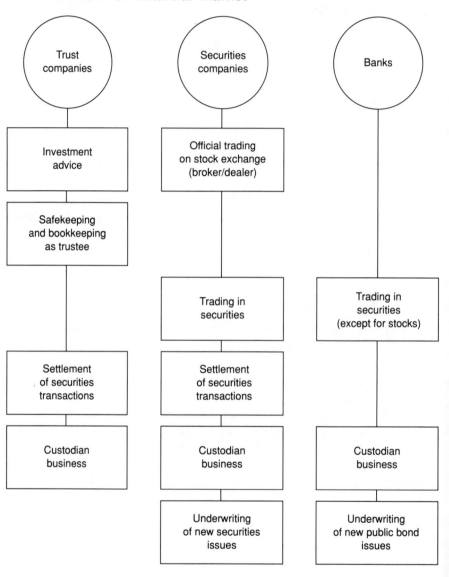

5.2 **Regulatory structure**

Overview

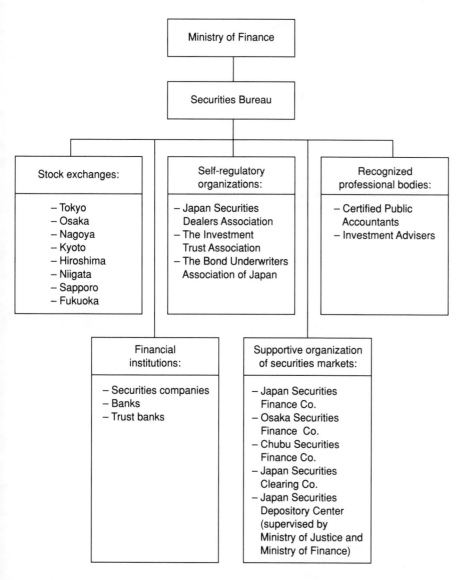

Responsibilities of regulatory bodies

All regulatory control and supervision is administrated by the Ministry of Finance's (MoF) Securities Bureau. Below are the divisions of MoF's Securities Bureau and their corresponding supervisory functions:

Name of body	Tasks/responsibilities	Legal basis
Secondary Market Division	The formation of fair prices in the securities market. Licensing and supervision of securities finance companies. Designation and supervision of central depository agencies	Securities and Exchange Law Securities and Exchange Law
Corporate Finance Division	Corporate financial disclosure system (acceptance of securities reports, etc. and their examination). The certified public accountant system	Securities and Exchange Law Certified Public Accountant Law
Securities Companies Division	Licensing and supervision of securities companies, foreign securities companies, investment trust management companies, and the securities business of banking institutions. Registration and supervision of investment advisers	Securities and Exchange Law, Law concerning Foreign Securities Firms and Securities Investment Trust Law Law for Regulating Securities Investments Advisory Business
Inspection Division	Inspection of securities companies	Securities and Exchange Law
Coordination Division	Supervision of securities-related corporations for public benefit	Securities and Exchange Law
Capital Markets Division	Planning, drafting and supervising policies relating to the issuing markets for capital increases, corporate bonds and yen-denominated foreign bonds	Securities and Exchange Law and Commercial Codes

Supervision of stock exchanges

The respective stock exchanges are organized according to the Securities and Exchange Law and are licensed by the Ministry of Finance (MoF). Due to the public nature of their activities, the exchanges' self-regulating rules cannot be changed without MoF's approval.

As the organizational structure and internal rules of the stock exchanges have been designed to enable their members to run and control the exchanges fairly and smoothly by themselves, the internal rules wield great power and are provided with a strict penalty system.

Supervision of clearing and central securities depository organization

The only clearing and depository organization in Japan is the Japan Securities Clearing Corporation, which is a wholly owned subsidiary of the Tokyo Stock Exchange. Its operation is based on the rules of the Tokyo Stock Exchange on the clearing system for domestic securities. It is directly supervised by the Tokyo Stock Exchange and therefore indirectly by MoF.

In order to implement a more comprehensive depository and clearing system, the Law concerning Depository and Book Entry for Share Certificates, etc. was enacted in 1984, and the Japan Securities Depository Center (JASDEC) is working on this new system towards its introduction in 1991. The MoF and the Ministry of Justice will be responsible for its supervision.

6 CUSTODIANS

Bank of Tokyo
3-2 Nihonbashi
Hongokucho 1-chome
Chuo-ku
Tokyo 103
Japan

Tel: 3 3242 0515
Fax: 3 3243 01588

Barclays Trust & Banking
Mitsubishi Building
5-2 Marunouchi 2-chome
Chiyoda-ku
Tokyo
Japan

Tel: 3 3214 2821
Fax: 3 3214 7537

Chase Manhattan
1-3 Marunouchi 1-chome
Chiyoda-ku
Tokyo 100
Japan

Tel: 3 3287 4150
Fax: call telephone number for fax

Citibank
Shin Otemachi Building
2-2-1 Otemachi
Chiyoda-ku
Tokyo
Japan

Tel: 3 3273 3751
Fax: 3 35566 1635

Dai-ichi Kangyo Bank
1-5 Uchisaiwaicho 1-chome
Chiyoda-ku
Tokyo 100
Japan

Tel: 3 3596 2520
Fax: 3 3596 6096

Daiwa Bank
1-1 Otemachi 2-chome
Chiyoda-ku
Tokyo 100
Japan

Tel: 3 3231 1231
Fax: call telephone number for fax

Fuji Bank
5-5 Otemachi 1-chome
Chiyoda-ku
Tokyo 100
Japan

Tel: 3 3216 2211
Fax: call telephone number for fax

Industrial Bank of Japan
3-3 Marunouchi 1-chome
Chiyoda-ku
Tokyo 100
Japan

Tel: 3 3214 1111
Fax: call telephone number for fax

Long Term Credit Bank of Japan
1-2-4 Otemachi
Chiyoda-ku
Tokyo 100
Japan

Tel: 3 3211 5111
Fax: call telephone number for fax

Manufacturers Hanover Trust
Company
6-1 Otemachi 2-chome
Chiyoda-ku
Tokyo 100
Japan

Tel: 3 3242 6511
Fax: call telephone number for fax

Mitsubishi Bank
7-1 Marunouchi 2-chome
Chiyoda-ku
Tokyo 100
Japan

Tel: 3 3240 1111
Telex: J22960
Fax: 3 3211 6645

Mitsui Bank
1-2 Yurakucho 1-chome
Chiyoda-ku
Tokyo 100
Japan

Tel: 3 3501 1111
Fax: call telephone number for fax

Morgan Guaranty Trust
New Yurakucho Building
12-1 Yurakucho 1-chome
Chiyoda-ku
Tokyo 100
Japan

Tel: 3 3282 6564
Fax: call telephone number for fax

Morgan Stanley International
Ote Center Building
1-3 Otemachi 1-chome
Chiyoda-ku
Tokyo 100
Japan

Tel: 3 3286 9000

Union Bank of Switzerland
  (Trust and Banking)
Hibiya Kokusai Building
2-2-3 Uchisaiwaichi chome
Chiyoda-ku
Tokyo 100
Japan

Tel: 813 3503 7771
Fax: 813 3503 7746

Yasuda Trust and Banking
2-1 Yaesu 1-chome
Chuo-ku
Tokyo 103
Japan

Tel: 813 3278 8111
Fax: 813 3281 6947

26 KOREA

1   PRINCIPAL STOCK EXCHANGE

Korea Stock Exchange
33 Yoido-Dong
Youngdeungpo-ku
Seoul 150-010
Korea

Tel: 82 2 780 2271
Telex: K28384 KOSTEX

2   PRINCIPAL REGULATORY AUTHORITY

Securities and Exchange Commission
FKI Building
28-1 Yoido-Dong
Youngdeungpo-ku
Seoul 150-600
Korea

Tel: 82 2 785 0061
     82 2 785 7593
Telex: 801 32230 (KOSEC)
Fax: 82 2 785 3475

3   TIME DIFFERENCE FROM GMT: +9 HOURS

4   FORMS AND TYPES OF SECURITIES

4.1   Forms of securities

***Bearer certificate* (Mukimyung Zungsuh)**   Certificates which are not regis-
tered on the books of the issuer.

Registered certificate **(Kimyung Zungsuh)** Certificates which are registered on the books of the issuer and can be transferred to another owner only when endorsed by the registered owner.

Allotment letter **(Shinjoo Insukwon Zungsuh)** In the case of a rights issue, subscription rights are distributed in the form of allotment letters.

4.2 Types of securities

Equities and warrants .

Common stock **(Botong Joo)** Common stocks do not have priority in payment of dividends. Dividends of common stocks are not fixed, but may be increased substantially if the company performs well. While common stocks are typically the most volatile type of corporate securities, they are also the securities with the greatest expected return. They are issued in registered form, and can also be issued in bearer form if specified in the Articles of Incorporation of the company. Shareholders can request the company to convert bearer shares into registered shares whenever they wish.

Non-voting preferred stock **(Woosun Joo)** Shares with preference rights with regard to dividend payments and any distribution of assets in the event of liquidation. However, the dividend does not represent a contractual commitment of the issuing corporation. (Issued in registered form.)

Warrant **(Shinjoo Insukwon Žungkwon)** The right which entitles the bearer to subscribe a specific number of shares of stock at a predetermined price during a specified period. Warrants are issued as a part of equity-linked bonds and are issued in bearer form.

Debt instruments

Fixed-rate coupon bond **(Hwakjung Ijabu Sachae)** Bond that pays a fixed rate of interest. (Issued in bearer form.)

Floating-rate note **(Kumni Yundongbu Sachae)** Bond with a variable interest rate. (Issued in bearer form.)

Discount bond **(Hahlin Sachae)** Bond which is sold at a discount of its face value, but is redeemed at face value on maturity date. (Issued in bearer form.)

Short-term bond **(Dangi Chaekwon)** Bond with a maturity of less than one year from the issuing date. (Issued in bearer form.)

Mid-term bond **(Junggi Chaekwon)** Bond with a maturity date over one year but less than ten years from the issuing date. (Issued in bearer form.)

Long-term bond **(Janggi Chaekwon)** Bond with a maturity date after ten years from the issuing date. (Issued in bearer form.)

Government bond **(Kukchae)**   Fixed-income securities issued by the central government. (Issued in bearer form.)

Municipal bond **(Jibangchae)**   Fixed-income securities issued by provincial or city governments. (Issued in bearer form.)

Corporate bond **(Hesachae)**   Fixed-income securities issued by local corporations. Usually corporate bonds are secured by collateral or a bank guarantee and issued at a fixed rate interest. (Issued in bearer form.)

Convertible bond **(Junhwan Sachae)**   Bond which provides an option for bondholders to exchange each bond for a specified number of shares of the underlying stock of the issuing corporation. (Issued in bearer form.)

Bond with equity warrant(s) **(Shinjoo Insukwonbu Sachae)**   Bond issued together with warrant(s) which entitle(s) the holder to buy a proportionate amount of new shares. (Issued in bearer form.)

Investment trust units

Beneficiary certificate **(Sooik Zungkwon)**   Listed securities which guarantee investors' rights to participate in the principal or trusted assets managed by an investment trust company. They are redeemed on the basis of net asset value. According to the Securities Investment Trust Law, beneficiary certificates are issued by investment trust companies only and need the approval of the Ministry of Finance. (Issued in bearer form.)

Money market instruments

Treasury bill **(Jejung Zungkwon)**   Promise of the Ministry of Finance to pay a stipulated amount on a stated maturity date less than one year from the issuing date. (Issued in bearer form.)

Certificate of deposit **(Yetak Zungsuh)**   A receipt for deposit of funds in a financial institution that permits the holder to receive interest, plus the deposit at maturity. (Issued in bearer or registered form.)

Commercial paper **(Sangup Uhum)**   A short-term unsecured promissory note issued at a discount from the face value by a financial institution or a large company. (Issued in registered form.)

Bonds with repurchase agreements **(Hwan Mechae)**   Repurchase agreements are collateralized loan contracts which run from overnight to several months. (Issued in bearer form.)

4.3   Securities Identification Code

Code name and structure

The Korea Stock Exchange uses securities codes for listed securities which consist of five digits for stocks and eight digits for bonds. The Securities Supervisory Board supervises the Securities Identification Numbering System.

Name and address of organization responsible for the Security Identification System

The Securities Supervisory Board
28-1 Yoido-dong
Yongdeungpo-ku
Seoul
Korea

Tel: 02 785 00 61
Telex: K32230
Fax: 02 785 34 75

4.4 Transfer of ownership

Transfer of bearer issues

The transfer of bearer issues is effected by physical delivery of the certificates. No transfer documentation is required.

Transfer of registered issues

Although the shares are registered in Korea, they need no endorsement of the transferor (the seller). Therefore the transfer of registered issues is effected in the same way as the transfer of bearer issues. The buyer may register his/her shares in his/her name but is not required to do so if he/she is not interested in exercising the shareholder's rights. If a client opens a safekeeping account and keeps the shares with a broker (securities house), the broker may deliver the shares to the Korea Securities Settlement Corporation (KSSC). The shares are cleared through a book entry clearing system among the members of the KSSC.

5 STRUCTURE AND REGULATION OF FINANCIAL MARKETS

5.1 Structure of financial activities

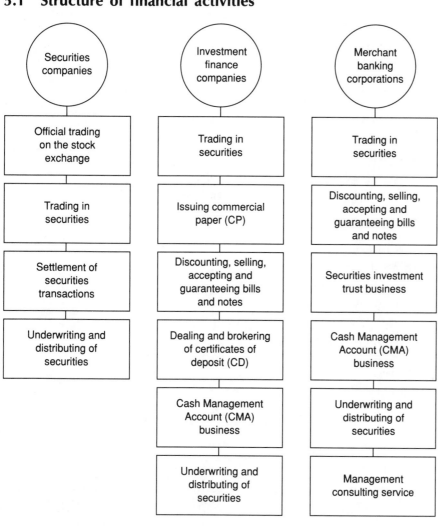

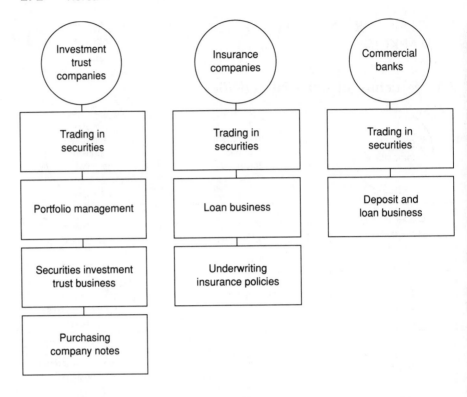

5.2 Regulatory structure

Overview

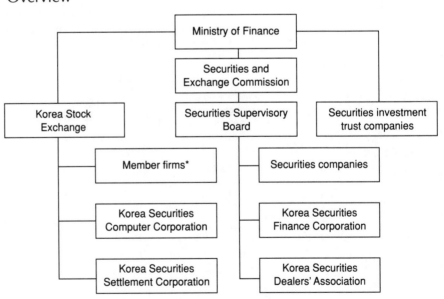

* Member firms are composed of 25 securities companies.

Responsibility of regulatory bodies

Name of body	Task/responsibilities
Ministry of Finance (MoF)	The MoF dominates policies for all financial sectors, including the securities markets. However, it generally delegates the implementation of its policies to a variety of governmental and semi-governmental agencies
Securities and Exchange Commission (SEC)	As an agency of the MoF, the SEC sets specific policies regarding the issuing of securities and the maintenance of market fairness, controls securities related institutions and supervises the staff of those institutions
Securities Supervisory Board (SSB)	As an agency of the MoF, the SSB is the enforcement arm of the SEC. It is directly involved in supervising and enforcing regulations pertaining to the registration of securities, the activities of listed companies and securities firms and general accounting standards as well
Korea Stock Exchange (KSE)	The KSE is responsible for maintaining a fair and stable market. The KSE sets requirements for listing companies' shares on the exchange and has the power to suspend trading or delist the securities if those requirements are not met
Korea Securities Dealers Association (KSDA)	The KSDA is a self-regulatory trade association composed of all member firms of the exchange

Supervision of the stock exchange

The MoF supervises the KSE to secure the safety of the market and to protect investors. The KSE must get approval from the MoF, after the consideration of the SEC, for the following activities:

– Change of the Articles of Incorporation
– Change of other regulations concerning the supervision of securities markets
– Listing or delisting of securities.

Supervision of clearing and central securities depository organization

The MoF, the SEC and SSB supervise the Korea Securities Settlement Corporation (KSSC).

Supervision of broker/dealers

The MoF, the SEC and the SSB supervise broker/dealers. As there are no custodian banks in Korea, securities companies carry out the custodian business.

Note: Foreign investors are not yet allowed to own securities in Korea directly, but must conclude an arrangement with a Korean bank which may agree to hold assets on a proxy basis.

6   CUSTODIANS

Bank of Seoul
10-1 Namdaemoon no, 2-ga
Chung-ku
Seoul
Korea

Tel: 2 776 8654
Telex: K23613
Fax: 2 774 3573

Citibank
KPO Box 749
89-29 Sinmunro 2-Ka
Chongro-ku
Seoul
Korea

Tel: 2 731 1303
Fax: 2 731 1987

Hongkong & Shanghai Banking
   Corporation
CPO Box 6910
6/F Kyobo Building
1 Chongro-1 Ka
Chongro-ku
Seoul 110-714
Korea

Tel: 2 739 4211
Fax: 2 739 1387

Korea Long Term Credit Bank
15-22 Yoido-dong
Youngdeungpo-ku
Seoul 150-010
Korea

Tel: 2 783 4362
Fax: 2 784 4277

Standard Chartered Bank
13/F Nae Wai Building
9-1 2-Ka Ulchi-Ro
Chung-ku
Seoul
Korea

Tel: 2 750 6114
Fax: 2 757 7444

27 LUXEMBOURG

1 PRINCIPAL STOCK EXCHANGE

Société de la Bourse de Luxembourg SA
Case Postale No. 165
L-2011 Luxembourg

Tel: 352 47 79 36 1
Telex: 2559 STOEX LU

2 PRINCIPAL REGULATORY AUTHORITY

Institut Monétaire Luxembourgeois
63 Avenue de la Liberté
2983 Luxembourg

Tel: 352 402929204
Telex: 2766
Fax: 352 492180

3 TIME DIFFERENCE FROM GMT: +1 HOUR

4 FORMS AND TYPES OF SECURITIES

4.1 Forms of securities

Bearer certificates **(Certificats au porteur)** Most of the securities traded in the Grand Duchy of Luxembourg are in bearer form.

Registered certificates **(Certificats nominatifs)** Registered securities have been issued mainly by companies specializing in investment management.

Book entry **(Forme scripturale)** Some investment trusts do not issue securities in bearer or registered form, but only in book entry form.

Depositary receipts **(Certificats de dépôt)** Certificates representing the deposit of an equivalent amount of foreign (mostly registered) shares, known as:

– BDR (Bearer Depositary Receipt)
– EDR (European Depositary Receipt)
– CDR (Continental Depositary Receipt), or
– IDR (International Depositary Receipt).

They are issued by banks or fiduciary companies to allow investors to buy bearer-type securities, payable in local currency, whereas the original underlying shares are registered in and payable in the currency of the home country.

Temporary global certificate (**Certificat global temporaire**) Provisional certificate embodying an entire (new) issue of Eurobonds to be deposited with a depository bank of an international central securities depository system against payment of the issue price and to be exchanged against the definitive bonds when they have been printed.

Permanent global certificate (**Certificat global permanent**) Certificates embodying an entire issue. No individual certificates may ever be claimed by holders. Introduced in recent times for warrants attached to Eurobonds. The permanent global certificate is usually held by one of the international clearing systems to allow for easy book transfers of the securities.

4.2 Types of securities

Equities and warrants

Ordinary share (**Action ou part sociale**) Security which represents an ownership interest in a company with full voting rights. (Issued in bearer or registered form; may be held as a depository receipt or in book entry form.)

Deferred ordinary share (**Action ordinarie différée**) A share with either the dividend or voting rights suspended until a future date.

Partly paid share (**Action libérée partiellement**) Shares for which the subscription price has not been fully paid. (Issued in bearer, if not quoted on a stock exchange, or registered form.)

Preferred share (**Action privilégiée**) Share having priority over ordinary shares regarding the distribution of dividends and liquidation proceeds. No or limited voting rights are attached (Issued in bearer or registered form.)

Cumulative preferred share (**action privilégiée cumulative**) Preferred share on which unpaid dividends are accumulated until enough earnings are available for payment. (Issued in bearer or registered form, may be held as a depository receipt.)

Note: In addition to the above-mentioned characteristics, shares may be convertible into other classes and/or redeemable.

Participation bond (**Action privilégiée participative et remboursable**) Share that provides participation in surplus profits beyond the fixed minimum dividend. (Issued in registered or bearer form.)

Subscription right **(Droit de souscription)**   Right of the shareholder to sub-scribe for new shares in the case of a capital increase in proportion to his present holding. (No security in the legal sense; in the case of bearer shares, usually embodied in a coupon.)

Bonus right **(Droit d'attribution gratuite)**   Right of the shareholder to par-ticipate in the distribution of bonus shares in the case of a capital increase in proportion to his present holding. (No security in the legal sense; in the case of bearer shares, usually embodied in a coupon.)

Note: Subscription and bonus rights are traded on the Luxembourg Stock Exchange during a limited period.

'SICAV' share **[Action d'une société d'investissement à capital variable (SICAV)]**   Share representing one part of ownership in an open-ended in-vestment company with a variable capital (SICAV). Certain companies issue capitalization and distribution shares. (Issued in bearer or registered form; may also be held in book entry form.)

'SICAF' share **[Action d'une société d'investissement à capital fixe (SICAF)]**   Share representing one part of ownership in a fixed capital in-vestment company. (Issued in bearer or registered form; may also be held in book entry form.)

Unit trust **(Part d'un fonds commun de placement)**   Participation unit in an investment fund (unit trust). Unit trust can issue capitalization and distribution units. (Issued in registered or bearer form; may be held in book entry form.)

Warrant **(Warrant)**   Issued either together with bond certificates or separ-ately, giving the holder the right to purchase within a specified period and at a fixed price securities or commodities. (Issued in bearer form; may be embodied in one global certificate.)

Debt instruments

Note that most of the instruments mentioned below are Eurobonds (except those issued in local currency). Eurobonds are predominantly issued in bearer form.

Straight bond **(Obligation classique)**   A fixed-income, interest-bearing debt security. The interest is usually paid yearly. Bonds containing no clauses granting conversion rights or other privileges.

Floating-rate note **(Obligation à taux variable)**   Medium- to long-term debt note with variable interest rate adjusted periodically. Interest rate floats at a fixed or variable spread over different interbank rates or government bond yields. Usually the interest rate is subject to a fixed minimum limit.

Step-up and/or step-down bond (or note) **(Obligation à taux progressif et/ou dégressif)**   Rate will go up and/or down as indicated in the terms and conditions of the notes.

Zero-bond **(Obligation à taux zéro)**   Bond without coupons. The special character of 'zero-bonds' consists in an issue price well below 100% with repayment on maturity at face value. The investor's only income is the difference between issue or purchase price and redemption or sale proceeds.

Capital growth bond **[Obligation (Bon d'Epargne) à capital croissant]**   Issue price 100%. Redemption at an increased principal amount. Mostly bonds issued by the government or public authorities of Luxembourg. (Issued in bearer form.)

Perpetual bond **(Obligation perpétuelle)**   Loans which are due for redemption only in the case of the borrower's liquidation. Interest rate can be fixed periodically.

Extendible bond **(Obligation prolongeable)**   The bondholder has the option at one or several fixed dates to extend the maturity.

Retractable bond **(Obligation retractable)**   Issuer and bondholder have the option for early redemption at one or several dates. Interest rate may be changed on these dates.

Bond with call option **(Obligation remboursable anticipativement au gré de l'émetteur)**   The issuer has the right to redeem the principal at a specified earlier date than the originally fixed final maturity.

Profit-sharing bond **(Obligation participative à rémunération variable)**   Interest consists of a fixed component, and a component depending on the results of the issuing company.

Bond with put option **(Obligation remboursable anticipativement au gré du porteur)**   The bondholder has the right to ask for redemption of the principal at a specified earlier date than at the originally fixed final maturity.

Government or state bond **(Emprunt d'état)**   Eight to 50 years loans issued in local currency by the Grand Duchy of Luxembourg. (Issued in bearer form.)

Public authority bond **(Emprunt émis par des pouvoirs publics)**   Luxembourg francs loans issued by the SNCI (Société Nationale de Crédit et d'Investissement), CFL (Chemins de Fer Luxembourgeois) and municipalities guaranteed by the government. (Issued in bearer form.)

Asset-backed securities **[Titres assis sur des créances d'actifs (p. ex. hypothèques)]**   Instruments backed by assets (e.g. mortgages).

Dual currency bond **(Obligation à deux devises)**   The issuer receives the proceeds of the issue in one currency, makes interest payments in the same currency, but redeems the principal at maturity in another currency according to a special formula fixed at the time of the issue of the bonds.

Multiple currency clause bond **(Obligation à option de change)**   Issue with the bondholder's option to choose the currency for redemption and sometimes also for interest payment or issue with the issuer's option to choose the currency for redemption.

Index, currency or gold-linked bond, etc. **(Obligation dont le remboursement est lié à la parité d'une devise, à un indice, au prix de l'or, etc.)** The redemption price is calculated according to a special formula based on an index, the exchange rate of a currency, the gold price, etc.

Convertible bond **(Obligation convertible)** Bond which may be exchanged for issuer shares or others, new bonds, gold bullion at a fixed price during specified periods, etc.

Equity note **(Obligation remboursable en actions)** Convertible bond which is redeemed at maturity by an automatic conversion into stock of the company.

Warrant issue bond **(Obligation avec warrant)** Bond with warrant issue which entitles to the purchase of issuer's shares or others (new bonds, gold bullion, currencies, etc.) at a fixed price during a specified period. The warrants are embodied in separate certificates or in a global certificate.

Private placement **(Placement privé)** Straight note which is not officially offered to the public, may be listed and traded on the stock exchange. (Issued in bearer or registered form.)

Eurobond **(Euro-obligation)** Bond issued free of any governmental regulations mostly in the form of bearer certificates, underwritten and marketed in several countries simultaneously by a syndicate composed of securities brokerage and banking firms from numerous countries. The currency is usually, but not always, different from the currency of the country where the issue is offered. Eurobonds are issued mostly as straight, convertible or floating-rate bonds or notes, whereby principal and interest are payable free of withholding tax. A great number of Eurobonds are listed on the Luxembourg Stock Exchange.

Certificate of deposit (CD) **(Certificat de dépôt ou Bon de caisse)** Issued against funds deposited for a definite period of time. Some CDs have a progressive interest rate, according to the certificate's duration. Certificate in LUF; minimum capital LUF 50 000.-; minimum duration six months. (Issued in bearer or registered form.)

Gold certificate **(Certificat-or)** Represents a quantity of gold bullion as indicated on the certificate. The bearer may exchange the certificate against physical delivery of the mentioned bullion. (Issued in bearer or registered form.)

4.3 Securities Identification Code

Code name and structure

No uniform securities identification numbers exist so far. The codes used on the Luxembourg Stock Exchange are the securities codes of Cedel. They are composed of six digits, to be extended to nine digits and later on to the 12 digit ISINs.

Name and address of organization responsible for the Securities Identification System

CEDEL SA
67 Boulevard Grande-Duchesse Charlotte
PO Box 1006
L-1010 Luxembourg

Tel: 44992 1
Telex: 2791 234

Cedel is also the national agency for the management of the ISINs (International Securities Identification Number) (see Chapter 3 on the Euromarket).

4.4 Transfer of ownership

Transfer of bearer securities

Title of ownership is transferred by delivery of the certificate, or by book entry, if both the seller and the buyer have securities accounts with banks which settle through a clearing system.

Transfer of registered securities

To register the transfer of ownership, the registrar or transfer agent must receive the endorsed certificate, the endorsement being duly authenticated or a transfer form completed and duly signed.

The registrar or transfer agency functions are provided by banks and/or by fiduciary trust companies in the case of investment mutual funds.

For companies which do not use a registrar or transfer agent, a buyer's and a seller's power must usually be provided to the broker in order to effect the transfer, subject to the company's Articles of Association.

5 STRUCTURE AND REGULATION OF FINANCIAL MARKETS

Structure of financial activities

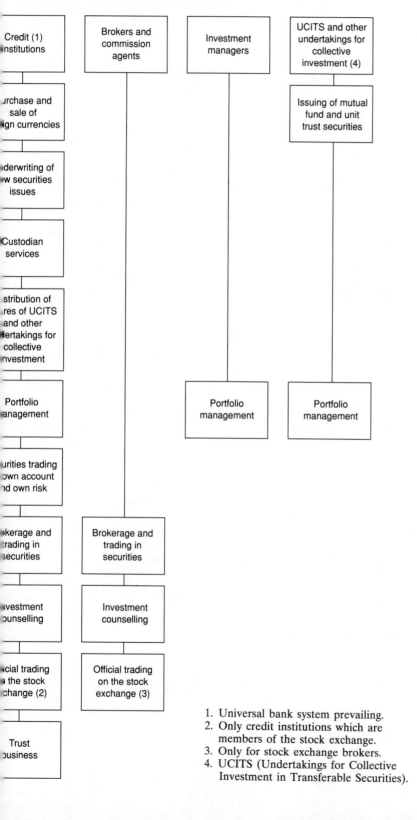

1. Universal bank system prevailing.
2. Only credit institutions which are members of the stock exchange.
3. Only for stock exchange brokers.
4. UCITS (Undertakings for Collective Investment in Transferable Securities).

5.2 **Regulatory structure**

Overview

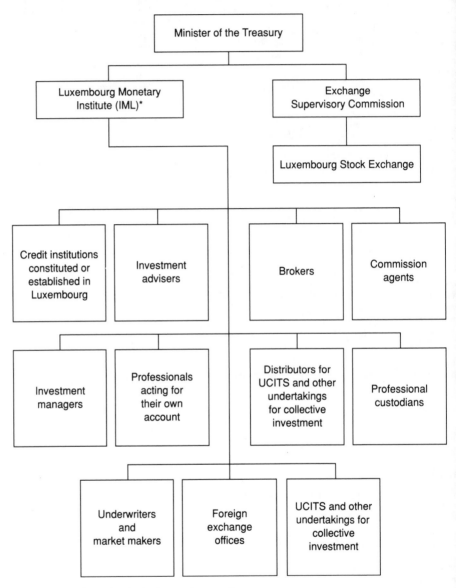

* IML = Institut Monétaire Luxembourgeois.

Responsibilities of regulatory bodies

Name of body	Responsibilities
Luxembourg Monetary Institute (IML) (Corporation under public law) (Legal basis: Law dated 20 May 1983)	Power of recommendation by: – IML circulars Adjudicatory power: – Regulatory supervision of credit institutions licensed under the modified law dated 27 November 1984 concerning the access to the financial sector and its supervision – Regulatory supervision of undertakings for collective investment licensed under the law dated 30 March 1988 relating to undertakings for collective investment Power of enforcement: – Power of injunction – Right of suspension of credit institutions – Possibility of requesting the suspension of payment, controlled management and the liquidation of credit institutions – Possibility of requesting the liquidation of undertakings for collective investment whose licence has been finally refused or withdrawn – Disciplinary power
Exchange Supervisory Commission (Legal basis: Article 1 of the Law on Exchanges dated 21 September 1990)	Adjudicatory power: – Regulatory supervision of stock exchange activities – Power of veto against certain decisions of the stock exchange authorities Power of enforcement: The Exchange Supervisory Commission has the authority to – Investigate, at any moment, at the office of the exchanges all books, accounts, registers, Acts and documents related to exchange transactions, including auditors' certificates and audit written reports and notes provided for by law and the regulations – Require from all professionals of the financial sector dealing in financial assets admitted to a regulated market, the delivery of any information which would be useful for the appreciation and conduct of general exchange activities, including settlement and payment operations, as well as the over-the-counter market and the transactions prices of assets traded in these markets

Name of body	Responsibilities
	– Require the exchanges to suspend or to strike off one of their members – Determine the rules regarding the scope of the audit mandate and the content of the audit report on the accounting documents of the exchanges. It may specifically charge an auditor to carry out an audit on one or more specified aspects of the operation of an exchange or of one of the members thereof in connection with exchange transactions – Prescribe to the exchanges, to the members thereof and to the professionals of the financial sector which deal in financial assets admitted to a regulated market, that, in case they do not comply with the laws, regulations and the measures based on theses laws and regulations, to remedy the ascertained situation within a specific time as determined by the Exchange Supervisory Commission
Luxembourg Stock Exchange (limited company, under supervision of the government) (Legal basis: Law on Stock Exchanges dated 21 September 1990 Grand-Ducal Decree dated 22 March 1928; Ministerial Decree dated 27 June 1985 approving the internal rulebook of the Luxembourg Stock Exchange Grand-Ducal Regulation dated 28 December 1990 regarding: – the contents, scrutiny and distribution of the prospectus for transferable securities to be offered to the public – listing particulars to be published for the admission of transferable securities to the official stock exchange listing)	Regulatory power through: – Luxembourg Stock Exchange Rules and Regulations Power of enforcement: – Imposing of disciplinary sanctions as provided for in the internal rulebook of the stock exchange Adjudicatory power: – Approval of prospectus before admission of securities to quotation on the Stock Exchange *Note*: The Exchange Supervisory Commission is responsible for the admission and examination of the listing applications

Supervision of the stock exchange

The Luxembourg Stock Exchange is supervised by the Exchange Supervisory Commission which ensures proper operation and safeguards the interests of both the government and the investor.

Supervision of clearing and central securities depository organizations

- Cedel SA: According to Part II of the modified law dated November 27 1984 concerning the access of the financial sector, Cedel SA is supervised by the Luxembourg Monetary Institute.
- Chambre de Liquidation at the Luxembourg Stock Exchange: Physical delivery of securities against payment is also possible via the 'Chambre de Liquidation', which is an institution supervised by the Luxembourg Stock Exchange.

Supervision of credit institutions, stockbroking firms and other activities of the financial sector

Credit institutions including custodian banks, stockbroking firms and other activities of the financial sector are supervised by the Luxembourg Monetary Institute.

6 CUSTODIANS

Banque Internationale de
   Luxembourg
2 Boulevard Royale
2953 Luxembourg

Tel: 352 45901
Fax: 352 45902164

Brown Brothers Harriman
   (Luxembourg) SA
33 Boulevard Prince Henri
BP 403
Luxembourg

Tel: 352 40 661
Fax: 352 0580

Cedel SA
67 Boulevard Grande-Duchesse
   Charlotte
L-1010 Luxembourg

Tel: 352 44 99 21
Fax: 352 4499 2210

28 MALAYSIA

☞ 1 PRINCIPAL STOCK EXCHANGE

The Kuala Lumpur Stock Exchange
3rd & 4th floor
Exchange Square
off Jalan Semantan
Damansara Heights
50490 Kuala Lumpur
Malaysia

Tel: 60 3 2546513/433
Telex: KLSE MA 30241/28009

☞ 2 PRINCIPAL REGULATORY AUTHORITY

Ministry of Finance
Block 9
Government Offices Complex
Jalan Duta
50592 Kuala Lumpur
Malaysia

Tel: 3 254 6000
Telex: MA 30242
Fax: 3 256 2819

3 TIME DIFFERENCE FROM GMT: +8 HOURS

4 FORMS AND TYPES OF SECURITIES

4.1 Forms of securities

Registered certificate All shares must be in registered form. Registered transfer of title is necessary in order to secure the rights of a shareholder in a particular company.

Bearer certificate   Certificate which is payable to the bearer.

Provisional letter of allotment   Issued to a shareholder to evidence provisional allocation of shares in a rights issue.

4.2   Types of securities

Equities and warrants

Share   Security which represents a portion of the owner's capital in a company. Owners of shares share in the success or failure of the business. This is measured by the amount of dividends they receive and by the price of the share quoted on the stock exchange (registered).

Ordinary share   Ordinary shares give holders rights of ownership of the company, such as the right to share in the profits, usually the right to vote in the general meeting and to elect and dismiss directors. Obligations of ownership are also conferred and may result in the loss of an investor's money if the company is unsuccessful. Ordinary shares usually form the bulk of a company's capital and have no special rights over other shares. In the event of liquidation, ordinary shares rank after all other liabilities of the company (registered).

Preference share   Share with preferential rights for dividends and for repayment in a liquidation. Partial or no voting rights. May be a combination of the following classes: convertible, non-convertible, redeemable, irredeemable, cumulative, non-cumulative and participating, non-participating (registered).

Participating preference share   Share entitling holder to participate in the profits beyond the fixed dividend by way of an additional, fluctuating dividend if the company is successful (registered).

Cumulative preference share   Share which apart from having a preferential right to a fixed dividend ahead of ordinary shares also carries the right to any arrears of the preference dividends which may have built up. Preference shares which are not entitled to such arrears in dividends are called non-cumulative preference shares (registered).

Redeemable preference share   Shares which may be redeemable by the company at a stated redemption price giving notice in advance. It is usual to set a redemption price above the par value to compensate the owner for the involuntary loss of his investment (registered).

Convertible preference share   Shares which carry the right to be made convertible, at the option of the holder, into another class of shares, normally into ordinary shares (registered).

Founders' share, management share   A share bearing a restriction that no dividend can be paid to the shareholder for a financial year unless ordinary shareholders are paid a certain amount for that year. Issued to the founders of a business (registered).

Property trust units   Units of a trust which mainly invests its funds in real estate.

Transferable subscription rights/warrants   Some loan stocks (see: 'Debt instruments') have subscription rights attached. These rights give the holders the right to subscribe for ordinary shares, at a known price and at a specific date in the future.

Debt instruments

Bond (straight, fixed and non-convertible) **(Bon)**   Security which represents an unsecured obligation of the issuer (Issued in registered or bearer form, can be held as depository receipt.)

Promissory note **(Surat Jaminan Corporate)**   Security which evidences a debt obligation of a company. (Issued in bearer form.)

Malaysian government security **(Surat Jaminan Kerajaan)**   Security issued by the Malaysian government in the domestic market with a maturity between three and twenty-one years. (Issued in registered form.)

Debenture   Loan securities which are either secured or unsecured by a charge on the assets of a corporation. Secured debenture-holders rank first in payment over the other unsecured creditors and ordinary shareholders in the event of a winding-up. Debentures can be convertible or unconvertible, redeemable or irredeemable. The interest rate is usually fixed.

Loan stock   Unlike a debenture, loan stocks are often unsecured. Loan stock holders rank alongside all other unsecured creditors when a company is liquidated. The loan stocks are usually convertible with a maximum maturity period of five years. Interest rate is also usually fixed. (Issued in registered form.)

Subordinated loan note   A debt instrument which ranks after all secured creditors in the event of a liquidation. (Issued in registered form.)

Money market instruments

Treasury bills **(Bil Perbendaharaan)**   Short-term government security with maturities not exceeding one year. (Issued in bearer form).

Bankers acceptance **(Penerimaan-penerimaan Jurubank)**   A usance bill of exchange drawn by a trader on his bank under an agreed line of credit extended by the bank (bearer).

Negotiable certificate of deposit (NCD) **(Sijil-sijil Simpanan boleh niaga)**   A document relating to money which has been deposited with the issuer. An NCD is a document which recognizes an obligation to pay a stated amount to the bearer. (Issued in bearer form.)

Trade bills (**Bil Dagangan**) Bill of exchange drawn by one trader on another to cover the financing of goods during the period of movement and/or during the course of processing. (Issued in bearer form.)

Government-issued investment certificates Monetary instrument to cater for the liquid asset requirements of the Bank Islam Malaysia and other Islamic institutions. They bear no interest income, but earn annual dividends that are not predetermined at the time of the issue. (Issued in bearer form.)

Floating-rate negotiable certificate of deposit (FRNCD) A document similar to the NCD, but with its interest rate refixed every three or six months based on the Kuala Lumpur interbank borrowing rates. (Issued in bearer form.)

Revolving underwriting facility Credit facility underwritten by a syndicate of banks to provide funds continuously over a specific period of time. (Issued in bearer form.)

Notes issuance facility Notes evidencing a debt obligation of a company provided by a syndicate of banks. (Issued in bearer form.)

Futures

Term in English	Reportable positions (in any delivery month)	Speculative position limits
Crude palm oil futures	100 or more contracts	500 contracts*
RBD palm olein futures	100 or more contracts	500 contracts*
Cocoa futures	100 or more contracts	150 contracts in one delivery month and 300 contracts total position.
Tin futures	100 or more contracts	200 contracts*
Rubber (SMR 20) futures	100 or more contracts	250 (10 tons)*

* In any one month or in all delivery months combined.

4.3 Securities identification code

There is no securities numbering system in Malaysia.

4.4 Transfer of ownership

Transfer of bearer issues

The value of bearer securities is embodied in the document or certificate. Consequently, the transfer does not necessitate special formalities and takes place by handing over the security.

Transfer of registered issues

The security, together with a transfer form signed by both the transferor and transferee, must be delivered to the company's registrar. The company is given one month to complete the transfer and have a new certificate issued for delivery.

5   STRUCTURE AND REGULATION OF FINANCIAL MARKETS

5.1   Structure of financial activities

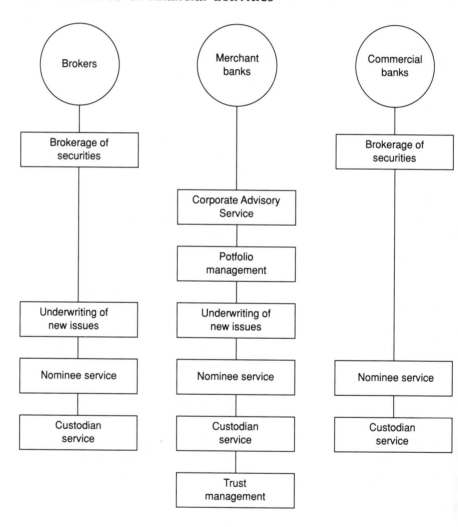

5.2 Regulatory structure

Overview

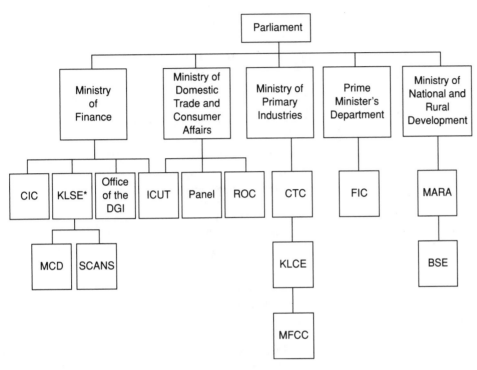

* Self-regulatory

CIC:	Capital Issues Committee.
KLSE:	Kuala Lumpur Stock Exchange.
SCANS:	Securities Clearing Automated Network Services, Sdn Bhd.
Office of the DGI:	Office of the Director-General of Insurance.
ICUT:	Informal Committee on Unit Trusts.
Panel:	Panel on Malaysian Code on Takeovers and Mergers.
ROC:	Registrar of Companies.
CTC:	Commodities Trading Commission.
KLCE:	Kuala Lumpur Commodity Exchange.
MFCC:	Malaysian Futures Clearing Corporation.
FIC:	Foreign Investment Committee.
MARA:	Majlis Amanah Rakyat (Council for the Advancement of Indigenous Races).
BSE:	Bumiputra Stock Exchange.
MCD:	Malaysian Central Depository, Sdn Bhd.

Responsibilities of regulatory bodies

Name of body	Responsibilities:	Legal basis
Capital Issues Committee (CIC)	Legislative/enabling power by: – Provision in the Securities Industry Act 1983 (SIA) – CIC policy guidelines	SIA 1983
Kuala Lumpur Stock Exchange (KLSE)	Legislative power by: – Memorandum and Articles of Association Adjudicatory power: – Regulatory oversight over stock broking companies under the SIA 1983 – Imposing of administrative disciplinary sanctions Power of enforcement: – Investigation of the financial and dealing position of stock broking companies	SIA 1983
Malaysian Central Depository, Sdn Bhd (MCD)	Legislative/enabling power by: – Securities Industry (Central Depositories) Act 1991 Adjudicatory power: – Monitoring compliance with the Rules of the Central Depository Power of enforcement: – Enforcement of the Rules of the Central Depository	
Office of the Director General of Insurance	Legislative/enabling power by: – Provision of the Insurance Act 1963 – Provision of the Insurance Regulations 1963 Adjudicatory power by: – Regulatory oversight over insurers, insurance agents, insurance brokers, adjusters – Imposing of administrative disciplinary sanctions	Insurance Act 1963

Name of body	Responsibilities	Legal basis
	Power of enforcement: – Investigation of potential violations Prosecution: – An errant insurer failing to comply with directives of the Director-General of Insurance will be prosecuted and, on conviction, will be liable to a fine or imprisonment or both	
Informal Committee on Unit Trusts (ICUT)	Legislative/enabling power by: – Provision of the Companies Act 1965 – Policy guidelines	Companies Act 1965
Panel on Malaysian Code on Takeovers and Mergers (Panel)	Legislative power by: – Provision of the Companies Act 1965 – Code on Takeovers and Mergers 1987 Adjudicatory power by: – Report to any authority as the Panel deems necessary on any breach of the code by parties concerned Power of enforcement: – Inquiry on any person involved in a takeover and merger exercise	Companies Act 1965
Registrar of Companies (ROC)	Legislative power by: – Provision of the Companies Act 1965 – Provisions of the SIA 1983 Adjudicatory power by: – Regulatory oversight over companies, directors, stock broking companies and individual dealers in securities Power of enforcement: – Investigations of potential violations – Prosecutorial functions	Companies Act 1965 SIA 1983

Name of body	Responsibilities	Legal basis
Commodities Trading Commission (CTC)	Legislative power by: – Provisions of the Commodities Trading Act 1985 Adjudicatory power by: – Regulatory oversight over the Commodity Exchange, the Clearing House and individuals concerned – Imposing suspension, penalty or reprimand as the case may be on errant parties Power of enforcement – In enforcing the provision of the Act the Commissioner is empowered to require the production of books from unauthorized persons, take possession of books, search, seize and investigate	Commodities Trading Act 1985
Foreign Investment Committee (FIC)	Enabling power by: – Government's guidelines for the regulation of acquisition of assets, mergers and takeovers	Governmental Decree
Bumiputra Stock Exchange (BSE)	Bumiputra Stock Exchange (BSE) is established and maintained by the Majlis Amanah Rakyat, a legal entity established under the Majlis Amanah Rakyat Act 1966. The operations and the management of BSE is based on its own internal Rules and Regulations and the provisions of the Securities Industry Act 1983 do not apply to it	Majlis Amanah Rakyat Act 1966

Supervision of the stock exchange

The Kuala Lumpur Stock Exchange (KLSE) is a self-regulatory organization with its own Memorandum and Articles of Association, as well as a set of rules which govern the conduct of its members in securities dealings. It is also responsible for the surveillance of the market and for the enforcement of its

Listing Requirements which define the criteria for listing, disclosure require-ments and standards to be maintained by public listed companies.

Supervision of the clearing organization

Securities Clearing Automated Network Services, Sdn Bhd (SCANS) oper-ates as the clearing house for the KLSE and is its subsidiary company. The operations of SCANS are supervised by the Board of SCANS comprising members of the KLSE Committee.

The Exchange has incorporated a new subsidiary called Malaysian Central Depository, Sdn Bhd (MCD) to manage and run the Central Depository System (CDS) in Malaysia. The CDS is operated under the book entry trans-fer system. The operations of MCD are supervised by a Board of Directors with the support of a management team.

Supervision of broker/dealers and custodian banks

The supervision of stockbroking companies falls under the duty of both the KLSE and the Registrar of Companies (ROC). The rules of the KLSE gov-ern the business and trading activities of the stock broking companies while the ROC, being the office that issues the various licences to deal in securities, ensures that the stock broking companies comply with the relevant provision of the Securities Industry Act.

6   CUSTODIANS

Chase Manhattan
Pernas International
Jalan Sultan Ismail
50250 Kuala Lumpur
Malaysia

Tel: 3 261 0011
Fax: 3 261 9010

Citibank
28 Medan Pasar
50050 Kuala Lumpur
Malaysia

Tel: 3 232 9039
Fax: 3 230 8758

Hongkong & Shanghai Banking
  Corporation
PO Box 10244
50912 Kuala Lumpur
Malaysia

Tel: 3 234 2358
Fax: 3 230 6944

Overseas Chinese Banking
  Corporation
Malaysia Central Office
Wisma Lee Rubber
Jalan Melaka
Kuala Lumpur
Malaysia

Tel: 3 292 0344
Fax: 3 292 6518

Security Pacific Asian Bank
Plaza See Hoy Chan
Jalan Raja Chulan
50200 Kuala Lumpur
Malaysia

Tel: 3 238 2919
Fax: 3 230 6986

Standard Chartered Bank
2 Jalan Ampang
50450 Kuala Lumpur
Malaysia

Tel: 3 234 4112
Fax: 3 232 7813

United Malayan Banking Corporation
Jalan Sultan Sulaiman
Kuala Lumpur
Malaysia

Tel: 3 230 9866
Fax: 3 232 2627

29 MEXICO

1 PRINCIPAL STOCK EXCHANGE

Bolsa Mexicana de Valores SA de CV
Uruguay 68 – Colonia Centro
Delegación Cuauhtémoc
0600 Mexico DF

Tel: 52 5 521 56 54
Telex: 017 73032/017 62233

2 PRINCIPAL REGULATORY AUTHORITY

Comisión Nacional de Valores
Barranca del Muerto 275
Col. San José Insurgentes
03900 Mexico D.F.

Tel: 52 5 660 0866
Telex: no number given
Fax: 52 5 651 8003
       52 5 651 6270

3 TIME DIFFERENCE FROM GMT: –6 HOURS

4 FORMS AND TYPES OF SECURITIES

4.1 Forms of securities

Registered certificate **(Titulo nominativo)**   Compulsory form for shares.

Bearer certificate **(Titulo al portador)**   Common form for bonds, with coupons, for issues before 1984. Since 1984 bearer securities are prohibited.

Jumbo certificate **(Macro titulo)**   One certificate represents a large number of shares of one issue.

Global certificate **(Titulo Unico)**   One certificate that represents the entire issue. At present, this type of certificate is used for money market securities.

4.2   Types of securities

Equities and warrants

Common stock **(Acción Comun)**   Ordinary ownership in a corporation, voting rights generally accompany possession. Only registered shares are available in Mexico.

Preferred stock **(Acción Preferente)**   Stock which pays to the holder a stipulated dividend. Preferred stock has claim prior to that of common stock upon the earnings of a corporation and upon the assets in the event of liquidation. In some cases, limited voting right in extraordinary meetings.

Non-voting shares **(Acciónes sin Derecho a Voto)**   Securities that do not permit a holder to vote on corporate resolutions. The holder only has pecuniary rights.

Accumulative preferred stock **(Acción con Dividendo Preferente Accumulativo)**   Preferred stock upon which dividends will accumulate until payment is made. A few Mexican corporations have issued this type of stock.

Certificates of Ordinary Participation (CPO) **(CPOs Certificados de Participación Ordinaria)**   CPOs are jumbo certificates issued by fiduciary institutions through trusts wherein ownership is formed by representative shares of the capital stock of corporations whose shares are quoted on the exchange.

Through CPOs, foreign investors may acquire 'A' shares previously reserved for Mexicans only.

Mutual funds **(Sociedades de Inversión)**   Trust which sells its shares to the public and whose assets are invested in a number of different securities. In Mexico these funds are open-ended, which means they continuously offer new shares for sale to the public.

In Mexico, there are three different kinds of such funds:

Sociedades de Inversión comunes – Common mutual funds which invest in fixed- and variable-yield securities.

Sociedades de Inversión de Renta Fija – Fixed-yield mutual funds which invest exclusively in fixed-yield securities. There are three types of this fund: one for individuals, one for corporations and one for trusts.

Sociedades de Inversión de Capitales – Venture capital funds which invest in securities issued by companies that require long-term resources and whose activities are involved in the national development plan.

Debt instruments

Bond, debenture **(Bono, Obligación)**   A fixed-income, interest-bearing debt security. Usually in bearer form with coupons attached (corporate bonds).

Straight bond **(Obligación Quirografaria)**   Bond containing no clauses granting special privileges and unsecured by the corporation's assets.

Mortgage bond **(Obligación Hipotecaria)**   Bond whereby a corporation pledges certain real estate assets as security.

Real estate participation bonds **[CEPIS (Certificados de Participación Immobiliaria)]**   Three-years draft issued on the capital market which offers to the issuers the possibility of financing building projects. The investor has the opportunity of investing in a security whose yield and amortization value is linked to the inflation rate of real estate.

Urban renovation bonds **(Bonos de Renovación Urbana)**   Draft issued to owners of properties expropriated following the 1985 earthquakes for a ten-year term expiring in 1995.

Bank development bonds **(Bonos Bancarios)**   Issued by Mexican development banks with a minimum term of three years at a yield above CETES (*see*: 'Treasury bill') or Bank Pagaré (*see*: 'Bank promissory note') rates.

Silver bonds **[CEPLATAS (Certificados de Plata)]**   Draft issued by the national credit societies on the capital market, standing for 100 ounces of silver.

Commodity bonds **(Bonos de Prenda)**   Issued by warehouses and backed by a deposit in a warehouse of commodities securing the issue.

Money market instruments

Treasury bill **[Certificado de la Tesoreria de la Federación (CETES)]**   Short-term obligation of the Mexican government. The bills are sold at a discount and are issued with maturities of 28, 56, 91, 180, 364 days depending on the issue.

Federal government development bonds **[BONDES (Bonos de Desarrollo del Gobierno Federal)]**   Draft issued in capital market with a minimum maturity of 364, 532, 728 days; the interest rate of Bondes is reset monthly at a fixed premium over the current Treasury bill rate, and interest is payable every 28 days.

Treasury promissory note **[PAGAFES (Pagarés de la Tesoreria de la Federación)]**   Drafts denominated in dollars issued by federal government and payable in pesos with maturities of 28, 56, 91, 180 and 364 days.

Bank promissory note **[Pagaré Bancario]**   Note issued by bankers for terms between one and 12 months with a fixed-interest rate.*

Banker's acceptance **(Acceptación Bancaria)**   Bill of exchange accepted by Mexican banks. Transactions are effected outside the stock exchange.*

---

* There are two kinds: public (issued by an enterprise and accepted by a bank); and private (issued and accepted by a bank).

Commercial paper (Papel Commercial)   Short-term unsecured promissory note, issued by large, creditworthy corporations with a fixed yield, with maturity up to 360 days.

Adjusted bond (Ajustabono)   Ajustabonos represent medium-term debt issued by the Mexican Federal Treasury. These bonds provide a hedge against inflation; each quarter the par value is reset according to the consumer price index. A fixed-interest rate, calculated on the adjusted par value, is paid quarterly, with maturities of 1092 and 1820 days.

Treasury bond (Tesobonos)   Draft denominated in USD issued by the federal government and payable in pesos which are calculated at the free rate, with maturities of 28, 71, 91, 98 and 182 days.

Repurchase agreements (Reportos)   A repurchase agreement is an operation in which a brokerage house (*reportado*) transfers money market securities (CETES, BAs, BONDES, etc.) to its client (*reportador*) for a fixed amount, at a previously determined rate of return and for a tenure of one to 45 days. At maturity, clients return the securities to the brokerage house and receive their money plus the agreed premium.

Currency hedges market (Mercado de Coberturas Cambiarias)   Instrument by which participants wishing to make US dollar operations (subject to exchange control regulation) at a future date can hedge the controlled or free exchange rate.

Federal government industrial development bonds [BONDIS (Bonos de Desarollo Industrial)]   Securities instruments issued by National Financiera to Promote Industrial Development. Interest is computed based on the CETES, plus a bonus rate.

4.3   Securities Identification Code

Code name and structure

The securities identification code in Mexico is assigned by the Mexican Stock Exchange (Bolsa Mexicana de Valores). This code consists of six alphabetical digits which are related to the company name of the issuer.

	Name of issuer company	*Code*	*Specification code*
Example:	Empresas Tolteca de Mexico SA	TOLMEX	B1003

For specification, a code of five alphanumeric digits is added, which relates to the issue series. The code is generally used for security transactions and specifically for just one issuer. In Mexico the code is called clave de pizarra ('ticker symbol').

Name and address of organization responsible for the Securities Identification System

Bolsa Mexicana de Valores, SA de CV
Paseo de la Reforma 255
Colonia Cuauhtémoc
Delegación Cuauhtémoc
06500 Mexico DF

4.4 Transfer of ownership

Transfer of bearer securities

The use of bearer securities has been prohibited in Mexico since 1984. Since then, all Mexican securities have to be in registered form. Under the old system, Mexican securities could be either in bearer or registered form.

Transfer of registered securities

Registered securities are transferred by the central depository INDEVAL, either by book entry or physical delivery. The transaction is registered in the name of the current stockholder and, if physical delivery is made, the stockholder's name must appear on the stock certificate. INDEVAL then advises the corporation about the changes to be made in its stockholder's register. In practice, registered shares are registered in the name of the brokerage firm which handles the account (street certificates) and never in the name of the beneficial owner to avoid back-and-forth shipments of stock certificates for endorsement (since there are no transfer deeds). The brokerage firm takes care of the allocation of stock and cash dividends and rights on behalf of the beneficial owners.

5   STRUCTURE AND REGULATION OF FINANCIAL MARKETS

5.1   Structure of financial activities

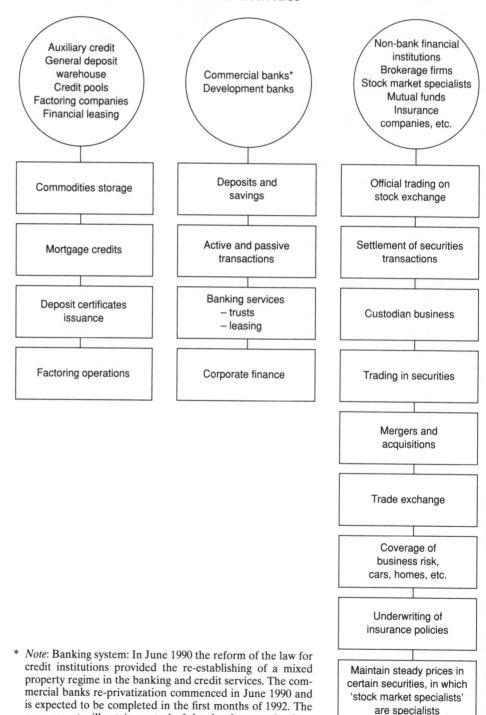

Auxiliary credit
General deposit
warehouse
Credit pools
Factoring companies
Financial leasing

Commercial banks*
Development banks

Non-bank financial
institutions
Brokerage firms
Stock market specialists
Mutual funds
Insurance
companies, etc.

Commodities storage	Deposits and savings	Official trading on stock exchange
Mortgage credits	Active and passive transactions	Settlement of securities transactions
Deposit certificates issuance	Banking services – trusts – leasing	Custodian business
Factoring operations	Corporate finance	Trading in securities
		Mergers and acquisitions
		Trade exchange
		Coverage of business risk, cars, homes, etc.
		Underwriting of insurance policies
		Maintain steady prices in certain securities, in which 'stock market specialists' are specialists

* *Note*: Banking system: In June 1990 the reform of the law for credit institutions provided the re-establishing of a mixed property regime in the banking and credit services. The commercial banks re-privatization commenced in June 1990 and is expected to be completed in the first months of 1992. The government will retain control of the development banks.

Financial groups

One of the most important changes in the financial system is the creation of financial groups. Subject to authorization by the federal government, a controlling company must hold at least 51% of the voting stock of the paid-in capital of each participant of the financial group. The law states that a financial group may only be formed by broker dealers, banks, factoring companies, general deposit warehouses, insurance and bond companies, leasing companies, currency and exchange houses and mutual fund operating companies. Each group shall include at least three of the above-mentioned financial intermediaries.

5.2 Regulatory structure

Overview

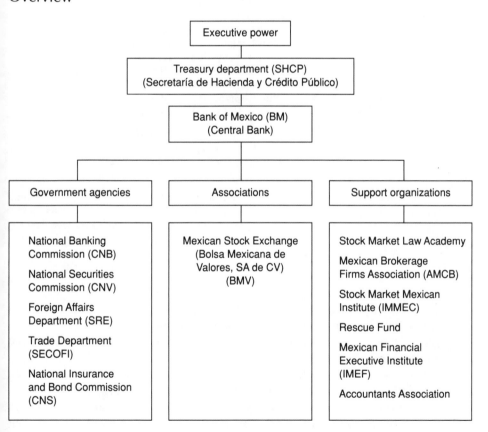

Responsibilities of regulatory bodies

Name of body	Task/responsibilities
Treasury Department (SHCP) (government agency)	Regulatory body of the financial market Rules of establishment Imposing of administrative disciplinary sanctions Investigation of potential violations Prosecutorial functions
Bank of Mexico (BM) (government agency)	Central bank Clearing house Establishment of monetary policies Exchange control Credit intermediary Only institution that can issue legal tender
National Securities Commission (CNV)	Promotion and regulation of stock exchange market Performance inspection of stock exchange, brokerage firms and market specialists Issue inspection of registered securities Investigation of violations of the stock market law Establishment of rules in order to supervise legal performance of the stock exchange, brokerage firms and stock market specialists
National Banking Commission (CNB)	Inspection and vigilance of banking institutions and those companies authorized to operate as credit organizations and in auxiliary credit activities
National Insurance Commission (CNS)	Inspection and vigilance of insurance institutions, bond companies and the remaining persons and companies that, according to Mexican law, carry out activities related to the insurance and bond business

Supervision of the stock exchange

The Stock Exchange (Bolsa Mexicana de Valores, SA de CV) is a private corporation and operates under the stock market laws passed by the government.

The National Securities Commission (CNV)(Commission Nacional de Valores) supervises the performance of the stock exchange.

The stock exchange is a private corporation whose shares are owned solely by the authorized brokers. The general meeting of the stockholders, which constitute the highest body of the stock exchange, elect each year the Board of Directors which is the governing body and consists of seven members. There is no direct government representation on the Board.

Members of the stock exchange are the brokerage firms and stock market specialists who act as intermediaries.

Supervision of clearing and central securities depository organization

The only central securities depository and clearing house for the transfer of stocks and bonds is the share depository institute INDEVAL (S.D. INDEVAL, SA de CV) which has its legal basis in the securities market law. In order to accept custodian accounts from brokerage firms, stock market specialists, stock exchange banks, insurance companies, mutual funds, etc., by law, the National Securities Commission must authorize brokerage firms to hold custody accounts at INDEVAL for their clients. The inspection and vigilance of this institution is carried out by the National Securities Commission.

Supervision of broker/dealers and custodian banks

Brokerage firms and stock market specialists are members of the stock exchange and therefore regulated by both the stock exchange and the National Securities Commission. The two authorities are supervised by the Central Bank and the Treasury Department.

6 CUSTODIANS

Acciónes y Valores de Mexico
Paseo de la Reforma 398, 4/F
06600 Mexico D.F.

Tel: 5 326 4848
Fax: 5 208 5048

Banamex
Av. Juarez 104-11 Piso
06040 Mexico D.F.

Tel: 5 720 7685 7240
Fax: 5 720 7390 7151

Bursamex
Isabel la Catollica
43 Colonia Centro
Cuauhtémoc 0600
Mexico D.F.

Tel: 5 747 2109
Fax: call telephone number for fax

Casa de Bolsa Inverlat
Bosques de Ciruelos No 120
Bosques de las Lomas
11700 Mexico D.F.

Tel: 5 325 3272
Fax: 5 259 0519

Chase Manhattan
Hamburgo 213
7 Piso
06600 Mexico D.F.
Mexico

Tel: 5 208 5666
Fax: 5 511 7306

Citibank
Paseo de la Reforma 390
Mexico City 06695
Mexico

Tel: 5 211 3030
Fax: 5 207 5129

Indeval
Paseo de la Reforma 253
Colonia Cuauhtémoc
06500 Mexico D.F.

Tel: 5 208 7228
Fax: 5 703 3935

Mexival
Paseo de la Reforma 359
06500 Mexico D.F.

Tel: 5 208 2044
Fax: 5 208 5215

Operadora de Bolsa
Rio Amazonas 62
Colonia Cuauhtémoc
06500 Mexico D.F.

Tel: 5 592 6988
Fax: 5 703 3369

30 THE NETHERLANDS

1 PRINCIPAL STOCK EXCHANGE

Amsterdam Stock Exchange
Beursplein 5
PÒ Box 19163
1000 GD Amsterdam
The Netherlands

Tel: 31 20 523 4567
Telex: 12302 EFBEU NL

2 PRINCIPAL REGULATORY AUTHORITY

Securities Board of the Netherlands
Postbox 11723
1001 GS Amsterdam
The Netherlands

Tel: 31 20 206 549
Telex: no number given
Fax: 31 20 206 649

3 TIME DIFFERENCE FROM GMT: +1 HOUR

4 FORMS AND TYPES OF SECURITIES

4.1 Forms of securities

K-securities **(Effecten in K-vorm)**   Bearer share or bearer bond in traditional, classical form with individual coupons attached (K-form).

CF-securities **(Effecten in CF-vorm)**   Bearer share or bearer bond of which the certificate itself and the coupon-sheet attached both have the size of a key punch card. The CF coupon sheet does not have individual coupons. The certificates can be kept in custody only by custodians which are participants in the CF system. Payment of dividend and interest takes place on the basis of the position of each CF custodian in the books of the CF office.

Registered securities **(Effecten op naam)** Securities which are made out in the name of the owner and can be transferred by assignment only.

Giral eligible securities **(Giraal leverbare effecten)** Securities admitted to Necigef.

Depository receipts **(Certificaten van aandelen)** Securities in the form of bearer certificates, issued by a Dutch Administration Office against the underlying original shares. The Office acts as trustee for the holders of the certificate and exercises the voting rights on the shares. There are three kinds of certificate: exchangeable against the underlying original shares, limited exchangeable and non-exchangeable.

Continental depository receipt **(CDR)** Bearer certificate representing foreign securities in original form, issued by Amsterdam Depository Company as a trustee, quoted in Dutch guilders.

Amsterdam security account system **(ASAS)** Foreign securities quoted on Amsterdam Stock Exchange in foreign currency and in original form and traded and settled according to the rules of the country of origin. No depository receipts are issued.

4.2 Types of securities

Equities and warrants

Ordinary bearer share **[Aandeel aan toonder (zonder bijzondere voorrechten voor de houder)]** Security of which the bearer is a shareholder in the company concerned.

Preference share **(Preferent aandeel)** Share providing the holder with preferential rights.

Cumulative preference share **(Cumulatief preferent aandeel)** Share upon which outstanding dividends will accumulate until payment is made.

Participating preference share **(Winstdelend preferent aandeel)** Share extending participation in earnings above the regular dividend.

Participating cumulative preference share **(Winstdelend cumulatief preferent aandeel)** Share with the right of accumulation of dividends until payment is made and with the right of participation in the earnings of the past year.

Priority share **(Prioriteits aandeel)** Share with special voting rights.

Founder's share **(Oprichtersbewijs)** Share without voting right. The owner has special benefits in case of distribution of profits after dividend payments.

Warrant **(Warrant)** Warrants are issued together with bonds or shares and usually entitle the holder to subscribe for new shares or bonds under specific conditions.

Falcon **(Langlopende call-optie op aandelen)** Fixed-term Agreement for Long-term Call Options on existing securities.

Unit trust **(Participatiebewijs)** Participation in an open-ended investment fund. If not quoted on the stock exchange, the issuing bank/broker makes a bid–ask quote.

Debt instruments

Straight bond **(Obligatie)** Part of a security debt issue with a (mostly) fixed interest. Bonds/debentures exist in bearer form and in registered form.

Subordinated bond **(Achtergestelde obligatie)** The debt is subordinated to those of other creditors in case of liquidation of the issuing company.

Convertible bond **(Converteerbare obligatie)** Bond convertible into shares.

Compulsory convertible bond **(Verplicht converteerbare obligatie)** The owner has to convert his bond into shares on request of the issuing company.

Index-linked bond **(Geïndexeerde obligatie)** Coupons and/or redemptions are linked to a certain index.

Income bond **(Inkomsten obligatie)** Bond the interest on which is subject to the income of the borrower.

Currency-linked bond **(Valuta gerelateerde obligatie)** A bond the payments of interest and principal on which are valued by reference to one currency though actually made in another.

Dual currency bond **(Obligatie met valuta clausule)** A bond denominated in one currency with interest and/or principal repayment in another currency at a predetermined rate.

Mortgage bond **(Pandbrief)** Bond issued by a mortgage bank.

Capital bond **(Kapitaal obligatie)** Subordinated bond usually issued by a commercial bank.

Zero-coupon bond **(Renteloze obligatie)** Bond with a nil coupon. Issued at a significantly lower price than the principal amount (100%) paid at redemption.

Bond-cum-warrant **(Obligatie met warrant)** Bond issued in combination with warrants.

Surplus bond **(Surplus obligatie)** Interest consists of two parts: a variable component linked to the capital market rate and a fixed rate as stated in the terms of the bond.

Profit-sharing bond **(Winstdelende obligatie)** Interest consists of a fixed component and a component related to the results of the company.

Premium bond **(Premie obligatie)** Bond paying only a part of the market interest rate. In addition, premiums are allotted to one or more certificate numbers by drawing at random.

Money market instruments

***Certificate of deposit* (Kortlopend schuldpapier uitgegeven door bank)**   Debt instrument with a lifetime of less than two years, issued by a bank.

***Commercial paper* (Kortlopend schuldpapier uitgegeven door andere dan banken)**   Debt instrument with a lifetime of less than two years, issued by a debtor which is not a bank.

***Floating-rate note* (Schuldpapier met een variabele rente)**   Short-term debt instrument the interest rate of which is revised regularly.

***Medium-term note* (Middellange termijn schuldpapier)**   Debt instrument with a lifetime of between two and five years.

***Future-rate agreement* ('Future Rate Agreement')**   Instrument for hedging of interest exposure.

***SWAPS* (Gelijktijdig contante aan/verkoop en termijn verkoop/aankoop)**   Simultaneous buy or sell in the spot market and a sell or buy in the future market.

Traded options

***Equity based* (Aandelen-opties)**   Option based on stocks.

***Index based* (Index-opties)**   Currently there are three indices:

(a)   The Dutch stock index; it covers 25 Dutch securities listed on the Amsterdam Stock Exchange.
(b)   The Dutch TOP-5 Index; it is made up of five Dutch internationals (Akzo, KLM, Royal Dutch, Philips and Unilever), listed on the world's leading stock exchanges.
(c)   The Major Market Index; it is based on 20 of America's leading blue chip industrial stocks, whose shares are quoted on stock exchanges around the world. The American Stock Exchange, situated in New York, introduced options on the Major Market Index in 1983. Since 1987 the Major Market Index options have also been traded on the EOE-Optiebeurs, thanks to a unique form of cooperation.

Through investing in options on these indices, the investor is exposed to the generalized trend of the underlying stocks rather than to an individual security.

***Interest based* (Obligatie-opties)**   An interest-based option is based on a Dutch government bond, or on the hypothetical bond future FTO (*see*: Futures). Investors can anticipate fluctuations of interest rates by investing in options on these Dutch government bonds.

***Currency based* (Opties op vreemde valuta's)**   Options based on the US dollar or the British pound, both quoted in Dutch guilders.

Precious metal based **(Opties op edele metalen)**   Options (as per March 1991 only) on gold.

Futures

Interest-rate based (FTO) **[Obligatie futures/Future op een hypothetische 7% (Staats) obligatie]**   The FTO future contract is based on a single hypothetical bond with a nominal value of NLG 250 000, and a coupon of 7%. This future contract will be actually delivered on the basis of the 'cheapest-to-deliver' principle.

Index based (FTI) **(Future op de EOE-aandelenindex)**   *See*: 'Traded options'.

4.3   Securities Identification Code

Code name and structure

The Dutch securities industry uses uniform code numbers (clearing code) for securities listed on the Amsterdam Stock Exchange (Official Market, Official Parallel Market, ASAS Market).

Name and address of organization responsible for the securities identification system

Effectencentrale van de Amsterdamse Effectenbeurs BV
Beursplein 5, Postbus 19163
NL-1000 GD Amsterdam
The Netherlands

4.4   Transfer of ownership

Transfer of bearer securities

The transfer of ownership can be effected in two ways with respect to both shares and bonds: the certificate is either physically delivered to the buyer, or the transfer is effected by book entry through the Netherlands' Central Institute for Giral Securities Transfer BV. If securities are eligible for the giral system, no physical delivery is permitted to settle stock exchange transactions.

Transfer of registered securities

The transfer of ownership of registered securities can be effected by means of endorsement and an assignment.

The transfer of registered shares may be subject to approval of the issuing company concerned, depending on the Articles of Association.

5 STRUCTURE AND REGULATION OF FINANCIAL MARKETS

5.1 Structure of financial activities

Financial activities take place on the Amsterdam Stock Exchange (ASE), the European Options Exchange (EOE) and the Financial Futures Market Amsterdam (FTA).

Amsterdam Stock Exchange (ASE) membership

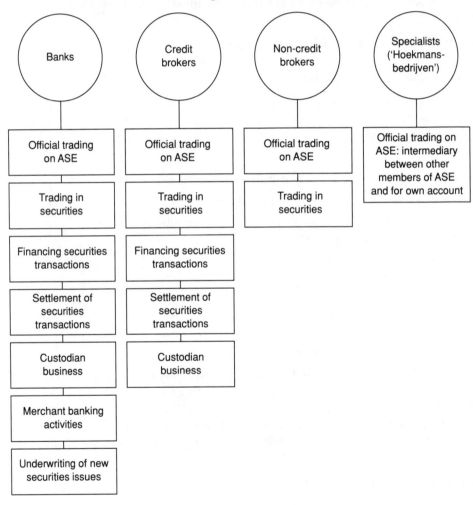

European Options Exchange (EOE) membership

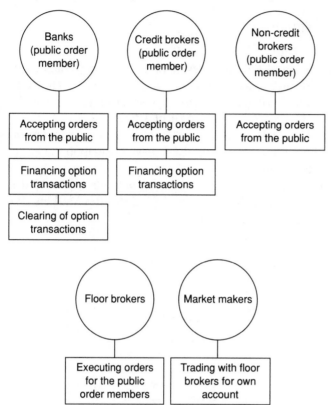

Financial Futures Market Amsterdam (FTA) membership

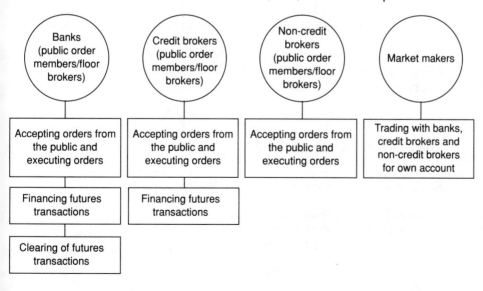

5.2 Supervision

Regulatory structure

In 1988, the Minister of Finance (MoF) presented to Parliament a bill regarding the supervision of the securities markets. It replaces the Stock Exchange Act of 1914. According to this Bill, which is to become effective in 1991, the Minister delegates his major supervisory powers to a newly created supervisor: the Securities Board (Stichting Toezicht Effectenverkeer). The Board, established in July 1988, has a committee of five independent members. The chairmen of both the ASE and the EOE have been appointed as counselling members of the committee.

The regulatory structure of the financial markets in the Netherlands according to the Bill on the Supervision of the Securities Markets (Wet toezicht effectenverkeer) will be as follows:

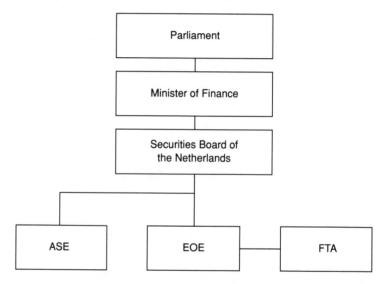

According to the Securities Giro Transfer Act (Wet giraal effectenverkeer, 1977), the Netherlands Central Institute for Giral Securities Transfer (Necigef) is supervised by the Minister of Finance.

Responsibilities of regulatory bodies

Name of Body	Legal Basis	Responsibilities
Securities Board of the Netherlands	Stock Exchange Act, to be replaced by the law regarding the supervision of the securities market	Legislative power, by law Regulatory supervision of members of the ASE, EOE and FTA

Name of Body	Legal Basis	Responsibilities
		Power of enforcement: the Foundation delegates the actual control of the departments of supervision of the ASE, EOE and FTA
Inspection Office of the Stock Exchange	Stock Exchange Act, to be replaced by the law regarding the supervision of the securities market	Regulatory supervision of non-credit brokers and jobbers (*hoeklieden*). Power of enforcement: – investigations of potential violations – investigations of the solvency of the members – prosecutorial function
Department of Compliance of the EOE and FTA	Stock Exchange Act, to be replaced by the law regarding the supervision of the securities market	Regulatory supervision of all members Power of enforcement: – investigation of potential violations – investigation of the solvency of all members – prosecutorial function
Dutch Central Bank	Act on the Supervision of Credit System	Regulatory supervision over all credit brokers and banks

Supervision of the stock exchange

The supervisory powers in the Netherlands are:

– Minister of Finance
– Securities Board of the Netherlands.

Supervision of clearing and central securities depositories

The clearing corporations of ASE and EOE are supervised by the Securities Board of the Netherlands. Necigef is supervised by the Minister of Finance. The clearing members of the EOE, the major Dutch (clearing) banks, are under the regulatory supervision of the exchanges and the Dutch Central Bank.

Supervision of brokers and custodian banks

Supervision of non-credit brokers (*see*: 'Financial Futures Market Amsterdam' is carried out by the Inspection Office of the Stock Exchange, supervision of credit brokers and custodian banks by the Dutch Central Bank.

6 CUSTODIANS

Amsterdam Rotterdam Bank
Securities Center
4800 de Breda
Amsterdam
The Netherlands

Tel: 20 289 393
Telex: 11006 AMRONL
Fax: 20 265 739

Bank Mees & Hope
Herrengracht 548
1017 AG Amsterdam
The Netherlands

Tel: 20 527 911

Barclays Bank Amsterdam
Wetteringschans 109
1017 SB Amsterdam
The Netherlands

Tel: 20 262 209
Fax: 20 266 511

Citibank
Herrengracht 545–549
1071 BW Amsterdam
The Netherlands

Tel: 20 551 5217
Fax: 20 5515 234

Kas-Associatie
Spuistraat 172
1012 VT Amsterdam
The Netherlands

Tel: 20 557 5911
Telex: 12286
Fax: 20 279 179

Pierson, Heldring & Pierson
Rokin 55
1012 KK Amsterdam
The Netherlands

Tel: 20 521 1188
Telex: 16388
Fax: 20 258 164

31 NEW ZEALAND

1 PRINCIPAL STOCK EXCHANGE

New Zealand Stock Exchange
Caltex Tower
286–292 Lambton Quay
PO Box 2959
Wellington
New Zealand

Tel: 64 4 727 599
Telex: 34 24 NZ

2 PRINCIPAL REGULATORY AUTHORITY

Securities Commission
102–112 Lambton Quay
39 The Terrace
PO Box 1179
Wellington 1
New Zealand

Tel: 64 4 729 830
Telex: no number given
Fax: 64 4 728 076

3 TIME DIFFERENCE FROM GMT: +12 HOURS

4 FORMS AND TYPES OF SECURITIES

4.1 Forms of securities

Registered certificate Virtually all New Zealand securities are in registered form. The certificate names the issuer and sets out the name of the holder and the number or amount of securities held.

Book entry security (Certificate not issued, CNI)   Special arrangement may be made with an issuer for a certificate not to be issued or a certificate surrendered, thereby allowing prompt delivery into the market either electronically or manually. Currently these facilities are restricted to brokers and major investment houses and will ultimately form the basis for the electronic transfer of securities in New Zealand.

Entitlement letters   Letter setting out an entitlement to an offer of new securities to existing security holders issued by the offering organization (*see*: 'Right').

4.2   Types of securities

Equities and warrants

Ordinary share   Representing an equity or part ownership of a company (registered).

Preference share   Share with preferential rights over ordinary shares as to claim on assets, earnings and dividends, ranking below creditors and debentureholders. Preference shares usually have a fixed dividend rate (registered).

Redeemable preference share   A preference share which is redeemable for cash on a fixed date. (New Zealand company law requires that redemption may be made only from profits of the company or a further issue of capital, registered.)

Convertible preference share   Share with a preferential right over ordinary shares as to claims on assets, earnings and dividends and including a right to convert to ordinary shares on either a fixed or optional basis on a future date or dates (registered).

Right (traded)   A transferable right to subscribe for new securities in the offering organization. These rights are traded on the NZSE and are utilized to offer capital increases to existing shareholders on advantageous terms (registered).

Right (non-renounceable)   The same purpose as the right, above, except that the rights must be exercised and subscribed for by the existing holder and cannot be traded until fully paid and accepted for trading on the NZSE (registered).

Debt instruments

New Zealand government stock   Stock issued and guaranteed by the New Zealand government. Issued for fixed maturities at fixed rates of interest (registered).

Local authority loan stock   Stock issued by semi-government bodies usually secured by a rating charge* on property. Issued for fixed maturities at fixed rates of interest (registered).

Debenture   Corporate securities with a fixed maturity date and fixed-interest rate secured by a charge on corporate assets (registered).

Unsecured note   Corporate securities with a fixed maturity date and fixed-interest rate but no charge on corporate assets (registered).

Convertible note   Unsecured notes of an issuer entitling the registered holder to convert the notes to shares either on a fixed or optional basis on a future date or dates. In the event of an optional conversion lapsing, the notes are repayable (registered).

Money market instruments

Reserve Bank Bill   Short-term bills issued by the New Zealand Reserve Bank.

Treasury Bill   90- and 180-day bills issued by the New Zealand Treasury.

Bank Accepted Bill   Bill of exchange accepted for payment by a bank. Customary means of effecting payment for merchandise sold in import–export transactions.

Certificate of Deposit   Money market instrument and negotiable claim issued by a bank in return for a short- to medium-term deposit.

Commercial Paper   The term applies to notes and acceptances originating from commercial transactions.

Futures contracts and options

The New Zealand Stock Exchange introduced a six-month pilot scheme on 9 July 1990. Call options were offered on five leading stocks. Contracts are for 1000 units of the underlying stock which must be deposited with the New Zealand Stock Exchange options account.

4.3   Securities Identification Code

Code name and structure

There is no standard security numbering system in New Zealand.

The New Zealand Stock Exchange provides a standard three-alpha coding

---

* Local authorities have the right to tax as a percentage of the valuation (government property valuation) to fund local authority activities. This revenue is used to fund local body expenditure such as sanitation, roadworks, libraries, etc. The ability to collect such taxes may be used to underwrite local authority capital raising or financial market transactions.

for all listed companies accompanied by a further two-alpha code to denote security. These codes are utilized in conjunction with a standard transaction numbering system to identify all interbroker stock exchange transactions for reporting, confirmation and settlement:

Example: MEC   Merchant Capital Corporation (NZ) Ltd
                    (registered share)
          MECOA Merchant Capital Corporation (NZ) Ltd
                    (Options)

The New Zealand Stock Exchange and the Reserve Bank are the joint agents for ISIN numbering in New Zealand. For the National Security Identification Number (NSIN), different coding structures are used by the NZSE and Reserve Bank for equity and debt securities respectively and a standard structure is being developed.

Name and address of organization responsible for the securities identification code

ISIN numbering agencies

Equities:
New Zealand Stock Exchange
8th Floor, Caltex Tower
286–292 Lambton Quay
PO Box 2959
NZ-Wellington
New Zealand

Tel: 64 4 727 599
Fax: 64 4 731 470

Debt Securities:
Reserve Bank of New Zealand
2 The Terrace
PO Box 2498
NZ-Wellington
New Zealand

Tel: 64 4 722 029
Fax: 64 4 738 554

4.4 Transfer of ownership

Ownership is transferred by the lodging for registration of a standard form of transfer (signed by the seller and the name of the buyer filled in) by an approved party (usually a broker, bank, solicitor or accountant) with the registrar for the company or corporation. The registrar records the change of ownership and issues a new certificate to the buyer.

Special transfers signed by both the seller and buyer are required for transactions undertaken outside New Zealand or not lodged by approved parties. The standard form incorporates special witnessing provisions in respect of transactions where the seller is resident outside New Zealand but the transaction is conducted through an approved New Zealand intermediary (see above).

Special forms are required for transactions in New Zealand government stock and rights.

5   STRUCTURE AND REGULATION OF FINANCIAL MARKETS

5.1   Structure of financial activities

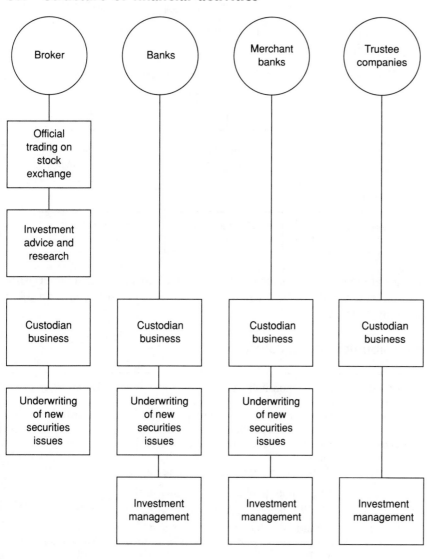

5.2 Regulatory structure

Overview

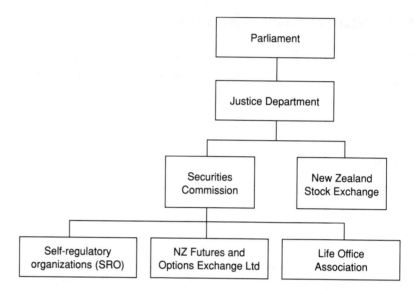

Proposals are in place to replace the Securities Commission with a Supervisory Authority and for the New Zealand Stock Exchange to become an SRO under that Authority.

Responsibilities of regulatory bodies

Name of body	Task/responsibilities	Legal basis
New Zealand Securities Commission	To supervise the law relating to the offering of securities to the public To review the law relating to bodies corporate To review practices relating to securities	Securities Act 1978
	To promote public understanding of the law and practices relating to securities	Securities Regulations 1983
	To authorize futures exchanges and persons authorized to undertake futures dealing To authorize life insurance companies	Securities Amendment Act 1988
Reserve Bank of New Zealand	To oversee registered banks operating in New Zealand	Reserve Bank Act

Supervision of stock exchange

Prior to the creation of the planned Supervisory Authority (*see*: 'Overview'), the New Zealand Stock Exchange is a self-regulatory body operating under the Sharebrokers Amendment Act 1981. The stock exchange has promulgated the following:

- the Rules of the New Zealand Stock Exchange
- the Regulations of the New Zealand Stock Exchange
- the Listing Requirements of the New Zealand Stock Exchange.

The Justice Department of the New Zealand government is responsible for recommending to the Governor-General in Council that the New Zealand Stock Exchange Rules and any amendments thereto are approved.

Supervision of clearing and central securities depository organization

There is currently no clearing house in New Zealand. The New Zealand Stock Exchange conducts a centralized clearing and accounting system for its members. This is based on same-day value for settlement funds.

There is no current central securities depository organization. Securities are usually registered in the name of the beneficial owner or a nominee which is usually the nominee company of a bank, broker or trustee company.

Proposals are underway to facilitate electronic transfer of securities in conjunction with the New Zealand Stock Exchange interbroker settlement system.

Supervision of broker/dealers and custodian banks

The New Zealand Stock Exchange is responsible for supervising its member firms. This is accomplished in two ways:

- Setting minimum net capital requirements in relation to outstanding balances.
- An independent inspection system to ensure capital and organizational requirements are met.

Registered banks and their custodial services are supervised by the central bank, the Reserve Bank of New Zealand.

6   CUSTODIANS

ANZ Banking Group of New
  Zealand
215–229 Lambton Quay
Wellington 1
New Zealand

Tel: 4 721 549
Fax: call telephone number for fax

Bank of New Zealand
BNZ Center
1 Willis Street
Wellington
New Zealand

Tel: 4 474 6999
Fax: 4 474 6883

Barclays New Zealand Custodian
  Services
Barclays House
36 Customhouse Key
PO Box 574
Wellington 6000
New Zealand

Tel: 4 726 926
Fax: 4 781 714

Citibank
Citibank Center
23 Customs Street East
PO Box 3429
Auckland 1
New Zealand

Tel: 9 307 1900
Fax: 9 302 1881

Hongkong & Shanghai Banking
  Corporation
4/F Hongkong Bank House
290 Queen Street
Auckland
New Zealand

Tel: 9 309 3800
Fax: 9 309 6681

National Australia Nominees
Level 2
United Bank Tower
125 Queen Street
Auckland
New Zealand

Tel: 9 302 2381
Fax: 9 302 2337

Westpac Nominees New Zealand
318–324 Lambton Quay
Wellington
New Zealand

Tel: 4 52144
Fax: 4 737 115

32 NORWAY

1 PRINCIPAL STOCK EXCHANGE

Oslo Bors
Tollbugt 2
Box 460 Oslo 1
Norway

Tel: 47 2 34 17 00
Telex: 77242

2 PRINCIPAL REGULATORY AUTHORITY

Kredit Tilsynet
PO Box 100
Bryn
0611 Oslo 6
Norway

Tel: 47 2 652 930
Telex: 56 77247 (TILSYN)
Fax: 47 2 630 226

3 TIME DIFFERENCE FROM GMT: +1 HOUR

4 FORMS AND TYPES OF SECURITIES

4.1 Forms of securities

Bearer security **(lhendehaverpapirer)**   Security not registered on the books of the issuing company. For premium bonds, the owner (investor) can choose either the bearer physical paper or the registered form.

Registered security **(Navnepapirer)**   Security that is recorded in the name of the holder on the book of the issuer or the issuer's registrar (mainly unlisted shares).

Allotment letter **(Tildelingsbevis)**   A temporary document of title issued to a successful applicant in the case of an offer of shares by a company to the public (mainly unlisted shares).

Book entry security **(VPS papirer)**   Security which is kept only in the form of an uncertificated holding, i.e. a computer-based record. All listed shares, all listed primary capital certificates, all bonds including all certificates (short-term bonds) and all options must be registered in the Norwegian book entry system for securities, Verdipapirsentralen (VPS). The securities are registered in the name of the owners. According to the Companies Act, information on ownership of shares and primary capital certificates is public and accessible at the company's head office. Debt instruments are treated as being in bearer form, thus neither the public nor the issuer have access to ownership information.

Unit trust part **(Fondsandeler)**   Security registered in book entry system kept by company managing the fund or registered in VPS.

Depository receipt **(Depotbevis)**   Listed depository receipts must be registered in VPS.

Global certificate **(Hovedgjeldsbrev/pantobligasjon)**   Represents an entire issue of bonds/certificates and is only an underlying document/security deposited with the agent/trustee of the loan.

4.2   Types of securities

Equities

Ordinary share **(Ordinaere aksjer)**   Securities which represent an ownership interest in a company. (Issued in registered form; may have to be in book entry form.)

(a)   Special types of shares with regard to voting rights
Free share **(Frie aksjer)**   Can be held by anyone, regardless of citizenship. Normally without voting rights. (Issued in registered form; may have to be in book entry form.)

A/B share **(A/B-aksjer)**   Some companies maintain shares with or without voting rights (separated into different series, e.g. A/B-shares).

Restricted share **(Bundne aksjer)**   Share which can only be held by Norwegians.

(b)   Special type of shares with regard to dividends
Preferred share **(Preferanseaksjer)**   Share with preferential rights with regard to dividend payments. (Issued in registered form; may have to be in book entry form.)

(c) Special type of shares with regard to claim in case of liquidation
Preferred share (**Preferanseaksjer**)   Certain preference shares have preference rights in case of liquidation. (Issued in registered form; may have to be in book entry form.)

(d) Other equities
Bonus share (**Fondsaksjer**)   Security which is issued through a transfer of funds in order to increase the share capital on a no-pay basis. (Issued in registered form; may have to be in book entry form.)

Primary capital certificate (**Grunnfondsbevis**)   Formally a debt instrument, but appears in a stock form. Savings banks, insurance companies and bond-issuing credit institutions can issue a perpetual loan in order to fulfil equity requirements. The parts kept by the investors can be compared with shares (also tax-wise), giving the holder e.g. dividend rights and certain voting rights.

Unit trust part (**Fondsandeler**)   Security which represents co-ownership in a mutual fund. Some funds have certain tax incentives for Norwegian residents. (Issued in registered form; held in book entry form.)

Subscription right (**Tegningsretter**)   Security which represents the right to obtain ownership of new securities (e.g. shares) normally in the issuing company. (Issued in registered form; may be in book entry form.)

Debt instruments and warrants

Bond (**Obligasjoner**)   An interest bearing debt instrument (book entry form).

(a) Special types of bonds with regard to interest
Straight bond (**Fastrenteobligasjoner**)   It is quite common that loans have the interest rate fixed only for a certain period. Thereafter, the interest rate must be renegotiated. The bond may have call options, both/either from the borrower's or the investor's part.

Floating-rate bond (**Flytenderenteobligasjoner**)   Coupon linked to an independent indicator, like LIBOR, NIBOR, etc.

(b) Special types of bonds with regard to maturity
Maturity fixed loans (bullet) (**Fastelan**)   The whole loan is paid back at maturity.

Retractable bond (**Serielan**)   The loan is repaid by drawings in equal lots (semi-annually/annually) over the whole loan period. May have call options for the borrower. A grace period may be provided.

Annuities (**Annuitetslan**)   As above, but repaid in semi-annual/annual annuities.

(c) Special types of bonds with regard to borrowers
The issues can be divided as follows, depending on the type of borrower:

– state loans
– state-guaranteed loans
– loans issued by boroughs, municipalities or guaranteed by such
– mortgage institutions
– bank/insurance companies
– others.

(d) Bond convertible into other securities
Convertible bond **(Konvertible obligasjoner)** Bond which may be converted by the holder into another security, mainly shares.

(e) Other instruments
Premium bond **[Premieobligasjoner (Gullfisk)]** Government bonds, issued normally for ten years. Premium bonds do not carry interest, the loan's total interest is paid out (tax-free) as lottery drawings (bearer).

Warrant **(Obligasjoner med Kjoepsrett)** Document giving the right, but not duty to buy securities at a certain price within a certain period. Not to be separated from the underlying bond/certificate (as long as not exercised). (Issued in bearer form; may have to be in book entry form.)

Money market instruments

Short-term bond **(Sertifikater)** Debt instrument with a maturity of up to 12 months (*see*: 'Book entry security').

Treasury certificate **(Statssertifikater)** Money market paper issued by the government (*see*: short-term bond).

Bankers Acceptance/certificate of deposits **(Banksertifikat pa tidsinnskudd)** Issued by banks for periods from one day to one year, normally between 14 and 180 days (*see*: short-term bond).

Commercial paper **(Lanesertifikater)** Money market instrument issued by credit institutions and private companies (*see*: short-term bond).

Traded options

Stock options **(Aksje Opsjoner)** At the end of March 1991, four stocks were listed as the underlying assets for trading in stock options on the Oslo Stock Exchange.

Option on the OBX Stock Index **(Aksjeindeks OBX)** OBX is an index composed of the 25 most heavily traded stocks on the Oslo Stock Exchange.

Futures

There is no organized futures market.

4.3   Securities Identification Code

Code name and structure

The full ISIN numbering standard is implemented for all instruments registered in VPS.

   Example: N00005620856   Tandberg

Name and address of organization responsible for the Securities Identification System

The securities identification numbering system is maintained by:

   Verdipapirsentralen (VPS)
   PO Box 6570 – Rodelokka
   0501 Oslo 5
   Norway

   Tel: 472 64 61 60
   Fax: 472 65 24 56

4.4   Transfer of ownership

Transfer of bearer securities

The value of these securities is embodied in a document or certificate. As no registration is necessary for bearer securities, the title to the security is transferred simply by delivery of the certificate.

Transfer of registered securities

The transfer of registered shares to a new owner takes place on the books of the company concerned in accordance with the company's Articles of Association and the Norwegian Companies Act. In case of a foreign portfolio investment, the company has to check whether the proposed registration does not cause the total foreign holding of shares in the company to exceed the statutory limit set at a certain percentage of the voting power. This does not apply to free shares.

   In the case of registered (physical) debt instruments, a new certificate is issued in the name of the new holder, usually for the whole amount of the holding. The holder of registered securities is not regarded as eligible to the rights which these securities carry until his name has been registered in the company's register.

   Norwegian banks keep registers of shareholders on behalf of several companies.

The Central Securities Registration System (VPS)

During 1986, a new computer-based securities registration system was introduced, thus abolishing the physical certificates for stocks and bonds quoted on the Oslo Stock Exchange. All listed securities must be maintained by this book entry system; Verdipapirsentralen (VPS), the Norwegian Registry of Securities, was established by law on 14 June 1985.

Each investor will have an account which will show his ownership of stocks and bonds. A change report will be sent from VPS directly to the account holder whenever there is a change in holdings. Although in a non-physical form, the shareholdership will be regarded as a registered security holding in relation to the Companies Act. In many companies, the board of directors may have the right to approve share transfers. Unless otherwise stated within two months, such an approval is regarded as given.

Clients of non-resident banks may have their holdings registered in the name of their foreign bank, through the intermediary of a Norwegian member of VPS which is licensed to keep such holdings. Such holdings are deprived of voting rights.

5   STRUCTURE AND REGULATION OF FINANCIAL MARKETS

5.1   Structure of financial activities

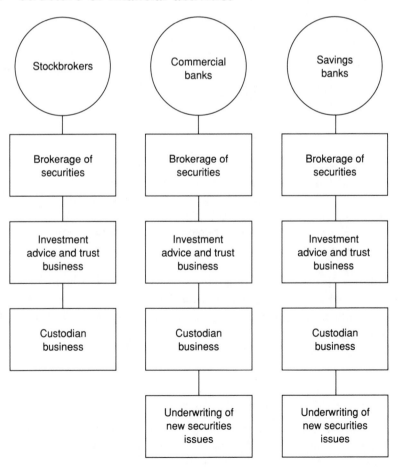

5.2 **Regulatory structure**

Overview

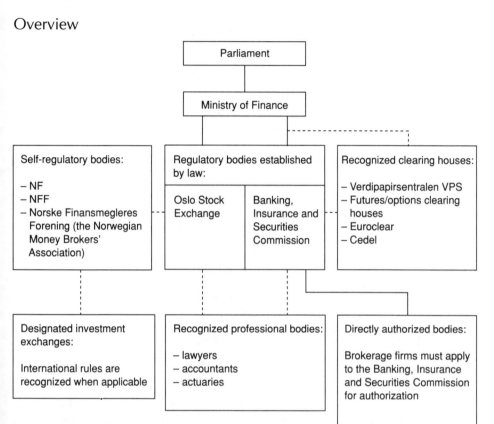

NF = Norges Fondsmeglerforbund (Norwegian Stockbrokers' Association).
NFF = Norske Finansanalytikers Forening (Norwegian Society of Financial Analysts).

Responsibilities of regulatory bodies

Name of body	Responsibilities	Legal basis
The Finance Department	Supervision of the securities market	The specific Acts
Oslo Stock Exchange (OSE) (supervised by the Ministry of Finance)	Adjudicatory power based on OSE rules: – On trading and new issues and parties involved therein (incl. insider trading) – OSE quoted securities/ prices/companies – Imposing of administrative disciplinary sanctions	Securities Exchange Act 1988

Name of body	Responsibilities	Legal basis
	Power of enforcement: – Investigation of potential violations – Prosecutorial functions	
Banking, Insurance and Securities Commission (supervised by Finance Department)	Supervision of the securities market according to the Act and to instructions of the Finance Department	The Act on Kredittilsynet of 1956
	Adjudicatory power: – Regulatory oversight over banks, insurance companies, brokers, etc. regulated by various Acts – Imposing of administrative disciplinary sanctions Power of enforcement: – Investigation of potential violations – Prosecutorial function	Various Acts regulating the markets
Recognized clearing houses:		
Verdipapirsentralen VPS (supervised by Banking, Insurance and Securities Commission)	Legislative power by: – Articles of Association, approved by the Finance Department – Organized EDP-systems/ functions within the securities industry – Exclusive rights to register securities, accounts and rights with the effect described in the Act	Act No. 62 of 14 June 1985 relating to the Norwegian Registry of Securities (amended by Act No. 8 of 9 January 1987 and Act No. 52 of 16 June 1989)
Self-regulative bodies:		
Norges Fondsmeglerforbund Norske Finansanalytikeres Forening Norske Kapitalmegleres	– Support the members and their interests within the securities markets – Recommend rules within the industry not already regulated by law, often on the basis of internationally acknowledged rules and practices	
Directly authorized bodies:		
Brokerage firms	Exclusive rights to deal, against commission; act as a middle-man in securities trading	Act on Securities Trading, etc. 1985

Name of body	Responsibilities	Legal basis
Recognized professional bodies:		
Advisers, e.g. – lawyers – accountants – actuaries	Such advisers will occasionally appear on behalf of parties in the market, and will adopt the market's rules and regulations	Laws regulating the relevant business, and the Acts within the securities area

Supervision of the stock exchange

Rules for quotation and admission have to be approved by the Ministry of Finance. The king, advised by his ministry, appoints the members of the Board of the Stock Exchange.

Supervision of clearing and central securities depository organization

Verdipapirsentralen, VPS, is supervised by the Banking, Insurance and Securities Commission. Its Articles of Association have to be approved by the Ministry of Finance. The king (ministry) appoints the members of the Committee of Representatives.

Supervision of broker/dealers and custodian banks

Broker/dealers and custodian banks are supervised by the Banking, Insurance and Securities Commission.

6   CUSTODIANS

ABC/Union Bank of Norway
PO Box 1172
Sentrum
0107 Oslo
Norway

Tel: 47 2 31 90 55
Fax: 47 2 42 13 61

Christiania Bank
PO Box 116
Sentrum
Oslo
Norway

Tel: 47 2 48 50 00
Fax: 47 2 48 43 63

Den Norske Bank
Kirkegatan 21
Oslo 1
Norway

Tel: 47 2 48 10 50
Fax: 47 2 48 28 96

33 PORTUGAL

☞ ## 1 PRINCIPAL STOCK EXCHANGE

Borsa de Valores de Lisboa
Praca do Comercio
1100 Lisbon
Portugal

Tel: 351 1 87 94 16
Telex: 44 751

☞ ## 2 PRINCIPAL REGULATORY AUTHORITY

Commissao Instaladora da CMVM
Bolsa de Valores de Lisboa
Praca do Comercio
1100 Lisbon
Portugal

Tel: 351 1 871 116
    351 863 180
Telex: 404 44751 (BVLISB P)
Fax: 351 1 877 402

3 TIME DIFFERENCE FROM GMT: NONE

4 FORMS AND TYPES OF SECURITIES

4.1 Forms of securities

Bearer certificate **(Titulo ao portador)** Certificates can be issued either to bearer or in registered form. However, most of them are issued in bearer form with the exception of those shares which, based on the company's by-laws, must be registered. Bearer certificates can be changed into registered certificates upon request. Charges arising thereof are at shareholder's cost.

Registered certificate **(Titulo Nominativo)**   In certain cases, shares must be registered, in particular when they have not been completely paid for, or when there is some restriction in the company's Articles of Association regarding the transfer of ownership. Registered shares may be converted into bearer shares, provided that the company's Articles of Association and the law allow it. Moreover, registered shares must be registered in the company's stock books, or with a credit institution.

Book entry securities **(Titulo Escritural)**   All types of public limited company securities may, or may not, take book entry form, following new legislation. The company's Articles of Association determine the form its securities take.

Provisional certificate **[Titulo Provisorio (Cautela)]**   Before the issuance of the definitive shares, the issuer may distribute provisional registered shares. Should the company request it and upon authorization from the stock exchange, they can be traded in the stock exchange non-official market.

4.2   Types of securities

Equities and warrants

Ordinary share **(Acçao Ordinaria)**   Share in the capital of a public limited company, entitling the owner to dividends and voting rights.

Preferred share **(Acçao Preferencial)**   Shares which entitle the owner to a prior claim in the profits or on the assets if the company goes into liquidation. There are also preferred shares without voting rights.

Debt instruments

Bond **(Obrigaçao)**   Debt security usually medium to long term (over three years).

Floating-rate bond **(Obrigaçao com Taxa de Juro Indexada)**   A majority of the Portuguese bonds are traded with indexed interest rates. There are three main indices: TRO, fixed by the Central Bank; APB, made public by the Portuguese Bankers' Association (APB); and a third type which is the weighted average of the last 12 Treasury bill interest rates (on a semi-annual basis).

Government bond **(Titulo de Divida Publica)**   Bonds issued by the state. The payment of interest and principal is guaranteed by the state.

Zero-coupon bond **(Obrigaçao de Cupao Zero)**   There is no periodic payment of interest. It can be accumulated and paid with the principal on maturity date, or more commonly the bond is bought at a discount on subscription date. The first issues were launched by the state in 1986.

Cash bond **(Obrigaçao de Caixa)**   Bonds issued on a continuous basis with total reimbursement on maturity date. The issuing company must be a financial institution, namely an investment bank or an investment company, and it can grant anticipated redemption to the bondholders, but not before 12 months after the issuing date.

***Medium-term Treasury bond* (Obrigaçao do Tesouro)**   Bond with 18 to 48 months' maturity, fixed-interest rate, sold in the primary market and reimbursed on maturity date. The interest is calculated and paid semi-annually. They are sold in auction in the primary market and are reserved to financial institutions which afterwards can place them among the public. They are tradeable on stock exchanges and only exist in book entry form.

***Convertible bond* (Obrigaçao Convertivel)**   Holders may exchange convertible bonds against shares, according to issuing conditions. Convertible bonds can only be issued by companies listed on the stock exchange.

***Warrant bond* (Obrigaçao com Warrant)**   Warrant bonds entitle holders to subscribe to one or several shares of the issuing company. The price, period and other conditions are set out at time of issuance. The subscription right (warrant) can be freely traded independently of the bonds, unless otherwise set out in the issuance terms. Issuing companies must be listed on the stock exchange.

***Participating certificate* (Titulo de Participaçao)**   Securities issued by public companies partly owned by the state for an unlimited period of time and with no voting rights. The income is twofold: a fixed part accounting for 60% to 80%, and a variable part depending on the company's results regarding the remaining 20% to 40%. The funds invested are equivalent to equity capital. The issuing company can redeem the certificates ten years after the issuance date. Certificates are also negotiable on the stock exchange.

Mutual investment funds

***Unit trust fund* (Fundo de Investimento)**   Unit trust funds are divided into equal units. Assets consist of securities or real estate in the case of real estate funds, both arising from the investment of capital received from the public. Both real estate and equity funds can be open- or closed-end funds depending on whether or not the capital to invest is fixed at the time of constitution of the fund.

As regards equity open-end funds, assets must include at least 6% of cash, bank deposits, Treasury bills or money market investments; a 25% minimum in public debt and a 75% minimum in quoted equities is also required. Other restrictions regarding assets which also apply to equity closed-end funds include a 10% maximum limit for unquoted securities, as well as for securities issued by a single issuer.

As regards real estate open- and closed-end funds, assets must consist of at least 75% real estate of which no more than 20% may be invested in a single project. Open-end funds must furthermore comply with a minimum 6% worth of cash, bank deposits, Treasury bills and money market investments.

The fund must be run by a fund management company, except equity closed-end funds, which can also be managed by banks. Unit trust fund's certificates can be represented by registered or bearer certificates, or be dematerialized securities.

Security funds include among others Treasury funds (Fundo de Tesouraria) whose assets generally include Treasury bills, CDs, CLIPs (*see*: 'Money market instruments') and money market investments, and are suitable for very short-term investments as the interest rate terms and the exact investment period can be arranged.

Other funds consist of assets which are a combination of shares, bonds, Treasury bills, other types of public debt and participation certificates which offer varying degrees of risk.

Money market instruments

Treasury bills **(Bilhetes do Tesouro)**   Treasury bills are issued by the Treasury for a period below one year in book entry form and are placed in the primary market by the central bank by auction and at a discount. The access to the primary market is reserved to financial institutions which can place the Treasury bills among the public with or without repurchase agreements by means of the optional issuance of registered certificates.

CLIPs **(Crédito em leilao ao Investimento Publico)**   A type of revolving underwriting facility with a six-month lifespan. In the CLIPs selling process there is a syndicate that underwriters each tranche and accepts other banks' bids which are made in terms of what interest rate the buying bank wants to be paid. For each auction, there is a maximum rate that the Treasury is willing to pay. This rate can be either linked to recent Treasury bills' interest rates or term deposits' interest rates. This financial instrument is available to the public in general, with a fiscal benefit.

Certificate of deposit **(Certificado de Deposito)**   Registered certificates representing banking deposits in Portuguese escudos for periods between 181 days and five years. The interest can be paid periodically or on maturity date and the interest rates can be fixed or variable. The minimum amount is PTE 5 million. Certificates of deposit can be traded in the secondary market, following endorsement.

5   STRUCTURE AND REGULATION OF FINANCIAL MARKETS

5.1   Structure of financial activities

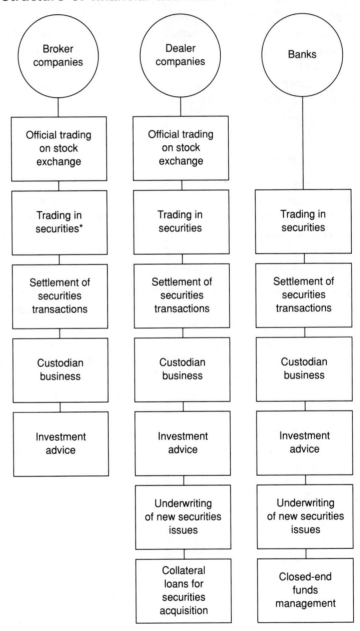

* Only on account of third parties.

5.2 Regulatory structure

Overview

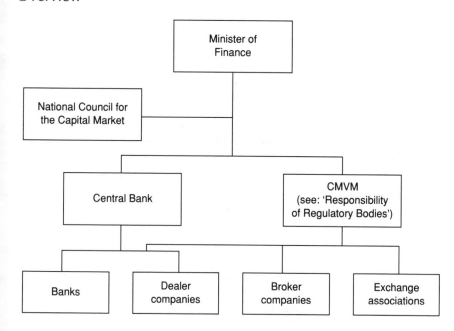

Responsibility of regulatory bodies

Name of body	Responsibilities	Legal basis
Minister of Finance	Further to responsibilities regarding economic and monetary policies: – he is the President of the National Council of the Capital Market – supervises the CMVM – he has the task of defining the regulations and organization of the markets, as defined by law	Codigo do Mercado de Valores Mobiliarios – Securities Market Act
Conselho Nacional do Mercado de Valores Mobiliarios National Council of the Capital Market	As a consulative body of the Minister of Finance, it has the following functions: – to give advice on the government's general policies for the capital market, on any new legislation directly concerning the market, the creation or closing of stock	

Name of body	Responsibilities	Legal basis
	exchanges, the creation of new types of markets, institutions, financial intermediaries or financial instruments, the adoption of exceptional measures in emergency circumstances – to periodically appraise the situation and development of the markets and to present relevant recommendations and suggestions in order to improve the structure and functioning	
Commissa do Mercado de Valores Mobiliarios, CMVM	The CMVM is responsible for regulating, monitoring, supervising and promoting the securities markets and all activities performed by every financial agent. It is also in charge of the cooperation with equivalent bodies of other countries. In its capacity as a regulatory body, the CMVM may enact general rules or instructions specially directed to a predetermined group of agents. Within its supervisory power it has the ability to carry legal actions against transgressors and to impose the respective fine	
Banco de Portugal – Central Bank	Together with the CMVM, it supervises the financial intermediaries under its authority. In order to ensure their liquidity it sets judicious financial limits, namely regarding the underwriting and placement of new issues	

5.3 Supervision of the stock exchanges

The stock exchanges are created and administered by Stock Exchange Associations. These Associations are non-profit-making institutions, with their own capital and corporate boards. Each Association may rule over more than one stock exchange. Each Stock Exchange Association is composed of associate members (broker and dealers) and associate non-members (financial institutions legally authorized to receive market orders and provide custody services). The Stock Exchange Associations have disciplinary power over the respective associates and, in general, over every individual present on the stock exchange premises.

Stock exchanges, Stock Exchange Associations and their boards are under the direct jurisdiction of the CMVM. The creation and activity of both the stock exchange and the Stock Exchange Associations requires the prior authorization of the Minister of Finance, preceded by a CMVM advice. The internal regulations of each stock exchange also require prior CMVM's approval.

5.4 Supervision of the clearing organization

The stock exchanges are responsible for the settlement and clearing of the operations through a nationwide system connected with a Central Securities Depository (Central de Valores Mobiliarios). The creation and maintenance of the Central is the responsibility of the Stock Exchange Associations which may together with other financial intermediaries create an independent association whose sole purpose is to create and manage the Central. This association is known as Interbolsa. The supervision of the settlement and clearance procedures, as well as the approval of their respective regulations, is the responsibility of the CMVM.

5.5 Supervision of brokers, dealers and custodian banks

All activities in the capital market of any financial intermediary are under the jurisdiction of the CMVM, including therefore the activities of dealer companies and custodian banks. Nevertheless, these two types of financial institutions are also under the jurisdiction of the Central Bank regarding activities – relevant or not to the capital market – that involve the granting of credit or that may affect their liquidity, such as underwriting and placement of new issues. Capital requirements and rules regarding financial limits fall under the jurisdiction of the Central Bank. The CMVM and the Bank of Portugal co-operate in these areas in order to avoid any conflict of assignment. In the case of the financial intermediaries that act as brokers in the stock exchanges, they are also subject to the supervision of the respective Stock Exchange Associations, which when appropriate may inspect their accounts.

6   CUSTODIANS

Banco Bilbao Vizcaya
Avenida da Liberdade 222
1200 Lisbon
Portugal

Tel: 1 535 171
Fax: 1 524 200

Banco Espirito Santo E Comercial
  de Lisboa
Apartado 2105
1103 Lisbon Codex
Portugal

Tel: 1 570 400
Fax: 1 577 884

Banco Portugues do Atlantico
110 Rua do Ouro
1100 Lisbon
Portugal

Tel: 1 346 1321
Fax: 1 321 307

Barclays Bank
50 Avenida da Republica
2nd floor
1000 Lisbon
Portugal

Tel: 1 793 5020
Fax: 1 779 9610

Citibank Portugal
48–50 Rua Alexandre
Herculano
1200 Lisbon
Portugal

Tel: 1 545 157
Fax: 1 576 524

Corretora Atlántico – Sociedade
    Financeira de Corretagem
Rua 1 de Dezembro 78–2nd
1100 Lisbon
Portugal

Tel: 1 346 5766
Fax: 1 346 5167

34 SINGAPORE

1 PRINCIPAL STOCK EXCHANGE

Stock Exchange of Singapore
1 Raffles Place
Singapore 0104

Tel: 65 535 37 88
Telex: RS 21853

2 PRINCIPAL REGULATORY AUTHORITY

The Monetary Authority of Singapore
Securities Industry Division
10 Shenton Way
MAS Building
Singapore 9001

Tel: 65 225 5577
Telex: 87 28174 (ORCHID RS)
Fax: 65 229 9697

3 TIME DIFFERENCE FROM GMT: +8 HOURS

4 FORMS AND TYPES OF SECURITIES

4.1 Forms of securities

Registered certificate A certificate represents an interest in the ownership in a company. The certificate bears the name of the registered owner whose name appears on the register of the issuing company.

Book entry securities Applies to securities listed on the SESDAQ market (second board market) and those new listings on the main board that have been listed since May 1990. Conversion of the existing main board securities began in June 1991. Underlying securities are immobilized and kept at the Central Securities Depository (Pte) Ltd.

Depository receipts   Certificates representing the deposit of an equivalent amount of foreign shares.

Jumbo certificates   Certificates of the SESDAQ market are registered in jumbo certificates in the name of the Central Securities Depository (PTE) Ltd. A number of marketable-lot certificates are also kept to meet withdrawal requirements.

Provisional allotment letter   In the case of the issuance of new shares through a rights issue for registered shareholders, these rights are issued and traded in the form of provisional allotment letters.

4.2   Types of securities

Equities and warrants

Share   Represents an ownership interest in a corporation. A very small proportion of the shares traded in Singapore are in bearer form. For registered shares, registered holders are entitled to voting rights.

Preference share certificate   Share with preference rights with regard to dividend payments and any distribution of assets on liquidation. Frequently without voting rights. (Issued in registered form.)

Deferred share   Share which is not entitled to dividends until the other share categories have a dividend paid on them or which remains without dividends for a stipulated number of years and is then automatically converted into an ordinary share.

Warrant   Warrants are normally issued together with a so-called warrant bond issue and usually entitle the bearer to subscribe to new shares or bonds under specific conditions. (Issued in registered form.)

Investment and unit trust certificates

Investment trust part   Part of the holdings of a closed-end investment company formed for the specific purpose of dealing or holding securities in other companies. (Issued in registered and held in allotment letter form.)

Unit trust part   Part of an open-end investment company which holds securities in trust for a large number of investors. It is obliged to re-purchase the units according to an agreed formula. Unit-holders have a direct legal interest in the portfolio because the fund is legally a trust.

Debt instruments

Straight bond   Bond without clauses granting conversion or warrant privileges. (Issued in registered form.)

Convertible bond   Bond issued by a corporation which may be converted by the holder into shares at a stipulated price within a certain period. (Issued in registered form.)

Warrant issue   Bond issue embodying the right to purchase shares or new bonds in the issuing company at a stipulated price within a certain period. (Issued in registered form.)

Floating-rate note   Note on which the interest can change under certain circumstances (e.g. linked to SIBOR, Singapore Interbank Offered Rate).

Money market instruments

The domestic money market comprises the interbank market and the discount market, both of which are closely interlinked. The market deals in short-term funds and instruments. Besides short-term commercial papers and short-dated government securities, the following instruments are issued, traded and redeemed in the money market:

Treasury bills   Issued by the Singapore government by weekly tender to financial institutions (discount houses and banks).

Singapore dollar negotiable certificates of deposit   Issued by banks for terms of three, six, nine and 12 months. Can be rediscounted in the money market.

Commercial bills   Issued by commercial houses and discounted in the money market.

In the interbank market funds are placed on an overnight basis or as loans with one to three months maturities. The purpose is for the borrowers to fulfil their statutory minimum cash balance requirements, for the lenders to invest non-yielding excess liquidity elsewhere.

The major participants in the money market are the commercial banks, discount houses, money brokers and the Monetary Authority. The discount houses act as intermediaries between the banks as well as between the banks on one hand, and the Monetary Authority on the other hand, by accepting short-term funds from commercial banks and investing them in the money market instruments.

There is not an active market in government papers (Treasury bills and stocks), as they are all picked up quickly by local institutions and generally held till maturity.

The Asian dollar market is essentially an international money and capital market where US dollars and other foreign currencies are pooled in the form of call and time deposits for onlending, mainly to countries in Asia. The market is predominantly an interbank market whose operators have to set up separate bookkeeping units, known as Asian Currency Units (ACUs), for such transactions.

Borrowers in the Asian dollar market can also raise medium- and long-term capital by tapping the Asian dollar bond market. Asian dollar bonds are bonds managed by an Asian institution and listed on the Singapore Stock Exchange. Most issues are denominated in US dollars. Besides straight bond issues, convertible bond issues and floating-rate notes linked to SIBOR (Singapore Interbank Offered Rate) are floated. Furthermore, US dollar negotiable certificates of deposit (USDNCDs, available for one to 12 months with a minimum denomination of USD 50 000) may be issued by ACUs after consultation with the Monetary Authority. These instruments are of two types, namely floating-rate or fixed-rate USDNCDs.

4.3 Securities Identification Code

There is no numbering system used for securities identification in Singapore.

4.4 Transfer of ownership

Transfer of bearer securities

The value of these securities is embodied in the document or certificate. As no registration is necessary for bearer securities, the title to the security is transferred simply by physical delivery of the certificates. However, bearer securities have to be deposited with a depository bank approved by the Monetary Authority of Singapore and depository receipts would be issued against the bearer securities.

Transfer of registered securities

The holder of registered securities is not regarded as eligible to the rights to which these securities carry until his name has been entered in the company's Register.

To effect a transfer the holder of the security must present it to the Registrar with a transfer instrument, duly endorsed and witnessed by a brokerage firm or bank stating the terms under which the transfer is to take place. Once the Registrar is satisfied that the transferee is the true owner, he issues the transferee with a new certificate bearing his name and updates the share register accordingly. The old certificate is then destroyed. Upon registration, all interest and dividend payments will be sent to the new owner.

Some companies maintain their own company's Register, though most companies engage professional Registrars to maintain the register of shareholders and to effect the transfer of their shares.

Transfer of registration for book entry shares is handled by the central depository, CDP, and takes place on settlement date in their records.

5   STRUCTURE AND REGULATION OF FINANCIAL MARKETS

5.1   Structure of financial activities

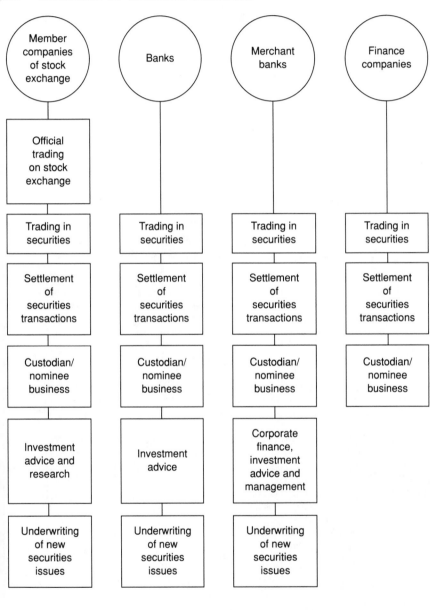

5.2   Regulatory structure

Overview

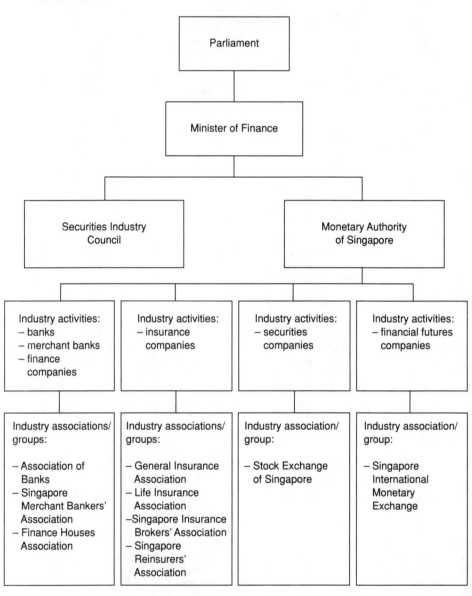

Responsibilities of regulatory bodies

Monetary Authority of Singapore (MAS, government agency)   Responsible for ensuring the stability and orderly development of Singapore's financial system and for the maintenance of high standards of prudential practice among its financial institutions. All commercial banks, merchant banks, finance companies, securities companies, futures brokers, money brokers and insurers must be granted licences by MAS before they are permitted to conduct financial business.

Legal basis: Monetary Authority of Singapore Act, Banking Act, Finance Companies, Securities Industry Act, Insurance Act and Financial Futures Act.

Supervision of stock exchange

The Singapore Stock Exchange, stockbroking companies and their representatives are regulated by the Securities Industry Act and Regulations which are administered by the Monetary Authority of Singapore.

The stock exchange is self-regulated by means of a nine-member Committee comprising four elected stockbroking members and five appointed members from outside the stockbroking industry. The management and regulation of the stock exchange is the primary responsibility of the Committee. It is responsible for making the major policies concerning the operation and development of the exchange. Stockbroking member companies must comply with the exchange's rules and by-laws in relation to all aspects of their business, financial conditions and organization.

Supervision of clearing and central securities depository organization

The Securities Clearing and Computer Services (Pte) Ltd (SCCS) is jointly owned by the Stock Exchange and all its stockbroking member companies. Its main functions include clearing and settlement of trades done on the main board, as well as the provision of computer facilities for trading and client accounting. It is supervised by a board of directors who are currently the committee members of the exchange. The Central Depository (Pte) Ltd (CDP) is wholly owned by the stock exchange. It acts as a central depository for immobilized securities of the main and second board. It provides clearing of trades done and book entry transfer of these securities. The CDP is managed and regulated by the stock exchange.

Supervision of broker/dealers and custodian banks

Stockbroking members of member companies of the stock exchange are regulated by the exchange's rules and by-laws, as well as the Securities Industry Act in relation to licensing and financial requirements.

Foreign stockbrokers who are licensed by the MAS to deal in securities in Singapore are supervised by the MAS. Banks who provide custodian services come under the supervision of the MAS under the Banking Act.

6 CUSTODIANS

Barclays Bank
50 Raffles Place
23-01 Shell Tower
Singapore 0104

Tel: 65 224 8555
Fax: 65 224 4717

Citibank Securities Services
UIC Building
01-00 5 Shenton Way
Singapore 0106

Tel: 65 320 5447
Fax: 65 222 5140

Development Bank of Singapore
6 Shenton Way
DBS Building
Singapore 0106

Tel: 65 220 1111
Fax: 65 221 1306

Hongkong & Shanghai Bank
21 Collyer Quay 02-00
Singapore 0104

Tel: 65 530 5043
Telex: HSBC RS 21259

Overseas Chinese Banking
  Corporation
65 Chulia Street
OCBC Centre
Singapore 0104

Tel: 65 535 7222
Fax: 65 532 6007

Security Pacific National Bank
Shell Tower
50 Raffles Place 01-03
Singapore 0104

Tel: 65 225 7016
Fax: 65 225 6316

Standard Chartered Bank
6 Battery Road
Singapore 0104

Tel: 65 225 8888
Fax: call telephone number for fax

United Overseas Bank
1 Bonham Street 01-00
UOB Building
Singapore 0104

Tel: 65 533 9898
Fax: 65 534 2334

35 SOUTH AFRICA

1 PRINCIPAL STOCK EXCHANGE

Johannesburg Stock Exchange
17 Diagonal Street
PO Box 1174
2000 Johannesburg
South Africa

Tel: 27 11 833 6580
Telex: 48 7663 SA

2 PRINCIPAL REGULATORY AUTHORITY

Ministry of Finance
Private Bag XII
Pretoria 0001
South Africa

Tel: 27 12 315 5111
Telex: no number given
Fax: 27 12 219580

3 TIME DIFFERENCE FROM GMT: +2 HOURS

4 FORMS AND TYPES OF SECURITIES

4.1 Forms of securities

Registered certificate   A certificate evidencing registered ownership in share(s) in a company or in loan stock (bonds) issued by the government or a local authority.

Bearer certificate   This form of securities is mainly common practice in financial instruments traded on the money market (see: 'Transfer requirements of bearer certificates').

Book entry This form of securities is exclusively used by the management companies of unit trusts. However, at the request of an investor a certificate will be issued. The usual practice is that only a statement is issued giving full details of the investment. Unit trusts are not tradable in the South African market, but are sold or repurchased directly by the management company to/from the public.

Allotment letter An allocation of shares in a rights issue.

Renounceable certificate A renounceable document of title representing an entitlement to new shares issued.

4.2 Types of securities

Equities

Ordinary share Represents partial ownership in a company, with voting rights. (Issued in registered form; may be held as a jumbo certificate.)

Preference share Share which pays to the holder a fixed rate of dividend. Preference shares have a claim prior to that of ordinary shares on the earnings of a company and upon the assets of the company in the event of liquidation. (Issued in registered form; may be held as a jumbo certificate.)

Cumulative preference share Share upon which dividend will accumulate until payment is made. Otherwise, the same as preference share. (Issued in registered form; may be held as a jumbo certificate.)

Participating preference share Share extending participation in earnings over and above its fixed dividend rate. Otherwise the same as preference share. (Issued in registered form; may be held as a jumbo certificate.)

Deferred share Represents share which only qualifies for a dividend after a prescribed minimum dividend has been paid to ordinary shareholders. (Issued in registered form; may be held as a jumbo certificate.)

Convertible preference share A share feature which allows the owner to exchange such shares in accordance with the terms of the issue. A common practice is converting preference shares into ordinary shares at a certain ratio stipulated at the time of issue. (Issued in registered form; may be held as a jumbo certificate.)

Debt instruments

Bond **(Straight bond)** Debentures and notes which carry no rights, but merely a fixed or variable interest rate for a fixed period after which they are redeemed. (Registered.)

Convertible debentures Secured debentures and notes which have inherent option rights, or which are convertible, either in whole or in part, into another class of security. (Issued in registered form; may be held as a jumbo certificate.)

Loan **(Ordinary loans)**   Unsecured loan bearing a fixed rate of interest and being redeemable after a certain period.

Gilt-edged security **(Government loan)**   The term 'gilt-edged security' is normally applied only to loan stocks of the central government issued at fixed rates and running for periods in excess of 12 months.

Semi-gilt-edged security **(Municipal/local authorities and statutory corporations)**   Semi-gilt-edged securities apply over a wider field and include stock of municipalities and public corporations such as Escom (Electricity Supply Commission), Iscor, etc. All these loan stocks are issued to satisfy long-term capital needs of the bodies concerned. They carry fixed rates of interest with prime coupon rates.

Unit trust certificates

Open-end trust   Unit trust fund which sells its units to the public and whose assets are invested in a number of different securities in which the unitholders have, in effect, an undivided interest. These unit trust funds continuously offer new units for sale to the public typically as demand increases. Open-end unit trust funds agree to redeem their shares at net asset value. (Held in book entry form.)

Closed-end trust   The number of units or shares in an issue remains unchanged, subject only to possible (but infrequent) increases in capital at the company's discretion. (Issued in registered form; may be held as a jumbo certificate.)

Money market instruments

There is no official money market, but money market transactions take place between the various financial and commercial institutions. The Banks Act 1965 will be replaced by the Deposit-taking Institutions Act 1990, which provides for the regulation and supervision of the business of public companies taking deposits from the public.

RSA Treasury bill   Government certificate of indebtedness issued for period of three months – minimum denomination ZAR 10 000.

Bill of exchange   Historically, the bill of exchange was accepted as the most suitable type of short-term investment governed by special legislation. It can be passed from one holder to another by mere endorsement. Being a negotiable instrument, a holder, in due course, and for value, is protected against fraud on the part of the previous holder. It has a short tenor of three to four months and is in itself proof of debt in a court of law.

Bills of exchange are of three main types
* Banker's acceptances (BA) – bills accepted by banks drawn by clients and transferable by endorsement. These bills conform to strict regulations and

those classifying as liquid banker's acceptances are rediscountable at the Reserve Bank.

- Trade bills – these bills have two commercial names as drawer and acceptor and have a bank's endorsement. They are categorized as liquid or non-liquid, the former being eligible for rediscount.
- Promissory notes – bills of exchange bear the signature of both the drawer and the acceptor, whereas promissory notes bear only the debtor's signature, being a promise to pay at a fixed or determinable future date a certain sum in money to the order of a specified person. Nevertheless, a second signature may be added as an endorsement, and this service is often performed by banks for clients who can provide documentary evidence that the notes represent genuine trade transactions and are not merely accommodation bills for loans of money.

Negotiable certificate of deposit (NCD) A negotiable certificate issued against funds deposited in a commercial, merchant or general bank for the wide range of maturities from three months to five years earning a specified rate of return. These deposits are normally in denominations of ZAR 1 million.

Land Bank bill To finance seasonal crop movements, the Land Bank is prepared to issue short bills of three or six months tenor as an alternative to the use of relatively costly bank overdrafts. Such bills rank as liquid assets, being eligible for discount at the Reserve Bank and are frequently held by commercial banks when there is a shortage of alternative short-dated papers.

Land Bank debenture Of longer maturity than Land Bank bills, these debentures also rank as liquid assets, if less than three months to maturity.

Traded options and futures

The JSE will commence trading traded options on equities in the second quarter of 1991. Some six equities and three index options are being proposed. Cash settlement will take place in all of the securities chosen and scrip settlement will be restricted to only one or two of the securities.

4.3 Securities Identification Code

Code name and structure

There is a Clearing House Code for securities traded on the stock exchange, consisting of three or four alphanumeric characters. This code appears on certain lists in the daily *Gazette* and the *Monthly Bulletin*, both issued by the Johannesburg Stock Exchange. The dealers and certain banks make use of this code.

Example: AAC = Anglo American Corporation (ordinary share)

All computer systems will be modified to incorporate the ISIN Identification Code as per the ISO standard.

The JSE has registered with the Association of National Numbering Agencies (ANNA) as the national numbering agency for South Africa but has agreed in principle with UNEXcor to retire from this in favour of UNEXcor, once it becomes a recognized clearing house.

Name and address of organization maintaining numbering system

The Johannesburg Stock Exchange
PO Box 1179
Johannesburg 2000
South Africa

Tel: 011 833 6580
Telex: 87663

4.4 Transfer of ownership

Transfer requirements of bearer securities

South Africans are neither allowed to hold any bearer securities nor are there any bearer securities on offer or available on the South African markets. Certain goldmining houses are allowed by exchange control to issue bearer shares quoted on overseas markets. Should these certificates be returned to South Africa, they must be converted into registered shares.

Transfer requirements of registered securities

All securities except bearer money market instruments are registered in name by a Transfer Secretary who can be in the employ of the issuer or who can be a separate company undertaking transfer secretarial work as its main business. The purpose of registration is to keep accurate records of ownership of the securities, which include the certificate number, in some cases transfer reference number, the holder of the security and the guaranteed signature of the holder. Interest or dividends are paid to the registered holder of the security.

Formalities for the transfer of registered securities

To effect a transfer of a security, it must be handed over to the Transfer Secretary with a transfer deed with two parts, A and B, on form CM42, duly completed.

Portion A consists of the full name of the issuer, number of shares, number of certificate, type of share and registered owner's name and signature. The signature of the registered owner must be dated at the time of signature and must be guaranteed by the placing of a stamp of the selling broker or the owner's banker. Up to this stage, the certificate plus the transfer deed will be fully negotiable. Portion B which consists of the new owner's full name and address, consideration, the name and address of the person lodging the document for registration and stamp duty, if applicable, must be completed before transfer. However, in terms of the Companies Act, it is not necessary for the buyer (transferee) to sign the transfer form.

Only after both of the above sections have been properly completed will the Transfer Office accept the document for transfer. To expedite deliveries, South Africa is using the Certified Deed System and has a Talisman Agency and ADR Depositories (*see*: 'Talisman Agency' and 'American Depository Agencies') to expedite movements of shares between Johannesburg and London and New York respectively.

Manner in which securities may be transferred

A security may be transferred by means of a securities transfer form accompanied by the respective share certificate, or a certified deed, or a broker's transfer form duly certified.

A certified deed can be obtained by lodging the original certificate registered by name with a transfer deed completed for a lesser number of shares than the certificate. The Transfer Secretary would retain the original document and issue a transfer deed certified to the effect that the original document has been retained by the Transfer Secretary and a balance receipt for the unused portion of the certificate. The transfer deed is then freely negotiable on the market. Should any further splits be required, a normal transfer deed must be signed by the owner and attached to the balance receipt for certification. This procedure can be repeated until all sales have been completed. Should a balance of shares be left in the owner's name, then the balance receipt can be surrendered for a certificate.

Stockbroker's position

When certificates with transfer deed or certified deeds are delivered to a stockbroker which are not in the denominations required for delivery, he can split them by using a broker's transfer form. These forms do not require the signature of the owner, but must bear the broker's signature and the original date of signature by the owner. Brokers' deeds are blue in colour to identify them from ordinary white transfer forms (CM42).

The total split required must add up to the number of shares surrendered to the Transfer Secretary, who will certify the broker's form to the effect that the original document has been surrendered to him. Brokers' transfer forms are freely negotiable.

On completion of portion B of the transfer deed accompanied by a certificate or a certified transfer deed or a broker's transfer form, the registration will be effected to the new owner's name which will appear as transferee.

Talisman Agency

The International Stock Exchange of the UK has established the Talisman Agency in Johannesburg, for the purpose of delivery and registration on settling arbitrage deals done on the two stock exchanges. The London brokers deposit the shares for registration in London into the name of their nominee company, while the Johannesburg Agency can certify in Johannesburg and vice versa. This operation results in no movement of physical scrip between the two centres.

American Depository Agencies

Various South African banks act as authorized depositories for American Depository Receipts (ADR) agents. This arrangement means that South African scrip quoted in New York is bought and deposited in South Africa, and ADRs are issued against it. Should the securities be sold, the receipt is surrendered in New York to the ADR agent and the underlying securities are released in South Africa for delivery to the market. As under Talisman, there is thus no movement of physical scrip between Johannesburg and New York.

5 STRUCTURE AND REGULATION OF FINANCIAL MARKETS

5.1 Introduction

The South African financial markets experienced changes in 1989 as far as the self-regulating organizations (SROs) provided for in the Financial Markets Control Act (FMCA) were concerned. The FMCA was passed by Parliament on 26 May 1989 and was promulgated on 10 August 1990.

Universal Exchange Corporation Limited (UNEXcor) is being developed by the banking sector as a recognized clearing house which will be capable of providing service to a multitude of SROs created under the terms of the FMCA. At present, UNEXcor focus on providing the service to the Bond Market Association only (service level 1).

As part of the UNEXcor development, a Central Depository is also being developed and in terms of current planning, it will become operative towards the end of 1991. Although the Central Depository Company is an entity that is completely separate from UNEXcor, the two entities will be linked by using the same computer facilities. The two systems are interdependent as the trading, settlement and risk management is linked to the safe custody of scrip on settlement of a trade. During the initial phase, only gilts will be immobilized in the Central Depository.

5.2   Structure of financial activities

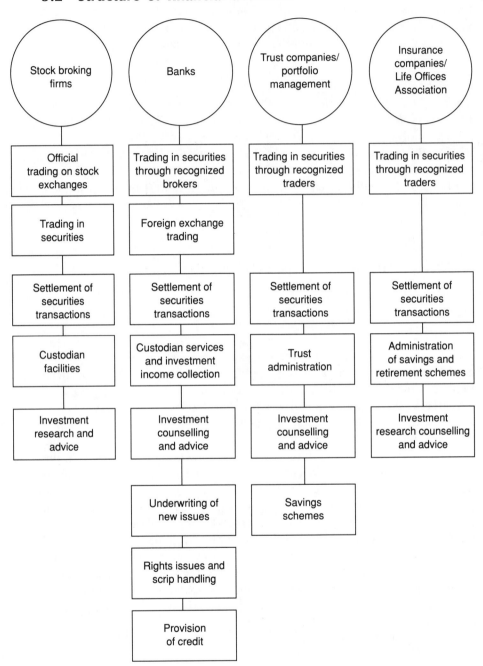

5.3 Regulatory structure

Overview

The organization of the financial markets at present is shown by the following:

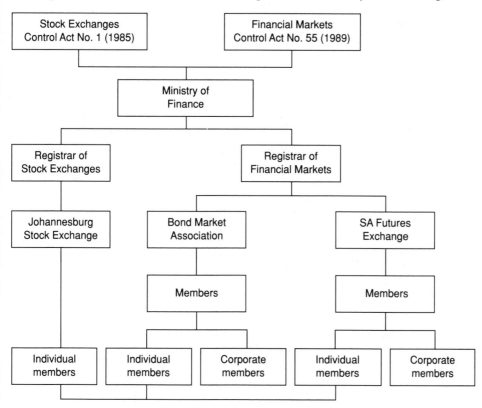

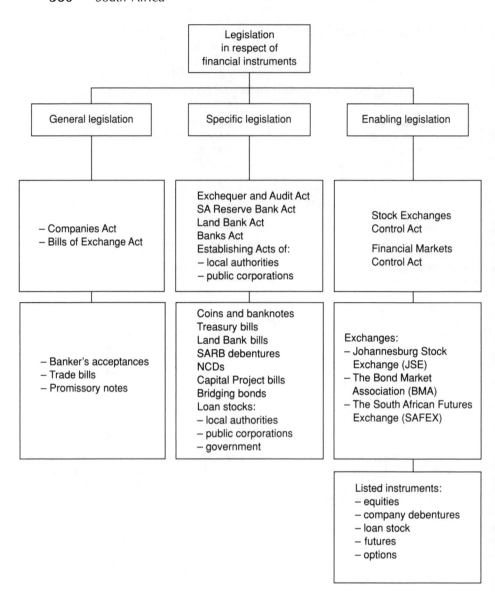

Responsibilities of regulatory bodies

(a) Introduction

There are two major statutes governing the South African securities markets: the Stock Exchange Control Act (SECA) of 1972 (amended in 1985), and the Financial Markets Control Act (FMCA) of 1989. Both Acts are enabling legislation to be complemented by the rules and regulations of the individual exchange associations. No formal market may operate unless it is licensed in terms of one of these Acts and that the regular traders of the market are registered as members thereof.

Equities markets and options on equities are licensed under SECA. Futures markets are licensed under FMCA, as will be the new bonds market once it is ready for operation. In the interim, the Johannesburg Stock Exchange will continue its market for bonds licensed in terms of SECA. SECA permits single capacity trading by members in equities; FMCA permits dual capacity trading in markets which are licensed under it.

The Acts are administered by the Financial Services Board (FSB), a private sector body created by the Financial Services Board Act 1990. The rules of each exchange must be approved by the Financial Services Board. An advisory body called the Financial Markets Advisory Board (FMAB) constituted of regulators and market practitioners provides guidance to the FSB over policy for the markets.

The Acts prescribe minimum requirements and guidelines as a framework for the development by the exchange of its rules and regulations in the administration of its affairs. These rules extend through entry requirements and standards, and business operations. Additionally, the SECA prescribes what instruments may be traded on the equities exchange. The Financial Services Board has, through the FMCA, the power to stipulate which instruments may be listed on the non-equities exchanges. Both Acts require that the rulebook of an exchange and amendments thereto are approved by the Financial Services Board; that the Financial Services Board may attend executive committee meetings; and that the Financial Services Board may issue directives declaring specific business operations and/or practices undesirable.

Finally, foreign exchange regulations provided for in the South African Reserve Bank Act and the Currency and Exchanges Act limit the activities of the exchanges geographically to the Republic of South Africa with the exception of arbitrage between markets across national borders.

Complementing these structures is the Securities Regulation Panel which has been established in terms of the Companies Act of 1973 with the responsibility for regulating takeovers and mergers and investigating insider trading.

(b) Role of the exchanges

A licensed exchange is responsible for the management of the securities which it lists, its members and the trading and settlement of the business conducted by the members. Each exchange is a private business entity owned by its members.

The rules of the exchange elaborate upon the guidelines and code contained within the Acts binding members, the listed companies/issuers and the investors in contractual terms. They are extended to cover pricing, trading, settlement, risk management, listing and disclosure requirements, surveillance, minimum capital requirements, performance guarantee, etc.

The Panel operates within the private sector and is self-regulating. It is given investigatory powers in insider trading matters, and if any proof thereof is found, the matter can be referred to the competent authorities for prosecution. Additionally, it is empowered to enforce its ruling on mergers and takeovers by obtaining the necessary civil relief from any court of competent jurisdiction. A formal Takeover Code with statutory backing has been promulgated by the Panel.

(c)   Role of the regulators

The role of the regulators is principally one of overseeing the exchanges and ensuring conformance by the exchanges to the securities laws and regulations issued by them under those laws. In addition, they carry investigatory powers which they may exercise.

The philosophy of enabling legislation and self-regulation (heavily reliant on honesty) is practised by the regulators and the exchanges in practical terms of cooperation. The regulators are concerned, first and foremost, with systemic issues: social efficiency; the avoidance of domino effects in the closely intertwined web of financial relationships; the integrity of the payments system; and capital requirements for the composite risk.

In support hereof, the regulators have additionally issued unwritten guidelines outlining their philosophy and objectives for the management of the markets. These extend through:

- Ensuring a high level of efficiency of the financial system by a strong bias towards competition – eliminating unnecessary restrictive practices, but retaining a desirable level of stability.
- Maintaining competitive neutrality – ensuring level playing fields through the same regulations for all categories of membership in the same market; free access to membership.
- All risk must be measured at current values.
- Legislation, rules and regulations must be practitioner-based. They should not be imposed, but developed on a participative basis.
- Flexibility to meet changing market requirements on a timely basis.
- Protection of the consumer, ensuring that the small investor is not exploited.
- The securities/financial market's need to be regulated from a functional viewpoint. The advent of corporate conglomerates being members of an exchange is additionally regulated through specific institutional Acts concerning banks, insurance, etc.
- An aim to have a single regulatory structure with one Act, one regulator and one exchange facility for processing clearing, settlement and risk management on behalf of all exchanges.

(d)   Conclusion

Clarity has been brought to the structuring and regulation of markets in an atmosphere of practicality. Change is exerting influence and pressure on all participants in the market, and further consequential modifications, restructuring and reorganization can be expected. Given the partnership type of relationship between the regulators and the exchanges, this should be successfully managed to the collective benefit of all markets and the users thereof.

The regulators have grasped the importance of successful financial market ingredients and are nurturing the markets at the macro-level in all of their dimensions.

Supervision of exchanges

Johannesburg Stock Exchange (JSE)

A committee, styled the Stock Exchange Committee, supervises its members and its operation and ensures that the provisions of the Stock Exchange Control Act, as well as the Stock Exchange Rules and Regulations, are adhered to.

Bond Market Association (BMA)

An elected Executive Committee supervises the operation of the exchange in accordance with the licence issued by the Registrar of Financial Markets.

South African Futures Exchange (SAFEX)

A committee, styled the Surveillance Committee, supervises the operation of the exchange and ensures that the provisions of the Financial Markets Control Act and the rules of the exchange are adhered to.

Supervision of clearing and central securities depository organizations

Clearing organizations

The Johannesburg Stock Exchange supervises the Johannesburg Stock Exchange Clearing House and the Gilt Clearing House.

The South African Futures Exchange has established a clearing house for futures. The Bond Market has appointed the Universal Exchange Corporation (UNEXcor) to provide clearing facilities upon licensing. The objective of Unexcor, who have the large banks and Reserve Bank as shareholders, will be to provide centralized clearing facilities to all markets.

Central Securities Depository

Banks offer safe custody services but an official central depository is not yet in operation. At present, a central depository is being developed by the banks and the South African Reserve Bank through a central depository company. During the first phase of development, only gilt and semi-gilt securities will be placed in the central depository and thus be immobilized.

Supervision of brokers, dealers and custodian banks

Brokers and dealers

(a) Brokers of the JSE are supervised by the General Committee as they must adhere to the Rules and Regulations applicable to members of the JSE. Dealers are employed by broking firms and have to pass certain examinations.

(b) The Bond Market Association will prescribe via its rules surveillance procedures, as well as minimum examinations to be written and passed by Financial Instrument Traders (brokers), Financial Instrument Principals and Compliance Officers. Although these have been agreed to in principle, a final decision will have to be taken on licensing of the exchange.

(c) The compliance and surveillance committee of SAFEX are empowered by the Rules to investigate the affairs of a member if there are reasons to believe that rules and/or regulations and/or procedures have been contravened. Dealers and compliance officers are required to write and pass prescribed examinations.

(d) Universal Exchange Corporation will have a set of procedures and principles applicable to a recognized clearing house. These are in the process of being formulated and will be implemented when UNEXcor becomes operational.

Custodian banks

The banks are supervised by the South African Reserve Bank in terms of the Deposit Taking Institutions Act (previously the Banks and Building Societies Act).

6   CUSTODIANS

First National Bank of Southern
   Africa
17 Diagonal Street
Johannesburg 2000
South Africa

Tel: 11 832 2544
Fax: 11 834 5380

French Bank
4 Ferreira Street
Johannesburg 2000
South Africa

Tel: 11 832 2433
Fax: 11 836 0626

Standard Bank of South Africa
Standard Bank Chambers
46 Marshall Street
Johannesburg 2001
South Africa

Tel: 11 632 2231

36 SPAIN

1 PRINCIPAL STOCK EXCHANGE

Bolsa de Comercio de Madrid
Plaza de la Lealtad
Madrid 28014
Spain

Tel: 341 589 2600
Telex: 27619 BOLMD E

2 PRINCIPAL REGULATORY AUTHORITY

Comision Nacional del Mercado de Valores
Paseo de la Castellana 19
Madrid 28046
Spain

Tel: 34 1 585 1500
Telex: 52 46 459 (TSRO E)
Fax: 34 1 585 1675

3 TIME DIFFERENCE FROM GMT: +1 HOUR

4 FORMS AND TYPES OF SECURITIES

4.1 Forms of securities

Macro title **(Macro titulo)** One certificate/document representing e.g. 10 000, 100 000, etc. units of a security. Mainly in use with the Nuevo Sistema de Liquidación y Compensación Bursátil (NSLB).

Multiple title **(Titulo multiple)** A certificate representing a variable number of bearer shares.

Extract of inscription **(Extracto de inscripción)** A certificate representing a variable number of registered shares.

Bearer certificate **(Certificado al portador)**   Unit-type security.

Registered certificate **(Certificado nominativo)**   Unit-type security.

Book entry **(Anotación en cuenta)**   Legal basis: Law of 28 July 1988. Issues in the form of book entry or securities converted from certificates into book entry form remain irreversibly book entries. The registers are kept (according to type of security) by a Sociedad de Valores or Agencia de Valores, the Servicio de Compensación y Liquidación de Valores and the Central de Anotaciónes. In time, this will become the most common form of security in Spain.

Depository certificate **(Certificado de depósito)**   Certificates representing participations in investment funds. This security is kept with the fund's managing company, which issues to the customer a 'Resguardo de participación', a participation receipt.

Global certificate **(Certificado multiple)**   Represents securities which are to be (or might be) issued at a later moment. (Mainly fixed-income securities within the Nuevo Sistema de Liquidación y Compensación Bursátil (NSLB).

Promissory note **(Pagaré)**   Security issued by the government (Pagaré del Estado) or by companies (Pagaré de Empresa) traded at the stock exchange. The document (physical) form of such securities is on the way out, being progressively substituted by book entries. (The government issues will probably cease to exist in the near future.)

4.2   Types of securities

Equities and warrants

Ordinary share **(Acción ordinaria)**   Ownership share with full rights. Issued in bearer or registered form and held in physical, jumbo or book entry form. (Some shares are issued as macro titulo, titulo multiple or extracto de inscripción.)

Unit trust share **(Participación)**   Security representing a share in an investment fund (*see*: 'Depositary certificate').

Preferred share **(Acción preferente)**   Differs in specific characteristics from ordinary shares as laid down in the company statutes (dividends, voting rights, liquidation; issued in bearer or registered form).

Syndicated share **(Acción sindicada)**   Refers to control over the composition of a company's shareholders. The transfer of ownership requires prior authorization from the Board of Directors, etc. (Issued in registered form and held as a macro titulo or global certificate.)

Special share **(Acción especial)**   Share which is equipped with special features – e.g. young shares from a capital increase not marketable for a determined period. (Issued in bearer or registered form and held as a macro titulo, titulo multiple or extracto de inscripción.)

Temporary dividend-right certificate **(Certificado temporal de dividendo)** Security with economic rights but without participation rights (e.g. voting rights). (Issued in bearer form.)

Warrant **(Warrant)**   Entitles the holder to subscribe for new issues. (Issued in bearer form, in some cases in different series.)

Debt instruments

Bond **(Bono)**   A medium-term (two to five years) debt instrument. (Issued in bearer form and held as jumbo or global certificate.)

Simple bond **(Bono simple)**   Security/debt instrument without any further right. (Issued in bearer form and held as jumbo or global certificate.)

Fixed-interest bond; variable-interest bond; zero-coupon bond **(Bono de interés fijo; Bono de interés variable; Bono de cupon cero)**   Bonds qualified according to interest characteristics. (Issued in bearer form and held as jumbo or global certificate.)

Fixed-term bond; extendible bond; bond with anticipated redemption **(Bono de plazo fijo; Bono de plazo extensible; Bono con amortización anticipada)** Bonds differing as to term characteristics, i.e. fixed, extendible or anticipated redemption. (Issued in bearer form and held as jumbo or global certificate.)

Government bond; bond issued by the communities and government institutions **(Bono del Tesoro o Bono de Autonomías; Bono de Comunidades; Bono de Organismos del Estado)**   Bonds differing as to issuer characteristics. (Issued in book entry form.)

Convertible bond **(Bono convertible)**   Bond convertible into shares. (Issued in bearer form and held as jumbo or global certificate.)

Matador bond **(Bono matador)**   Peseta-denominated debt issued by non-Spanish entities. (Held as jumbo or global certificate.)

Note **(Obligación)**   A long-term debt instrument (more than five years). (Issued in bearer form and held as jumbo or global certificate.)

Government note **(Obligación del estado)**   Government debt. (Issued in bearer and book entry form.)

Perpetual debt **(Deuda perpetua)**   Government debt without term of redemption. (Issued in bearer form.)

Mortgage notes **(Obligación hipotecaria; cédula hipotecaria)**   Security issued mainly by financial entities against mortgage loans granted. (Issued in bearer form and held as jumbo or global certificate.)

Money market instruments

Government promissory note (Pagaré del Tesoro)   Government instrument, characterized by its short term. (Issued in book entry form) (*see also*: 'Forms of securities'). A draft of new tax laws provides for the disappearance of this instrument.

Treasury bill (Letra del Tesoro)   Marketed (government) issue. (Issued in book entry form.)

Company promissory note (Pagaré de Empresa)   Security issued by private companies. (Issued in bearer form and held as jumbo or global certificate.)

4.3   Securities Identification Numbering System

Code name and structure

The Spanish securities number consists of eight digits having the following meaning:

1st digit:	1 = shares
	2 = notes (obligaciones)
	3 = bonds
	4 = notes (mortgages, cédulas)
2nd to 6th digit:	identification of issuing company
7th and 8th digit:	identification of the issue.

Name and address of organization responsible for the Securities Identification System

Comision Nacional de Mercado de Valores
Agencia Nacional de Codificación de Valores
Paseo de la Castellana 19
E-28046 Madrid
Spain

Tel: 34 1 585 16 31/2

The identification code is mainly used in settlements and transfers of securities.

4.4   Transfer of ownership

Transfer requirements of bearer securities

Transfer of the ownership of securities is quite formal in Spain. All transfers of property are subject to the intervention of either a 'Sociedad de Valores y Bolsa' or an 'Agencia de Valores y Bolsa'. The buying broker issues a contract note titled *póliza de operaciones al contado*, or *poliza* for short, when the investor acquires ownership.

The *póliza* indicates: place and date, identification of the owner (purchaser), name of the company (issuer), number of shares or bonds, nominal value and rate of exchange (but not the name of the seller), and it is considered as title of ownership – i.e. the physical possession of securities is not legal proof of ownership. When selling, the *póliza* must be remitted to the selling intermediary when the ownership is transferred.

The transaction is complete when the seller delivers the securities and signs the *vendi* (certificate of sale), which has the same contents as the *póliza*. Usually the bank signs the *vendi*, if a selling order is transmitted through it.

In case of jacket custody (individual deposit with segregation per client), the securities are additionally identified by the listing of their numbers in the *póliza*. In consequence, this converts bearer certificates virtually into registered certificates. This additional identification is not required if the securities are fungible and kept in a collective deposit (Nuevo Sistema de Liquidación y Compensación Bursátil, NSLB).

Transfer requirements of registered securities

In the case of registered shares, the same procedure as above applies. Furthermore, the name of the new owner has to be inscribed in the company's register.

In the case of foreign financial institutions which transact business for their clients, or in the case of central depository organizations operating outside Spain on behalf of banks connected to the respective system, they act as nominees and appear in the company's register in lieu of the last owner.

Transfer of ownership under the Spanish Securities Market Act 1988

The new Spanish law and regulations that brought about deep changes as from 29 July 1989 no longer recognizes the individual intermediary. He has been substituted by either the Sociedades de Valores y Bolsa (securities companies) or Agencias de Valores y Bolsa (securities agencies). The fate of the *póliza* is uncertain. Maybe it will disappear as the tax which formerly constituted its basic element has been abolished.

5   STRUCTURE AND REGULATION OF FINANCIAL MARKETS

5.1   Structure of financial activities

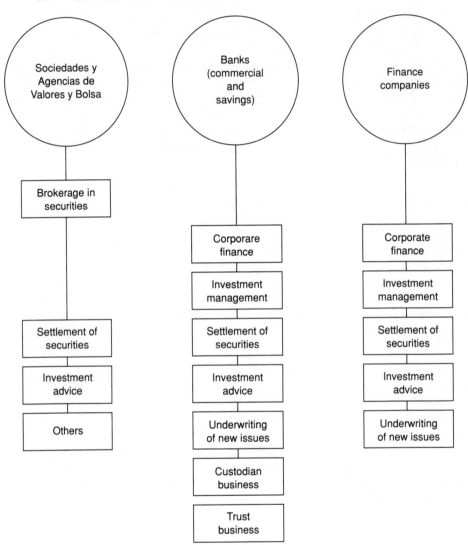

5.2   **Regulatory structure**

Overview

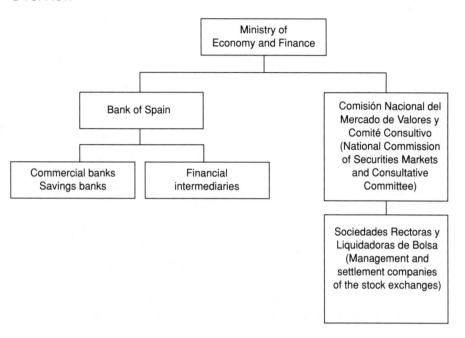

Responsibility of regulatory bodies

Name of body	Tasks/responsibilities	Legal basis
Bank of Spain	Legislative power by: – Rules and releases Adjudicatory power by: – Regulatory oversight over banks and certain financial intermediaries – Imposing of administrative disciplinary sanctions Power of enforcement: – Investigation of potential violations	Several banking laws

For description of the other regulatory bodies see following sections.

Regulatory structure under the Spanish Securities Market Act 1988

Under the new regulatory structure of the Spanish Securities Market Act 1988, in force since 29 July 1989, a new body for the surveillance and supervision of the financial markets has been created: the Comisión Nacional del Mercado de Valores (CNMV). Together with the Banco de España, the CNMV will control the securities markets, as well as the individuals and corporate bodies related to these markets; i.e. the CNMV will oversee the transparency of the securities markets, the correct fixing of the prices on these markets, the protection of investors and promote the disclosure of any information necessary in order to attain these aims. The CNMV is a public agency with independent legal status and full public and private legal capacity.

The Comisión Nacional del Mercado de Valores is governed by a Board of Directors (Consejo de Administración) consisting of:

- A Chairman and a Vice-Chairman appointed by the government upon nomination by the Ministry of Economy and Finance.
- The Director-General for the Treasury and Financial Policy and the Deputy Governor of the Bank of Spain.
- Three directors, appointed by the Ministry of Economy and Finance from among persons of acknowledged competence in securities market matters.

In addition, a Secretary and Comité Consultivo de la Comisión Nacional del Mercado de Valores (Consultative Committee consisting of representatives of the members of the Stock Exchanges, of the issuers and of the investors) will support the CNMV in its task.

Supervision of stock exchanges

The stock exchanges operate under the supervision of the Ministry of Economy and Finance which is responsible for their regulation, organization and operations.

Supervision of clearing and central securities depository organizations

There is no central securities depository in Spain. Traditionally, the banks have been the institutions providing the depository services. Due to their banking status, they are supervised by the Bank of Spain.

To date, there is no central clearing house as the trades are cleared and settled through the settlement services of the stock exchange in which they were executed.

6   CUSTODIANS

Banco Bilbao Vizcaya
Castellana 81
Madrid 28046
Spain

Tel: 1 582 6000

Banco Central
OP Alcala 41
Madrid
Spain

Tel: 1 431 1845
Fax: 1 575 0597

Banco Hispano Americano
Plaza de Canalejas
1/Madrid 28014
Spain

Tel: 1 531 8010
Fax: 1 522 1823

Banco Santander
Foreign Securities Dept
Paseo de la Castellana 75
Madrid 28046
Spain

Tel: 1 581 3000
Fax: 1 581 3388

Bancoval
Alfanso XI
Madrid 28014
Spain

Tel: 589 2551
Fax: 589 2028

Barclays Bank SAE
Stock Exchange and Custodian
  Services
Lagasca 42
Madrid 28001
Spain

Tel: 1 410 2800
Telex: 49440 BRCLA E
Fax: 1 276 4174

Citibank
José Ortega y Gasset 29
Madrid-6
Spain

Tel: 1 435 5190

Midland Bank of Madrid
Surcusal en España
José Ortega y Gasset 29-1
Madrid 28006
Spain

Tel: 1 431 0613
Telex: 48015 MIDM
Fax: 1 43 0010

Morgan Guaranty Trust
José Ortega y Gasset 29
Madrid 28006
Spain

Tel: 1 435 6041

37 SWEDEN

☞ ## 1 PRINCIPAL STOCK EXCHANGE

Stockholms Fondsbors
Box 1256
S-111 82 Stockholm
Sweden

Tel: 46 8 613 8800
Telex: 13551 BOURSE S

☞ ## 2 PRINCIPAL REGULATORY AUTHORITY

Bankinspektionen
Postadres B 16096
10322 Stockholm
Sweden

Tel: 46 8 242 120
Telex: no number given
Fax: 46 8 241 335

3 TIME DIFFERENT FROM GMT: +1 HOUR

4 FORMS AND TYPES OF SECURITIES

4.1 Forms of securities

Book entry system **(Kontobaserade värdepapper)**   All VPC securities are book entry securities without paper certificates, only registrations in securities accounts. The registers are kept in the VPC's computers but responsibility for registration lies with an 'account operator', normally a Swedish bank or broker, appointed by the respective owner. Book entry systems are also used for mutual funds, foreign securities and options traded at the Stockholm Stock Exchange. As of June 1991, a book entry system will gradually come into force for debt instruments.

Bearer certificates (**Innehavarpapper**)   Security not registered on the books of the issuing company. Certificates are issued for the holder. Mainly used in the money market.

Registered certificates (**Registrerade värdepapper**)   Securities registered in the books of the issuing company. Certificates are issued in the beneficial owner's name or in a trustee's name. Mainly used among smaller joint-stock companies not using the VPC system and for some of the debt instruments.

Depositary receipts (**Svenska Depabevis**)   Used for a few foreign companies whose shares are traded at the Stockholm Stock Exchange.

4.2 Types of securities

Equities and warrants

Common share (**Stam Aktie**)   Shares may have differentiated voting rights. Present company law allows a maximum difference of one to ten. Some companies still have, in accordance with earlier law, shares with a 1/100 or 1/1000 vote (see below).

Shares with different voting rights are divided into series, usually designated 'A' for full voting power and 'B' for restricted voting power. However, the shares of the series A and B rank equal in all other respects. Even C-class shares exist with voting power as for B-class.

A Swedish company cannot issue non-voting shares.

Preference share (**Preferens Aktie**)   Share with preference rights with regard to dividend payment.

Restricted share (**Bunden Aktie**)   Share which can only be owned by a Swedish citizen.

Free share (**Fri Aktie**)   Share which can also be owned by a non-Swedish citizen. Restricted and free shares can be combined with any voting class (A, B or C).

Mutual fund share (**Andelsbevis**)   Participation certificate of a mutual fund. All funds are open-ended. They are regularly held in book entry form.

Tax incentive mutual fund (**Allemansfond**)   A tax incentive scheme for small savings in shares for individuals in force since 1984. The savings, limited to a certain amount per person and month, are put into special mutual funds. The mutual fund shares cannot be transferred or sold, only redeemed. Dividends, if not reinvested by the fund, and capital gains, are taxed at the reduced rate of 20%.

Warrant (**Teckningsoption**)   Entitles the owner to subscription for shares within a certain time at a specified price.

Debt instruments

Bond/debenture **(Obligationer/Förlagslan)** An interest-bearing debt certifi-cate issued by the government, mortgage banks, banks, industrial companies, etc. (Issued in bearer or registered form; see also below.)

For some years, practically no new issues of bonds (except convertibles) have had the interest fixed for the whole life of the bond. The interest is adjusted every one, two-and-a-half, four or five years in accordance with the movement of the new issue yield of a corresponding bond (or a standard bond). Private debtor bonds may be subordinated to all other debt of the debtor (*förlagslan*, usually called 'debentures').

Since the beginning of 1986, some issues of floating-rate notes have been made. The interest rate is fixed every three months at a certain spread over the current rate for three-months government debt certificates.

Convertible debenture **(Konvertibelt skuldebrev)** Bond which may be con-verted by the holder into shares of the issuing company. Usually *förlagslan*. Fixed interest rate.

Convertible participating note **(Konvertibelt vinstandelsbevis)** Bond which may be converted by the holder into shares of the issuing company. The interest rate is adjustable.

Premium bond **(Premieobligation)** Government 'lottery' bond. Issued by the government with small denominations (SEK 200–1000) which do not carry interest. The total interest on a loan is paid out as premiums by lottery drawings. These stock exchange quoted loans normally run for ten years and are freely transferable. (Issued in bearer form.)

Savings bond **(Sparobligation)** Government bonds issued from time to time to private individuals only in limited amounts with a tax-free interest premium if held for a given time. The aim is to encourage the placing of small savings in government securities. They are non-transferable and non-marketable. (Issued in registered form.)

Treasury notes **(Riksobligationer)** Treasury notes are interest-bearing bonds made out to a certain person or order. The holder must be registered at the National Debt Office when interest is paid (registered notes). They are straight loans with no amortization (bullet loan). The maturities range from two to ten years from issue. Fixed-coupon rate with interest paid annually.

Interest-bearing bond loans **(Räntelöpande obligationslan)** Interest-bearing bond loans made out to a certain person or order. The holder must be registered at the National Debt Office, VPC or the borrower when interest is paid (registered notes). Usually they are straight loans with no amortiza-tion (bullet loan). Usually fixed coupon with interest paid annually.

Mortgage institutions borrowing bonds **(Bostadsobligationer)** Interest bearing straight bonds and amortization loans. The maturities range from one to ten years. Interest is paid annually or semi-annually, sometimes based on interest rate adjustment clauses.

Money market instruments

Treasury bills (**Stadskuldväxlar**)   Promissory notes issued to the holder (bearer note). The maturities range from six to 12 months from issue. They are discount securities.

Commercial papers (**Företags/Bankcertifikat, Marknadsbevis**)   Promissory notes made out in both registered and bearer form. The maturities range from a few days up to 12 months. They are discount securities.

Mutual funds

Interest and bond funds (**Ränte och obligations fonder**)   Mutual funds for smaller investors in Treasury bills, government bonds, etc. (Issued in book entry form.)

Traded options and futures

OM Stockholm
OM Stockholm is a subsidiary of the OM Gruppen AB (OM Group), a company listed on the O-list of the Stockholm Stock Exchange. OM Gruppen AB has approx. 1600 shareholders, including most Swedish banks and brokerage firms. The proportion of institutional ownership is 55%.

OM Stockholm organizes a market-place and clearing house for trading in financial derivative instruments. Current products are options and futures contracts on individual stocks, the OMX stock index and notional bond options. OM Stockholm also provides clearing facilities for the futures on notional bonds traded in the Interbank money market.

Traded options:	A right but not an obligation to buy/sell underlying securities under certain conditions.
– equity based:	put and call options related to a certain equity.
– index based:	put and call options related to the OMX index, which is based on the 30 most traded equities.
– interest rate based:	options related to certain notional bonds.
Futures:	an agreement to buy/sell underlying securities at a fixed price at a fixed time.
– index based:	future related to the OMX index, which is based on the thirty most traded equities.
– stock based:	future based on a certain equity.
– interest rate futures:	futures based on five- and ten-years notional bonds and a six-months notional Treasury bill.

4.3   Securities Identification Code

Code name and structure

The Swedish financial community has agreed to use the international ISIN-code (ISO 6166) as a common uniform numbering system.

The code structure is:

- pos. 1–2:   SE for Sweden
- pos. 3–11: decided by VPC
- pos. 12:   check digit number

Example of security code:

Security: Alfa Laval, series B free
Code: SE0000100315

The Swedish ISIN Codes are merely running numbers and contain no classification information.

Name and address of organization responsible for the securities identification system

The Swedish Securities Register Centre:

Värdepapperscentralen VPC AB
S-171 18 Solna
Sweden

Tel: + 46 8 799 06 00
Fax: + 46 8 98 24 92

4.4   Transfer of ownership

Transfer of bearer securities

The title to bearer securities is transferred simply by physical delivery of the certificate.

The same applies to some of the money market instruments that are registered but endorsed in blank and treated as bearer instruments.

Transfer of registered securities

For VPC securities, the legal right of ownership is established by registration in a securities account. Transfer of ownership is settled by book entry from the seller's account to the buyer's. Responsibility for the registration lies with the owner's 'account operator', normally a Swedish bank or broker. The books of the respective company are consequently updated in the VPC registers.

For registered securities issued with certificates, transfer of ownership is established by endorsement on the certificate. To be entitled to dividend/interest, where this is not payable against a coupon, the certificates must be sent to the issuing company for re-registration in its books. This also applies for receiving principal at maturity, etc.

5 STRUCTURE AND REGULATION OF FINANCIAL MARKETS

5.1 Structure of financial activities

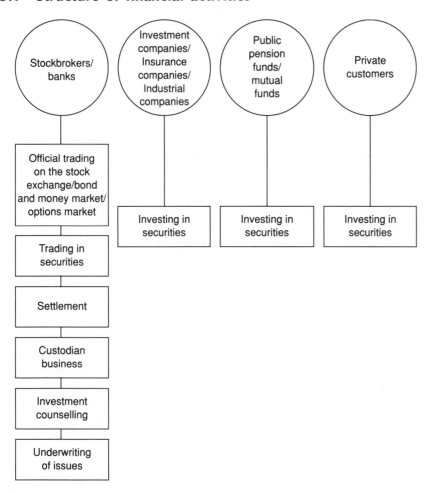

5.2 Regulatory structure

Overview

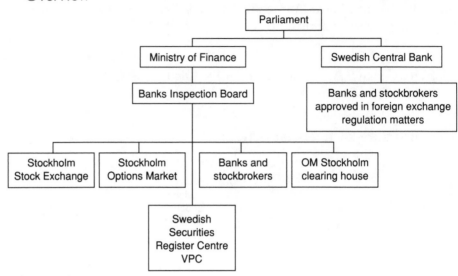

Responsibilities of regulatory bodies

Name of body	Tasks/responsibility	Legal basis
The Bank Inspection Board	To supervise banks, stockbrokers, finance companies, the Stockholm Stock Exchange, Värdepapperscentralen VPC AB, etc. Promulgates common directives	Bank Act 1987, Act on Stockbroking 1979 Act on Securities Market 1985 Act on the Stock Exchange 1987
Swedish Central Bank (Sveriges Riksbank)	To supervise banks and stockbrokers in foreign exchange regulation matters Promulgate ordinances	Act governing payment to/ from another country 1990 Ordinance governing payment to/from another country 1990 Foreign Exchange Control Act 1990

Supervision of stock exchange

- Legal basis: Law on the Stockholm Stock Exchange of 1979; Decree for the Stockholm Exchange of 1979; rules for the quotation of securities were issued by the Stock Exchange

Board in 1979 and have since received some amendments.

- Stock exchange control: Bank Inspection Board (a government body).
- Options market control: Bank Inspection Board (a government body).

The governing body of the Stockholm stock exchange is the Board which consists of 11 members.

Supervision of clearing and central securities depository organization

The Bank Inspection Board supervises the Swedish Securities Register Centre VPC and OM Stockholm Clearing House.

Supervision of broker/dealers and custodian banks

Broker/dealers and custodian banks are supervised by the Bank Inspection Board and the Swedish Central Bank.

6   CUSTODIANS

Skandinaviska Enskilda Banken
Kungstradgardsgatan 8
10640 Stockholm
Sweden

Tel: 46 8 763 5000
Fax: 46 8 763 8389

Svenska Handelsbanken
Institutional Custody Services
  Department
Blasieholmstorg 12–14
10670 Stockholm
Sweden

Tel: 46 8 701 2145/2988
Fax: 46 8 611 7275

38 SWITZERLAND

☞ ## 1   PRINCIPAL STOCK EXCHANGE

Zurich Stock Exchange
Bleicherweg 5
8021 Zurich
Switzerland

Tel: 41 1 229 2111
Telex: 813065

☞ ## 2   PRINCIPAL REGULATORY AUTHORITY

Association des Bourses Suisses
Tallstrasse 15
BP 8021
Zurich
Switzerland

Tel: 41 1 212 0404
Telex: no number given
Fax: 41 1 212 0520

🕐 ## 3   TIME DIFFERENCE FROM GMT: +2 HOURS

4   FORMS AND TYPES OF SECURITIES

4.1   Forms of securities

Bearer certificate **(Inhaberpapier)**   Bearer certificate is any security which is made out to the bearer – i.e. the person who holds or possesses the instrument.

Registered certificate **(Namenpapier)**   A registered certificate is any security which is made out in a specific name. Its transfer requires a written declaration which need not be written on the security. It differs from instruments made out 'to order', such as registered shares (*see*: 'Order certificate'), which are transferable by endorsement only.

Order certificate (**Orderpapier**)   Security which is transferable by endorsement only. A security can be designated as an order certificate, either by the drawer (with a special clause 'to the order of') or by law. Order certificates determined as such by law (such as registered shares, bills of exchange, promissory notes, cheques) always take the form of order instruments, even though the special clause 'to the order of' may be missing on the certificate.

Global certificate (**Globalurkunde**)   A global certificate represents an entire issue of bonds, notes or investment trust units. Global certificates are usually kept in safekeeping with a central securities depository.

Jumbo certificate (**Jumbo Zertifikat**)   Certificate of large denomination representing 1000 shares or a nominal value of Sfr. 100 000 or more. Jumbo certificates are normally safekept by banks or a central securities depository.

Book entry claim (**Buchforderung**)   Claim that is not incorporated in a document, but only recorded in an accounting system, and therefore legally not a security under Swiss law. The person entitled and the respective rights are evidenced by the book entry. Transfers are effected by debits and credits. There are money market claims against the Swiss Confederation, the Cantons of Berne, Basle and Geneva, the City of Zurich and against the companies Ciba-Geigy and Winterthur Insurance. The claim is entered in a specific debt register, held with SEGA (the Swiss Securities Clearing Corporation). On behalf of the issuer, SEGA is maintaining the main register, whereas the SEGA participants maintain the sub-register on a detailed basis. SEGA has no knowledge of the investors' identities. The immobilization in a paperless form is irreversible, but transfers into other names are possible. The book entry claims are accepted in the SEGA Clearing System in order to facilitate custody and transferability.

Certificate with deferred printing (**Wertpapier mit aufgeschobenem Titeldruck**) Registered shares which are recorded in the shareholders' register, but not issued in certificate form as along as the shareholder does not expressly ask for delivery of a certificate. This uncertificated form permits fungibility and eligibility of Swiss registered shares in the Swiss depository organization SEGA. Consequently, book entry transfers between SEGA members – without the printing and movement of physical certificates – are possible.

Swiss certificate (**Schweizer Zertifikat**)   Original share certificate of a foreign company, mainly originating in the USA, Canada or the UK, which is listed on a Swiss stock exchange, registered in a nominee name and endorsed in blank. In 1988, the former four nominees (Swiss 'Nominee Banks') which were Crédit Suisse, Swiss Bank Corporation, Union Bank of Switzerland and Société Nominee de Genève established a commonly owned nominee company for the registration of foreign registered shares listed in Switzerland. This company, which is called Snoc Swiss Nominee Company, acts as of 1 July 1991 as the only nominee for stock traded on the Swiss stock exchanges. Now only foreign shares registered in the name of Snoc Swiss Nominee

Company represent 'good delivery' to settle stock exchange transactions in Swiss certificates.

4.2   Type of securities

Equities and warrants

Bearer share **(Inhaberaktie)**   Most Swiss shares are in bearer form with a coupon sheet attached, but many Swiss companies have issued both bearer and registered shares. The par value of a Swiss share must be at least Sfr. 100.– (most used: Sfr. 100.– for registered shares and Sfr. 500.– for bearer shares).

Registered share **(Namenaktie)**   Share belonging to a person who is recorded in the register of shareholders of the company concerned. Usually the acquisition of registered shares is reserved for Swiss citizens and Swiss-controlled companies and subject to approval by the board of directors. In general, registered shares have a lower nominal value than bearer shares. The principle 'one share one vote' allows Swiss control, despite possible minority of Swiss ownership in terms of equity.

Dividend-right certificate **(Genussschein)**   Security incorporating the right to participate in the net profit and the liquidation proceeds of a company, as well as in rights issues. However, the holder has no membership rights, in particular, he cannot attend shareholder meetings. The dividend-right certificate may be in bearer or registered form.

Participation certificate **(Partizipationsschein)**   Bearer security incorporating the same rights as the dividend-right certificate and thus similar to that. It is issued for the purpose of raising capital, and its nominal value is part of the equity of the company. (Issued in bearer form.)

Warrant **(Optionsschein)**   Warrants are normally issues together with so-called warrant or option bond issues and usually entitle the bearer to subscribe to new shares or bonds under specified conditions. Warrants can be traded separately from the bonds of a warrant issue. (Issued in bearer form.)

'Naked' warrants for Swiss-registered shares (single company or basket) **(Stillhalteroptionen für Namenaktien)**   'Naked' warrants are not issued in combination with another instrument and embody the right to purchase Swiss-registered shares during a predetermined period at a predetermined price and are mainly intended for foreign investors. However, the exercise of the option to purchase registered shares at a predetermined price will be restricted to persons admitted by the company concerned. Therefore, before the 'naked' warrant can be exercised, a foreign investor will have to sell it to a person admitted by the company as a registered shareholder. Such warrants have been issued for shares of a specific company or for a basket of such registered shares.

***Cash or equity option* [COTO (Cash oder Titel Option)]**   A dividend with the option exercisable during a limited period:

(a)   to draw the dividend in the form of stock
(b)   to collect the dividend in cash, or
(c)   to sell the option in the market.

Similar to a stock dividend in an appreciating stock market, COTOs have been issued in order to augment retained earnings for the company and save taxes for the investors. After several companies issued COTOs in 1990, the Federal Tax Administration decided that as from 1991 all COTOs would be subject to 35% withholding tax, regardless of the option chosen, thus eliminating the tax advantages of this instrument. Since then, no more COTOs have been issued. Nevertheless, as the Federal Administration's decision has not yet been challenged, the tax status can be considered as pending.

***Investment trust unit* (Anlagefonds-Anteilschein)**   Share evidencing participation in an investment trust (mutual fund) in which investors pool their capital for joint investment. The assets are held and managed by a bank (or managed by a special management company) for account of the investors. In Switzerland, only open-end investment trusts are allowed. They are permitted to issue new shares continuously and are obliged to redeem shares at net asset value. Although a trust may stop issuing new shares, it is still obliged to redeem them.

***Part in cooperative society* (Genossenschafts-Anteilschein)**   Document denoting membership or participation in a cooperative. No security.

Debt instruments

***Straight bond* (Festverzinsliche Obligation)**   Obligation of a bond issue with a fixed interest rate during the whole life of the security. (Issued in bearer form.)

***Floating-rate bond* (Variabel verzinsliche Obligation)**   Bond whose interest rate depends on the actual interest rate of another financial product, mostly from the money market, and is adjusted regularly. (Issued in bearer form.)

***Zero-coupon bond* (Null-Coupon Obligation)**   Interest is discounted for the whole life at the time when the bond is issued. Rare because tax treatment varies among cantons and because new regulations may be forthcoming. (Issued in bearer form.)

***Fixed-term bond* (Obligation mit fester Laufzeit)**   Security which matures after a predetermined fixed lifetime in accordance with the terms and conditions of the loan. (Issued in bearer form.)

***Perpetual bond* (Obligation mit ewiger Laufzeit)**   No specific date for redemption is fixed for these bonds ('until liquidation of company'). Special terms and conditions may apply.

Extendible bond **(Obligation mit verlängerbarer Laufzeit)** In accordance with the terms and conditions, the life of the securities can be extended.

Federal bond **(Anleihe der Eidgenossenschaft)** Bond issued and backed by the full faith and credit of the Swiss government. Issued in bearer form or as a book entry claim recorded in the Federal Debt Register.

Public authority bond **(Anleihe der öffentlichen Hand oder einer öffentlich-rechtlichen Körperschaft)** Bond issued and/or backed by the full faith of a canton, or other public authority of Switzerland. (Issued in bearer form.)

Mortgage bond **(Pfandbrief)** Security issued for the long-term financing of first mortgages granted by banks and offering far-reaching, legally stipulated collateral. Such bonds are issued in bearer form by two central mortgage bond institutions.

Swiss franc bond of foreign debtor **(Sfr.-Auslandanleihensobligation)** Bond placed on the Swiss capital market by foreign borrower (company, government agency or state). The issues are divided into bearer debentures of Sfr. 5000 and Sfr. 100 000 each. Swiss bonds of foreign debtors are exempt from the 35% withholding tax on interest.

Bank-issued medium-term note **(Kassenobligation)** Medium-term certificate of indebtedness issued continuously by a bank upon demand with maturities of two to eight years. Usually they are used by banks for refinancing a portion of the mortgages granted. There is no established market. With their varying dates of issue, they belong to the category of individual securities and are therefore not fungible. Issued in bearer form; often with deferred certification if deposited with issuing bank.

Convertible bond (into equity) **(Wandelanleihensobligation)** Bond which may be converted by the holder into shares or participation certificates of the same or another company within a specified time period and at a specified price. (Issued in bearer form.)

Convertible bond (into debt) **(Wandelanleihensobligation)** Bond which may be converted by the holder into debt of the same borrower within a specified time period, with specified terms and at a specified price. (Issued in bearer form.)

Bond with warrant (into equity) **[Optionsanleihensobligation (mit Aktien-Optionsschein)]** Bond with warrant(s) attached embodying the right to purchase shares or participation certificates of the issuing company at a stipulated price within a certain period. (Issued in bearer form.)

Bond with warrant (into debt) **[Optionsanleihensobligation (mit Obligationen-Optionsschein)]** Bond with warrant(s) attached embodying the right to purchase bonds of another debt issue of the same borrower at a stipulated price within certain period. (Issued in bearer form.)

Bond with call/put option **(Vorzeitig tilgbare Obligation)** Bond which – according to the terms and conditions – can be prematurely called for redemption by the borrower or collected by the holder exercising the put option. (Issued in bearer form.)

Dual currency bond (**Doppelwährungsanleihensobligation**) US dollar-denominated bond which is paid for in Swiss francs on subscription with interest payments in Swiss francs, but final redemption to be effected in US dollars. (Issued in bearer form, US dollar could be substituted by another currency.)

Notes, private placement (**Notes, Privat-plazierung**) Medium-term obligation consisting of a written, unconditional promise to pay. Notes are privately placed by the underwriting bank or a syndicate of banks. Compulsory deposit of the notes with the issuing bank or respectively a member of the underwriting syndicate or the Swiss central depository SEGA. Physical withdrawal is not possible, as such notes usually exist as global certificates, or in very large denominations only.

Money market instruments

Mainly due to federal turnover stamp duty on securities, there is only a rudimentary money market in Switzerland. Consequently, Swiss banks have been going abroad for most of their money market transactions. Instruments available in Switzerland:

Bill of exchange (**Wechsel**) Unconditional written order, addressed by one person to another, calling on the person to whom it is addressed to pay, on demand or at a fixed or determinable future time, a sum of money to the order of a specified person or to the issuer himself (*see also*: 'Order certificate').

Treasury note (**Schatzanweisung**) Short- and medium-term certificate of indebtedness in bill of exchange form issued by the federal government with maturities of one to two years, occasionally also for as little as three months. Treasury notes may be discounted by banks at the Swiss National Bank (SNB) if the remaining life is less than three months.

Rescription (**Reskription**) Special kind of Treasury note issued by the federal government, a canton or a municipality with a maturity up to four years. Rescriptions are used to raise funds for public authorities for limited periods, or by the Swiss National Bank to achieve cyclical or capital market objectives (sterilization rescriptions).

Money market book entry claims against the Swiss Confederation, cantons, cities or corporations (**Geldmarkt-Buchforderungen gegenüber der Eidgenossenschaft, Kantonen, Städten oder Unternehmen**) These book entry claims are recorded with SEGA, the Swiss Securities Clearing Corporation. On behalf of the issuer, SEGA is maintaining the main register, whereas the SEGA participants maintain the sub-register with customer details. SEGA has no knowledge of the investors' identities. In order to facilitate custody and transferability, SEGA accepts such claims in its clearing system. These claims are usually offered on a discount basis for minimum amounts of CHF 50 000. Subscription is public by means of a tender offer or continuously, depending on the issue, and restricted to residents. Legally not securities, they are not subject to the federal turnover stamp duty. So far, there is only a rudimentary secondary market in these issues.

Book entry money market claims against foreign borrowers (**Geldmarktbuchforderungen gegenüber ausländischen Schuldnern**)   Short-term borrowing programmes set up by Swiss banks for foreign debtors such as Unilever, World Bank, Electrolux, Beecham Finance, N.V. Philips. Each issue constitutes a claim of the intermediary bank against the issuer whereby the bank acts as representative of the investor. These investments are free of Swiss stamp duty and payment of interest is free of withholding tax. Continuous offering with maturities of one, three or six months.

Loan with sub-participation (**Schuldscheindarlehen**)   Similar to a note but as the *Schuldschein* qualifies as a receipt of a payment of a loan amount and not as a security instrument under Swiss law, it can avoid Swiss withholding tax and stamp duty triggered by ordinary note issues, provided the number of sub-participants does not exceed 40 creditors. The borrower must not be a bank. The issuer issues only one *Schuldschein* for the total loan amount, whereas investors participate in form of sub-participations in book entry form.

Derivative instruments

Options and futures (SOFFEX)

Currency-linked money market investments (**Geldmarktanlage mit Währungsoption**)   Fixed-rate money market investment with guaranteed returns on investment and a currency option permitting an additional limited profit potential through exchange rate fluctuations. An innovation on the Swiss capital market – e.g. CLOU issued by Union Bank of Switzerland, or GIFTS issued by County NatWest Securities Ltd.

Index-linked money market investments (**Geldmarktanlage mit Indexoption**)   Fixed-rate money market investment with guaranteed return on investment and an index option giving an additional limited profit potential in stock market fluctuations. An innovation on the Swiss capital market – e.g. GROI issued by Swiss Bank Corporation, or SMI Deposit issued by Crédit Suisse.

Low exercise price option (**LEPO**)   Standardized SOFFEX traded call option with a fixed exercise price of CHF 1 enabling holder to buy the underlying Swiss stock for CHF 1. Created for short-term (max. six months) trading, in order to avoid Swiss stamp duty.

Three-months interest rate futures contract (**Drei-Monats-Zinsterminkontrakt**)   The three-months Euro-CHF interest future is traded at SOFFEX (Swiss Options and Financial Futures Exchange AG) with March, June, September and December maturity and a minimum trading unit of CHF 1 000 000.

Traded index futures (**Standardisierte Index-Futures**)   Futures on the SMI (Swiss Market Index) or the Eurotop 100 with a contract amount of CHF 50 maturing January, July or October.

Traded options (equity based) [**Standardisierte Optionen (Aktienoptionen)**] Options (call/put) on underlying Swiss stocks (bearer or registered shares). The options are traded on the Swiss Options and Financial Futures Exchange (SOFFEX).

Traded options (index based) [**Standardisierte Optionen (Index-optionen)**] The Swiss Market Index (SMI) and the Eurotop 100 are used as contract indices for options trading on SOFFEX.

Synthetic instruments (OTC)

Convertible Money Market Units (**CMM-units**)   Combination of an equity and a money market investment with a maturity of one year. If one year later the underlying stock exceeds the exercise price, the investor will receive the exercise price in cash. If the underlying stock remains under the exercise price, the investor will receive the stock itself. An innovation on the Swiss market issued by Swiss Bank Corporation.

Index-linked call or put warrant (**Call oder Put auf einem Markt-Index**)   Call warrant on a market index which can be changed during the first two months into a put warrant. An innovation on the Swiss capital market – e.g. COP on the Swiss Market Index (SMI), or on the Major Market Index (XMI) issued by Swiss Bank Corporation.

Interest options (**Zins-Optionen**)   Option on underlying spot or forward interest rate – e.g. calls and puts on the Euro-CHF-Future (three-month or five-year LIBOR), or the CHF-five-year-SWAP rate. Innovations on the Swiss capital market – e.g. SBV Zinsoptionen auf 5-Jahres-LIBOR issued by Swiss Bank Corporation.

Long-term bond future (**Long-term bond future**)   Underlying is the average market value of all in Zurich-traded Swiss Franc bonds with remaining maturity between $8\frac{1}{2}$ and 12 years. Long-term bond futures are cash settled.

Low exercise price option (**LEPO**)   Call option with an exercise price fixed at 0.01% of the underlying bonds' face value, enabling holder to avoid the Swiss stamp duty for short-term (up to six months) trading positions. An innovation on the Swiss market – e.g. LEO issued by Bank Leu AG.

Precious metal linked money market investment (**Geldmarktanlage mit Edel-metall Gewinnchance**)   Fixed-rate money market investment with guaranteed return on investment and an additional precious metal exposure, giving a limited profit potential in precious metal market fluctuations.

4.3   Securities Identification Code

Code name and structure

Swiss banks use the uniform Telekurs Securities Identification Numbers (Valorennummer), consisting of up to six digits.

Example: 135799 Bearer Share Swiss Bank Corporation

As of 1 January 1986, printing regulations of the Association of Swiss Stock Exchanges require that the 12-digit International Securities Identification Number (ISIN) be printed on the listed securities. (For detailed information about ISIN see Chapter 3 on the Euromarket.) Telekurs AG plans to change to the ISIN standard by the end of 1992.

Organization responsible for the Security Identification System

Telekurs AG
Neue Hard 11
CH-8021 Zurich
Switzerland

Tel: 01 279 42 60
Telex: 823548

4.4 Transfer of ownership

A security is any document in which a right is incorporated in such a way that it cannot be claimed nor transferred to others without the document (Article 965, Swiss Code of Obligations SCO).

Bearer securities

A security is deemed to be a bearer security if it is apparent from the wording or the form of the document that any holder shall be recognized to be legally entitled thereto. The obligor, however, is no longer allowed to pay when he has been prohibited by court or police order from making such payment (Article 978, SCO).

Transfer does not require any special formalities and takes place either by handing over the security or by entries in the securities accounts of the banks (in case of collective safecustody of securities with the central depository SEGA or immobilization in a bank's vaults). Swiss securities are predominantly in bearer form.

Registered securities

To transfer ownership of a security, or to create a limited right in them, the transfer of possession of the document is required in all cases. Securities made out 'to order' require, moreover, an endorsement (Article 967, SCO) (*see also*: 'Order certificate').

Registered shares of many listed companies have restricted transferability (*vinkulierte Namenaktien*). The restrictions may be laid down specifically in the by-laws of the company, or all transfers may generally be subject to the approval of the Board of Directors of the company. The Board may e.g. refuse a transfer without giving any reasons or make it dependent on certain conditions. As a rule, only individuals of Swiss nationality residing in Switzerland, and Swiss-controlled corporations, will be accepted as registered shareholders.

Exceptions: BBC, Ciba-Geigy, Forbo, Georg Fischer, Landis & Gyr, Mikron, Nestlé, Rieter Holding, SMH and Sandoz, which are open also to foreign investors up to a limited percentage of the voting share capital. In addition, the registered shares from Ciba-Geigy and Nestlé can be cleared through Euroclear and CEDEL if they are registered in Euroclear's or CEDEL's nominee name which requires disclosure of ownership details on request of the company. As of 1993, all shares registered in the name of 'Snoc Swiss Nominee Company' will be clearable through SEGA and Intersettle.

The Swiss Parliament is in the process of changing the Swiss companies law (*Aktienrecht*) with, among others, the goal to require explicit reasons in the by-laws of a listed company for refusing to register a new shareholder.

Additional characteristics of listed Swiss registered shares are the following:

(a) Shareholder's application and endorsement
The transfer of registered shares to a new holder usually requires the endorsement in blank of the registered holder on the share certificate or on a separate form (*fliegende Blankozession*), as well as a signed application form (*Eintragungsgesuch*) by the new owner giving his name, nationality and address, and declaring that he has acquired the shares for his own account. If the company has no objections to the transfer, it will alter the registration in the share register and return the old (or issue new) certificates in the name of the new shareholder(s).

(b) 'One-way' certificates
Most listed Swiss-registered shares are so-called 'one-way' certificates with no coupon sheet attached. A new certificate is issued at every change of ownership. One single certificate may represent the entire holding of a shareholder. The transfer can be further facilitated by including a power of attorney in the application form, authorizing the company to endorse the certificate on behalf of the shareholder. Such a power of attorney is valid until revocation and simplifies transfer formalities very much – e.g. in the case of the sale of the shares or the shareholder's death.

(c) Deferred printing of registered shares
On 2 September 1988 a new system for the handling and safekeeping of Swiss-registered shares was launched by SEGA, the Swiss Central Securities Depository. The system of issuing 'one-way' certificates led to the deferred printing of registered certificates. Provided there is an appropriate provision in the articles of association, the company is authorized to dispense with printing a share certificate as long as the shareholder does not ask for it. Holdings of 'uncertificated' registered shares will of course be recorded in the company's shareholder register and corresponding entries will be made in the books of the custodian bank for each of its securities customers and

by SEGA. However, SEGA only knows the aggregate shareholdings per custodian bank: no information concerning individual portfolios or other shareholder particulars are known to SEGA. Companies wishing to adopt this practice have to make the necessary amendments to their Articles of Association. This new system permits factual fungibility of vinculated registered shares within SEGA and greatly facilitates timely settlement, while reducing risks and costs.

5   STRUCTURE AND REGULATION OF FINANCIAL MARKETS

5.1   Structure of financial activities

The universal banking system prevails, i.e. a bank may combine all functions under one roof, whether it is a commercial, mortgage, savings or investment bank, a broker/dealer or investment manager, a state-owned bank, a regional or local private bank.

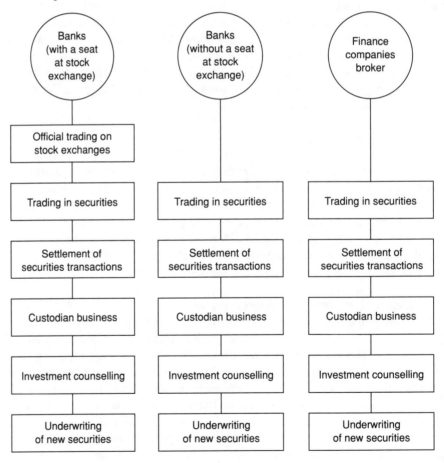

5.2 Regulatory structure

Overview

(a) Banking community (organized under federal law)

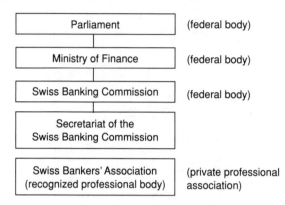

Parliament	(federal body)
Ministry of Finance	(federal body)
Swiss Banking Commission	(federal body)
Secretariat of the Swiss Banking Commission	
Swiss Bankers' Association (recognized professional body)	(private professional association)

(b) Stock exchanges (organized under cantonal law)

All three stock exchanges (Zurich, Geneva, Basle) are members of the Association of Swiss Exchanges (Vereinigung der Schweizer Börsen).

As of 1993, the three stock exchanges, Basle, Geneva and Zurich, will start operating the Electronic Stock Exchange of Switzerland (EBS). At the beginning, trading will be limited to fixed-interest bearing securities. However, the system could be upgraded such that trading in other securities will be possible. The system will be a fully electronic, order driven trading system with the option of providing support for market making. In addition, it will enable automatic matching, continuous pricing and the automatic calculation of the opening price according to the principle of the maximum tradeable volume. As a non-governmental legal body, the EBS will have to fit into the existing legal and political environment, especially the legal base for the three main existing stock exchanges.

Structure of the Zurich Stock Exchange:

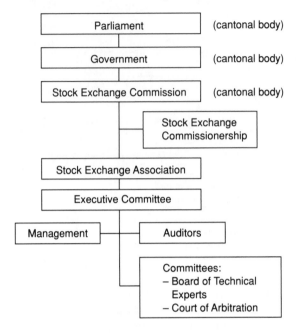

Responsibility of regulatory bodies

(a) Banking community

Name of body	Tasks/responsibilities
Federal Parliament	Setting the legislative basis – i.e. Federal Act on Banks and Savings Institutions
Ministry of Finance	Enforcing the banking law with delegation of relevant power to the Swiss Banking Commission
Swiss Banking Commission (government body)	Legislative power by: – Directions in the form of Circular Letters (*Kreisschreiben*) Adjudicatory power: – Regulatory oversight over banks and savings institutions licensed under the Federal Act on Banks and Savings Institutions. (Since 1990, large finance companies, issuing houses and firms active in derivative instruments are also subject to supervision) Power of enforcement: – Investigation of potential violations – Suspension of banking licence
Secretariat of the Swiss Banking Commission (government body)	Administrative body of the Swiss Banking Commission

(b) Stock exchanges

Name of body	Tasks/responsibilities
Cantonal Parliaments	Setting the legislative basis: – Gesetz betreffend den gewerbsmässigen Verkehr mit Wertpapieren (Securities Trading Law) of 21 December 1912 for the Zurich Stock Exchange – Börsengesetz (Stock Exchange Law) of 1944 and the new law of 14 January 1982 for the Basle Stock Exchange – Loi de la Bourse (Stock Exchange Law) of 1856, reformed in 1958 and 1959 for the Geneva Stock Exchange The stock exchange in Berne has changed from open outcry auctions to telephone trading as of 1 July 1991. It is subject to the new statutes of the Stock Exchange Association of Berne of 1991 (a private body). The name of the Stock Exchange is: Telephon-Börse Bern (TBB). Trading hours are from 9 a.m. to 11 p.m.
Government of the Canton	The stock exchanges are under control of the government of the canton in which they are located. The relevant authorities for the three main exchanges are: – The Stock Exchange Commissionership (Börsenkommissariat) and the Stock Exchange Commission (Börsenkommission) for the Canton of Zurich – The Cantonal Stock Exchange Commission (Börsenkommission) and the Cantonal Office of the Stock Exchange Commissioner (Börsenkommissariat) for the Canton of Basle – The Cantonal Stock Exchange Commission (Commission Cantonale de la Bourse) and the Stock Exchange Commissionership for the Canton of Geneva
Stock Exchange Commission (government body)	Issuance of licences for securities trading Approval of Stock Exchange rules and regulations Monitoring of securities trading Publication of the quotation sheet
Stock Exchange Association (self-regulating)	The so-called 'ring' banks (licensed to trade securities on the floor) must be members of the Stock Exchange Association. Its purpose is to safeguard and facilitate the trading in securities by organizing regular trading sessions. The Stock Exchange Association has issued, among others, Stock Exchange regulations, standing customs and rules governing the listing of securities
Executive Committee (self-regulating)	The general assembly of the Stock Exchange Association elects six to eight members to the Executive Committee
Association of the Swiss Exchanges (self-regulating)	The stock exchanges of Zurich, Geneva and Basle are members of the Association of Swiss Exchanges (Vereinigung der Schweizer Börsen) whose Board of Directors consists of representatives of the three Stock Exchanges and the main trading houses (banks)

Supervision of stock exchanges

Government bodies: Stock Exchange Commission through the Stock Exchange Commissionership

Self-regulating bodies   Association of the Swiss Exchanges
of the industry: Stock Exchange Association through the Executive Committee.

Supervision of clearing and central securities depository organization

SEGA, the Swiss Securities Clearing Corporation, is self-regulated. Based on the Articles of Association, the following bodies have to be considered:

- General assembly of the shareholders
- Board of Directors
- Executive Committee of the Board of Directors
- Management.

Up to now, SEGA has admitted as full members only institutions which are subject to supervision by the Swiss Banking Commission.

Intersettle, the Swiss Corporation for International Securities Settlements, is for the time being self-regulated. It is being examined whether Intersettle will have to apply for a banking licence which would result in supervision by the Swiss Banking Commission. The bodies of Intersettle in accordance with its articles of association are:

- General assembly of the shareholders
- Board of Directors
- Executive Committee of the Board of Directors
- Management

Supervision of broker/dealers, custodian banks and other financial institutions

Broker/dealers are under supervision of the respective cantonal government and self-regulating bodies for their trading activities on the stock exchange. Custodian banks are under supervision of the Swiss Banking Commission.

Large finance companies, issuing houses and firms active in derivative instruments, too, are subject to supervision by the Federal Banking Commission, provided that they refinance themselves substantially outside their group or that they underwrite new issues for public placement in the primary market.

6 CUSTODIANS

Bank Julius Baer
Bahnhofstrasse 36
8010 Zurich
Switzerland

Tel: 1 228 5111
Fax: 1 432 7530

Bank Leu
Bahnhofstrasse 32
8001 Zurich
Switzerland

Tel: 1 219 1111
Fax: 1 219 3197

Banque Scandinave en Suisse
11 Cours De Rive
CH-1211 Geneva 3
Switzerland

Tel: 22 787 3111
Fax: 22 735 3370

Barclays Bank
10 Rue d'Italie
CH-1204 Geneva
Switzerland

Tel: 22 286 460
Fax: 22 286 460

Citicorp
Seestrasse 25
8022 Zurich
Switzerland

Tel: 1 205 7111
Fax: 1 202 2820

Credit Suisse
Paraddeplatz 8
CH-8001
Zurich
Switzerland

Tel: 1 333 1111
Fax: 1 211 9966

Lombard Odier & Cie
11 Rue de la Corraterie
1211 Geneva 11
Switzerland

Tel: 22 709 2111
Fax: 22 709 2111

Morgan Guaranty
Stockerstrasse 38
8022 Zurich
Switzerland

Tel: 1 206 8460
Fax: call telephone number for fax

Pictet & Cie
29 Boulevard Georges-Favom
1204 Geneva
Switzerland

Tel: 22 705 2211

Swiss Bank Corporation
6 Aeschenvorstadt
CH-4002 Basle
Switzerland

Tel: 61 202020
Fax: call telephone number for fax

Swiss Volksbank
Bundesgasse 26
CH-3001 Bern
Switzerland

Tel: 31 32811
Fax: 31 327503

Union Bank of Switzerland
Bahnhofstrasse 45
8021 Zurich
Switzerland

Tel: 1 234 1111
Fax: call telephone number for fax

39 UK

☞ ## 1 PRINCIPAL STOCK EXCHANGE

The London Stock Exchange
London EC2N 1HP
UK

Tel: 071 588 2355
Telex: 886557

Note: The London Stock Exchange, and stock exchanges in Belfast, Birmingham, Bristol, Dublin [*see Eire*], Glasgow, Liverpool, Manchester and Newcastle are all part of the International Stock Exchange of the United Kingdom and the Republic of Ireland (ISE); as such, the exchanges all share most ISE services, including settlement services

☞ ## 2 PRINCIPAL REGULATORY AUTHORITY

Securities and Investments Board
Gavrelle House
2–14 Bunhill Road
London EC1Y 8RA
UK

Tel: 44 71 638 1240
Telex: 51 291829 (TLXG)
Fax: 44 71 382 5900

3 TIME DIFFERENCE FROM GMT: NONE (ALTHOUGH CLOCKS GO FORWARD 1 HOUR ON THE LAST SUNDAY IN MARCH AND BACK ONE HOUR ON THE SUNDAY FOLLOWING THE LAST SATURDAY IN OCTOBER FOR BRITISH SUMMER TIME (BST))

4   FORMS AND TYPES OF SECURITIES

4.1   Forms of securities

Registered stock   Registered stock is represented by certificates which identify the legal owner – i.e. the name placed on a company's share register.

Renounceable documents   Renounceable documents constitute temporary evidence of ownership. In the case of allotment letters and renounceable certificates, these are quasi-bearer. In each case, the owner's name is recorded in a temporary register and enfaced on the document. Subject to all payments being made, and there being no registration by a new owner, registered definitive certificates are produced in the allottee's name. There are four main types:

- Allotment letter: a temporary document of title issued to a successful applicant in the case of an offer of shares by a company to the public. (Issued in bearer form.)
- Provisional allotment letter: substantially the same as an allotment letter (above). It is issued to evidence the provisional allocation of shares in a rights issue. (Issued in bearer form.)
- Renounceable certificate: a renounceable document of title representing an entitlement to new shares issued by way of capitalization or takeover. (Issued in bearer form.)
- Split receipt/allotment: any of the above-mentioned documents may be split into separate denominations. The original has to be renounced and the request made before the last date for splitting published on the original document. (Issued in bearer form.)

On renunciation by the allottee, the transfer of renounceable documents of title takes place by simple delivery. Each document explains action required by the holder. The newly issued shares can be registered in his or her name, or renounced in favour of somebody else. This facility applies for a strictly limited time.

Book entry securities   Securities for which the issuing company maintains an uncertificated holding (i.e. a computer-based record).

Taurus eligible securities   UK and Irish securities quoted on the London Stock Exchange for which the issuing company maintains an uncertificated register.

Bearer certificate   Primarily used as evidence of title for short-dated money market instruments (i.e. normally up to 12 months maturity). Also used for stock, represented by certificates and transferable by delivery.

Global securities   In very limited use, other than for Eurocurrency issues, where they represent an entire issue prior to the availability of definitive certificates.

American depository receipts (ADR)   A registered security issued by a US depository bank which represents shares in foreign (UK) stock or bonds held abroad by the sub-custodian of the American depository bank (*see*: USA, 'Forms of securities').

4.2   Types of securities

Equities and warrants

Ordinary share   Ownership share with full voting rights. Commonly known as 'equities'. Ordinary shares are usually issued in registered form.

Restricted/non-voting ordinary share   Ownership share without a vote or with limited voting powers. Often described as 'A shares'. (Issued in registered form.)

Preference share   Part of the share capital of a company, ranking after secured creditors but before ordinary shareholders in the event of liquidation. Preference rights are defined in the Articles of Association of the relevant company but may relate to dividend, voting rights, distribution of surplus assets, etc. (Issued in registered form.)

Participating preference share   These preference shares have further rights which are normally linked to the relevant company's profits or dividend payment on ordinary shares. (Issued in registered form.)

Other preference shares   These will have the rights of standard preference shares, but may also be:

– cumulative (i.e. income arrears are carried forward to the next payment date)
– convertible (into ordinary shares)
– redeemable (at a fixed date or contingent on a special event), or
– permanent (not redeemable except at issuers' option). (Issued in registered form.)

Deferred ordinary   A deferred ordinary share is an ownership share with either the dividend or voting rights suspended until a future date. (Issued in registered form.)

Packaged securities   A basket of shares in different companies, usually utilities, assembled in accordance with a preset formula.

Founder/golden share   Share issued to the founders or the government (especially in recent strategically important privatizations). These may give certain privileges, especially in the event of a takeover. (Issued in registered form.)

Investment trust share   A share of a company bound by a trust deed, formed to invest in specific types of securities. Shares in an investment trust can usually only be bought and sold through the stock exchange. Sometimes referred to as a 'closed-end' fund. (Issued in registered form.)

Unit trust units   A unit of an open-end fund governed by a trust deed with specific investment objectives. The funds are pooled under management and the price of units is based on net asset value. Purchases and sales are largely directed through the managers. (Issued in registered form.)

Warrant   A warrant is an instrument which gives the holder the right but not the obligation to acquire a prespecified amount of ordinary shares or other securities at a specific price at some time in the future. It is normally issued as part of a loan stock, but quoted as a separate instrument after issue.

Debt instruments

Loan stock   Domestic debt security usually in registered form issued by government, local authority, public board or corporate entity.

Unsecured loan stock   An unsecured loan stock gives the holder no prior call on the assets of a company in the event of liquidation. (Issued in registered form.)

Mortgage debentures   Loan secured on a specific part of the assets of a company, normally land and buildings. There may also be a floating charge on other assets. (Issued in registered form.)

Debenture stock   Loan secured by a floating charge over the assets of a company remaining after meeting the prior claims of other creditors. (Issued in registered form.)

Subordinated unsecured loan stock   Loan issued by financial institutions whereby the rights of the stockholder are subordinated to the interest of other specified creditors. (Issued in registered form.)

Convertible loan stock   This may be any of the types identified above, with the additional right to exchange for another form of security (normally ordinary shares) at a pre-specified rate and date declared at the time of issue. (Issued in registered form.)

Floating-rate loan stock   Loan stock with a variable yield, linked to a market rate of interest (normally LIBOR). (Issued in registered form.)

All loan and debenture stocks may be issued by creditworthy companies for maturities normally between five and 20 years, although exceptions can arise.

Gilt-edged stock
– Fixed interest (issued in registered and/or book-entry form): a stock whose interest and capital are guaranteed by the British government. The issues are divided into four categories:

- short gilts – due to be repaid at par within five years
- medium gilts – due to be repaid between five and 15 years
- long gilts – due to be repaid at more than 15 years

- undated gilts (e.g. War Loan) – with no redemption date (issued in registered and bearer form.)

– Index-linked stock (issued in registered form): a stock with an interest rate linked to the retail price index working six months in arrears. There are no restrictions on the ownership of such stock. Although there is the benefit of indexation against inflation, there is no facility whereby exemption from tax on the income so paid can be obtained for owners resident outside the UK.

Local authority stock, corporation and county stock   Fixed-interest stock issued by local authorities, county councils or city corporations. Many issues are comparatively small and are usually held by institutions. Such smaller issues are rarely traded on secondary markets. (Issued in registered form.)

Bulldog bonds   Fixed-interest stock issued by foreign governments in the domestic sterling bond market. These may be of varying maturities. (Issued in registered form.)

Short-dated bond   Short-term debt issued by local authorities, the interest rate being fixed on issue. Often referred to as a 'yearling bond'. (Issued in registered form.)

Money market instruments

The money market is an open market for lending and borrowing short-term funds and for dealing in negotiable instruments. The latter are issued with a short maturity (usually three to 12 months). The following instruments are available on the British money market:

Treasury bill   Bearer certificate of indebtedness issued for periods of three to 12 months, backed by the full faith and credit of the government. The minimum denomination is GBP 5000. (Issued in bearer form.)

Certificate of deposit (CD)   A negotiable certificate issued against funds deposited in a commercial bank for a definite period of time (normally one to 12 months) and carrying a rate of return, either fixed or linked to market rates. The minimum denomination is GBP 50 000. (Issued in bearer form.)

Euro-commercial paper   Bearer promissory note denominated in USD or ECUs issued for a maturity from seven to 364 days. A note may be interest bearing or issued at a discount to the face value.

ECU bonds   UK government bonds, denominated in ECUs with capital and interest payable without deduction of withholding taxes to non-residents of the UK.

Sterling commercial paper   Substantially similar in concept and operation to Euro-commercial paper but denominated in sterling.
   Since March 1989, eligible issuers have been:

– Companies whose ordinary and preferred stock have a market capitalization of at least GBP 50 million and are listed on the London Stock Exchange.
– Certain unlisted companies, companies quoted on some non-UK exchanges, banks, building societies, international organizations and foreign public sector bodies. (The market is regulated by the Bank of England, but since March 1989 new issues no longer require timing consent from the Bank of England). (Issued in bearer form.)

Bank accepted bill   Bill of exchange accepted by an authorized bank. The minimum denomination is GBP 50 000. If it is related to a trade debt, a bank accepted bill is eligible for re-discount at the Bank of England. (Issued in bearer form.)

Local authority bill   Bill drawn on a local authority for acceptance by a bank. The minimum denomination is GBP 50 000. (Issued in bearer form.)

Options and futures

Option   An option is the right to buy or sell a specified asset or intangible at a pre-determined price at a time in the future. The initial price represents a premium to acquire the rights in the option and the cost will be a function of time and volatility. Options may relate to indices, interest rates, currency rates, gilt-edged warrants and other investment vehicles (e.g. gilt-edged warrants and negotiated options).

Traded options   An option which is traded in the traded options market of the London Stock Exchange and will have a value for either the writer (issuer) or holder.

Futures   Contracts for the delivery or purchase of assets at a date in the future. Futures are used as hedges and for speculative purposes with delivery of the underlying relevant asset rarely being effected. Futures are common in most commodities and financial instruments.

Negotiated option   An instrument giving a right to buy or sell a minimum GBP 100 000 nominal value of the gilt-edged stock underlying the option. Negotiated options are not capable of being traded and have a maximum life of 12 months.

Gilt warrants   An instrument giving a right to buy or sell gilt-edged stock underlying the warrant. Gilt warrants are capable of being traded in either the American or European form.

Pincs   An equity interest in a single investment property represented by a share certificate in the company which owns the freehold or leasehold of the property. Investors receive a share of the property's income and flow and any capital growth. Investors are exempt from Capital Gains Tax.

4.3 Securities Identification Code

Code name and structure

Sedol A uniform stock code is used to identify uniquely all securities issued in the UK or Eire. These include all UK-authorized unit trusts, offshore and overseas funds shown daily in the *Financial Times*.

This Code comprises a seven-digit number allocated by the Master File Service of the London Stock Exchange which is the National Numbering Agency for the UK and Ireland and recognized by ISO standard 6166. This code is known as the SEDOL (Stock Exchange Daily Official List) system. Sedol numbers are also allocated to foreign securities traded and held in the UK or Eire. The Sedol code is the basis for the ISIN code for UK securities.

Name and address of organization responsible for the Security Identification Code

The service is administered by:

Master File Services
The London Stock Exchange
GB-London EC2N 1HP

Tel: 071 588 2355
Fax: 071 588 5456

From October 1991 all the settlement services operated by the London Stock Exchange (including Checking, Talisman and INS and when implemented Taurus) will use the ISIN number as the security identification code in place of the Sedol. However, the Sedol will continue to be used in those cases where an ISIN has not been issued for a non-UK security by the competent overseas numbering agency.

4.4 Transfer of ownership

Transfer requirements of bearer securities

The transfer of bearer securities is effected by physical delivery of the certificates. No transfer documentation is required.

Transfer requirements of registered securities

Evidence of ownership of a registered security is represented by an entry in the register. Companies will either maintain their own share and stock registers or employ a service registrar to carry out this function. The Bank of England maintains the register of all registered gilt-edged securities.

Transfer requirements of renounceable certificates

Full details of Talisman are incorporated in this part (see below) and expand on the details given in the section above ('Forms of securities') in respect of the transfer requirements of renounceable certificates.

With effect from 1992 (as a result of the introduction of Taurus), UK and Irish corporate securities (equities, fixed income and warrants) may be settled in dematerialized form. The changes to the process resulting from the introduction of Taurus are noted as appropriate in each relevant section.

Talisman securities
1. Market transactions
Sold market transactions in Talisman eligible securities for settlement through Talisman are generally effected by the selling member firm depositing a Talisman sold transfer for each sold transaction, together with the appropriate certificate(s).

Since 1979, such sold deposits have been registered out of the selling client's name (the transferor) into the LSE Talisman service's uncertificated nominee Sepon Limited.

Under Taurus, the Talisman sold transfer and the stock certificate will be replaced by book entry transfer instructions and, for non-Taurus participants, considered to be in the main private investors, a share statement. The latter will provide details of ownership but not be regarded as evidence of ownership.

Where a client has bought stock, subsequent to Talisman settlement of the bought market contract, a Talisman Bought Transfer is prepared by the LSE to register the stock out of Sepon into the name(s) required by the buying client.

Any shares held by the LSE prior to and during the process of settlement are held in trust by the London Stock Exchange on behalf of the underlying owner whose interests are protected at all times.

Under Taurus, the Talisman bought transfer is replaced by a book entry transfer instruction.

2. Off-market transactions
Transfers arising from non-market transactions are effected by means of the stock transfer form and, on occasions, by a subsidiary transfer known as a broker's transfer form. If the transferor's holding is being divided and transferred to different transferees (i.e. the buyers), a separate stock transfer will be required for each amount.

The appropriate rate of stamp duty is affixed to the transfer, which is then sent to the registrar to have the new owner's name inserted on the register and a certificate issued.

Under Taurus, transfer forms and stock certificates are replaced by book entry transfer facilities for off-market transactions. Stamp duty is scheduled to end with the introduction of Taurus.

Non-Talisman securities
In the event of a transfer arising from a market transaction in gilt-edged, local authority or other security not settling through

Talisman, the transferor must sign a stock transfer form. The form must be duly completed and stamp duty affixed if necessary. The stock transfer form is then lodged with the Registrar, who will register the securities in the name of the transferee (i.e. the buyer).

Book entry securities (Central Gilts Office) A system of dual inputs is employed. The seller inputs transaction details and then authorizes these as correct. Once the buyer inputs acceptance of the details, the transaction is processed.

Book entry securities (Central Moneymarkets Office) A similar system as for the Central Gilts Office. The office is run by the Bank of England and covers short-dated sterling money market instruments.

5   STRUCTURE AND REGULATION OF FINANCIAL MARKETS

5.1   Structure of financial activities

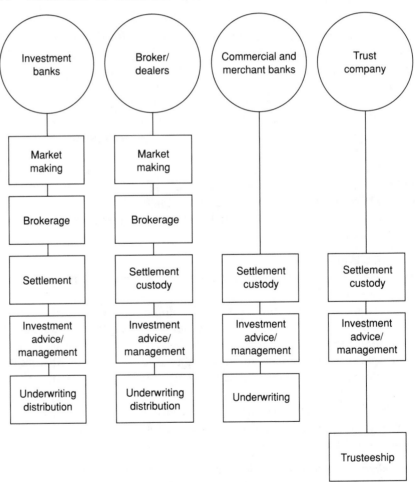

5.2 Regulatory structure

Overview

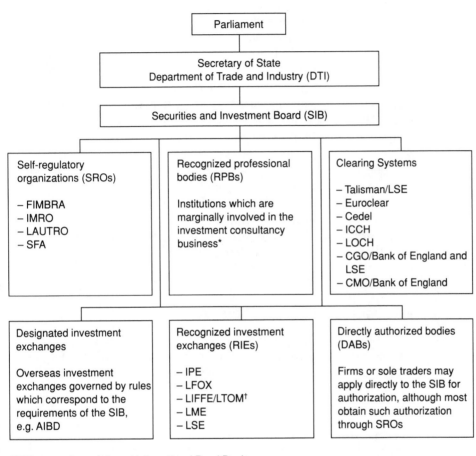

AIBD   – Association of International Bond Dealers
FIMBRA   – Financial Intermediaries Managers and Brokers Regulatory Association
ICCH   – International Commodities Clearing House
IPE   – International Petroleum Exchange
IMRO   – Investment Management Regulatory Organization
LAUTRO   – Life Assurance and Unit Trust Regulatory Organization
LIFFE   – London International Financial Futures Exchange
LME   – London Metal Exchange
LOCH   – London Options Clearing House
LSE   – The London Stock Exchange
SFA   – Securities and Futures Association

* For example, accountants, lawyers, secretaries, actuaries, etc.
† LIFFE/LTOM merger is planned for 1992 to form the London Derivatives Exchange (LDE).

The Financial Services Act 1986 introduced a wide-ranging review of the UK securities industry. Essentially the Act provides that no one may carry on investment business in the UK unless they are an authorized or exempted person. Investment business includes the dealing in, arranging deals in, managing and advising on investments and the establishment, operation and winding-up of collective investment schemes.

The Act ensures that, with few exceptions, everyone carrying on investment business in the UK (unless exempted) is subject to regulation. It therefore impacts on brokers, market makers, underwriters and investment managers, investment advisers, insurance intermediaries,' unit trust and offshore fund managers. The Act has a much wider application than the Prevention of Fraud (Investment) Act 1958 which it replaced.

Whereas the Act provides certain transaction-related exemptions (e.g. principal dealings, overseas residents), care needs to be taken as to whether or not the exemption applies.

Authorization may be achieved in any one of seven ways. The majority achieve this by membership of a self-regulatory organization (SRO). Alternatives are primarily direct authorization by the Securities and Investment Board (SIB) or certification by a recognized professional body (RPB).

Responsibility of regulatory bodies

The regulatory scheme is 'practitioner-based statute-backed regulation'. The government has delegated its regulatory powers to the SIB, its designated agent. The SIB, in turn, operates through SROs, RIEs, RCHs and RPBs.

(a) Principal regulatory bodies

Name of body	Responsibilities	Legal basis
Securities and Investment Board (SIB) (government agent)	Recognition and withdrawal of SROs, RPBs, direct application, RIEs and RCHs: – Making of rules and regulations concerning conduct of business, investment funds and segregation of clients' money – Carrying out investigations and exercise of enforcement powers – Supervision of collective investment schemes	The Financial Services Act 1986
Self-regulatory Organizations (SROs*)	Authorization of members: – Supervision of capital adequacy and conduct of business	The Financial Services Act 1986

Name of body	Responsibilities	Legal basis
The Securities and Futures Association (SFA)	Resulting from the merger of the Securities Association (TSA) with the Association of Futures Brokers and Dealers (AFBD), in 1991, comprising primarily members of both organizations – e.g. stock, futures, commodities and options dealers	
Financial Intermediaries Managers and Brokers Regulatory Association (FIMBRA)	Comprising a wide range of smaller securities firms, investment managers, advisers and intermediaries in life insurance and other pooled investments	
Investment Management Regulatory Organization (IMRO)	Comprises investment and fund managers and advisers, generally drawn from merchant banks, investment trusts pension fund managers, unit trust managers and insurance companies	
Life Assurance and Unit Trust Regulatory Organization (LAUTRO)	Comprising insurance companies, unit trusts, friendly societies (companies with no shareholders; all profits paid to policyholders) and others producing and selling pooled investments	

* The rules of an SRO must afford investors protection at least equivalent to the rules of the SIB applicable for directly authorized persons. The SRO must have effective arrangements and resources for monitoring and enforcement of its rules and must ensure that its members are 'fit and proper' to carry on investment business. The SRO's authorization procedures must be fair and reasonable.

Supervision of recognized investment exchanges (RIEs)

Each RIE is, pursuant to Schedule 4 of the Act, responsible for ensuring that there is a proper and orderly market for the protection of investors and for the settlement of any trades dealt on the RIE. There is also a need for the RIE to have adequate arrangements and resources for the monitoring and enforcement of its rules and investigation of complaints. It is required to promote and maintain a high degree of integrity and fair dealing and to share information with other persons having responsibility for the supervision or regulation of investment business.

Unless otherwise exempt, an RIE will be required to be authorized by an SRO. The RIE's rules are monitored by the SIB to ensure that the requirements of Schedule 4 are met. Each RIE member will be required, before effecting any transactions for or with a client, to discharge its obligation to its SRO.

The principal RIEs are, at present:

- The London Stock Exchange (LSE)
- The International Petroleum Exchange (IPE)
- The International Financial Futures Exchange (LIFFE) (to merge with the London Traded Options Market to become the London Derivatives Exchange (LDE))
- The London Metal Exchange (LME)
- The London Futures and Options Exchange (LFOX).

Supervision of recognized clearing houses (RCHs)

In certain cases, the RIE provides its own settlement and clearing arrangements, the Stock Exchange being a good example as it provides for equity settlement through its Talisman clearing house. The clearing system is not recognized separately from the stock exchange.

In other circumstances, clearing houses have obtained recognition as an RCH, their function being to provide clearing services for transactions dealt on an RIE by matching contracts and guaranteeing their performance. The rules are monitored by the SIB to ensure that the RCH has adequate arrangements and resources for the monitoring and enforcement of its rules and investigation of complaints. RCHs are required to promote and maintain a high degree of integrity and to share information with other persons having responsibility for the supervision or regulation of investment business.

The following is the list of RCHs:

- The International Commodities Clearing House (ICCH)
- Euroclear
- Cedel.

Recognised professional bodies (RPBs)

RPBs are to regulate the practices of a profession; no RPB regulates investment business.

Supervision of broker/dealers and custodian banks

The two main SROs (SFA and IMRO) have attempted to cover as many different categories of investment as possible. This has been done by them agreeing to regulate activities outside their main scope rule if they are incidental or ancillary activities. It is therefore the case that a broker/dealer may be solely authorized by the TSA and a custodian bank by IMRO. Where this cannot be achieved and a firm needs to register with more than one SRO, to avoid conflict, a 'lead' regulator will be appointed. This may well be the SRO responsible for the largest part of the firm's business.

Broker/dealers are supervised by their SRO for the purposes of capital adequacy, conduct of business and by their RIE in relation to trading and settlement.

Custodian banks are subject to supervision by the Bank of England for general regulatory purposes. Most custodian banks are members of the Investment Managers Regulatory Organization (IMRO).

The rules relating to the conduct of custodian business are established by IMRO through reference to the SIB rulebook, while the Bank of England regulates the overall banking business and capital adequacy of the individual banking groups.

6 CUSTODIANS

Bank of America
26 Elmfield Rd
Bromley
Kent
BR1 1WA
UK

Tel: 081 634 4338
Fax: call telephone number for fax

Bank of Scotland
Securities Department
Broad Street House
55 Old Broad Street
London EC2P 2HL
UK

Tel: 071 601 6666
Fax: 071 374 4415

Bankers Trust Company
Dashwood House
69 Old Broad Street
London EC2A 2HE
UK

Tel: 071 982 2500
Fax: call telephone number for fax

Barclays Bank
168 Fenchurch St
London EC3P 3HP
UK

Tel: 071 626 1567
Fax: 071 588 3229

Boston Safe Deposit and Trust Co.
   (UK) Limited
Princess House
Bush Lane
London EC4R 0AN
UK

Tel: 071 623 0800
Fax: 071 283 7648

Chase Manhattan Bank
Woolgate House
Colman Street
London EC2P 2HD
UK

Tel: 071 726 5303
Fax: 071 726 5859

Chemical Bank
180 Strand
London WC2R 1ET
UK

Tel: 071 380 5239
Fax: call telephone number for fax

Citibank
7 Savoy Court
London WC2R 0EA
UK

Tel: 071 438 0926
Fax: call telephone number for fax

Clydesdale Bank
PO Box 124
The Guildhall
57 Queen Street
Glasgow G1 3EA
UK

Tel: 041 204 1010
Fax: 041 204 0828

Continental Bank
Continental Bank House
162 Queen Victoria Street
London EC4V 4BS
UK

Tel: 071 236 7444
Fax: 071 236 9247

Coutts & Company
15 Lombard Street
London EC3V 9EQ
UK

Tel: 071 628 1010
Fax: 071 623 0747

Kleinwort Benson Group
20 Fenchurch Street
London EC3P 3DB
UK

Tel: 071 623 8000
Fax: 071 623 4069

Lloyds Bank
Capital House
1–5 Perrymount Road
Haywards Heath
West Sussex RH16 3SP
UK

Tel: 0444 459 144
Fax: 0444 418 528

Manufacturers Hanover
7 Princes Street
London EC2P 2LR
UK

Tel: 071 315 6341
Fax: 071 588 3354

Midland Securities Services
5 Laurence Pountney Hill
London EC4R 0EU
UK

Tel: 071 260 0863
Fax: 071 260 5933

Morgan Guaranty Trust
Morgan House
I Angel Court
London EC2R 7AE
UK

Tel: 081 555 3111
Fax: call telephone number for fax

Morgan Stanley International
Kingsley House
1 A Wimpole Street
London W1 AM 7AA
UK

Tel: 071 709 3000
Fax: 071 709 3937

NBO Bank NA
28 Finsbury Circus
London EC2M 7AU
UK

Tel: 071 920 0921
Fax: 071 628 3273

National Westminster Bank Trust
Juno Court
24 Prescott Street
London E1 8BB
UK

Tel: 071 714 6054
Fax: 071 714 6031

Northern Trust Company
155 Bishopsgate
London EC2M 3XS
UK

Tel: 071 628 2233
Fax: 071 982 5200

Royal Bank of Scotland
Regent's House
PO Box 348
42 Islington High Street
London N1 8XL
UK

Tel: 071 833 2121
Fax: 071 833 3968

Security Pacific National Bank
Security Pacific House
4 Broadgate
London EC2M 7LE
UK

Tel: 071 374 1087
Fax: 071 374 7385

State Street
Lloyds Chamber
1 Portsoken Street
London E1 8BT
UK

Tel: 071 480 7388
Fax: call telephone number for fax

Swiss Bank Corporation
99 Gresham Street
London EC2P 2BR
UK

Tel: 071 606 4000
Fax: 071 606 2284

Union Bank of Switzerland
The Stock Exchange Building
London EC2N 1EY
UK

Tel: 071 929 4111
Fax: call telephone number for fax

40 USA

1 PRINCIPAL STOCK EXCHANGES

New York Stock Exchange
11 Wall Street
New York
NY 10005
USA

Tel: 212 656 3000
Telex: 710 581 5464

American Stock Exchange
86 Trinity Place
New York
NY 10006
USA

Tel: 212 306 1610
Telex: 96 1672

2 PRINCIPAL REGULATORY AUTHORITY

Securities and Exchange Commission
450, 5th Street NW
Washington DC 20549
USA

Tel: 202 272 2000
 202 272 2300
 202 272 2306
Telex: 89518 (WU TLSE WSH)
Fax: 202 272 7050
 202 272 7051

3 TIME DIFFERENCE FROM GMT: −5 TO −8 HOURS

4 FORMS AND TYPES OF SECURITIES

4.1 Forms of securities

Registered certificate A security certificate whose owner is designated on records maintained for this purpose by a registrar. Certificates are generally registered in a bank, broker or depository nominee name.

Book entry security (with certificates available to investors)   Combines the services of a book entry organization, usually a central depository, and the issuer's transfer agent. Certificates, including jumbo certificates, underlie the book entry records of ownership. Availability of book entry services reduces the issuer's costs of printing and signing certificates, transferring them and making dividend or interest payments. In this category are US Treasury notes and bonds issued physically prior to July 1986 and recorded in the Federal Reserve Book Entry System and many other types of physical securities eligible for the services of a central depository.

Book entry security (without certificates available to investors)   Global certificate, or no certificate at all, underlies records of ownership at a book entry organization. Sometimes referred to as 'book entry only' or 'pure' book entry, this option eliminates the issuer's costs of printing and signing certificates, transferring them and making dividend or interest payments to multiple owners. In this category are uncertificated US Treasury and Agency securities processed in the Federal Reserve Book Entry System, certain corporate and municipal bonds, and notes, certificates of deposit processed by a central depository.

Bearer certificate   A security certificate whose owner is not registered on the records of a Registrar, and therefore presumed to be owned by the person who holds it. The Internal Revenue Code imposes penalties on the issuance of securities in bearer form after 30 June 1983, with the exception of short-term issues or obligations of a type not generally offered to the public.

American depositary receipt (ADR)   A registered security issued by a US depositary bank which represents shares of foreign stock or bonds held abroad by the foreign sub-custodian of the American depositary bank. ADR issues may either be sponsored by the foreign corporation or unsponsored. In a typical unsponsored issue, the investor pays the American depositary bank fees. For sponsored issues, the company pays the fees. (Registered; may be held in book entry form.)

Global certificate   A single certificate, in either bearer or registered form, representing the whole of an issue of securities. Such certificates are often used in book entry systems in cases where the issuer is obliged under state law to issue its securities in certificated form. In these cases, the issuer issues a global certificate which is then lodged in the facilities of a securities depository or other book entry agent and safekept by the agent. The securities are available to purchase only in book entry form, and no definitive certificates can be obtained.

Jumbo certificate   A certificate for a registered security which is in an unusually large denomination. Persons who hold large amounts of securities (e.g. securities depositories, large institutional investors) often keep most of their holdings in jumbo certificate form, to minimize the need for vault space.

4.2 Types of securities

Equities and warrants

Common stock Securities that represent ownership in a corporation, the one type of security that must be issued by a corporation. The two most important common stockholder rights are the voting right and the dividend right. Common stockholder claims on corporate assets are subordinate to those of bondholders and preferred stockholders and general creditors. (Registered; may be held in book entry form.)

Some important terms which apply to common stock are:

– Authorized common stock is the amount of stock that the corporation has the legal authority to sell
– Issued-and-outstanding common stock is stock that is owned by shareholders
– Unissued common stock is stock that the corporation is authorized to sell but that remains unissued
– Treasury stock is issued stock that the corporation has bought back from its shareholders.

Special classes of common stock US corporations typically issue one class of common stock. Some, however, have issued voting and non-voting common. Such classes may have restricted voting rights, a different number of votes per share, etc. (Registered; may be held in book entry form.)

Letter stock Also called restricted stock. A special issue of common stock a corporation is legally permitted to sell without SEC registration to a small group of investors. The buyer must sign a letter of intent stating that the purchase is for investment purposes and will not be sold. 'Letter bonds' can also be issued. (Registered; physical form.)

Preferred stock Stock which pays to the holder a stipulated dividend. Preferred stock has claim prior to that of common stock upon the earnings of a corporation and upon the assets of the corporation in the event of liquidation. Frequently without voting rights. (Registered; may be held in book entry form.)

Callable preferred stock Callable preferred stock can be repurchased by its issuer at a specified price. (Registered; may be held in book entry form.)

Convertible preferred stock Convertible into common stock at the option of the owner. (Registered; may be held in book entry form.)

Protected preferred stock A protected stock has its dividend guaranteed in case the corporation does not earn a profit in a certain year. A special fund established from previous corporate earnings pays the dividend when it is due. (Registered; may be held in book entry form.)

Cumulative preferred stock Cumulative preferred stock has a feature which entitles it to receive at a later date those dividends which accumulate (dividends in arrears) during profitless years. During such years, common stock and regular preferred stocks generally are paid no dividends. (Registered; may be held in book entry form.)

Participating preferred stock   Participating preferred stock allows its holders to receive dividends in addition to the fixed amount, in years in which the common stock dividend exceeds a specified level. (Registered; may be held in book entry form.)

Prior preferred stock   A class of preferred stock which has senior rights over other classes of preferred stock. (Registered; may be held in book entry form.)

Warrant   Warrants are securities given to stockholders or bondholders by an issuer, which entitle the owners to subscribe to other securities, typically common stock of the issuing company. They normally have a life of some three to five years, but some exist for up to 20 years. A few are issued with no expiration date. Exercise of subscriptions based on warrants is irrevocable. (Registered; may be held in book entry form.)

Rights   Many US corporations provide shareholders with pre-emptive rights, and therefore must offer existing common shareholders the first opportunity to buy new shares in amounts proportionate to their holdings. This privilege of buying new shares on a proportionate basis is called a 'right'. A right will indicate the amount of shares the shareholders will be entitled to purchase, the price per share of the offering, and the expiration date of the offer. (Bearer or registered; may be held in book entry form.)

Debt instruments – corporate

Debenture   Debentures are long-term debt securities on which interest payments are usually made semi-annually or annually. They typically have a maturity of ten or 20 years. Debentures are unsecured loans. Special bond features include convertible and callable features, as well as attached stock warrants. (Bearer or registered; may be held in book entry form.)

Mortgage bond   Mortgage bonds are secured by real property, and may be closed or open-end, depending on whether the indenture permits additional bonds to be issued under the original indenture. (Bearer or registered; may be held in book entry form.)

Equipment trust certificate   These debt instruments are secured by machinery or equipment such as railroad cars or airplanes. (Bearer or registered; may be held in book entry form.)

Collateral trust bond   These bonds are backed by securities portfolios, often held by a trustee. (Bearer or registered; may be held in book entry form.)

Guaranteed bond   Guaranteed bonds have their interest or principal, or both, guaranteed by a third party. (Bearer or registered; may be held in book entry form.)

Medium-term notes (MTN)   Corporate notes (MTNs) differ from bonds, in that a trustee is not retained to protect the investor's interest, therefore they require no indenture. Maturities range in most cases from nine months to 12 years. They are continuously offered by the issuer as parts (tranches) of shelf-registrations with the Securities and Exchange Commission. (Bearer or registered; may be held in global or book entry form.)

Promissory notes   *See*: commercial paper under 'Money market instruments'.

Debt instruments – municipals

Bond   Municipal bonds are debt instruments of state and local governments, agencies or authorities. Interest payments on municipals are exempt from federal income tax and, in many cases, also exempt from state income taxes in the state of issue. (Bearer or registered; may be held in book entry form.)

General obligation bond   General obligation bonds are secured by the full faith and credit of the issuer and may be supported by the issuer's taxing power. (Bearer or registered; may be held in book entry form.)

Revenue bond   Bonds issued to raise funds to build public facilities such as airports, bridges and hospitals and secured by the income received by the facility in the form of fees, tolls and rents. (Bearer or registered; may be held in book entry form.)

Special tax bond   Bonds secured by a specific tax. If it also carries the issuer's pledge of full faith and credit, it is considered a general obligation bond and is often referred to as a double-barrelled bond. (Bearer or registered; may be held in book entry form.)

Industrial revenue bond   Bonds issued by a state or local government to construct facilities to be leased to a public corporation. These bonds are backed by the credit of the corporation, rather than the issuer. Currently, economic development and pollution control bonds are the types most frequently issued. (Bearer or registered; may be held in book entry form.)

Refunding bond   Refunding bonds are issued to replace a bond issue that has been called. They are usually sold with lower interest rates than the bonds they replace. (Bearer or registered; may be held in book entry form.)

Note   Municipal notes are issued by state and local governments as interim financing for a period usually less than one year. The notes may be TANs, RANs or BANs (see below). (Registered; may be held in global or book entry form.)

Tax anticipation note (TAN)   TANs are the most common type of municipal notes. They are sold in anticipation of tax receipts. If the issuer knows that taxes will be paid by a certain date, it can borrow that amount on a temporary basis and pay interest to the note-holders. (Registered; may be held in global or book entry form.)

Revenue anticipation note (RAN) RANs are issued in expectation of revenue from a particular project or projects. (Registered; may be held in global or book entry form.)

Bond anticipation note (BAN) BANs are issued in anticipation of the sale of a new bond issue. When the new bond issue is sold, the notes will be repaid with interest. (Registered; may be held in global or book entry form.)

Variable rate demand obligation (VRDO) Variable rate demand obligations are a type of municipal debt issuance distinguished by two characteristics: an interest rate that varies at frequent periods; a demand or put feature whereby the holder may tender the securities either periodically (no less frequently than the interest rate change) or at will for their par value plus accrued interest. (Registered; may be held in book entry form.)

Tender option bond Tender option bonds are obligations which grant the bondholder the right to require the issuer or a specified third party acting as agent for the issuer to purchase the bonds, usually at par, at a certain time or times prior to maturity or upon the occurrence of specified events or conditions. (Bearer or registered; may be held in book entry form.)

Debt instruments – US Treasury securities

Treasury bill Treasury bills are also called T-bills. They are short-term obligations of the US government (*see*: 'Money market instruments'). (Only in book entry form.)

Treasury bond Securities backed by the full faith and credit of the US government. Issued with maturities ranging from ten to 40 years. (Registered; since mid 1986 only in book entry form.)

Treasury note Securities backed by the full faith and credit of the US government. Issued with maturities ranging from one to ten years. (Registered; since mid 1986 only in book entry form.)

US savings bond Non-marketable securities issued by the US Treasury. Several series are outstanding – series E, H, EE and HH. (Registered.)

Foreign targeted issues *See*: 'Euromarket' (Binder A-K).

US government agency securities

US government agency security Securities sold by government agencies are not direct obligations of the USA, but carry some form of government guarantee or sponsorship. Types of securities issued by the agencies are: common stock, debt obligations, short-term notes, stripped securities (zero-coupon bonds), subordinated convertible obligations and mortgage-backed securities (*see*: 'Mortgage-backed securities'). (Registered; in book entry form.)
  Agencies issuing these securities are:

- Farmers Home Administration
- Bank of Cooperatives
- Federal Intermediate Credit Bank
- Federal Land Bank
- Federal Financing Bank
- Federal Home Loan Bank (FHLB)
- Student Loan Marketing Association (Sallie Mae)
- Federal National Mortgage Association (Fannie Mae)
- Federal Home Loan Mortgage Corporation (Freddie Mac)
- Government National Mortgage Association (Ginnie Mae)
- Resolution Trust Corporation (RTC).

Foreign targeted issues   *See*: Chapter 3 on the Euromarket.

Mortgage-backed securities/asset-backed securities

Mortgage-backed security (MBS)   A generic term that refers to securities backed by mortgages, including pass-through securities, mortgage-backed bonds, mortgage pay-through securities and CMOs (see below).

Pass-through mortgage-backed security   A security representing an ownership interest in an underlying pool of mortgages. The cash flow from the underlying mortgages is 'passed through' to the security-holder as monthly payments of principal, interest and prepayments. Pass-through securities have been guaranteed/issued by the Government National Mortgage Association (GNMA), the Federal National Mortgage Association (Fannie Mae) and the Federal Home Loan Mortgage Corporation (Freddie Mac), as well as private institutions. (Registered; in book entry form.)

Private pay-through security   These securities are secured by mortgage collateral, and are issued by private financial entities (sometimes called 'private conduits') with no guarantees by any government or government-sponsored agency. Some securities are issued via public offering (registered with SEC), and others are marketed through private placement. (Registered.)

Collateralized mortgage obligation (CMO)   CMOs are debt obligations of an entity established by a financial institution or other sponsor. They are collateralized by whole mortgage loans or by mortgage-backed pass-through securities guaranteed by the Government National Mortgage Association (GNMA), the Federal National Mortgage Association (FNMA) or the Federal Home Loan Mortgage Corporation (FHLMC). CMOs are sold in multi-maturity classes called tranches. (Registered; in book entry form.)

REMIC   An acronym for Real Estate Mortgage Investment Conduit. A REMIC is a vehicle created under the Tax Reform Act 1986 for issuing mortgage-backed securities. REMICs may be structured as corporations, partnerships, trusts or as a segregated pool of assets and will not be subject to taxation at the issuer level if in compliance with the requirements of the Act. (Registered; in book entry form.)

Asset-backed security (ABS) A security collateralized by loans, leases, unsecured receivables or installment contracts on personal property, automobiles or credit cards. The cash flows generated by the underlying obligations are used to pay principal and interest to the ABS-holders.

Money market instruments

Money market instrument A generic term to describe a wide variety of low-risk, short-term securities traded among dealers and institutional investors.
   The following instruments are available on the US money market:

Treasury bill (T-bill) Government obligation backed by the full faith and credit of the USA, issued for periods of three to 12 months. T-bills are traded on a discount basis, with a minimum denomination of USD 10 000. T-bills are the most liquid form of short-term investment. (In book entry form only.)

Banker's acceptance (BA) Bill of exchange accepted by large American banks. BAs bear interest for periods of three to six months. BAs constitute an irrevocable primary obligation of the drawer and of any endorsers whose names appear upon them. The minimum amount accepted is USD 10 000. BAs primarily serve to finance imports and exports. (Bearer.)

Commercial paper (CP) Short-term unsecured promissory notes issued by large, creditworthy corporations. Interest is usually paid on a discount basis and maturities range from 30 to 270 days. The minimum amount is usually USD 100 000. (Bearer or registered; in book entry form.)

Negotiable certificate of deposit (CD) A negotiable certificate issued against funds deposited in a financial institution for a fixed period of time, earning a specified rate of return. Normally available for periods of one month to five years. The minimum amount is usually USD 100 000. (Bearer or registered; in book entry form.)

Investment fund securities

Registered Investment Company (RIC) An investment company, registered with the Securities and Exchange Commission (SEC), which sells its shares to the public and whose assets are invested in a portfolio of different securities in which the shareholders have, in effect, an undivided interest. (Generally referred.)

Callable bond A bond which may be redeemed before the stated maturity date at a specified price, usually at or above par. It is not a distinct investment vehicle, but rather a feature of many types of securities. Preferred stock and many types of debt instruments have call features. (Bearer or registered.)

Zero-coupon bond An original issue discount bond on which no periodic interest payments are made, but which is issued at a deep discount from par, accruing (at the rate represented by the offering yield at issuance) to its full value at maturity. (Bearer or registered.)

Repurchase agreement (REPO)   A contract between a seller and a buyer of federal government or other securities in which the seller agrees to buy back the securities at a specified price after a stated period of time. In the interim, the seller has the use of the buyer's funds, for which the seller pays the buyer interest at an agreed-upon market rate. (Registered; usually in book entry form.)

Private placements   The sale of securities by an issuing corporation directly to a sophisticated institutional investor. They are highly structured deals with protective convenants for lenders, usually structured as an unsecured obligation at a fixed or floating rate. Exempt from SEC registration requirements. (Registered.)

Traded options and futures

Traded option   A contract that gives its owner the right (the option) to buy or sell a security at a certain price within a designated time period. There are two types of options: puts and calls. A call option gives its owner the right to buy a security at a fixed price until expiration date; a put allows the owner to sell a security for a predetermined price on a future date.

Futures contract   Futures are contracts traded on an exchange which call for the future delivery or receipt of physical products (like gold or grain) or financial instruments, on a given date at an agreed-upon price.

Foreign currency futures   Foreign currency futures are simply contracts for the delivery of a fixed amount of foreign currency.

Interest rate futures   Interest rate futures allow the purchase of a fixed-income short-term security (Treasury bills, notes and bonds, Ginnie Mae bonds, Eurodollars, and CDs) at a specified price.

Stock index futures   Stock index futures are a form of financial future written on the three widely quoted stock indexes:

– Standard & Poor's 500 Stock Index (S&P500)
– New York Stock Exchange Composite Stock Index
– Value Line Composite Index.

Each stock index tracks a different group of companies.

4.3   Securities Identification Code

Securities identification numbers

(a)   The CUSIP system (for North American securities)

CUSIP is an acronym for Committee on Uniform Security Identification Procedures developed by the American Bankers' Association and maintained by Standard & Poor's Corporation. This numbering system is the standard method utilized throughout the US financial community for identifying domestic securities. Over one million securities issues are identified under the CUSIP system.

A CUSIP number is a nine-digit alphanumeric number permanently assigned to each issue and identifying that single issue and no other. This CUSIP number may be used in all phases of security dealings – comparisons, communications, reports, delivery tickets, transfers, dividend claims, trading and bookkeeping – thus eliminating confusion and delays arising as a result of a multitude of numbering systems. Securities covered by the CUSIP numbering system must meet the minimum requirements:

– Municipal and US government issuers or its agencies with USD 500 000 or more of outstanding debt. There is no debt limitation when the issuer is already listed in the CUSIP system.
– Securities of publicly held corporations which have either filed, or are exempt from filing, registration statements with the SEC.

(b) CUSIP International Numbering System (CINS) for non North American securities

To enable US domestic financial organizations to identify non North American securities in a nine-digit format (similar to the CUSIP format for North American securities), Standard & Poor's Corporation has developed the CUSIP International Numbering System (CINS).

(c) International Securities Identification Directory (ISID)

The ISID Directory is co-produced for the CUSIP Agency by Standard & Poor's Corporation and Telekurs NA, Inc. The directory lists more than 200 000 securities, providing CUSIP numbers for US/Canadian issues, CINS numbers for non North American issues and cross references to the International Securities Identification Number (ISIN) system and 12 other major national securities numbering systems from Europe and Asia.

Organization providing the Securities Identification Numbers

The facilities manager for CUSIP, CINS and ISID is:

CUSIP Service Bureau
Standard & Poor's Corporation
25 Broadway, 19th Floor
New York, NY 10004
USA

Tel: 212 208–83 47

4.4   Transfer of ownership

Transfer requirements of bearer securities

Bearer securities (payable to the bearer according to its terms and not by reason of any endorsement) are negotiable and thus transferable upon delivery. To evidence a change in ownership of a bearer security all that is needed is to give physical or book entry possession of the security to the new owner.

The transfer agent, normally a bank or trust company, acting as agent for an issuer of securities has the duty to be certain that all of the requirements of a valid transfer of ownership are present before changing the records, which includes:

– endorsement
– signature guarantee
– tax ID number
– payment of Transfer Tax, if applicable.

There are two basic steps involved in the transfer process:

• The transfer agent must first cancel the security certificate (or debit an account in a book entry system) and remove the name of its original owner – the seller – from the corporate records.
• The second step is to issue another certificate or effect a book entry credit in the name of the new owner – the buyer – and record the new owner's name in the corporate books. The new owner will then receive any interest or dividend payments and any shareholder communications.

Registration can also be in the name of a nominee (e.g. of a custodian bank or a central securities depository) or broker's name on behalf of the beneficial owner of the securities. This is usually referred to as 'street name' registration.

5 STRUCTURE AND REGULATION OF FINANCIAL MARKETS

5.1 Structure of financial activities

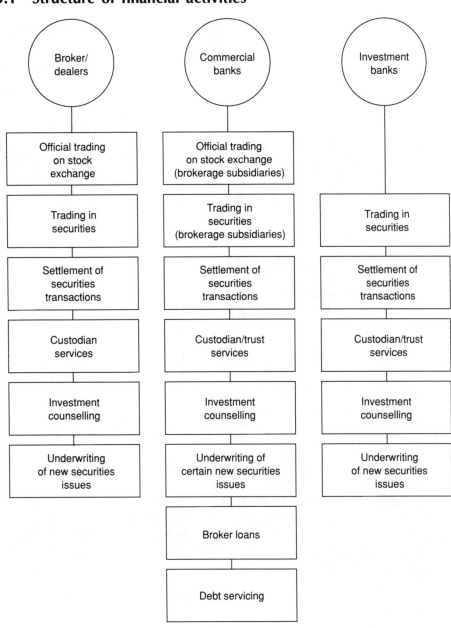

5.2 Regulatory structure

Overview

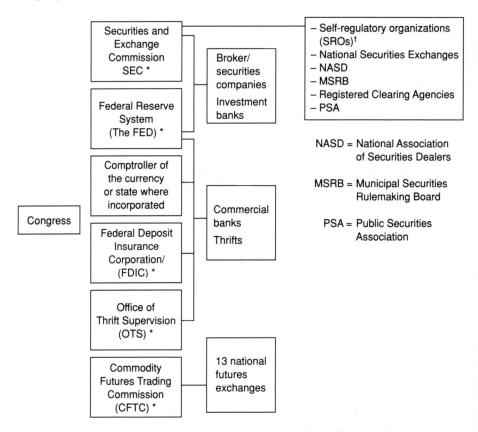

* Board members appointed by President with consent from Congress.
† Quasi-public organizations which set their own rules for their members, subject to filing them with the SEC and, in some cases, getting prior approval from the SEC.

Responsibilities of regulatory bodies

The description of various US laws appearing below is only intended as a brief and general overview of some of the significant features of US regulation of banks and broker/dealers and should not be relied on by a person attempting to determine the effect of such US laws on it and particular transactions. Persons should consult with their own advisers in making such determinations.

Name of body	Responsibilities	Legal basis
Securities and Exchange Commission (SEC)	*Scope*:	
	– Regulates disclosure in connection with offering, purchase and sale of securities	Securities Act 1933
	– Provides for oversight of brokers, dealers, clearing houses, associations and exchanges licensed under the Securities Exchange Act 1934	Securities Exchange Act 1934
	– Regulates disclosure by issuers with publicly traded securities, tender offers and insider trading	
	– Provides for registration and regulation of investment companies such as mutual funds	Investment Company Act 1940
	– Provides for registration and regulation of investment advisers	Investment Advisers Act 1940
	Power of enforcement and regulation:	
	– Investigation of potential violations	(Under one or more of the above laws)
	– Civil enforcement (criminal enforcement referred to and handled by the US Department of Justice)	
	– Seeks to prevent fraud and deception in the purchase and sale of securities	
	– Obtains court orders against acts and practices that operate as a fraud upon investors or otherwise violate laws	
	– Suspends or revokes registrations of brokers, dealers, investment companies and investment advisers who wilfully engage in prohibited acts and practices	
	– Imposes civil penalties, including e.g. dollar fines, and rescission of transactions	
Commodity Futures Trading Commission (CFTC)	*Scope*:	
	– Regulates trading of the various US futures exchanges (contract markets), public brokerage houses, futures commission merchants and commodity trading advisers	Commodity Futures Trading Commission Act 1974

Name of body	Responsibilities	Legal basis
	Power of enforcement and regulation: – Approves rules under which an exchange proposes to operate – Monitors the various exchanges' enforcement of rules (i.e. customer funds must be kept in accounts separate from accounts maintained by firms for their own use) – Investigates potential violations – Reviews terms of proposed futures contracts – Suspends or revokes registrations	
Federal Reserve System, consists of Federal Reserve Board and Regional Federal Reserve Banks	*Scope*: – Serves as nation's central banking system – Influences lending/investing activities of commercial banks – Regulates the money supply – Establishes the reserve requirements applicable to all depository institutions – Regulates the foreign activities of member banks and Edge Act corporations – May supply credit to virtually all depository institutions – Handles government deposits/debt issues – Plays a key role in the payments system such as cheque clearance and wire transfer of funds – Shares regulatory jurisdiction with the states over about 1000 state-chartered banks that are members of the Federal Reserve System, and with the Comptroller of the Currency over national banks – Primary regulator of bank holding companies *Power of enforcement and regulation*: – Enforces various laws and regulations by a variety of means such as cease and desist authority and the power to impose fines – Examines bank holding companies and state member banks	Federal Reserve Act 1913 Bank Holding Company Act 1956 Edge Act 1919

Name of body	Responsibilities	Legal basis
Federal Deposit Insurance Corporation (FDIC)	*Scope*: – Provides insurance for US domestic banks and thrifts deposits up to USD 100 000 – Serves as the primary federal regulator for state-chartered banks that are not members of the Federal Reserve System – Legislation enacted in 1989 granted the FDIC authority over savings and loan associations *Power of enforcement and regulation*: – Performs periodic examinations of insured state-chartered banks not members of the Federal Reserve System – Enforces various laws and regulations by a variety of means such as cease and desist authority and the power to impose fines	Glass Steagall Act 1933
Securities Investors Protection Corporation (SIPC)	*Scope*: – A non-profit entity which provides insurance protection for customers' accounts at brokerage firms, in the event of a broker's insolvency. The broker buys this insurance, which has an upper limit of protection of USD 500 000 per customer account, but no more than USD 100 000 can represent cash left with the SIPC member broker	Securities Investors Protection Act 1970
The Comptroller of the Currency (Comptroller) (Division of US Department of the Treasury)	*Scope*: – Charters and regulates national banks *Power of enforcement and regulation*: – Examines national banks – Enforces various laws and regulations by a variety of means such as cease and desist authority and the power to impose fines	National Bank Act

Supervision of stock exchange(s) and associations

The individual exchanges have rules relating to trading and operational practices of member firms of the respective exchanges. The exchanges derive their extensive self-regulatory control from federal securities laws. The various regional exchanges in cities other than New York have responsibility over trading in their market-places, as well as to ensure compliance with federal laws.

The New York Stock Exchange (NYSE) is the best-known US self-regulatory organization. The NYSE has responsibility for regulation of the internal affairs of all its member firms in trading on its exchange.

The American Stock Exchange's responsibility is to regulate trading in its exchange.

The largest self-regulatory organization, the National Association of Securities Dealers (NASD), is a registered securities association and regulates the internal affairs of member firms that are not members of the NYSE or Amex. The NASD is also responsible for supervising trading practices of the over-the-counter markets.

Ultimately, the SEC oversees each exchange's self-regulatory practices. The SEC also has review power over disciplinary actions, as well as giving advance approval to proposed rule changes for an exchange or an association.

Supervision of clearing and central securities depository organization(s)

Depositories, such as the Depository Trust Company, the Midwest Securities Trust Company, the Philadelphia Depository Trust Company and the Participants Trust Company, were organized as state-chartered limited-purpose trust companies. They are held to the same regulations as any such trust company. Therefore they are responsible to their state banking regulations. In addition, as members of the Federal Reserve System, they are subject to Federal Reserve examination and are also subject to regulation by the SEC.

In addition, the Federal Reserve System provides the depository for certain federal government and agencies' securities.

Clearing agencies other than depositories which perform comparison, clearing and settlement functions, such as the National Securities Clearing, International Securities Clearing, the Government Securities Clearing, Midwest Clearing and Stock Clearing Corporation of Philadelphia, are regulated solely by the SEC.

Supervision of broker/dealers and custodian banks

A custodian banking institution may be subject to regulation by three federal regulators plus, as to certain types of banks, the bank and securities regulators of one or more states. The federal banking regulators are:

– The Comptroller of the Currency
– The Federal Reserve Bank
– The FDIC.

Broker/dealers are regulated both by the federal government and the states. Applicable federal laws are administered by the SEC and the Federal Reserve. The Federal Reserve regulates margin trading, and the SEC regulates all other activities of broker/dealers. Brokerage activities performed by banks are subject to federal and state regulations.

6 CUSTODIANS

Bank of America
335 Madison Avenue
New York
NY 10017
USA

Tel: 212 503 7000
Fax: call telephone number for fax

Bank of Bermuda
6 Front Street
Hamilton
HM 11
Bermuda

Tel: 809 295 4000
Fax: 809 295 7093

Bank of New York
48 Wall Street
New York
NY 10286
USA

Tel: 212 495 1784
Fax: call telephone number for fax

Bankers Trust
34 Exchange Place
Jersey City
New Jersey 07302
USA

Tel: 201 860 2986
Fax: 201 860 7536

Boston Safe Deposit & Trust
The Boston Company Building
1 Boston Place
Boston
Mass. 02108
USA

Tel: 617 722 7000
Fax: call telephone number for fax

Brown Brothers Harriman
40 Water Street
Boston
Mass. 02109
USA

Tel: 617 742 1818
Fax: 617 589 3178

Chase Manhattan Bank
1 Chase Manhattan Plaza
New York
NY 10081
USA

Tel: 212 552 2222
Fax: 212 425 3460

Chemical Bank
55 Water Street
New York
NY 10041
USA

Tel: 212 820 5314
Fax: 212 820 6418

Citibank
111 Wall Street
24th floor
New York
NY 10043
USA

Tel: 212 657 9033
Fax: 212 509 0591

Fiduciary Trust Company
  International
2 World Trade Center
New York
NY 10048
USA

Tel: 212 466 4100
Fax: call telephone number for fax

Manufacturers Hanover
7th floor
40 Wall Street
New York
NY 10001
USA

Tel: 212 623 4444
Fax: 212 482 5245

J.P. Morgan
23 Wall Street
New York
NY 10015
USA

Tel: 212 483 2323
Fax: 212 483 1529

Northern Trust
50 South Lascelles Street
Chicago
Illinois 60675
USA

Tel: 312 630 6000
Fax: 312 444 7236

Security Pacific Corporation
The Sequor Group
Global Custody Services
127 John Street
New York
NY 10038
USA

Tel: 212 952 2851
Fax: 212 785 3021

Standard Chartered
160 Water Street
New York
NY 10038
USA

Tel: 212 269 3100
Fax: call telephone number for fax

State Street Bank
Master Trust Division
1 Enterprise Drive
North Quincy
Mass. 02171
USA

Tel: 617 847 2511
Fax: 617 847 2294

Sumitomo Trust and Banking
  Company (USA)
Global Custody Department
527 Madison Avenue
New York
NY 10022
USA

Tel: 212 303 9253
Fax: 212 644 3077

GLOSSARY

Application language   A computer programming language (*q.v.*) dedicated to a particular application or set of applications.

Beta   A measure of the extent to which the price of a particular investment instrument changes in relation to an overall change in the relevant market index.

Clearance   In securities markets, the process of determining exactly what counterparties owe, and what they are due to receive, on settlement date.

Computer security   A term used to describe a range of measures aimed at preventing unauthorized or illicit access to, or use of, information held on computer.

Correlation coefficient   As used in quantitative analysis, a measure of the extent to which a change in the price of one investment instrument alters in relation to a change in the price of another investment instrument.

Custodian   Any financial institution providing domestic (*q.v.*) or global custody (*q.v.*) services.

Depository   A national organization which immobilizes or dematerializes securities, thereby facilitating the efficient, speedy and low-risk processing of securities transactions.

Domestic custody   An umbrella term for a group of services provided in order to administer and handle domestic investments.

EDI   An abbreviation of 'electronic data interchange': the computer-to-computer interchange of inter-company data, based on the use of agreed communications standards.

Efficient Markets Hypothesis, the (EMH)   A theory which states that financial markets are efficient, in that the prices on the market reflect and embody all the information that is currently available. A logical consequence of the Efficient Markets Hypothesis is that no trader or investment manager should be able to make consistently abnormal profits on a financial market.

Encryption   An encoding technique, designed to prevent computer-held data from being read by unauthorized persons.

Fault tolerance   An attribute of any computer system which is designed to continue operating in the event of a component or software fault, with the fault in no way affecting the operation.

Fundamental analysis   A method of analysing investment instruments, and attempting to forecast their likely price fluctuation, by detailed investigation of 'fundamental factors' relating to the economic or financial well-being of the organization which issues the instruments.

Global custodian   Any organization, most usually a commercial bank, which provides global custody services.

Global custody   An umbrella term for a group of services provided in order to administer and handle cross-border investments.

Global custody system   A computerized system designed for use by an investment manager or custodian to facilitate the reception or provision of a custody service.

Hacking   Obtaining illicit access to computer data, usually via an external communications system.

Indexation   An investment management technique which involves the creation and management of a fund (or 'index fund') designed to replicate as closely as possible a market index.

Investment instrument   Any financial instrument in which an investment manager may invest. Investment instruments are more often known as 'securities', but this term can be misleading, as securities are very rarely completely secure.

Investment management organization   Any financial organization which has as a principal part of its business the investment management of funds held either on behalf of the organization's own customers or on behalf of external clients. Examples of investment management organizations are insurance companies and pension funds. These are also often referred to as 'institutional investors', as distinct from private investors.

Lead custodian   In any network involving sub-custodians (*q.v.*), the principal custodian with which the client is dealing.

Local Area Network (LAN)   Computer networks that operate in-house.

Message authentication   An encoding technique, designed to allow the recipient of a piece of computer-held information to detect if the information has been tampered with.

Operating system   A protocol for allowing the electronics of a computer to operate an application.

Programming language   A means for a computer to be instructed to carry out a useful task.

Proprietary network   A network of branch offices, located in different countries, all owned by the same custodian.

Quantitative analysis   An investment management technique that involves the formation and management of investment portfolios which are created with the objective of ensuring, as far as possible, that the portfolio embodies certain risk and return profiles.

Real-time processing   An attribute of any communications system within which information is transmitted to recipients simultaneously with it being inputted. Real-time processing is regarded as taking place instantaneously.

Return   A measure, over a period in the past (usually one year), of the income accruing from holding an investment instrument, plus any change in the market value of the instrument. Return is usually assessed exclusively of transaction costs. In quantitative analysis, estimated *future* return is an important concept.

Risk   A measure of the likelihood that a particular level of return will be achieved in the future. For future levels of return, risk can only be estimated. It is usually estimated by calculating the standard deviation of relevant historic returns.

Settlement   The making of payment for a securities purchase; the final process in any securities transaction.

Sub-custodian (agent bank)   A custodian subcontracted by a lead custodian to undertake part of the custody service, particularly in a country where the lead custodian has no representation.

Technical analysis   A method of analysing investment instrument and market price fluctuations, and attempting to forecast their likely price fluctuations, by extrapolating historic fluctuations into the future according to various theories of the likely relationship between historic and future fluctuations. Often also known as 'chartism'.

INDEX